AMERICAN COLLEGE ATHLETICS

BY

HOWARD J. SAVAGE

STAFF MEMBER, CARNEGIE FOUNDATION FOR THE ADVANCEMENT OF TEACHING

AND

HAROLD W. BENTLEY, JOHN T. MCGOVERN, DEAN F. SMILEY, M.D.

WITH A PREFACE BY

HENRY S. PRITCHETT

PRESIDENT OF THE FOUNDATION

BULLETIN NUMBER TWENTY—THREE

NEW YORK

THE CARNEGIE FOUNDATION

FOR THE ADVANCEMENT OF TEACHING

522 FIFTH AVENUE

1929

D. B. UPDIKE · THE MERRYMOUNT PRESS · BOSTON

CONTENTS

CONTENTS

PREFACE

ATHLETICS, AN ELEMENT IN THE EVOLUTION OF THE AMERICAN UNIVERSITY

*Instead of holding the universities in contempt, we ought
rather to endeavor to recall them to more sober studies.*
Erasmus to Luther, May, 1519

THE university grew in Europe. It was transplanted to the Americas. It is an association of scholars and students whose primary aim is the development of the intellectual life. The name *universitas* given to this association was not intended to indicate the effort to teach universal knowledge. The term connotes simply the whole body of teachers and students associated together. The quality of a university will therefore depend upon the scholarship of its teachers and the intellectual quality of the students it gathers unto itself and by their attitude toward the things of the mind. While the university in every civilized country will reflect, to a greater or less extent, national ideals and habits of mind, its primary function in every country is to serve as an exponent of its highest intellectual life. This is the reason and the justification for its existence and the basis of its appeal for support.

II

Nothing in the educational régime of our higher institutions perplexes the European visitor so much as the rôle that organized athletics play. On a crisp November afternoon he finds many thousands of men and women, gathered in a great amphitheater, wildly cheering a group of athletes who are described to him as playing a game of football, but who seem to the visitor to be engaged in a battle. He is the more mystified when he discovers that of the thousands of onlookers, not one in a hundred understands the game or can follow the strategy of the two teams. At the end, the vast majority of the onlookers only know, like old Kaspar of Blenheim, that "'t was a famous victory" for one university or the other.

When the visitor from the European university has pondered the matter, he comes to his American university colleagues with two questions:

"What relation has this astonishing athletic display to the work of an intellectual agency like a university?"

"How do students, devoted to study, find either the time or the money to stage so costly a performance?"

III

This study undertakes to answer these questions, not for the foreigner so much as for thoughtful Americans both in and out of the university. In undertaking this study the Foundation has sought sincerely after the facts. It has got information at first hand and has aimed to marshal it, in this report, in such form as will enable the student of education to apprehend the process through which the present athletic situation has come about, and the reaction of this development upon the scholarly and social life of the universities, colleges and schools.

The study has been carried out, and its results are here set forth, in no captious or faultfinding spirit. It has been assumed that there is a legitimate place in the secondary school and in the college for organized sports, that such sports contribute, when employed in a rational way, to the development both of character and of health. The report is a friendly effort to help toward a wise solution as to the place of such sports in our educational system. It has been necessary, in order to render this service, to set forth the abuses and excesses that have grown up. This has been done with the most painstaking effort to be fair, as well as just. A statement with respect to each institution mentioned has been communicated to its officers before going to press.

IV

The study relates to colleges in the Dominion of Canada as well as to those in the United States. The Carnegie Foundation has the same relations to the colleges in each country. Furthermore, it is impossible to discuss educational institutions in one of these nations without some reference to the other. Speaking a common language, having common traditions, and living side by side, in constant interchange of intellectual and social conceptions, the educational ideals of the two countries inevitably react the one on the other. It is a fortunate relation for both.

As this report shows, the state of organized sports in Canadian colleges is somewhere between that in the colleges of the United States and that in those of Great Britain.

V

This study is the third publication of the Carnegie Foundation dealing with the subject of athletics. The first described athletic sports at some twenty American colleges and universities and depended almost exclusively upon printed materials. Its conclusions are set forth in the Twentieth Annual Report of the Foundation (1925). In 1927, Bulletin Number Eighteen of the Foundation was issued. It was prepared from information obtained by personal visits and dealt with games and sports at British schools and universities. Those interested in the subject of college sports should read that bulletin as an introduction to the present study of athletics in North American schools and colleges.

The present study was authorized by the trustees of the Foundation in 1926. It has been carried out by Dr. Howard J. Savage, member of the Staff, and author of the study on sports in British schools and universities.

VI

The college president or teacher interested in the place of organized sports in American colleges and the effects of these upon the intellectual life of his college will desire to go carefully into the details as set forth in the chapters of this report. On the other hand, experience shows that few busy men find the time to read a detailed report. It is also realized to-day, in all fields of public action, that the facts must be presented in a form available to the intelligent layman as well as to the professional student. In the matter of the public health, for example, it is clear that the public must be educated in the knowledge of the fundamental facts concerning health and disease before any great advance in the health of the nation can be effected. The same thing is true of education. The public must gain some clear notion of the tendencies, the limitations, and the cost of our school system before any general advance in educational effectiveness is likely to result. I have therefore sought to condense into a single chapter the essential facts brought out by this study, and to indicate their relation to the process of public education as conducted in present-day American universities, colleges, and schools. The great expansion of college sports is not an isolated fact in our educational development. It is characteristic of the transformation through which the college has gone in the last five decades.

To make clear to the reader what has happened, one can scarcely do better than to answer the questions of the European visitor just quoted. What has organized sport to do with the work of an intellectual agency which the university and the college are conceived to be? And how can college boys find the time or the money to maintain so costly a display for popular entertainment?

VII

In brief these questions can be answered in the following terms:

In the United States the composite institution called a university is doubtless still an intellectual agency. But it is also a social, a commercial, and an athletic agency, and these activities have in recent years appreciably overshadowed the intellectual life for which the university is assumed to exist.

In the second place, the football contest that so astonishes the foreign visitor is not a student's game, as it once was. It is a highly organized commercial enterprise. The athletes who take part in it have come up through years of training; they are commanded by professional coaches; little if any personal initiative of ordinary play is left to the player. The great matches are highly profitable enterprises. Sometimes the profits go to finance college sports, sometimes to pay the cost of the sports amphitheater, in some cases the college authorities take a slice of the profits for college buildings.

VIII

The process by which football has been transformed from a game played by boys into a profitable professional enterprise can only be understood by a review of the transformation of the American college of fifty years ago into the present-day American university.

Fifty years ago our highest institutions of learning called themselves colleges. Their courses of study were not so widespread as they are today, but the college conceived of itself as an intellectual agency. To train the habits and the powers of mind was its function. All other matters were incidental to this fundamental purpose.

Students began with certain required studies. In our oldest college, Harvard, the freshman of fifty years ago was required to study Greek, Latin, mathematics, a foreign language, and certain scientific studies, generally chemistry or physics. Many electives were offered in the following years.

About this time, colleges in the United States began to be sensitive over the fact that they were not on a plane of scholarship and research comparable with that of the European universities, and particularly of the German universities to which American students were beginning to resort in increasing numbers. The American college did not pretend to be a university. It aimed to offer to a youth a general cultural education, and to send him out into the world a cultivated man, knowing his mother tongue and some Greek and Latin and mathematics, in touch with literature and science, and with a mind so trained as to enable him to take up a profession or a business with intelligence and success. There were men in the colleges — Agassiz, Gibbs, Young, and others — who were engaged in research, but their researches were in the main personal. The conscious purpose of the college was to teach and, as a teaching agency, to bring the college youth to an understanding and appreciation of the intellectual life, — in a word, to teach the boy to think.

In their haste to become universities, our colleges adopted the name and then proceeded as rapidly as possible to grow up to it. This was effected by superposing a graduate school on the old college. Two disparate educational agencies were merged into one. It was the first great merger.

IX

The graduate students, most of whom are candidates for the doctor's degree in science, literature, education, or the professions of law and medicine, have little in common with the youths in the undergraduate college who make up, in most cases, the majority of the whole body of students. But the yoking together of the graduate university and the undergraduate college had a profound effect upon the ideals and methods of the college. The obligation to teach was subordinated to that of research. The college youth now shares the freedom of the man or woman in the graduate school. Teaching as a disciplinary process was considered out of place in a university. College teaching became, more and more, a process of handing out information in all fields of knowledge, rather than a vigorous intellectual experience. Examinations and coaching agencies to help college boys to acquire the necessary credits multiplied amazingly.

The university, as so constituted, soon began to conceive of itself not merely as an agency for training students to think hard and clearly, but as a place where, without fundamental education, young people can acquire the elementary technique of business, banking, accounting, transportation, salesmanship, journalism, and, in effect, all the vocations practiced in a modern industrial state. From the exposition of esoteric Buddhism to the management of chain grocery stores, it offers its services to the enquiring young American.

It is under this régime that college sports have been developed from games played by boys for pleasure into systematic professionalized athletic contests for the glory and, too often, for the financial profit of the college. It is important to trace out the process by which this has come about. But such an enquiry is only a section of a much larger one, namely, an evaluation of the intellectual quality of the agency which has suffered such a transformation.

<h2 style="text-align:center">X</h2>

The American college as it had grown up since our Colonial days was a product of our national life and civilization. The United States was a young country. Its people generally lived close to the soil. The industries were only beginning. The college was the expression of the national ideal of intellectual culture growing out of two hundred and fifty years of such life. The American university represents no such long growth. It was made by building a university structure, mainly borrowed from Germany, upon the existing institution of higher learning.

In comparison with this, the European university is the fruitage of a thousand years. It began before there was a system of general education, before the conception of popular education had been accepted as a necessary duty of civilized society. It has been gradually adjusted to this conception and rests on a secondary school, which in turn rests on a common school, appropriately called in Germany the people's school. The people's school is free and attendance upon it compulsory. It covers the ages from six to ten or twelve. Upon this is placed the secondary school, for which tuition is charged, and which leads at about nineteen to the University, sought only by those who desire, or believe they desire, scholarly and professional training. The university conceives of itself strictly as an intellectual agency. The student has complete freedom. He may work or not as he pleases. He is dealt with as a man, not as a boy. Marks and credits do not enter into the life. At the end of his study he may present himself for a doctor's degree, when a thesis and a searching examination must be met. The seminar, which brings together students and professors in thoughtful scholarly groups, is the avenue through which the examination is approached. Of all who go to the university for study, only a fraction go up for degrees. The machinery of marks and credits through which every youth in an American university expects to be advanced to a bachelor's degree is unknown.

In the European system of education, from the people's school to the university, there are doors at convenient intervals that open from the elementary school or the secondary school into trade schools. These are almost wholly lacking in our system of education. Such business or commercial schools as do exist are mainly private enterprises. They are not related to the public system of education. Nevertheless the commercial colleges, as they are called, have served a real purpose. The training is sharp and practical. They teach even the college graduate, who sometimes resorts to them, to write a legible hand and to spell correctly.

To-day the American university offers its school of business or of "business administration," a somewhat misleading term. While these schools touch many fields—the theory of business, cost accounting, analysis of business cases, salesmanship, and other subjects—they offer a highly theoretical substitute for the intensive practical régime of the commercial and industrial schools of Europe. In the German trade school, for example, the boy who wishes to enter foreign trade will learn to speak the language of the country in which he plans to work. It cannot be assumed that the American boy—though a college graduate—can speak and read his own language with precision.

XI

The question is whether an institution in the social order whose primary purpose is the development of the intellectual life can at the same time serve as an agency to promote business, industry, journalism, salesmanship, and organized athletics on an extensive commercial basis. The question is not so much whether athletics in their present form should be fostered by the university, but how fully can a university that fosters professional athletics discharge its primary function. It is true the athletes belong (in recent years) to the college half of the university. Now and again one hears from the graduate school side of the university a protest against the all-absorbing glamour of the athlete, and from the college side a complaint that the graduate students lack college "patriotism." But the fact remains that the same administration that is seeking to promote sholarship and research in the graduate school is responsible for the stadiums, the paid coach, and the gate receipts in the college.

How far can an agency, whose function is intellectual, go in the development of other causes without danger to its primary purpose? Can a university teach equally well philosophy and salesmanship? Can it both sponsor genuine education and at the same time train raw recruits for minor vocations? Can it concentrate its attention on securing teams that win, without impairing the sincerity and vigor of its intellectual purpose? It is to these questions that the thoughtful man is finally led if he seeks to reconcile the divergent activities of the present-day American university. The matter of athletics is only one feature in the picture, but a significant one.

XII

A word should be said with respect to the counter-influence of the American college as it exists to-day apart from the university.

The independent college has not wholly escaped the tendencies of the time. Some of them have been drawn into the well nigh universal passion to exploit athletics and to offer courses in journalism or business or salesmanship. But the group of strong, independent colleges, whose standing is acknowledged among college men, represents to-day our most consistent exponent of higher education according to an ideal of intellectual culture which has grown out of our own racial history, national experience, and intellectual striving.

Most institutions, however, suffer from that weakness of our rapid educational growth in the last four or five decades which is due to our national tendency to compete and imitate. Colleges and universities watch each other with an eye on competition rather than on scholarship. They are strongly moved to do exactly the same things, to be all of one type, lacking individuality.[1]

It is a misfortune to a nation when its educational agencies follow a single type and each tries to teach every subject that any other teaches. More individuality in the colleges, fewer courses, better teaching will deepen the quality of their service, and the tendencies in this direction are more promising to-day in the independent college than in the universities.

Perhaps no more stimulating demonstration could be offered to-day to higher education in our country than that of a university devoted to the pure intellectual ideal *sans* athletics, schools of business, of salesmanship, and of other commercial vocations.

XIII

Our method of mass production in education deserves credit for the notable service it has rendered to democracy during a period of economic complexities and of social confusion. The presence in our schools, colleges, and universities of children and youth from all economic groups in the body politic has constituted a political and social service of great significance. The absence of class feeling, the recognition of equal opportunity for rich and poor, and the kindly relations that permeate the social structure in the United States are due in no small measure to the democratic nature of the school constituency. It may well be that the political service of the present-day system of schools is its greatest contribution. But is it necessary to sacrifice the intellectual ideal in order to be democratic? There is nothing more democratic than the ability to think. To recognize and act upon that principle is a profound test of durable democracy.

[1] "Easy methods seem to be a dogma with Americanizers. Easy is the word one hears all the time in connection with the art of teaching." Abbé Ernest Dimnet, *The Art of Thinking*, New York, 1929, page 64.

XIV

The preceding pages have dealt with a complicated situation of which organized athletics are but one factor. It remains to summarize the particular defects and excesses of present-day athletic contests as set forth in detail in the chapters of this report. The game of football looms large in any account of the growth of professionalism in college games. This does not mean that other sports are untouched by the influences that have converted football into a professional vocation.

The unfavorable results upon students through the athletic development may be briefly stated in the following terms:

1. The extreme development of competitive games in the colleges has reacted upon the secondary schools. The college athlete begins his athletic career before he gets to college.[1]

2. Once in college the student who goes in for competitive sports, and in particular for football, finds himself under a pressure, hard to resist to give his whole time and thought to his athletic career. No college boy training for a major team can have much time for thought or study.

3. The college athlete, often a boy from a modest home, finds himself suddenly a most important man in the college life. He begins to live on a scale never before imagined. A special table is provided. Sport clothes and expensive trips are furnished him out of the athletic chest. He jumps at one bound to a plane of living of which he never before knew, all at the expense of some fund of which he knows little. When he drops back to a scale of living such as his own means can afford, the result is sometimes disastrous.

4. He works (for it is work, not play) under paid professional coaches whose business it is to develop the boy to be an effective unit in a team. The coach of to-day is no doubt a more cultivated man than the coach of twenty years ago. But any father who has listened to the professional coaching a college team will have some misgivings as to the cultural value of the process.

5. Inter-college athletics are highly competitive. Every college or university longs for a winning team in its group. The coach is on the

---

[1] "The predominance of sports in schools, in the national life, in the press, not only crowds out what is, or should be, more important, but it creates an atmosphere in which these important things are made to appear superfluous." Abbé Dimnet, *The Art of Thinking*, page 61.

alert to bring the most promising athletes in the secondary schools to his college team. A system of recruiting and subsidizing has grown up, under which boys are offered pecuniary and other inducements to enter a particular college. The system is demoralizing and corrupt, alike for the boy who takes the money and for the agent who arranges it, and for the whole group of college and secondary school boys who know about it.

6. Much discussion has been had as to the part the college graduate should have in the government of his college. In the matter of competitive athletics the college alumnus has, in the main, played a sorry rôle. It is one thing for an "old grad" to go back and coach the boys of his college as at Oxford or Cambridge, where there are no professional coaches and no gate receipts. It is quite another thing for an American college graduate to pay money to high school boys, either directly or indirectly, in order to enlist their services for a college team. The process is not only unsportsmanlike, it is immoral to the last degree. The great body of college graduates are wholly innocent in this matter. Most college men wish their college to win. Those who seek to compass that end by recruiting and subsidizing constitute a small, but active, minority, working oftentimes without the knowledge of the college authorities. This constitutes the most disgraceful phase of recent inter-college athletics.

7. The relation of organized sports to the health of college students is not a simple question. The information to deal with it completely is not yet at hand. A chapter of the report is devoted to this subject. In general it may be said that the relation of college organized sports to the health of the individual student is one dependent on the good sense exhibited by the college boy in participating in such sports, and to the quality of the advice he receives from the college medical officer.

8. For many games the strict organization and the tendency to commercialize the sport has taken the joy out of the game. In football, for example, great numbers of boys do not play football, as in English schools and colleges, for the fun of it. A few play intensely. The great body of students are onlookers.

9. Finally, it is to be said that the blaze of publicity in which the college athlete lives is a demoralizing influence for the boy himself and no less so for his college.

XV

It goes without saying that fifty thousand people (not an unusual attendance) could not be gathered to witness a football game, through the mere pull of college loyalty or interest in the sport. The bulk of the spectators do not understand the game. They are drawn to this spectacle through widespread and continuous publicity. The relation of the press to the inter-college sports is described in detail in a chapter devoted to that subject. It is sufficient here to add a brief statement.

The American daily, or weekly, paper lives on its advertising, not on the subscriptions paid by its readers. The news policy of the paper is determined by this fundamental fact. It desires to print the things that will be eagerly read by the great body of everyday men and women who shop in the stores. The working woman likes to read of the fine clothes of the society belle, her husband delights in the startling accounts of fights or the details of the professional baseball games. The paper, being human, supplies the kind of news the advertisers like. It prints much for those of wider interests, but it follows the desires of its great advertising constituency all the time.

This has led to a form of personal news-telling unknown in any other country. In no other nation of the world will a college boy find his photograph in the metropolitan paper because he plays on a college team. All this is part of the newspaper effort to reach the advertiser. The situation is regrettable alike for journalism and for the public good. But it exists.

Into this game of publicity the university of the present day enters eagerly. It desires for itself the publicity that the newspapers can supply. It wants students, it wants popularity, but above all it wants money and always more money.

The athlete is the most available publicity material the college has. A great scientific discovery will make good press material for a few days, but nothing to compare to that of the performance of a first-class athlete. Thousands are interested in the athlete all the time, while the scientist is at best only a passing show.

And so it happens that the athlete lives in the white light of publicity and his photograph adorns the front pages of metropolitan (which means New York, Boston, Chicago, San Francisco, Los Angeles, New Orleans, and a hundred other) dailies. It must be an unusual boy who can keep his perspective under such circumstances. Why should the college boy be subjected to this régime merely to enable some thousands of attractive young reporters to make a living?

XVI

The process of developing our composite four-story educational structure—elementary school, secondary school, college, and university—was, until recently, highly competitive. The colleges of twenty years ago competed for students in much the same way in which the railroads competed for passengers. Admission requirements were cut as the railroads cut rates. The attractions of athletic distinction were added to the other reasons for choosing a particular college. In some states the colleges depleted the secondary schools in order to fill their own ranks.

The process has been successful beyond all expectations. An artificial market in college attendance has been created beyond the ability of the colleges to supply. The pressure to seek students has gone by. The problem to-day is how to deal with the ever-increasing army of applicants for admission to the college door. The elementary school points the boy to the secondary school, and the secondary school points the youth of eighteen or nineteen to the college. Down the long vista of the years from six to eighteen our educational system points to one door—the college-university.

Consequences of great moment result from this rigid organization. Many boys and girls whose usefulness and happiness would be best sought in a commercial or industrial trade are carried into the college by the mere sweep of the tide. Insensibly but inevitably the intellectual quality of the college is softened in order to meet the capacity of those who must be cared for. In some institutions, notably in some tax-supported universities, where graduation from any high school automatically admits to the state college, the incoming class is in large measure got rid of in the examinations of the freshman year, a costly process and one entirely unjust to a great number of the youth of both sexes.

In the third place, the program of carrying great masses of young people through college, with little regard to their intellectual fitness, translates itself in terms of cost that is growing at an alarming rate. In no other nation is mass production in higher education attempted at public cost. Aside from the social and intellectual objections to such a process, the financial load will in time become too heavy even for our rich nation.

In this situation the athletic competition has played a minor part. The number of those who go to college or who remain in it for the sake of engaging in its commercialized and highly advertised college sports is relatively small. But as far as it goes the history of inter-college athletics points straight at the fact that our system of public education, democratic as it is, has been evolved in great haste under the stimulus of competition and with all too little of wise thinking either as to the intellectual quality of the higher institution or the economic and vocational needs of the great body of children who enter the elementary school and find therein their ideals of life and their choice of a means of support. We hear much inspiring talk touching the ideals of college life. This is as it should be. But no nation can afford in its educational system to forget that to the great mass of mankind an honest job, performed in good spirit, is the road to moral soundness and to social contentment.

We need now to deal with the educational system as a whole with the purpose both to serve the needs of the great majority who ought not to go to college and to preserve at the same time the intellectual quality of those who can and ought to seek the higher education. Fortunately, justice to the vocational need and ministry to the intellectual aspirations lie along the same path.

The weakness of the American university as it exists to-day lies in its lack of intellectual sincerity. It stands nominally for high intellectual ideals. Its effort at intellectual leadership is diluted with many other efforts in fields wholly foreign to this primary purpose. Inter-college athletics form only one of these.

Our competitive stage of university building ought now to cease. We have more universities in name than we need, if they are to be universities in the sense of sincere scholarship. We have passed the pioneer stage of nation building. Our nation has traveled at a rapid pace this last generation. The duty of to-day is to readapt our public educational system as a whole to a sincere conception of education conceived to meet the actual needs and aspirations of all the people, which shall be sincere alike in the things of the mind and the spirit as well as in those of the daily job. To inaugurate such a fundamental and far-reaching study of what can and ought to be done is the most important national problem that confronts us. The college and the university were merged not as the result of deliberation but hurriedly. Whether they ought to remain permanently united is yet to be determined. Our situation to-day is one of confusion. Thoughtful and able men are concerned both for the American college and for the university. To integrate our composite structure in terms of the intellectual, social, and moral aspirations of the whole people is the vital need that confronts us.

XVII

This is, after all, a report on college athletics. It is fitting that the last word in this review should bring the reader back to the immediate subject of the report.

The thoughtful reader who has become aware of the transformation of college sports into professional athletic contests directed by paid coaches will wish to have answers to two questions.

Who is responsible for the athletic transformation? and what is now to be done about it?

The changes that institutions in the social order undergo are complicated by many factors. All human agencies—government, the church, the university—are influenced by the tendencies of the time. It was inevitable that the growing wealth and luxury of society, the transformation of the nation from a predominantly agricultural stage to an industrial stage would be reflected in its highest institutions of learning. It is no criticism of the university that its life and its functions have been affected by these universal tendencies, and that its organization and its attitude to the world have undergone a change. How far an intellectual agency such as a university, or a religious agency such as a church, ought to stand against those tendencies of society that run counter to the cause for which the university or the church stands, is a complicated matter to gauge. Leadership as a rule does not come from institutions as such. It comes from men who have the vision to see and the quality to lead. Institutional piety cannot take the place of personal righteousness. In any period of rapid industrial and social adjustment, such as the United States is going through, institutions are almost sure to drift until they find their bearings in the new order and develop the leadership to meet the new conditions. Sometimes the process results in a gradual and peaceful readjustment; sometimes a new institution divides the field with the old and established ones. At the beginning of this paper is a brief quotation from a letter of Erasmus to Luther. Both men were keenly alive to the low state in which the church and the university had fallen in their day. Erasmus believed that reform could be brought about within the old church. He pleaded that the unity of Christendom ought to be preserved, that if it split into two bodies it would undoubtedly split into innumerable sects, a prediction that has been amply confirmed. Luther was more determined. He would reform promptly or divide. Whether in the face of the weakness of the Popes of that day reform could have been compassed in the church it is now idle to enquire.

It is a useless enquiry at this day to ask who were responsible for the development in the colleges of commercialized sports. The tendencies of the time, the growing luxury, the keen inter-college competition, the influence of well-meaning, but unwise, alumni, the acquiescence in newspaper publicity, the reluctance of the authorities of the university or the college to take an unpopular stand,— all these have played their part.

But there can be no doubt as to where lies the responsibility to correct this situation. The defense of the intellectual integrity of the college and of the university lies with the president and faculty. With them lies also the authority. The educational governance of the university has always been in their hands. There have been cases in the past quarter century when a politically minded governing board, or an excited group of alumni, has sought to override the decision of the faculty in such matters. Such incidents to-day are rare though not entirely unknown. The president and faculty have in their power the decision touching matters affecting the educational policy and the intellectual interests of their institution. If commercialized athletics do not affect the educational quality of an institution, nothing does. The responsibility to bring athletics into a sincere relation to the intellectual life of the college rests squarely on the shoulders of the president and faculty.

What ought to be done?

The paid coach, the gate receipts, the special training tables, the costly sweaters and extensive journeys in special Pullman cars, the recruiting from the high school, the demoralizing publicity showered on the players, the devotion of an undue proportion of time to training, the devices for putting a desirable athlete, but a weak scholar, across the hurdles of the examinations — these ought to stop and the inter-college and intramural sports be brought back to a stage in which they can be enjoyed by large numbers of students and where they do not involve an expenditure of time and money wholly at variance with any ideal of honest study. Extensive statistics have been gathered as to the comparison between the college performance of those taking part in inter-college contests with that of students who take no part in athletics. Some of these tabulations are given in this report. They mean little. When the intellectual life of a body of college students is on a low plane, the difference between the formal credits of men in training for inter-college contests and those of the ordinary student who is not in training, may be inappreciable. But it requires no tabulation of statistics to prove that the young athlete who gives himself for months, body and soul, to training under a professional coach for a gruelling contest, staged to focus the attention of thousands of people, and upon which many thousands of dollars will be staked, will find no time or energy for any serious intellectual effort. The compromises that have to be made to keep such students in the college and to pass them through to a degree give an air of insincerity to the whole university-college régime. We cannot serve every cause—scholarship, science, business, salesmanship, organized athletics—through the university. The need to-day is to re-examine our educational régime with the determination to attain in greater measure the simplicity, sincerity, and thoroughness that is the life blood of a true university in any country at any age.

For the kindly coöperation of the universities and colleges in the United States and Canada, that has made this study possible, the Foundation is deeply grateful. Endowed and tax-supported institutions, and those under the control of religious bodies, whether Catholic or Protestant, have alike welcomed the enquiry and have given their assistance to a thorough and sincere prosecution of the study.

HENRY S. PRITCHETT.

July, 1929.

AMERICAN COLLEGE ATHLETICS

CHAPTER I
THE STUDY OF ATHLETICS
IN AMERICAN UNIVERSITIES AND COLLEGES

THE present enquiry has for its object to ascertain the significant facts concerning college athletics in the United States and Canada, to analyze these facts in relation to American college and university life, with such reference to school and college athletics in other countries as may shed occasional light upon our problems, and to present a summary of American college athletics, their merits and their defects, together with such suggestions looking to their improvement as may grow out of the materials in hand. The ideal of all who have been concerned with the work has been to offer an unbiased treatment as full and as accurate as circumstances permit. Of the numerous facts collected in the course of the enquiry, only a tithe can be set forth in detail. For the generalizations which the study contains it is believed that the data in hand afford ample justification. The purpose is not to add to the already vast bulk of educational theory, even though some attention is paid to the bearings of college athletics upon the principles and practice of education.

I. History and Extent of the Enquiry

Authority to pursue the enquiry rests solely upon the generosity and kindly coöperation of individuals and institutions. Before January 8, 1926, when the trustees of the Carnegie Foundation, through their executive committee, formally authorized the enquiry, they had considered a number of requests that such a study be undertaken. These requests, coming from influential and important bodies, such as the Association of American Colleges and the Association of Colleges and Secondary Schools of the Southern States, and from numerous individuals, included also that of the National Collegiate Athletic Association. In 1925 the Foundation had gathered materials concerning college athletics from some twenty colleges and universities in the United States and from the universities and schools of Great Britain. The discussions of this subject which have appeared in recent annual reports of the Foundation, notably the Eighteenth and the Twentieth, and in Bulletin Number Eighteen, are therefore to be regarded as reports *ad interim*. Useful as they have been in their own way, they affect little if at all the present discussion and conclusions; they represent merely a preliminary clearing of the ground.

A. Steps in the Study

As a preliminary to the present enquiry requests were sent to eighty-three persons, well qualified by their experience and interests, for suggestions as to what phases of American college athletics should be selected for study and by what means this study should be pursued. The replies showed careful consideration, and an attitude of helpfulness that has afforded one of the pleasantest aspects of our task. Although the great majority of suggestions proffered proved to be both useful and important, upon a few that will be noticed shortly it has seemed impossible to proceed.

Next, advice and assistance were sought from every person suggested as qualified to give them. It might be expected that a policy of consulting so many individuals would lead to a dispersion of the aims of the enquiry. This has not proved to be the case. Those who have been appealed to, whether for preliminary counsel or for information in the course of the enquiry, have shown an astonishing unanimity in the topics and materials which they have offered for consideration. Apparently there is no lack of general agreement concerning what problems are most important to college athletics.

As early as the spring of 1926, it became evident that no trustworthy results could be obtained by a general use of the questionnaire in studying so complex a subject. As a result, after much consultation, five members of the enquiry's staff visited a total of 130 schools, colleges, and universities. These may be classified as follows:

INSTITUTIONS VISITED

Section	Total	Colleges and Universities			Secondary Schools		
		Publicly Controlled	Privately Controlled	Total	Publicly Controlled	Privately Controlled	Total
Mid-Atlantic	40	4	26	30	7	3	10
South Atlantic	12	5	7	12			
West North Central	9	5	4	9			
East North Central	14	6	7	13	1		1
New England	22	2	15	17		5	5
Pacific States	9	4	3	7	2		2
Rocky Mountain States	8	6	2	8			
West South Central	5	2	3	5			
East South Central	4	2	2	4			
Canada	6	4	2	6			
Newfoundland	1		1	1			
	130	40	72	112	10	8	18

A complete list of these institutions is presented in the Appendix. In addition, hundreds of students, teachers, alumni, and other persons at these and other institutions have discussed matters that were pertinent to the enquiry. For the hospitality and kindly patience of all those who have contributed to the materials thus collected we desire to express our gratitude.[1] Professor W. Carson Ryan, Jr., of Swarthmore College, read the voluminous literature of college athletics, and the results of his work are published as Bulletin Number Twenty-four of the Foundation. By the summer of 1928 the great bulk of data had been collected and analyzed. On April 17, 1929, a summary of the information received from each of the colleges and universities of the enquiry was sent to each presiding officer. Pertinent excerpts from the eighty and more replies received appear in numerous footnotes throughout the present volume, especially in Chapter X.

B. Omissions from the Study

Among those proposals with which it has been impracticable to proceed, two may be selected for discussion. Both of them involve the rating of colleges and universities.

1. Ratings Respecting Athletic and Educational Standards

The suggestion was earnestly made that universities and colleges be rated as regards their athletics and the methods employed in administering them; more specifically, that the institutions be listed that "enforce the amateur rule, make athletics a part of the curriculum and encourage mass participation, have faculty direction and control, use good administrative methods, and make training the mind of primary importance while athletics are secondary." After much consideration such a rating was adjudged to be impracticable. At best the enquiry could represent general tendencies in American college athletics only by a sampling of the colleges of the United States and Canada; its validity must depend in part upon the size and nature of the sampling. Moreover, the arbitrary fixing of a scale of values prerequisite to such a rating would require a minuteness of detail which no agency at present constituted could undertake to secure. An insistence upon one or another requirement might have worked injustice to comparatively large numbers of institutions at which other requirements were conscientiously subserved. The present study therefore attempts to offer no rating of American colleges in respect to their conduct of athletics. It is to be hoped, however, that some of these matters will find answers in the pages that follow.

2. Training in Physical Education

Another request was to the effect that institutions that prepare teachers of physical education should be studied in detail and then rated on a basis of standards and performance. Upon careful inspection this procedure proved to be impractical, first,

[1] Two Southern universities failed to accord what is to be regarded as full coöperation. The promises of one officer at the University of Georgia to send complete data and materials as requested in the course of a field visit were not fulfilled. The only institution at which official coöperation in the study was requested and was flatly refused is Oglethorpe University. There coöperation was confined to interviews with the president; when interviews were sought with faculty members and students, and permission was requested to examine books and records as they were examined at other coöperating institutions, both were refused and the field agent was bidden to cease his enquiries.

because to do it justice would have distorted the project as a whole, and, secondly, because it is too important a matter to be relegated to a subordinate position in a general enquiry.

C. PRINCIPLES EVOLVED

As the work progressed a few general principles began to take form and upon these the enquiry as far as possible was based:

1. Facts have more weight than opinions, except perhaps when opinion itself has become fact. Adherence to this principle has caused us to seek confirmation of facts of whose validity the persons offering them were absolutely convinced. If it is never pleasant to appear to doubt another's word, it is still less pleasant to cross-examine a man who has proffered information with the sole object of helping one to ascertain the truth. We bear witness to the generous forbearance of numbers of persons in what might easily have become situations of some embarrassment.

A portion of the facts which the enquiry has brought to light is unsavory. At the beginning of the study it was confidently stated by one whose advice was sought and whose opinions are much respected that it would be impossible to uncover the truth concerning the subsidizing of athletes without employing private detectives. No private detectives have been employed. During field visits the following general procedure was usual. Official letters of introduction were presented through appropriate university officers, usually the president, and through them appointments were sought with other officials, professors, and undergraduates. Only one or two exceptions to this policy have been made, and in those cases conversations with the president were delayed because of absence or other reasons. In a number of instances individuals have expressed astonishment at the openness of the enquiry and the frankness with which information was sought and given. This open frankness suggests that changes in American college athletics will depend first and last upon the extent and trustworthiness of the knowledge in the hands of university and college officers.

2. Any description of conditions or any recommendations which result from the enquiry must take into consideration both the past and the present as well as the future, must be as nearly unprejudiced as possible, and must be grounded in verifiable fact.

3. Each member of the special staff of the enquiry must be kept at all times informed of every phase of the work, for the sake of maintaining a uniform point of view.

4. Authorized discussion of any phase of the enquiry must await the publication of the study.

Of these general principles the most difficult to maintain has been the last, especially in the case of newspaper men and college executives. When college officers have requested suggestions in the solution of some of their major administrative problems, we have been forced in some cases to avoid specific suggestions and to deal in very general terms with matters that deserve a most exact individual treatment.

D. Special Problems

Among the special problems of method encountered in the course of the enquiry, a word should be said concerning three : the treatment of rumor, the duration of visits to individual institutions, and the study of recruiting and subsidizing.

1. The Treatment of Rumor

It is not the purpose of the present study to add to the considerable bulk of rumor and scandal which darkens American college athletics. Of the numbers of well-intentioned persons who early in the enquiry brought to us talk of the inducements and subsidies offered to athletes, very few would or could give the names of the men involved. Fewer still were willing that their own names should be mentioned. Although it appeared to be considered unfair to attach these tales to individuals, almost all exhibited no compunction in indicating freely the universities, colleges, and schools which they believed "*must* be offering inducements." As the work advanced, however, the number of persons who discussed these problems frankly increased almost from day to day. If those who invent unfounded rumors of subsidizing and recruiting or speed them on their way had the task of verifying or disproving even a few of their products, they would be more cautious in such activities.

2. Duration of Visits

At the beginning of the enquiry a field visit to a college or a university consumed from two to six days. As the work went forward it became possible to reduce the average time devoted to field visits by advance notification, so that material could be prepared before the arrival of the field agent, by increased knowledge of what would probably be pertinent to the work, and, above all, because of the increased skill of field agents. Thus information which in 1926 might have taken six days to gather could have been collected in 1928 in from one-third to one-half of the time. To those institutions which needed further study a second, and in one instance a third, visit was paid, but in the absence of special considerations no more than a single visit was required. The information collected is therefore not referred specifically to any single date. For the most part it relates to conditions as they existed at the time the field visit was paid.

3. The Study of Recruiting and Subsidizing

Obviously an enquiry that includes recruiting and subsidizing involves vastly different problems from one that touches upon such comparatively innocuous matters as athletic facilities or organization. The search for facts respecting the solicitation and support of athletes often leads along devious paths to individuals or groups far removed, in distance and in point of view, from the college campus. Under these conditions the gathering of trustworthy information becomes an arduous task. In such quests valuable assistance has been rendered by many college and university officials who indicated channels of enquiry and established fruitful relationships. On the other hand, in a few instances officials have been short-sighted enough to resent a genuine study of facts. Apparently such men failed to realize that if an enquirer, officially received, comes upon information which excites his curiosity, then refusal, evasion, or concealment on any particular topic arouses a suspicion which is often worse than the facts involved. Moreover, if an enquirer possessing only moderate discernment merely remains on the campus, he can scarcely fail to arrive at the truth.

It should be noted that athletes themselves exhibit a high degree of honesty and straightforwardness when approached in the same spirit. Even when athletes have been warned in advance concerning questions or have feared the consequences of giving information, conversation with them has proved enlightening. Perhaps these facts will suggest to college officers who really wish to learn the truth, a ready source of knowledge.

II. Standards and Criteria

It is inevitable that the present study should attempt to evaluate many phases of our college athletics. These values are summarized and discussed in Chapter XII. But it is equally inevitable that the assumptions underlying these critical evaluations should color numerous earlier pages of the discussion. It therefore seems appropriate that a few of the considerations that have guided us in our task be set down in the sections that follow.

A. American and European Sport

Standards for American college athletics must be sought in America. They are not to be found in England, where traditionalism, the organization into colleges, and conditions of university life, especially at Oxford and Cambridge, set that country, however admirable may be its ideals of sport, quite apart from the United States. The English national life and English university life have been slow of growth. American life and, in the main, American university life are the products of a century and a half. The intimate connection in tradition, practice, and operation with the mother country associates some aspects of Canadian college athletics more closely with sport in England than with college sport in the United States. Thus, although an appreciation of American college athletics must be based upon the tenets upon which the Union is founded and life in the United States is lived, nevertheless the athletic tradition of the universities of England and Canada deserves examination in order that its best may be considered in the light of its applicability to the problem of the colleges and the university. The underlying principles of college sport in various countries present striking similarities, but these principles are modified by geographical considerations, educational practices, and national ideals of initiative and achievement. This fact stands out sharply when consideration is directed to international athletic competition.

B. The Uses of Games

Recent discussions of the uses and purposes that various branches of college athletics may serve have brought forth two important observations. In the first place, certain contests, being games of youth, are useful almost exclusively during school and college days. Among this number are to be found most of the contests of "personal encounter," or bodily contact, such as football, basketball, hockey, lacrosse, boxing, and wrestling. Although these provide players and spectators with much diversion, only in comparatively few instances have they important relation to life after graduation. The principal exceptions are those college athletes who later become professional players.

The second group of pastimes contains those games which are suitable for participation until relatively late in life : Tennis, golf, handball, squash, and in less degree baseball, commenced in school or college can be played after graduation as facilities offer. Other ball games also have their place in the recreation of later years.

It is therefore obvious that those who are charged with the education of youth are in duty bound to determine the use and emphasis to be accorded to games and contests of these two types. If it is to be accepted as fact that the great spectacles afforded by college football contests are of value in providing "emotional explosions" for large groups of undergraduate spectators, the question must be pressed a step further to an analysis of the right of the alumnus to expect his college to provide for him a means of escape from the dreary round of every day. Certainly present-day college football encourages in the man of thirty no very ardent desire to don a suit and subject himself to the rigors of training, even if it provides a paramount topic of conversation and a ground of common interest and lively — albeit gradually waning — enthusiasm. To assist those who are interested in arriving at their own evaluation of such matters is one of the aims of the present study.

C. Rules and Their Observance

Only the slightest consideration is necessary to validate the proposition that "rules do not enforce themselves, and the athletic standing of a college is in no way determined by its rules." Whatever college athletic regulations respecting recruiting and subsidizing of players may be in vogue, they must be regarded as ideals to which a very large number of institutions have not yet attained. It is safe to say that if as much ingenuity were expended upon discovering and eliminating those cases in which young athletes accepted secret assistance for unworthy motives, as now is devoted to infringing rules and corrupting youthful sportsmen, our college athletics would soon take on an entirely different complexion. It is one thing for older and presumably wiser persons to entertain lofty ideals for the general run of undergraduates. It is quite another matter to cause individual young men and young women, as well as persons of maturer years, to feel the force of such ideals, to make them their own, and finally so to shape their conduct as to approximate them or at least not deliberately to contravene them. The value of any rule of conduct lies in its observance.

III. Definitions

Athletics in American colleges and universities form a part of those diversions of college life generally termed either *outside activities*, in the sense that they lie beyond the academic requirements of the institution, or *student activities*, as representing one means whereby students may exercise their abilities and predilections apart from the strictly educational or academic routine. *Extramural athletics* are understood to be those branches of competitive sports and games in which duly authorized under-graduates representing a university, a college, or a school meet in contests representa-tives of other institutions or organizations. Thus, strictly speaking, a college soccer team which plays against the team of a local amateur club participates in extramural but not intercollegiate athletics. *Intercollegiate athletics* are those branches of under-graduate sports and games in which duly authorized representatives of one institution of higher education meet in contests with those of another. Similar distinctions should be borne in mind respecting school athletics. *Intramural athletics* comprise those games and contests in which duly matriculated students, undergraduates, graduates, or both, contend against other contestants of similar status in the same institution. In the course of an intramural schedule, however, a dormitory team which plays principally against fraternity, other dormitory, and class teams, may undertake a game with a school or some other body that is not an integral part of the institution to which the team belongs.

Mention should also be made of three distinctions which, although too little recog-nized, have grown in importance since 1913. The first of these distinctions is connoted by the terms *control* and *guidance*. The second is the essential difference between, on the one hand, the regulation of college athletics by faculty members whose professional interests centre primarily upon things of the mind, and on the other, control by faculty members whose professional interests concern the development of the body, or "physical education" in its accepted sense. The third distinction lies between (1) a college program of physical education which includes only such matters as athletic sports and games, intercollegiate and intramural, corrective exercises, and rather per-functory discussion of certain aspects of social hygiene set forth in a few lectures to large groups, and (2) a college program which includes some or all of these matters, but has for its ultimate and sincere purpose the fitting of young men and women to understand in a general way the relationships of hygiene in the broadest sense of the term to their own lives, to the end that they may intelligently conduct this phase of their own careers.

In the present study *physical education* denotes primarily that phase of college or school instruction which has for its principal purpose the development of bodily strength and well-being and muscular coördination among its participants. The wider implications of the term include, as just indicated, instruction in personal and social hygiene, in exercises calculated to correct physical or nervous defects, and in the use for purposes of instruction of competitive games and contests that until recent years have figured principally as college pastimes. Physical education, therefore, extends its field to deal with mental, physical, social, and moral health. Frequently the terms *educational* and *education* are employed in contrast to commercialism.

Commercialism in sport is the placing of a higher value upon monetary and material returns, whether direct or indirect, from any athletic activity than is placed upon its returns in recreation, health, and physical and moral well-being.

A sentence uttered by Professor Percy Hughes, of Lehigh University, at the dedication of the University of Nebraska stadium, expresses a contrast which is all too often ignored in considering college athletics: "We train the body, only the mind is capable of education." Finally, it must be taken for granted that *sportsmanship*,[2] which in its essential manifestations is merely the operation of the golden rule and of the attitude of the gentleman (in the American sense) in competitive contests, is a desirable social phenomenon. The development of the qualities included in the term "sportsmanship" is possible not alone in all species of contests and games but in all of the other social aspects of life.

Conclusion

The present situation in American college athletics could be described and efficacious remedies proposed merely by setting forth a series of quotations from materials published before 1900. The complaints that have been voiced since 1900 have been in the

[2] Speaking after a luncheon of the Sportsmanship Brotherhood in New York City on May 15, 1929, Professor Charles W. Kennedy of Princeton said in part: "It will always be difficult to frame a definition of sportsmanship that will be completely accurate and comprehensive, for sportsmanship is so subtly rooted in the reactions of human spirit, so various in its possible gestures, and so intricately interwoven with the elements of individual character and personality that it is by its very nature not susceptible of being caught and held in any net of words. Nevertheless, there are elements of sportsmanship so clear that he who runs may read. A sportsman is one who loves the game for its own sake; who has a scrupulous regard for the rules of fair play and strives under these rules to pit his best against the best of an opponent whom he respects; who admires excellence in the game for its own sake and who pays an instinctive tribute of respect to excellence whether it be his own or that of an opponent; who in the stress of competition strives to the uttermost without descent to breach of rule or vindictive spirit; who hates a quitter, an alibi, or a boast; who in the course of the game preserves courage in the face of odds, and dignity, self-respect and good will in the presence of defeat; who wishes an amateur game to be played by amateurs and not by masquerading professionals; who delights to meet all comers upon the democratic fields of sport with a recognition that it is well for youth to have this early training in the knowledge that in the life of a great democracy he is the better man who proves it. These, though by no means all, are some of the important elements in that fine and subtle attitude of mind called sportsmanship." Professor Kennedy's address is printed in *Sportsmanship*, the publication of the Sportsmanship Brotherhood, for June, 1929.

main echoes or amplifications of the adverse criticisms of previous years. Some of the reasons these cries have gone unheeded are to be found in their general nature and lack of specific modern instances, but especially in the fact that the interests of individuals and the special pleadings which have been used to buttress and justify their complaints have obscured the truth of their utterances. The present study is not the final word on American college athletics. Although very possibly it contains more generalizations than will please numerous readers, a formula for remedying the defects of college and school athletics is not proposed. So complex and so overlaid with the interests of individuals are our athletics that, with their bearing upon self-pride and the maintenance of reputation and esteem, they yield few approaches for amendment by any means other than a long continued amelioration of habits in youth.

It is, of course, impossible to make the study appear true to all the facts in the individual experience of any reader. The emphasis and importance assigned to various parts must differ from those that others would assign. It is inevitable that weaknesses should receive an emphasis that to some persons may appear quite disproportionate to their place in any scheme of values. Doubtless college athletics possess many more merits than are numbered in the pages that follow. If abuses seem to be overemphasized it is because the developments during the last two decades of American college athletics have been very great and the ideals to be served very high.

In the United States, what is needed in college and school athletics is not more law but a more genuine regard for existing law, not uniformity of requirements respecting eligibility and kindred matters but uniformity and recognition of fundamental principles, especially as affecting the exemplification of sportsmanship ; not because sportsmanship is fashionable, but because, even more than it is to-day, it should be appreciated and sincerely regarded in every form of athletic competition.

CHAPTER II

THE GROWTH OF COLLEGE ATHLETICS

THE student of American college athletics who considers the vastness of the material and social fabric that they now involve will ask, first, how this structure came to occupy its present place in our university life, and, secondly, what relationship it bears to the status of the amateur. These two subjects are inextricably interwoven, but because college athletics are of the college, while the amateur status touches not alone college athletics but all athletic sports and games, the bearings of both will be clearer if they are considered separately.

The development of athletics in the colleges of the United States falls into four fairly well-defined periods:

I. The Beginnings of College Athletics, the development of undergraduate sports and games up to 1852, when the first recorded intercollegiate contest took place.

II. The Intensification of College Sports, the growth in popularity of contests in all branches up to 1885, with a rather clearly marked division at the year 1880.

III. The Expansion of College Athletics and Its Results, from the abolition of football at Harvard up to 1906, one year after the formation of the first national athletic association.

IV. The Struggle for Control, which began to gain headway about 1906 and is not yet concluded.

I. THE BEGINNINGS OF AMERICAN COLLEGE ATHLETICS (TO 1852)

Although an anthropologist would remind us that games go back to the earliest history of the human race, and that even animals play, a less remote genesis of athletics in the American college may be found beyond the college walls of colonial and revolutionary days in the pioneer life of the colonists and the earlier citizens of the Republic. A game at football is recorded in Virginia as early as 1609. In New England and the Middle Atlantic colonies it is to such aspects of the community life as market days, barn-raisings, and huskings that the seeker for the origins of American athletic sports must turn. The New England Thanksgiving custom of men kicking a football about their backyards bears little semblance to a team game, nor, for that matter, do the athletic contests that grew up about the observance of Independence Day. The participants in such exertions were generally younger men, although occasionally older persons engaged in them. With the growth of social organizations of various kinds and the rise of militia companies, rivalry between such bodies led naturally to tests of athletic skill and thus to a semblance of group contests, which, however, exerted little if any influence upon the life of colleges and schools.[1]

A. College Games and Contests

Such contests as have just been mentioned were essentially of the people. In colonial days the young man who proceeded from school to college and who thus entered the life of learning and scholarship, thereby set himself apart from his friends and neighbors. Before 1800 he was apparently little given to such indulgences and pastimes as they pursued. In the early American college, as Francis A. Walker pointed out, "there was more than indifference, there was contempt for physical prowess. A man known to be especially gifted in this way was thereby disparaged in public estimation; if he was known to make much of it, he was more likely to be despised. It was taken for granted that he could not be good for much else. Brains and brawn were supposed to be developed in inverse ratio; strength was closely allied to brutality." Doubtless the fact that a large proportion of the undergraduates of those days were intending to enter the Christian ministry had much to do with this attitude; it was more than half a century before the discovery was made that Christianity could be muscular.

On the other hand, sporadic attention, often of a repressive nature, was directed to games at some colleges. A minute of the Princeton faculty of May, 1761, frowns upon students "playing at ball." Hockey, "baste ball," and "prison baste" are mentioned as of 1786. Another Princeton minute, dated November 26, 1787, prohibited students and grammar scholars from playing a certain game with sticks and a ball, — probably

[1] Of the published materials bearing upon the history of American college athletics, the valuable contributions of Edward Mussey Hartwell, usually published, from 1884 on, in the Reports of the United States Commissioner of Education, must be regarded as the foundation. Reference should be made also to Francis A. Walker's discussion of "College Athletics," *Harvard Graduates Magazine*, 1893; Professor Henry D. Sheldon's important treatise on *Student Life and Customs*, 1901; the studies of Professor George L. Meylan in the *Cyclopaedia of Education*, 1911; President Thwing's discussions in numerous volumes; Walter Camp's *Sixty Years of American Football*, 1924; Major A. M. Weyand's *American Football*, 1926; and Professor Amos Alonzo Stagg's *Touchdown!* 1927. B. H. Hall's *Collection of College Words and Customs*, 1856, and Andrew P. Peabody's *Harvard Reminiscences*, 1888, contain illuminating passages. Among studies descriptive of life at American colleges and universities, the athletic and other histories of Dartmouth by John H. Bartlett and John G. Gifford (1893), and by H. G. Pender and Raymond McPartin (1923), of Brown, Princeton, and Yale, together with Horace M. Lippincott's *University of Pennsylvania* (1888), are important. Critical excerpts from all of these books and many others bearing upon the subject will be found in Professor W. Carson Ryan, Jr.'s, study of the literature of college athletics, published as Bulletin Number Twenty-four by the Carnegie Foundation for the Advancement of Teaching, 1929.

shinty or shinny. In the eighteenth century, as Hartwell shows, quoting the sixteenth of the *Ancient Customs of Harvard College*, the freshmen were required to "furnish bats, balls, and footballs for the use of students, to be kept in the buttery." "Occasionally the students at Harvard and Yale kicked a football about on the Common, or in the street, and a yearly game took place between the sophomores and freshmen, which partook largely of the nature of a modern rush." Most of the college faculties perforce tolerated free-for-all fights between student classes, and it is not unlikely that, in the initiation of freshmen, tests of skill or strength had their part. So far as athletics were concerned, the century was characterized in American colleges by an almost complete absence of anything approaching organization, rules, or what we now regard as team games, as distinguished from contests between sides.

The early history of a few of the modern college games can be traced with a degree of certainty.

1. Cross-Country Running

If any man deserves the title of the father of American college athletics, it is Charles Follen, a former pupil of F. L. Jahn's system of Graeco-German gymnastics. Coming to Harvard in 1824, after the political and social disorders that attended the rise of the Jena Burschenschaft, Dr. Follen, while teaching German and introducing gymnastics into Harvard College, used to lead "the entire body of students, except the few lame and the fewer lazy, on a run without pause, from the Delta to the top of the hill now crowned by the most conspicuous of the Somerville churches, and back again after a ten-minute halt." These young men were taught "to run with a minimum of fatigue, with the body thrown slightly forward, the arms akimbo, and breathing only through the nose." Dr. Follen's activities in the teaching of gymnastics upon the Jahn system, with those of his fellow-exile, Dr. Beck, were even more important than his leading of cross-country runs.

2. Gymnastics

Harvard is usually said to be the first college to have a gymnasium, in one of its dining halls during 1826. In September of the same year the Yale Corporation appropriated three hundred dollars for the clearing and preparation of ground for an outdoor gymnasium. One year later gymnastic apparatus was set up at Brown, Williams, and Amherst, which is usually credited with having inaugurated in 1860 the first college department of physical training or education.[2] The training thus initiated at these five

---

[2] "The School of Messrs. Cogswell and Bancroft, in Northampton, Mass., was the first institution in this country that introduced gymnastick exercises as a part of the regular instruction, in the Spring of 1825." (Beck, *A Treatise on Gymnasticks, taken chiefly from the German of F. L. Jahn*, 1828, preface, noted by Dr. Hartwell in his paper on the *Rise of College Gymnasia in the United States*, 1886.) Dr. Beck also taught Latin in Harvard College. As Dr. Hartwell indicates, the impulse to establish these early gymnasiums came from Prussia, "where, during the last fifteen years of the eighteenth century and the first two decades of the nineteenth, Guts Muths and Jahn accomplished a great work in reviving physical education."

institutions did not, however, develop into a systematic program of physical education. It is referable to the group of sporadic outcroppings of interest in physical exercise, German in origin, which dot the early decades of the American university. It was thirty years before the first Princeton gymnasium was built, partly by faculty subscription, in 1859.

3. Football

The first authoritative reference to football as a college pastime concerns the Princeton of 1820. In 1827, Bloody Monday at Harvard included among its activities a contest at football between freshmen and sophomores. The game was played at West Point between 1840 and 1844, and at about the same time class football contests were popular at Harvard, Yale, and Princeton, Amherst and Bowdoin. Accounts of these matches indicate that the game resembled modern soccer rather than the college football of the present day.

4. Baseball

Baseball, with its probable origins in the English "rounders," the early nineteenth century American schoolboy game of "one-old-cat" and "town-ball" played in Canada and in Philadelphia in 1833, first became an organized game in 1839 under the guidance of Major Abner Doubleday. Rudimentary forms of the game may have been enjoyed by undergraduates as recreation and exercise before the middle of the century. At smaller colleges, like Amherst and Bowdoin, a kind of baseball appears to have enjoyed some popularity without any particular organization, but the game apparently had little standing in colleges before 1852.

5. Other Land Sports

During the earlier period other games were played at the colleges along the Eastern seaboard. For instance, Amherst undergraduates indulged in cricket, wicket, the pitching of loggerheads and quoits, and round ball. Bowdoin men enjoyed walking. At Princeton, handball and cricket were in vogue, and shinny and its derivatives, hawkey and hurley, continued in sporadic popularity. It has been said upon good authority that Yale students showed little inclination toward physical exercise on land, and probably much the same is true of other colleges where water for swimming and boating was easily accessible.

6. Rowing

Yale and Harvard took the lead in developing rowing as a college pastime. As early as 1843 Yale undergraduates purchased their first racing boat and formed their first boat club. Nine years later Harvard defeated Yale in a race in eight-oared barges over a two-mile course on Lake Winnepesaukee. "The character of this first contest," says

Dr. Thwing, citing Richard M. Hurd on *Yale Athletics*, "may be inferred from a remark made by one of the Harvard crew that they had only rowed a few times for fear of blistering their hands. The chief idea of training was avoiding sweets on the actual day of the race," a practice that is certainly not in accord with modern training methods. In 1852, also, the Yale Navy was formed. Rowing, then, appears to have been, in the United States, the first sport in which intercollegiate competition took place.

B. Developments in England

Organized athletics appeared in English schools and colleges somewhat earlier than in the United States. The first Eton-Harrow cricket match was played as early as 1822, to be followed five years later by the first match between Oxford and Cambridge. The game had been a schoolboys' pastime since the middle of the seventeenth century. Of course, the genesis of Rugby football is definitely marked by the iconoclastic run of William Webb Ellis in 1823. In 1829, Eton and Westminster rowed their first race, and records of boating exist at both institutions beginning with 1811 and 1813, respectively. The first Oxford-Cambridge eight-oared race took place at Henley in 1829.

Notwithstanding the priority of dates, the statement frequently heard that American school and college games had their roots in English university and school sports must be regarded as "not proven" in its entirety. It is true that cricket and Rugby football reached an early popularity in the United States at such colleges as Princeton and Harvard, and it is probable that American football would be to-day an entirely different game were it not for the influence of English Rugby, as played in this country. Nevertheless, the inclination toward outdoor sports among the people of the United States, in the early nineteenth century, referable in part to the decline of pioneer life, was of sufficient force to have developed college athletic pastimes without the modifying influence of English university contests.

C. Athletics and Faculties

The attitude of the American undergraduate toward college athletics during the closing years of the eighteenth century and the earlier years of the nineteenth has been outlined. The attitude of faculties may be summarized as on the whole tolerant of undergraduate pastimes, except when they became either rowdy or dangerous to life or college property. Only in such circumstances do repressive measures appear to have been exerted. At Princeton in 1787 the faculty, after first stating its *locus parentis*, remarked that "there are many amusements both more honorable and more useful" for undergraduates than shinny. The later refusal of the Amherst faculty to sanction the laying out of bowling alleys reflects somewhat the same notion. On the other hand, the Princeton faculty of 1849 permitted the building of a handball court. This fact and the early introduction of gymnasiums at Amherst, Harvard, and Yale may be taken as an indication that not all college faculties opposed exercise by undergraduates, provided it was conducted with decorum and in a manner in keeping with the scholarly life which the young gentlemen were supposed to lead.

II. The Intensification of American College Athletics (1853–1885)

The years between 1853 and 1885 were characterized by a comparatively slow growth in college athletics up to about 1870, by a more rapid growth thereafter, and by an increasing tendency in the direction of organization. By 1870 athletics had taken their place in American college life. Thereafter the influence of the older English universities becomes direct. The closing years of the period are marked by an intensification of interest, by the growth of an intercollegiate rivalry which had manifested itself previously in a far milder form, and by attempts to abolish football about 1885.

A. Intramural Contests

The influence of the English college system coupled with English rowing is probably responsible for the division, in 1859, of the Yale undergraduate body into twelve intramural boating clubs of twenty men each. These persisted for some nine years, at the end of which the clubs were superseded by a system of inter-class crews and the Yale University Boat Club. At about this time bumping races were rowed at more than one Eastern college. American inter-class baseball began with the Princeton competitions of 1864, which have been accepted as the origin of most of the organized intramural baseball series of the country. Although a Princeton football club may have been organized in 1857, nevertheless Princeton football of 1858, if good authority is to be credited, was a rough-and-tumble affair played with an inflated bladder by sides of indeterminate number in the quadrangle formed by college buildings. The game had many resemblances to soccer, which, by 1860, a dozen Eastern colleges were playing with some regularity. It was six years before the resuscitated Princeton Football Club became the most popular undergraduate activity. Meanwhile a similar development was under way at Harvard. After a gradual increase in the popularity of class football teams and games, in 1872 the Harvard Football Association was organized to supplement them. Field days for many branches of track and field sports came to be held at the University of Pennsylvania, Princeton, and Yale. The intramural contests of the earlier portion of the period, although intense with class and club rivalry, were informal and comparatively disorganized affairs conducted principally for the amusement of the undergraduates.

B. Extramural Matches

Respecting extramural matches, it will be well to enquire in what sports they first developed and then to note the comparatively rapid growth of formal associations and rules for games.

1. Formal Contests

Professor Stagg tells the story of the first organized football clubs, from information furnished to him by Gerrit Smith Miller, Esq., whose experience at football began in 1856. From the playground games at the Epes Sargent Dixwell Private Latin School, Boston, and the Boston Public Latin School, Boston English High School, Roxbury High School, and Dorchester High School, apparently sprang the first interscholastic football contests. The game was certainly soccer, the rules for which were codified in England by the Football Association in 1863. From twelve players at the Dixwell school, two from the English High School, and one from the Boston Latin School, was formed the Oneida Club during the summer of 1862. Although in 1867 a Princeton all-college team defeated Princeton Seminary at football, it was not until the following year that the first Princeton 'Varsity Football Club was constituted. During the spring of 1869 Princeton defeated Rutgers at baseball, and, spurred on by the loss of this contest, the Rutgers'Varsity Football Club challenged the Princeton organization to a game which is generally considered to have been the first American intercollegiate football match. Rutgers won. This game also was soccer. The influence of the English public schools upon American college football is to be noted in the revival at Yale, about 1870, of football under the tutelage of D. F. Scharf, an old Rugbyan. From about 1869 to about 1877, intercollegiate soccer games were played intermittently under local rules by Columbia, the College of the City of New York, Harvard, Haverford, New York University, the University of Pennsylvania, and Yale.

During the eight years following 1852, Harvard and Yale rowed some six races under varying conditions on three different courses. At last, in 1864, boat races between the two universities under standardized conditions were inaugurated on Lake Quinsigamond, near Worcester. This regatta, which was the occasion for the first sensational newspaper accounts of intercollegiate competition, marked also the beginning of a series of five successive annual Harvard victories culminating in the sending, 1869, of a Harvard crew to England, where it was defeated by Oxford. Thus, rowing provides a second connection between sport at the older English universities and American college athletics. At a number of colleges, rowing attained very great importance, and there was much discussion of the advisability of mitigating the rigors of races.

It would appear that organized college baseball began at Princeton in 1858, when an unusually expert group of players entered the freshman class. The nine was called the Nassaus, and the first match outside of Princeton was played in 1860. One year earlier Amherst had organized her first baseball team. It was not until 1865, however, that undergraduates at Yale took a similar step, possibly influenced thereto by the success of Princeton in the field. Eighteen sixty-eight witnessed the first baseball game in the annual Harvard-Yale series. During the eight years following 1860, college baseball reached a definite status in intercollegiate competition,— indeed, by 1870 baseball was played in all of the more prominent Eastern colleges. The years following 1870 were characterized by a number of attempts to codify and regularize competition in many sports.

2. Rules and Associations for College Matches

This development can be sketched only in the briefest terms. In 1871, rules for the game of football are said to have been first written down. One year later the Yale Football Association was organized. In 1873, the first Oxford-Cambridge 'varsity Rugby match took place, and in the following year Harvard adopted Rugby Union football rules and played her first football game against the University of California, at Cambridge. As regards the rules for football matches, not alone in the East but in other parts of the United States, the confused conditions of the day were productive of little intercollegiate good will. It is, therefore, not astonishing to find that in 1876 at a convention of representatives of American colleges held at New York, an intercollegiate football association was organized and the Rugby Union rules were adopted officially to govern matches, with a few slight modifications. Those modifications, however, in time expanded into a corpus of playing usage that has definitely severed American football from English Rugby, from its offshoot, the Canadian game, and from soccer.

Intercollegiate rowing continued to advance apace. In 1870, there was organized the Rowing Association of American Colleges, which included most of the institutions in New England and three or four in New Jersey and New York State. Under the auspices of the Association six annual races were held, the first three on the Connecticut River at Springfield, the remaining three at Lake Saratoga. Participation in these regattas was variable and the membership of the Association changed rapidly. To one regatta as many as seventeen colleges sent their crews; to the next, only seven. The long standing rivalry between Harvard and Yale disrupted the membership of the Association. Feeling ran high and contests among the spectators were not infrequently more bitter than those between the crews. Finally, in 1876, both Yale and Harvard withdrew from the organization. Bowdoin, Brown, Dartmouth, and Trinity endeavored unsuccessfully to continue it.

Apparently track athletics was one of the branches that developed more slowly. The Intercollegiate Association of Amateur Athletes of America was founded in 1875, and in the following year its first intercollegiate track and field meeting was held at Saratoga. The first college baseball league of 1879 included Amherst, Brown, Dartmouth, Harvard, and Princeton. Yale joined in 1880.

Thus the conditions engendered and fostered by intercollegiate competition led to the formation of associations to the end that teams and crews might meet each other in athletic competition on a uniform and accepted basis. At the same time, the rivalries which grew out of one such association in the course of years proved to be its undoing, for partisanship replaced sportsmanship, and organization broke under the stress of rivalry.

C. Training, Coaching, and Management

Up to about 1880 neither training nor coaching in American college athletics had become specialized. Training tables were unknown; uniforms were of the simplest. What coaching existed was done by members of faculties, by graduates, and by those undergraduates whose schools had provided them with sufficient experience to justify their being chosen for the work and its responsibilities. Management appears to have been entirely in the hands of undergraduates. Usually participants in matches away from home grounds or waters paid their own expenses, although it is possible that some of the college athletic clubs received from their members subscriptions to help defray the costs of travel. Consciously or unconsciously, the athletic usages and customs of the period regarding such matters bear many resemblances to those of Oxford and Cambridge. The doctrine of equal opportunity for competition among all undergraduates regardless of means had not yet been invoked to enable the impecunious student to participate in intercollegiate contests. To these observations a few individual exceptions may be taken, but as far as information serves they represent with fair accuracy the situation in the United States during this earlier period of athletic development.

D. The Faculties; the Press

The year 1880 has been set as a dividing line between the old régime and the new. After this date the attention devoted to sports increased rapidly and coincidentally with the rise of their popularity in the universities of England. For a time American faculties tolerated with a few rather ineffectual protests the development of pursuits which many of their members already regarded as inimical to the best scholarly interests of the colleges. In 1871 both the Harvard and the Yale faculties prohibited intercollegiate soccer contests, and it has been suggested that the agreement of 1878 between twelve colleges for contests in public speaking, essay writing, and exercises in Greek, Latin, mathematics, and mental science marked an attempt on the part of their faculties to abate some of the enthusiasm that athletics aroused. There may also have been some resentment of the intrusion of newspapers into the field of college sports. For instance, in 1874, the New York *Herald* Olympian Games were inaugurated. These constituted an intercollegiate championship meeting in which athletes from Columbia, Cornell, Dartmouth, Harvard, Princeton, and Yale competed, and they continued for several years. Be these suppositions as they may, there is little doubt that the football of the 1880's amply justified President Eliot's epithet "brutal." In 1884, after repeated protests against the roughness of the game, the Harvard faculty by formal vote abolished football at Cambridge. The prohibition lasted for two years. Similar but less drastic attempts to control football were made at other colleges. The attitude of most faculties toward athletics appears to have been not opposition but tolerance or *laissez-faire.* There was a general lack of comprehension respecting the implications of college sport and a complete failure to foresee the development that it was destined to undergo.

III. The Expansion of College Athletics and Its Results (1886–1906)

The third period of American college athletics is marked by a sudden break with the past and by a rapid development of many of the characteristics of the period that was to follow. The informality of the earlier day had been superseded by organization and elaboration. Some of the commentators became as optimistic as their present-day successors over the moral and physical benefits to be derived from well-regulated athletics. Indeed, later writers in support of college athletics have added very few if any important arguments to those of their predecessors. But there were other comments of a warning nature. The tendencies noted as having been initiated about 1880, which gave rise to a gathering alarm over the expansion of athletics and the flock of evils that beset their progress, resemble in kind those which characterize certain aspects of the present day. It is far from a pleasure to note that a part of this third period was darkened by a sinister influence that proceeds from college alumni, — who of all men should have been scrupulous in keeping untarnished those sports to which they as undergraduates had been devoted. This is not to imply that college teachers then were or now are the only true repositories of athletic righteousness or ethical standards; it is merely an attempt to present facts which our college history has come to accept as valid. By 1890, all or practically all English public schools had adhered to either the Rugby Union code or the Association code for football. Had a similar choice been possible in the United States during the period under consideration, the future of American college football and other branches of athletics might have been less variegated.

A. Control, 1887–1906

During most of what we have called the second period of American college athletics, the direction and management of sports and games rested, in general, with the undergraduates. About 1880, expansion began. More branches of athletics were introduced. Training was intensified and elaborated, and trainers were employed. Coaching began to be a progressively technical task, and paid coaches grew to be rather the rule than the exception. Not a few of the leaders of the present who demand that athletics be administered by faculty members alone, began their careers as hired coaches of teams before 1906. Equipment ashore and afloat grew in amount, in complexity, and, above all, in cost. All of these factors were reflected in a rapidly rising expenditure for athletics, which called for increased funds for their support, whether from subscriptions or from gate receipts or from both. Charges for admission to football contests, the origin of which is obscure, advanced in some instances to $1.50. Special financial support began to be solicited from alumni. One result was that alumni who made generous contributions to college athletics received, openly or covertly, in return, a generous share in their control; and alumni who became active in that control gained or retained their power and prestige by their own contributions of money and by subscriptions which they solicited from other alumni and from friends of the college. The reciprocity that underlay this situation was generally regarded as a fair exchange.

The motives among alumni that led to their acquisition of influence and, in many instances, their domination of college athletics, have been unjustly impugned. There was betting on college contests in the 1880's and '90's, and there is betting to-day; but it is doubtful if the amounts of money that the rank and file of graduates wager on college games have ever bulked very large in the personal economics of most individuals. Although a winning team at football or baseball always will be pleasing to a graduate, only a very small proportion of men wager such large sums that a bet makes any real difference to them, whatever its issue. Motives in the struggle for athletic control must be sought in other aspects of personality. For the most part they are to be found, on the one hand, in college loyalty, which is akin emotionally to patriotism, and on the other in that flattering sense of power, of consequence, and even of social prominence in certain circles, which comes from a connection with large affairs, or affairs that are much in the public eye, — an enjoyment which may lead either to a comparatively innocent feeling of self-gratification, or to an insatiable and offensive lust for power. Nor must the motive of service to youth be overlooked. As yet comparatively rare, it is of the highest value.

Meanwhile, most members of faculties appear to have played the rôle of the traditional pedant in holding aloof from athletics and their administration, in maintaining their attitude of *laissez-faire*, and in concerning themselves with the study and the lamp, rather than with all the affairs of college life. Attempts were made to "control" athletics, but at most institutions their results were negligible. Dr. Hartwell was moved to write in the Report of the United States Commissioner of Education for 1897–98, "The powerlessness of our educational leaders to originate, and their failure to adopt, effectual measures for evolving order out of the athletic and gymnastic chaos over which they nominally preside, constitutes one of the marvels of our time." In consequence, there was scarcely a struggle for the control of college athletics; the alumni, or such of them as concerned themselves actively with the matter, achieved dominion almost by default. The importance of undergraduates to college athletics began to diminish. From the point of view of the extravagances into which their administration had fallen, their loss of power is not to be regretted. On the other hand, new abuses sprang up to crowd the old. The reputation of a college came to be regarded as uncomfortably low unless its teams won more than a fair share of victories.

A few college administrative officers, however, saw the dangers into which athletics had been permitted to drift. The revival of football at Harvard was followed (1887–90) by the inauguration of what later became known as the "central committee plan," whereby alumni, undergraduates, and faculty united in one body for the regulation of athletics. Some of the principles underlying this plan are embodied in the present-day methods of control at Harvard, Princeton, and Yale, and from them much good has flowed at more than one other institution.

At the end of the century, Professor Sheldon discerned three sorts of athletic government: First, Harvard's highly centralized tripartite type, in which faculty, alumni, and undergraduates coöperated, had spread to Amherst, Bates, Bowdoin, the University of Maine, Wesleyan, and, in the South, Tulane. Second, in the West and South, a dual plan was common, under which faculties and undergraduates shared the burden. Finally, at Princeton, the University of Virginia, and Yale, all of which were "noted for the strength of their student traditions," the management of athletics was in the hands of students, "faculty interference" being almost eliminated, although graduate influence was "sometimes present in great force." It is interesting that the sections of the country in which the demand for the "faculty control" of athletics has been loudest in recent years are those in which faculties have had, nominally at least, most responsibility for athletics since about 1900.

B. The Opposition During the 1890's

As early as five years after the inauguration of the committee plan at Harvard, President Eliot, in his annual report for 1892–93, first set forth both the benefits and the disadvantages of college athletics. The fact is usually lost sight of that he referred these disadvantages not necessarily to the sports themselves, but to their "wanton exaggeration." A flock of do-or-die defenders of college athletics rose up, but there were also those who, like Walter Camp, pleaded for moderation and reproved extravagance in training, playing, and press reporting. It was not long before the controversy became general. The attackers were led by E. L. Godkin and other editors, especially of church and religious periodicals. The defenders found that without serious danger to their cause they could divide their efforts between repelling the charges of their opponents and consolidating their own positions. Recruited principally from the ranks of college graduates and former players, the champions of athletics found their materials of war ready to their hands in the convictions which had grown from their own experience. In

general, the bitterness of the attack and the vigor of the defense have not been sur-
passed in even the most heated of subsequent athletic controversies.

The accusations against athletics current in the last decade of the century might
easily have served as a source-book for their later opponents. They included charges of
"over-exaggeration," demoralization of the college and of academic work, dishonesty,
betting and gambling, professionalism, recruiting and subsidizing, the employment and
payment of the wrong kind of men as coaches, the evil effects of college athletics upon
school athletics, the roughness and brutality of football, extravagant expenditures of
money, and the general corruption of youth by the monster of athleticism. The defense
denied the accusations, one and all, pointed to the bodily vigor and mental alertness of
athletes, their manly character, their loyalty, and the qualities of leadership that their
own participation in atheltics had engendered; scoffed at the notion that any college
athlete could be recruited or paid; and generally sought by assertion to deny all appearance of evil.

In the midst of the tumult stood the college teacher. The year 1905 found him
exerting his disciplinary power to abolish American football at Columbia, Massachusetts Institute of Technology, the University of California, Nevada, Stanford, and
a few other institutions. Apparently only at the Institute did intramural contests gain
permanently by this measure. At the three Western institutions Rugby football was
substituted for the American game. To judge from what the college teacher published
over his own signature, his perception of the province and uses of athletics, their merits
and their defects, was keener than that of any detractor or enthusiast. Second to him
stand a few alumni, whose reasoning leads one to believe that they had profited as
much from their studies as from their games. However keenly the college teacher
analyzed the athletic problems of that day, he seems to have done comparatively little
about them, except to abolish football at the institutions just indicated. Upon many
regulatory committees he stood among the minority, and not infrequently his faculty
colleagues who were members of college athletic committees and alumni as well, sided
in close votes with the groups of their older allegiance. Only in the West and South did
the faculty member tend to claim on nominally equal terms with undergraduates his
share of the control of athletics.

In Canada, the situation during the period 1886–1900 was vastly different. At the
English-speaking Canadian universities, such as Dalhousie, McGill, Queen's, and
Toronto, and even at the newly opened University of British Columbia (1894), a
natural adherence to the English tradition of games and sports, the recollection, on the
part of members of the staff, of undergraduate days at Oxford, Cambridge, Edinburgh,
or some other of the older British universities, and, apparently, a predilection for
scholarship on the part of undergraduates, all served to keep athletics in a position
different from that which they were coming to occupy in the United States. The Eng-

lish controversy over the merits of the Rugby Union and Association codes and the bitterness of the struggle against professionalism in Rugby had their reflections in Canadian university athletics. On the whole, the results of these disputes were beneficial, if only because they kept before Canadian eyes the necessity of frankness and openness in all matters bearing upon university sport.

C. CENTRALIZING ORGANIZATIONS

The period under examination is characterized also by a growing recognition of common interests among colleges and universities of the United States. In the absence of any central agency to deal with the relationships between college and school, interest in common problems on the part of administrators led first to the formation of associations to deal with or at least to consider such matters, and later to a recognition of the value of discussing other phases of mutual concern, including athletic competition.

1. Associations of Colleges

Although by 1880 a body of practice respecting the accrediting of schools for college entrance after the Prussian method had spread somewhat among the universities of the West, beginning with Michigan in 1870, nevertheless the Eastern usage in such matters was most disparate. A recognition of the need of a somewhat more regularized procedure led in 1879 to a conference of New England colleges at Trinity College, Hartford, at which entrance requirements were examined and discussed. So fruitful was this conference that the New England Association of Colleges and Preparatory Schools was formed to continue its activities. This body was followed in 1887 by the formation among some fifteen colleges of the College Association of Pennsylvania, in 1888 by the Association of Colleges and Preparatory Schools of the Middle States and Maryland, in 1892 by the North Central Association of Colleges and Secondary Schools, and in 1895 by the Association of Colleges and Preparatory Schools of the Southern States. By 1905, a distinct tendency toward nominal uniformity in requirements for admission and for the granting of degrees is discernible among the strongest colleges and universities of the country. This movement had importance for college athletics in two aspects: first, and directly, as demonstrating the advantages of free discussion of common interests; secondly, and rather more indirectly, as affecting standards of eligibility for intercollegiate competition.

2. Athletic Conferences and Associations

The last decade of the century was marked by the founding of three organizations among colleges and universities that furthered mutual interests and facilitated intercollegiate competition. The first of these bodies were regional in membership and extent; and of the first three, two were deliberative assemblies rather than organizations to promote competition. These differed materially from the Intercollegiate Association of

Amateur Athletes of America, which had been founded by undergraduates in 1875. The Southern Intercollegiate Athletic Conference was formed in 1894, in the Mid-West the Intercollegiate Conference, colloquially known as the "Western Conference" or "Big Ten," in the following year, and the Maine Intercollegiate Track and Field Association in 1896. The advantages of such organizations, which are discussed more fully in subsequent pages, were soon felt. After the turn of the century, came the Northwest Conference (1904), and in 1905 the first nation-wide attempt to unite in one body all of the reputable colleges and universities supporting intercollegiate competition, resulted in the formation of the Intercollegiate Athletic Association, with thirty-nine member colleges, which in 1910 became the National Collegiate Athletic Association. Almost at once the good results of informal, open discussion of problems were so apparent that to many it seemed as if the athletic millennium had come. The Canadian Intercollegiate Athletic Union was founded in 1906.

D. PROBLEMS OF ELIGIBILITY

About the matter of eligibility for intercollegiate competition during the 1890's clustered many of the abuses which have persisted even to the present day. Then, as now, they bulked largest in connection with football. The origins of recruiting and subsidizing, the bestowal of nominal jobs, the relaxation of standards, and the granting of favors of all sorts to athletes are referable in part to the laxity of college standards for entrance, attendance, and graduation. For such requirements during the 1890's as well as at the present time, college and university faculties under the leadership of presidents and deans have been responsible. Between 1890 and 1929 the requirements appertaining to these matters have been materially strengthened. Even as early as 1898 the eligibility codes for athletics at Columbia, Harvard, and Pennsylvania included requirements respecting academic status and an intention to remain in college throughout the year, minimum programs of work, a one-year residence transfer rule, and a four-year eligibility rule. At Harvard many of these features were adopted through the influence of faculty members serving on the Committee for the Regulation of Athletic Sports. At Columbia, undergraduate dissatisfaction with conditions had had much to do with recent changes. At both Columbia and Pennsylvania the influence of faculty members was considerable, and apparently it was felt at a number of other Eastern institutions. Yet a great portion of the current improvement is to be ascribed to the work of the college associations and athletic organizations and conferences which had their inceptions before 1906.

In this respect, then, the influence of college teachers has been productive of good. The reasons it has not more generally eliminated the abuses in question are to be referred to at least three general causes : first, a certain softening and sentimentalization of college education in the United States, which happily, as these words are written, appears to be abating; secondly, the usurpation of athletic control by alumni, whose studied intent too often has been to depreciate the scholastic values of our college education and disproportionately to exalt the benefits to be gained by undergraduates through participation in "outside activities," whatever their nature; and thirdly, on the part of college teachers themselves, a lack of concern with the true value and functions of study and scholarship, and a lack of ability to make clear and binding upon others their own convictions through action. In short, the control of college athletics would probably have followed naturally a suitable directing of college life and standards of value on the part of faculties. This matter is now past history, and it is comparatively easy to say what might have been. College athletics assumed Gargantuan proportions before faculty members in general understood, much less considered, the implications of their exaggerated growth. Apparently the first causes contained less of educational insincerity than of general inattention, preoccupation with other matters, and administrative unsteadiness.

1. Recruiting in the 1890's

The soliciting of impecunious but skilled athletes, especially football players, in the '90's was conducted openly by captains or managers. At least, little successful attempt was made to conceal it. Apparently, there were comparatively few direct offers of money, but nominal employment, promises of social favor and athletic success, and the allurements of college life, dangled before the naïve recruit, seem to have been even more powerful in their attraction. The practice of dressing up the butcher's boy, the iron molder, the boiler maker, or even a bond salesman, in football clothing, which in those days concealed from partisan and opponent alike almost every distinguishing feature, was more than merely scandalous. Over such practices American humor shed its mellowing ray to obscure the fundamental issues, and the deception was so common and so amusing that at this distance it is almost impossible to appraise its viciousness. Probably this abuse was less prevalent at the great universities. At less widely known institutions, which by the lights of the time seemed to have all to gain and nothing to lose, it was flagrant. Such dishonesty was practiced as much by undergraduates as by coaches or trainers or alumni.

2. Proselyting and Tramp Athletes

One phase of the progress of American college athletics toward decency during the past forty years may be gauged by the disappearance of the tramp athlete. From 1890 to 1905 he was to be found upon most college football teams. It was common practice for partisans of certain larger institutions to make almost regular annual campaigns for drawing players away from smaller colleges. The ease with which an undergraduate at one institution might transfer to another, following an importation of the principle of migration among European universities, was furthered by the fact that registration of special students in a single subject was common practice. Fortunately, to-day a just appreciation of the functions of migration on the part of administrative officers, the strengthening of college standards, the adherence of conferences to the one-year and three-year rules, and, above all, the enlightenment of college opinion have practically eliminated the tramp athlete and his cousin the "ringer."

3. The Effects upon School Athletics

These abuses placed upon school athletics a blight from which they are only to-day recovering. It would be difficult to overestimate the handicaps from which they suffered through facile and almost universal imitation on the part of schoolboys, whether in public or in private schools, of the more spectacular and generally the least beneficial aspects of college life, not alone as regards games, but also in respect of secret societies (pale shadows of the college fraternity), social pursuits, and dissipation, as accompaniments or influences in athletics. From the blight of such troubles, it has taken school athletics a full quarter-century to emerge.

E. Summary

The twenty years between 1886 and 1906 contain the origins of those defects which are to be traced in our college athletics of the present day. The exuberance of the development at that time supplied a large part of the momentum which actuates modern college sports and games. It must be remembered that athletics of that period harbored the possibilities of both beneficent and harmful development in later years. That so many of their evils persisted beyond the first quarter of the twentieth century is due to the rankness of growth which they were permitted to attain during the time of their most rapid expansion. On the other hand, since 1906 the merits of athletics, their value, and their place in college life have come to be better understood. Apparently, to attempt to kill any branch of athletics by prohibiting it will not cure it or the whole body of the troubles that afflict them.

IV. The Faculties Take a Stronger Hand (1907–1928)

The most recent period of college athletics in the United States reflects the preoccupations and the changes of interest of the men who have exerted most influence in the councils of the National Collegiate Athletic Association. For the present, our concern is less with those changes and preoccupations than with their manifestations in athletics. It would be too sweeping to say that the Association has dominated athletics in American colleges, but it is entirely just to say that the changes that have taken place in college sports have had their counterparts in the proceedings of the Association.

A. The Decline of Formal Gymnastics

With the spread of the practice of requiring physical exercise or gymnasium work for a degree, which had begun before 1900, the popularity of formal gymnastics waned rapidly. Their vogue among undergraduates had never been very great. A few attained a proficiency that lent enjoyment to their pursuit, but the great majority of students were mildly diverted by them during periods of exercise and endured them as one necessary step toward a degree. The gymnasiums of that day were dirty and unsanitary. The teachers were in some cases ill-equipped for their posts. Again, the use of corrective exercises for remedying physical defects doubtless had something to do with the rising unpopularity of gymnastics for all. Moreover, an absence of the competitive motive, the rise of basketball, handball, fencing, boxing, and other indoor sports, and the development of intramural athletics, all united to deprive gymnastics of their former place among the beneficial diversions of college life.

B. The Rise of Intramural Athletics

Even during the periods when the expansion of intercollegiate competition threatened to absorb all of the interest and the energies of college athletes, less formal contests between teams representing fraternities, clubs, and classes went on apace to produce their leaven of healthful diversion in college life. The fact that the intenseness and bitterness of the inter-college rivalry of the day did little to abate interest in those games and contests which undergraduates organized for their own immediate pleasure, testifies to the vitality of such pastimes. It should be clearly understood that the undergraduate and not the director of physical education, the coach, or the faculty member, was the founder of intramural athletics.

When, however, interest in gymnastics fell rapidly, and a means had to be found of introducing the competitive element into physical training, a rather highly developed structure of inter-club, inter-class, and inter-fraternity baseball, bowling, handball, and basketball games was ready to hand. What the masters in English secondary schools were forced to devise anew through the adaptation of the "house system" from the structure of the English public school, the American teacher of physical training found awaiting his needs. About 1907 the notion began to spread that participation in some branch of intramural competition could be made possible for any healthy undergraduate, and those in charge of physical training were not slow to seize upon the opportunity thus afforded. Between 1900 and 1910 at the University of Missouri, Professor Clark W. Hetherington carried forward work in physical education which had been begun as early as 1894 at Stanford University and continued in 1896 at the Whittier State School, through a "department organization which controlled all the physical activities, inter-collegiate and intra-collegiate, of both men and women students." A department of intramural athletics was established by the athletic association at the University of Michigan in 1913–14, and Ohio State University followed closely after. "In these early steps toward intramural athletics," as Professor Elmer D. Mitchell has written in his *Intramural Athletics*, "the athletic association had a more or less selfish idea that intramural athletics would furnish a recruiting ground for future 'varsity material." To this process many directors of physical training, anxious that their adaptation of intramural athletics should succeed, gave willing acquiescence.

The West and the Middle West were the sections of the country in which intramural athletics, thus formalized, prospered best. In the East and Northeast a tradition of undergraduate independence stood somewhat in the way of rapid and full development under the supervision of teachers of physical training and others appointed to the work. When, a little later, the values of "athletics for all" became recognized, the good results of such programs provided a fruitful source of persuasion and advertising. From the studies of two competent historians of college athletics, Professor Sheldon and Professor Meylan, it appears that undergraduate participation increased from about twenty per cent in 1900 to thirty-two per cent in 1910. This decade witnessed the expansion of athletics from the essentially intercollegiate basis to the combination of intercollegiate and intramural competition.

C. The Faculties Assert Themselves

The somewhat scattered but constantly growing attempts on the part of faculties to secure over college athletics a control which in some sections of the country they had apparently never exercised have grown out of a number of causes, of which probably the most commendable is the conviction that a college or university should be an institution of learning. Into the matter enter other considerations, the relative importance of which will vary according to the individual judgment.

In the first place, the advancement of coaches or teachers of physical training to faculty appointment or directorships of physical education at a number of institutions led to a natural feeling on the part of less favored colleagues at other colleges that their work should be similarly dignified. To this conviction the interchange of sentiments at meetings of conferences and other bodies and the strength manifested by various groups and associations lent force. In the West, especially, the number of conferences and associations increased rapidly after 1906, owing to emulation of the Intercollegiate Conference and its success, and the power of the National Collegiate Athletic Association grew steadily because of the injection of a kind of crusading spirit directed to the spreading of the gospel of "faculty control." Some of the origins of this spirit are to be traced in the professional training which certain schools of physical education dispense; others, in the intrinsic attractiveness of the new conception of the purposes of college athletics and the honor and power which it promised to men who hitherto had enjoyed less than what they and many others considered their fair share of both.

In the second place, the widening conception of education as a process having at least two-fold bearings, on mind and on body, gave currency to a definition of physical education that includes all bodily activity, — even sport itself. From these premises, nothing was more logical than that those charged with the oversight of the mental phases of education should be charged also with the oversight of its physical phases. The importance of this concept in its most extreme aspects is its implied exaltation of things physical to a theoretical parity with the things of the mind and of the spirit.

These and other factors operating in varying force at large numbers of colleges and universities have had their effects upon every aspect of college athletics. Above all, they have lent force to the rallying-cry that athletics are "educational." ·

D. Athletics Continue to Expand

With the control of athletics nominally in the hands of faculty members at numbers of universities and colleges, it might be expected that by some means their expansion would be diminished or at least regulated with a degree of strictness. Such has not proved to be the case. Since 1906 their intensity has not abated, intercollegiate rivalry has not grown appreciably kinder, and specialization has much increased; costs have mounted amazingly. A part of the growing expenditure has been due to improvements in buildings, playing-fields, and equipment of all kinds, and a portion of the money thus paid out has benefited the building investments of universities. Popular interest has been deliberately stimulated by many types of newspapers and periodicals, including the college press. At the same time, at some institutions problems of student discipline have apparently become less acute, and at many others they have become different in character. More young men and women are being led to health-giving diversions. There can be little doubt that since 1924 a number of changes for the better have come into college athletics.

E. Abuses and Secrecy

Whatever the reason, it is certain that the seriousness with which college athletics are nowadays taken has driven certain well-recognized abuses under cover, but at the same time has propagated and intensified them. As a consequence, the observer is confronted, on the one hand, with the most lofty ideals and, on the other, by rumors and even well-authenticated statements of questionable practices, deception, and hypocrisy which constitute the very antithesis of the exalted sentiments in whose light they multiply. This paradox is less puzzling if examined in the perspective of years. The abuses which reached open crises about 1890, 1900, and 1905 have not by any means been eliminated even by the guarded publicity that they have recently received; they are probably more deliberately practiced but more carefully covered than they have been at any previous period.

Conclusion

The competitions and contests, the delight in bodily activity, the loyalties, and the honor that form a part of that vast organism called college athletics are the reflections in our college life of characteristics that are common to the youth of the world. In the pages that follow, these and other less pleasing phenomena of college athletics will be examined in the hope that those aspects which are good may in course of time achieve an unassailable predominance over those which are less worthy to survive. There can be no question of abolishing college athletics, nor should there be. What can be looked for is a gradual establishment through concrete action of a few general principles, to which all men would agree in the abstract. Even this slow change will be impossible without the sanction of an enlightened college and public opinion.

After some account of the development of the amateur status which, although it applies to all competitive games and sports, pertains especially to college athletics, it is purposed, first, to treat rather generally of athletics in schools, next, to discuss in detail a number of aspects of college athletics, and, finally, to enquire concerning the values that now inhere or could be brought to inhere in this aspect of American college life.

CHAPTER III
THE DEVELOPMENT
OF THE MODERN AMATEUR STATUS

ALTHOUGH the modern conception of the amateur status, so far as the United States is concerned, is less than a quarter of a century old, the amateur convention is almost as old as sport itself. The essential differences between the amateur and the professional in athletics were clearly understood among the ancient Greeks.[1] Unfortunately the history of such older conceptions has had little bearing upon the American amateur convention; we are too young a nation to listen to the ancients. The present phase of this study is therefore concerned principally with the development of the concept "amateur" in the United States. Because its growth in Great Britain and Canada is partly contemporaneous, reference is also made to these aspects of the British sports tradition. But before these matters can be outlined, attention must be directed to one phase of the relation of amateurism to eligibility that has been all too infrequently pondered.

I. Amateurism as a Phase of College Eligibility

Any valid definition of the amateur must apply equally to all those athletes at whom it is directed and to no others. Traditionally, American college athletics have been the games and sports of the amateur. On the other hand, the fact has not always been recognized by college men or by others, that except where requirements for eligibility overlap definitions of the amateur or the professional status, eligibility to compete in college athletics is not essentially concerned with amateurism.

A. American Amateurism

Without reference at the moment to the controversial phases of the matter, the definition of an amateur most widely current in the United States is as follows:

---

[1] Cf. Forbes, *Greek Physical Education*, New York, 1929, pages 90–91, 262, and *passim*. Other important references in the history of amateurism in relation to education are set forth in Professor Ryan's *Literature of School and College Athletics*, 1929.

An amateur sportsman is one who engages in sport solely for the pleasure and physical, mental, or social benefits he derives therefrom, and to whom sport is nothing more than an avocation.[2]

In connection with this definition it is important to note that (1) the amateur participates in sport *solely* for (*a*) pleasure and for (*b*) physical, mental, or social benefit; (2) for him sport is not a means of livelihood. The antithesis of amateurism is, of course, professionalism. Now, a professional athlete may receive from participation as much pleasure and physical, mental, and social benefit as the amateur, although these returns may be of a somewhat different sort, but they are not his sole interests; he receives in addition monetary or material benefit which the amateur by definition foregoes. Hence, to the professional, sport is much more than an avocation; it provides a return in money or in kind. This factor differentiates him from the amateur, and the obscurity between the two types of athlete is due to confusion over this single point. The matter involves both the presence or absence of material considerations and also a body of spiritual considerations, which accrue to the amateur, but which in the case of the professional are necessarily outweighed by the material benefits that he receives.

B. ELIGIBILITY

From the point of view of college athletics, eligibility is a somewhat broader matter. Certain of its phases rightly touch upon amateurism; others have little direct bearing upon it. For instance, the number of years spent in college, the program of work carried, the grades and number of credits attained, questions of time in migration and similar matters have *per se* no bearing whatever upon the question whether a man or a woman is receiving or foregoing monetary or material benefits from sport. Beyond college walls eligibility turns upon amateurism more often than within them.

Failure to appreciate the distinctions that are implied by the terms "amateurism" and "eligibility" and to understand the relationships between the two concepts has led to confusion and even to distrust of the validity of both conventions.

II. NOTES ON THE DEVELOPMENT OF THE AMATEUR STATUS IN THE UNITED STATES

Although for convenience the development of the amateur convention will be sketched first in the United States, next in Great Britain, and lastly in its relation to world competition, it must be noted that the phenomena thus isolated have been in some measure interdependent. The somewhat scanty notes which are here presented in tracing the development make no claim to be a history of the convention. Collected

[2] It is interesting that the term "Corinthian" is employed to indicate an amateur yachtsman, especially in the United States. According to the *New English Dictionary* a Corinthian is an amateur in any sport who rides his own horse, steers his own yacht, etc. Apparently the meaning is derived from the profligate elegance of ancient Corinth, but the *N. E. D.* notes the use of the word in *Blackwood's* as early as 1823, the year of the Christ Church-Brasenose controversy over professional assistance to amateur oarsmen in Oxford inter-college rowing.

principally from published documents, they represent only a few of the convictions which grew or flourished for some time before being legislated into definitions, rules, or agreements. At best, the skeins of the development are tangled. For purposes of presentation the evolution in the United States is divided into three general periods, without reference to the periods assigned to the development of American college athletics in Chapter II.

A. Eligibility and Professionalism up to 1888

Apparently the first American sport in which professional playing bulked large was baseball. As early as 1860 semi-professionalism had begun; even at this time the "throwing" of games was frequently charged. The year 1868 saw the formation of the first wholly professional baseball club, the Cincinnati Red Stockings. Three years later, in 1871, the line of cleavage between amateurs and professionals was recognized by the establishment of two associations, one with professional and one with amateur jurisdiction. The National Baseball League, formed in 1876, and the American Association, organized in 1882, continued the professional development. Thus the sport in which questions of professionalism have proved most troublesome in many parts of the country was the first in which the professional status was recognized in fact.

In the United States, as in England, the first college sport seriously to involve the question of professionalism was rowing. As early as the rowing contests of the 1850's between Harvard and Yale, charges of professionalism were bandied freely.[3] Up to the period of the Saratoga regattas, however, there was little general concern over professionalism in American college athletics. The number of contestants in intercollegiate competition was small, and each knew most of the others personally. In 1876, the lack of rules for competition and the activities of the bookmakers at Saratoga led to a very large amount of betting on the first meeting held by the Intercollegiate Association of Amateur Athletes of America, and thence probably arose the question of professionalism as a factor in the victory that should yield large winnings to bettors.

1. The Intercollegiate Association of Amateur Athletes of America, 1876

Although the controversy was acute, the relationship of amateurism to eligibility appears not to have been of great concern in college athletics at the moment. The first constitution of the Intercollegiate Association of Amateur Athletes of America, adopted in 1876, contained no statement concerning eligibility. The amateur status was evidently taken for granted.

2. The National Association of Amateur Athletes of America, 1879

Meanwhile, outside of the colleges, athletic sports, growing yearly in popularity,

---

[3] Emmett A. Rice, *Brief History of Physical Education*, 1928, page 217. Respecting England, see *Games and Sports in British Schools and Universities*, 1927, page 194.

began seriously to involve the question of amateurism. The "Amateur Championship" established by the New York Athletic Club in 1876 was turned over three years later to the newly formed National Association of Amateur Athletes of America, to which at first "clubs owning or leasing running paths or enclosed grounds" were eligible, but in which "boat, lacrosse, and cricket clubs" were not entitled to vote.[4] A later qualification provided that any athletic club that "held a meeting with not less than five events open to all amateurs" was eligible to membership. It seems likely that certain features of the organization and composition of the National Association were primarily responsible for the subsequent objections that were raised, especially in the Middle West, against combining in one body the powers of definition, arbitration of standards, and sport promotion. Some of these features were perpetuated in the successor of the Association.

The first definition of the amateur adopted by the National Association of Amateur Athletes of America in 1879 was briefly as follows:

> An amateur is any person who has never competed in an open contest, or for a stake, or for public money, or for gate money, or under a false name; or with a professional for a prize, or where gate money is charged; nor has ever at any period of his life taught or pursued athletic exercises as a means of livelihood.

Fundamental features of this definition had been adopted as early as 1872 by the National Association of Amateur Oarsmen of the United States,— some seven years before the Henley Stewards set forth their very strict qualifications. Its essential clauses opened the amateur definition of the League of American Wheelmen (1880). Of these three sets of regulations, only those of the National Association of Amateur Athletes of America bear directly upon subsequent legislation. For the later development of the convention of amateurism in the United States, one fact concerning this definition is noteworthy, — its negative phrasing. A subsequent amateur definition by the same body, effective in 1885, continued the negative attitude and particularized in much detail the circumstances in which an amateur becomes a professional. Thus amateurism of the day was defined as absence of professionalism. This negative attitude permeates all attempts to define the amateur status during the next thirty years. Its bearing upon American college athletics is of the first importance. The modern affirmative definition was framed only after the negative definition had given rise to a legalistic attitude of mind and shown by its prohibitions how to "beat the rules."

3. The Colleges and the Rules

Up to 1880, in college athletics, eligibility in its broadest sense was the chief concern of the law-givers. At about that time professionalism began to take its place as a con-

[4] The earlier development is outlined in F. W. Janssen's *History of American Amateur Athletics and Aquatics . . . 1829–1888*, New York, 1888, which bears very little, except at this point, upon American college athletics.

dition and a force to be actively opposed. In 1882, at Princeton, "it was found necessary to amend the eligibility rules so as to exclude all students whose college expenses were paid" [5] on account of their participation in athletics. Apparently the sport over which most concern was felt was baseball. Although rumors of payment to college athletes flew fairly thick between 1885 and 1890, the most prevalent evils appear to have been extravagant expenditure, excess training, newspaper notoriety, and the roughness of football contests. Writing in 1886,[6] even so acute a critic as Dr. Hartwell used the term professionalism in a somewhat loose sense: "By professionalism, we mean the purpose to win a game by any means, fair or foul." In the midst of such confusion it is not to be doubted that matters of college eligibility were uppermost in the minds of those who in 1888 revised the rules of the I.C.A.A.A.A. This code, which is too long and complicated to quote here, was regarded as desirably stringent. According to modern notions, it imposed a mistaken emphasis upon the negative aspects of eligibility. It did, however, oppose professionalism; the athlete was prohibited from competing for money prizes and from selling or realizing upon the trophies that he won.

4. The Amateur Athletic Union of the United States, 1888

By 1887 professionalism in extracollegiate sport was causing even more concern than in college athletics. The National Association was accused of being national only in name and its definition and administration of amateurism had given rise to dissatisfaction. As a result the Amateur Athletic Union of the United States was formed on January 21, 1888, with fifteen athletic clubs as charter members, an increase of five clubs over the number that had sent delegates to the preliminary conference of October 1, 1887. The Union's first constitution served to reinforce the previous method of definition. According to it,[7] an amateur is

> One who has not entered in an open competition; or for either a stake, public or admission money or entrance fee; or under a fictitious name; or has not competed with or against a professional for any prize or where admission fee is charged; or who has not instructed, pursued or assisted in the pursuit of athletic exercises as a means of livelihood, or for gain or any emolument; or whose membership of any Athletic Club of any kind was not brought about or does not continue, because of any mutual understanding, express or implied, whereby his becoming or continuing a member of such club would be of any pecuniary benefit to him whatever direct or indirect, and who shall in other and all respects conform to the rules and regulations of this organization.

This adherence to the negative form of amateur definition served to give standing to a method of approach which, from the points of view of logic, education, and human conduct, leaves much to be desired.

[5] Presbrey and Moffatt, *Athletics at Princeton*, New York, 1901, page 37.
[6] Circular of Information, *Physical Training in American Colleges and Universities*, United States Bureau of Education, 1886.
[7] Janssen, *History of American Amateur Athletics and Aquatics*, 1888, page 13.

5. Summary

The initial stage of the development of an amateur convention in the United States thus closes with the formation of a strengthened "governing" body for non-professional contests in many fields of sport and with the adoption of eligibility rules by the principal college track and field organization in the country only after twelve years of operation. For the most part, all of the rules involved were stated in the negative. As respects college sport, amateurism was at first taken for granted. Then an attempt was made to resist the encroachments of professionalism. Finally, with the revision of the I.C.A.A.A.A. code in 1888, eligibility became a very much involved and confused affair in which prohibitions and injunctions against the acceptance of money by players were more emphasized than any affirmation or positive statement of what an amateur is.

B. The Amateur Convention in the Light of College Eligibility, 1889–1916

As indicated in Chapter II, one of the tendencies of the years 1889–1916 in the history of American college athletics was toward the formation of groups and associations to deal with both academic and athletic problems. Respecting the development of the American concept of amateurism, this phase is marked in some quarters by a gradual weakening of the prohibitory attitude against professionalizing tendencies. A feeling that amateurism is a positive virtue rather than a negation of its opposite culminated in the affirmative amateur definitions of 1916. Meanwhile, notably in the Eastern states, there is discernible a tendency for colleges and universities to attack the problem of professionalism on an individualistic basis. West of the Alleghenies, however, the usual approach appears to have been through the conference and its mutuality of interests. The decade beginning in 1886 witnessed in England a sharpening of the issues, and in the United States more controversy over them than they had previously called forth. By the late 1880's, the age of innocence as regards professionalism in American sport was fast waning.

1. In the East

For Eastern college athletics, individual universities and groups of two or three institutions took steps to cope with certain abuses that involved the amateur status. The Harvard-Princeton controversy of 1889 dealt in mutual accusations of recruiting and subsidizing, in which Yale also was involved.[8] The contemporary "Harvard reforms" gave to the Committee on the Regulation of Athletic Sports power to reinstate violators of the amateur rule, a provision to which Princeton could not subscribe. During the following decade recruiting and proselyting increased amazingly among American colleges, and the importation of "ringers" for a season or a single game

---

[8] Presbrey and Moffatt, *Athletics at Princeton*, 1901, pages 577 ff.

grew at some institutions to be so usual as to excite only perfunctory comment. The Eastern universities continued their struggle for sound provisions of eligibility. In 1896, Columbia and the University of Pennsylvania adopted for participation in athletics rules which definitely opposed professionalism. Four years later the Princeton eligibility code for contests with Yale contained the provision that "no professional athlete, nor any man who has ever received any pecuniary profit by reason of his connection with athletics, shall take part in the game of baseball between the two (2) Universities hereinbefore provided for." In the East, then, it was the intention of those who controlled or guided college athletics, including baseball, that they should be exclusively amateur sports.

The associations which presided over intercollegiate contests at this time were of the same opinion. Along with the professionalizing force of league baseball, another influence made itself felt in track and field sports; namely, the money prizes offered in bicycle racing. Now, the membership of the Intercollegiate Association of Amateur Athletes of America was predominantly, if not exclusively, Eastern. One attempt to deal with cash prizes in general was embodied in the I.C.A.A.A.A. rule that no award should exceed twenty-five dollars. In passing, it may be noted that the limit imposed by the Amateur Athletic Union from about 1891 to 1916 was thirty-five dollars. But the I.C.A.A.A.A. did not stop at the limitation of cash prizes; it continued to deal rather thoroughly with the whole matter of eligibility, including amateurism. The capitalizing by college athletes of their athletic reputation, the commercializing of their abilities, proselyting, and low scholastic standards had already led in 1886 to the adoption by the I.C.A.A.A.A. of an eligibility code which, except for increased stringency, has remained to the present day.

Thus far, the development of a conception of college amateurism in the Eastern states has followed a discernible course, although that course is far from logical and although the confusion of eligibility with professionalism has made it somewhat devious. It had its beginnings in a tacit acceptance of an undefined amateur standard. Then the inroads of clearly recognizable professionalism called forth repressive measures that took the form of prohibitions.

2. The Westerly Developments: the Intercollegiate Conference, 1895

Westward from the Atlantic seaboard the prohibitory attitude spread with conviction and rapidity, but in slightly varied form.

With the founding of the Intercollegiate Conference in 1895 a new motif appears. On January 11th, the Faculty Conference, which was the source of all amateur, eligibility, and similar provisions in the Intercollegiate Conference up to the formation of the Directors Conference in 1922, passed a rule relating to compensation and prizes which was destined to have a far-reaching effect:

Rule 6. Compensation and Prizes

Section 1. No student shall participate in any intercollegiate contest who has ever used, or is using, his knowledge of athletics or his athletic or gymnastic skill for gain; or who has taken part in any athletic contest in which money prize was offered, regardless of the disposition made of the same. In case of minor infractions, prior to entering college, the Conference will entertain applications for reinstatement. . . .

Section 2. No person who receives a regular annual or monthly compensation from the university for services rendered shall be eligible to play on any team.

In this rule the primary emphasis falls upon preventing the use of athletic or gymnastic skill for gain. The scope of the prohibitory attitude is thus notably widened. Probably the feeling was spreading that the gainful use of athletic talent really lay at the bottom of all impairment of the amateur status. At any rate, the phrasing of the Intercollegiate Conference rule gathered many adherents in the West. During the period under examination it appeared under the guise of the "Definition of an Amateur" adopted by the Missouri Valley Conference in 1908, and later, as will be noted subsequently, it shows itself in other sets of conference regulations. Wherever it went it carried with it the prohibitory attitude.

3. The Definitions Questioned, 1899–1904

At about this time, other questionings of the standard involved in the definition of professionalism from the point of view of money receipt were voiced, even in New England. A speaker at the Twentieth Annual Meeting of the New England Association of Colleges and Secondary Schools, although admitting that the rule on money or its equivalent in the definition of professionalism led to absurdities, favored its retention. With this position one or two prominent educators took issue. Among them, the president of Trinity College maintained that the monetary distinction was an importation from England and would not be accepted in this country, — this in spite of the fact that it had been for seventeen years a part of the eligibility provisions of the Amateur Athletic Union of the United States, and had been the cornerstone of the provisions of the earlier National Association of Amateur Athletes of America.

In 1903–04, the Committee on the Regulation of Athletic Sports at Harvard passed a rule that no student "of Harvard University who has played on any semi-professional nine, or on any so-called summer baseball nine shall represent Harvard University in any public athletic contest until he has received special permission from the Committee." Although from one point of view this action merely re-affirmed the tenet of 1889, from another it reflected the growing questions whether summer baseball could really be controlled, whether in any event the receipt of money for summer baseball at a hotel or in a professional league should impair a college amateur's standing, and, if it did, whether the player's own university was not after all the best judge of his status.[9]

4. A National College Athletic Association, 1905

In 1905 the Intercollegiate Athletic Association came into being with thirty-nine member institutions. Five years later the body became the National Collegiate Athletic Association. Between 1906 and 1915 the Association added little in clarification of the amateur status. Its Proceedings for those years set forth eligibility rules, which were not a requirement for membership in the body, on the understanding that the authorities of each institution should decide upon methods of preventing the violation of the principles laid down in Article VI of the Association's constitution. The "Principles of Amateur Sport," as these rules were entitled, were designed to prevent (1) proselyting, (2) recruiting, (3) the playing of those ineligible as amateurs and students in low or irregular standing, and (4) improper and unsportsmanlike conduct on the part of any one connected with college athletics. The provisions were suggested as minima to "be made more stringent where local conditions permit." Whatever good purposes they may have served, they tended to add to the confusion then existing concerning the amateur status and eligibility.

5. Affirmative Definition Begins

In 1909, the Association constituted a committee on the amateur law which, in reporting at the meeting of the next year, recommended the following distinctions:

> 1. An amateur in athletics is one who enters and takes part in athletic contests purely in obedience to the play impulses or for the satisfaction of purely play motives and for the exercise, training, and social pleasure derived. The natural or primary attitude of mind in play determines amateurism.

> 2. A professional in athletics is one who enters or takes part in any athletic contest from any other motive than the satisfaction of pure play impulses, or for the exercise, training, or social pleasures derived, or one who desires and secures from his skill or who accepts of spectators, partisans, or other interests, any material or economic advantage or reward.

Although these distinctions may appear to be somewhat technical, involved, and doctrinaire, they have the merits of any attempt to achieve scientific accuracy. More important still, they make up, so far as can be ascertained, the first attempt affirmatively to define an amateur. But practical adherence to negative regulation had not by any means kept pace with the progress of the theory of amateurism. As early as 1901 Professor Sheldon had noted with satisfaction that the eligibility rules of the

---

[9] This attitude toward summer baseball playing by Harvard athletes, although sincere, has had at certain other New England colleges a negative bearing which is reflected in the Minutes of the Twenty-first Annual Meeting of the Association of New England Colleges for Conference on Athletics, 1928 (page 15): "The general opinion seemed to be, from many of those participating in the discussion, that summer baseball could not be controlled, and therefore it was futile to legislate against it."

leading American colleges were "iron-clad in opposition to professionalism : a student who in any way, either individually or as a member of a team, has accepted a remuneration for playing or for training athletes, is excluded from representing the college." During the decade following the writing of Professor Sheldon's words, professionalism and evasions of rules made serious encroachments upon American college sport.

By 1911 the National Collegiate Athletic Association recognized that the amateur problem had become acute. It is possible that the influence of Dean Briggs of Harvard may be read between the lines of the report of its committee on amateurism in 1912, the year in which Dean Briggs entered upon the first of his five terms as president of the Association. The committee noted that troubles arise not "so much out of the difficulty of determining whether an actual violation of the *letter* of the law has occurred but whether there has been a violation of the *spirit* of the rule with the consequent tendency to take the easier way and rule on the letter and ignore the spirit."

The last stage of negative defining appears in the official handbook of the I.C.A.A.A.A. for 1913 :

> An amateur is a person who has never competed in an open competition, or for money, or under a false name ; or with a professional for a prize ; or with a professional where gate money is charged ; nor has at any time taught, pursued, or assisted at athletic exercise for money, or for any valuable consideration.

The chaos to which attempts at negative definition of amateurism and eligibility had led is illustrated by a writer on athletics and the college in the *Atlantic Monthly* for February, 1914 : "To my view there is no place in college athletics between amateur and professional ; that a man be a *bona fide* student of the institution he represents is all we have a right to ask." This notion still persists in some quarters.

Between the enunciation of the affirmative definition in 1909, and 1916, conditions rapidly became intolerable. On December 29 and 30, 1915, a congress assembled by the I.C.A.A.A.A. to deal with the matter provoked intense discussion. At the same time, the recognition of the difference between the spirit and the letter of the rules was bearing fruit. For example, the Rules of Eligibility for Athletic Teams and Crews adopted by Harvard, Yale, and Princeton in June, 1916, are introduced as follows :

> With a view to keeping the spirit and the associations of professionalism out of college sports without the unreasonable hampering of them by the mere letter of rules, and with a view to maintaining in mutual confidence at these three universities the same theory and practice in matters of eligibility, we adopt the following statement of principles.

Although, according to these principles, no person who has received a pecuniary reward or its equivalent is permitted to represent his university, nevertheless the respective university committees on eligibility under the approval of the Committee of the Three Chairmen were free to interpret this provision in accordance with its spirit rather than its letter.

Wider legislative results followed when the Amateur Athletic Union in November, 1916, and the National Collegiate Athletic Association in December reached substantial agreement in defining an amateur sportsman as "one who engages in sport solely for the pleasure and physical, mental, or social benefits he derives therefrom and to whom sport is nothing more than an avocation." The N.C.A.A., however, phrased the definition somewhat differently : "An amateur athlete is defined as one who participates in competitive physical sport only for the pleasure, and the physical, mental, moral, and social benefits derived therefrom." The immediate source of the phrasing adopted by all of these bodies was the work of the Athletic Research Society in conjunction with numerous previous committees of the National Collegiate Athletic Association, which had been considering the matter since 1909.

Thus, with the Amateur Athletic Union, the Intercollegiate Association of Amateur Athletes of America, and the National Collegiate Athletic Association in literal or substantial agreement concerning the meaning of the term amateur, the doctrine of amateurism may be regarded as established. From that year onwards at least one definition of the amateur may be regarded as standard.

C. Agreement and Disagreement, 1917 and thereafter

The process of clarification respecting the relationship between amateurism and eligibility brought another important step by the National Collegiate Athletic Association, which probably reflected a state of mind among its constituents. Beginning in 1916, the Proceedings of the Association omitted the detailed eligibility rules previously printed, but included a statement to the effect that "the secretary of the Association will furnish on request a set of eligibility rules that are recommended to colleges wishing to adopt such rules." Apparently the feeling was that the eligibility rules formerly set forth had been outgrown and that the constituent colleges were capable of interpreting the amateur status in its bearing on eligibility without direct advice from the Association.

Five years after other national bodies had promulgated the "standard" amateur definition, it was embodied in the constitution of the newly formed National Amateur Athletic Federation. In 1921, also, the constitution of the National Collegiate Athletic Association, which was then revised to its present form, first contained the standard phrasing. Even more important in some respects are the revised Principles of Amateur Sport that follow the definition :

> In the opinion of the National Collegiate Athletic Association the spirit of amateurism carries with it all that is included in the definition of an amateur and much more. It stands for a high sense of honor, honesty, fair play, and

courtesy. It stoops to no petty technicalities and refuses to twist or avoid the rules of play or to take unfair advantage of opponents.

For the first time the ethical connotations of amateurism as regards sportsmanship are affirmed. These considerations apply equally to sportsmanship in professional athletics.

But the conception of amateurism as a negation of professionalism, through restricting participation in intercollegiate competition to those who have not used their athletic skill for gain, continued to attract adherents. In 1922 the Ohio Athletic Conference employed this means of defining the amateur status, after the manner of the Missouri Valley Conference (1908) and the (Mid-Western) Intercollegiate Conference (1895). Further departures from the standard usage and a belated insistence upon the negative attitude are to be noted in the constitutions of other athletic conferences, notably the Southwest Conference (1926) and the Pacific Coast Intercollegiate Conference (1926). This divergence from better current practice may be due in part to a desire to employ unhackneyed phrasing adapted to particular local conditions, and in part to a feeling that a standard national definition needed, not reaffirmation, but local particularization.

D. Summary: Unity in American Definitions of the College Amateur

From the point of view of American college athletics, the concepts "amateur" and "amateurism" which have evolved since 1888 may be regarded as fairly well unified in purpose and spirit, if not in phrasing. To-day men are in a very substantial agreement as to what an amateur sportsman is. Differences of opinion arise principally from attempts to interpret and apply the definition in the light of facts and events.

In general, two states of mind are discernible. One adheres to the affirmative "standard" position as set forth in the amateur definitions of the larger and more representative sports bodies. The other upholds certain negative definitions, that generally prohibit the use of skill for gain or the receipt of pecuniary rewards, compensation, or valuable considerations. The situation thus engendered leads to a legalistic frame of mind and tempts to evasion when desires for material or monetary returns come into conflict with the established conception of amateurism. From every point of view in college athletics, affirmation of a principle is preferable to the negation of its opposite.

III. Developments in Great Britain and Canada

Between the development of the idea of amateurism in the United States and similar developments in Great Britain and Canada a few similarities are discernible, but for the most part the British and Canadian processes are much more closely related one to the other than either is to the American.

A. AMATEURISM IN ENGLAND

To comprehend the principles which underlie the development of the amateur ideal in Great Britain, and especially in England, it must be clearly understood that British amateurism has always been much more the concern of the representative bodies governing and legislating for individual sports than of any one centralizing organization. This fact has a few parallels in the United States. Thus, for example, American soccer, lawn tennis, golf, and swimming associations endeavor to apply their own definitions of amateurism, due regard being had to their relationship, if any, with the Amateur Athletic Union; but with respect of those sports over which jurisdiction is claimed by the Amateur Athletic Union of the United States, the amateur provisions of the Union take at least theoretical precedence over those of individual organizations. Roughly, the British situation would obtain in the United States if all individual sports bodies exercised their own jurisdiction over their respective branches, — if, for example, not only the American Lawn Tennis Association but the Football Rules Committee and the Basketball Association possessed identical powers respecting the amateur status. This illustration is intended, not as an accurate summary of the two national situations, but merely as a means of clarifying certain important distinctions between two general types of procedure.

The critical period for the amateur status in English sport began with the year 1879, when the Henley Stewards promulgated their very strict definition of an amateur oarsman. In the following year the Amateur Athletic Association legislated for track and field athletics. In 1880, also, payments to soccer players for "broken time" began, and these were legalized by the Football Association for soccer five years later, when registration of amateurs and professionals in that sport commenced. The issues sharpened in 1886. The Rugby Football Union set its face against professionalism, and during 1892 and 1893 the question of "broken time" disrupted this body and resulted in the formation of the Northern Rugby Union. By 1896 wide differences of opinion in most of the British sports had led to a clear differentiation of the professional from the amateur, although ever since that time defenders of the amateur status have continued on the alert. Cricket has no amateur definition; the game is controlled by the Marylebone Cricket Club, a private body.

This very brief outline merely hints at the bitterness of the struggle to preserve amateurism in the British Isles.[10] The upholders of the amateur status have come gradually, and hence perhaps the more strongly and militantly, to believe that the whole matter hinges upon the player's personal integrity rather than upon his social standing. At the present day, whatever the origin of the long and bitter controversy, it may be said that amateurism in England is a matter principally of social standing

---

[10] Further details will be found in *Games and Sports in British Schools and Universities*, Bulletin Number Eighteen, Carnegie Foundation for the Advancement of Teaching, pages 185 ff.

only in two sports : rowing, under the laws of the Henley Stewards and the Amateur Rowing Association, but not of the National Amateur Rowing Association : and cricket, where the distinction between "gentlemen" and "players" is still maintained. Many an oarsman or cricketer would welcome a more rational distinction between professionals and amateurs in those sports.

B. In Canada

Although the history of the amateur concept in Canada owes much to the influencing traditions of the mother country and at the same time something to the contiguity of the United States, it need not concern us at this point. In general, Canadian amateur organizations of to-day bear many resemblances to our own, but with this difference, that the traditions of the "game for the game's sake" and "playing the game" are far more powerful as motives in its preservation than they are south of the boundary.

The relation of the Amateur Athletic Union of Canada to other amateur sports bodies exhibits many parallels to that of the Amateur Athletic Union of the United States to similar organizations as regards jurisdiction and affiliation, but it appears to be far closer and less controversial. The "standard" Canadian amateur definition is as follows :

An amateur is one who has never :

(A) (1) Entered or competed in any athletic competition for a staked bet, moneys, private or public, or gate receipts.

(2) Taught or assisted in the pursuit of any athletic exercise or sport as a means of livelihood.

(3) Received any bonus or payment in lieu of loss of time while playing as a member of any club or engaged in any athletic sport or exercise, or any consideration whatever, for any service as an athlete except actual travelling or hotel expenses.

(4) Sold or pledged his prizes.

(5) Promoted an athletic competition for personal gain. (Note.— An athlete guilty of any of the above offences can never be reinstated.)

(B) An athlete who has competed with or against a professional for a prize or where gate receipts are charged or a collection taken up (except as may be specially provided for by the By-laws of the A.A.U. of C.) or has entered in any competition under a name other than his own, shall be ineligible for registration and competition as an amateur. (Note.— Such an athlete may be eligible for reinstatement.)

(C) All others shall be considered eligible for registration and competition in the C.I.A.U.

(D) Physical directors who have not become professionalized for any other reason shall be regarded as non-competing amateurs.

Parks or playgrounds instructors or persons engaged in similar work, who have not become professionalized for any other reason, shall not lose their amateur standing by engaging in such work, provided that during the time of such occupation they shall not be eligible to compete in amateur contests.[11]

The relation of Canadian university athletics to the Amateur Athletic Union of Canada may be gathered from the fact that the Canadian Intercollegiate Athletic Union is an "allied body" of the Amateur Athletic Union, upholding the same amateur definition. The articles of alliance provide that "each body . . . shall have supervision and control of the amateur standing of individuals under its jurisdiction, and all penalties of suspensions and disqualifications upon individuals shall be respected by the other party." Matters of eligibility rest in the hands of the individual universities, which are required to send to the secretary of the C.I.-C.A.U. four days before each inter-'varsity contest a certificate of eligibility for proposed players, in accordance with the provisions of the Union, signed by each player, by a professor whose classes he is attending, and by the academic head of the institution. A separate certificate is submitted for each branch of athletics, and provision is made for late registrations up to one week after a contest. The names thus forwarded are entered in a register of amateurs, and lists are sent as soon as possible to all of the university and other athletic associations concerned. In case eligibility is questioned, a board of reference, consisting of three members, each from a different university, is empowered to deal individually and collectively with the matter, consulting where necessary with the academic head of the institution of which the questioned player is a member.

In Canada, representative sports bodies similar to those of Great Britain control the various branches of athletics. For example, the Canadian Rugby Union sets as its objective "the furtherance of Amateur Rugby Football throughout the Dominion, including the enforcement of the rules of the game," and the holding of a series of Canadian amateur championship matches between teams from its affiliated unions.

[11] Examination of the amateur rulings and definitions of some eight English representative sports bodies discloses numerous parallels between them and the Canadian definition. The Canadian prohibitions against entering or competing in any athletic competition for a staked bet, moneys private or public, or gate receipts, are found in the provisions of the Football Association, Ltd., the Amateur Boxing Association, the Amateur Rowing Association, the National Amateur Rowing Association, the Henley Stewards, the Amateur Swimming Association, and the Amateur Athletic Association (track and field). Competing for a prize is forbidden by the three English rowing associations and by the Rugby Football Union without the Union's permission. Teaching or assisting in the pursuit of any athletic exercise or sport as a means of livelihood is not countenanced by the three English rowing bodies and the boxing and athletic associations, nor by the swimming association except with reference to teachers in schools and colleges. Payments for broken time, which the Canadian rules define as the receipt of "any bonus or payment in lieu of loss of time while playing as a member of any club or while engaged in any athletic sport or exercise," or accepting any consideration whatever for any service as an athlete except actual traveling or hotel expenses, are not countenanced in cricket, according to a statement of the secretary of the Marylebone Cricket Club, Rugby football, swimming, and track and field athletics, although the Football Association, Ltd., still permits compensation for broken time at soccer. Competing against a professional for a prize or where admissions are charged or a collection taken up is prohibited in English boxing and rowing by all bodies, while competing with "one who is not an amateur" is permitted not at all in track and field, and in swimming only in military service, and then only in service competitions. The Rugby Football Union forbids playing with or against a professional, and competing under an assumed name. Selling or pledging an athlete's prizes is "strongly deprecated" by the Amateur Athletic Association and forbidden by the National Amateur Rowing Association and the Amateur Swimming Association. The Canadian provisions respecting the promotion of athletic competition for personal gain, physical directors, and parks or playground instructors find no English counterpart.

These bodies are five in number : the Canadian Intercollegiate Rugby Football Union, the Interprovincial Rugby Football Union, the Ontario Rugby Football Union, the Quebec Rugby Football Union, and the Western Canada Rugby Football Union.

The concern of the Canadian Rugby Union passes far beyond such matters as the playing rules, eligibility, and the amateur status. Its Football Code touches upon the ethical bearings of play and the game as an institution :

THE FOOTBALL CODE
CANADIAN RUGBY UNION

You may meet players and even coaches who will tell you that it is all right to hold or otherwise violate the rules if you do not get caught. This is the code of men whose sense of honor is sadly lacking.
The football code is different. The football player who intentionally violates a rule is guilty of unfair play and unsportsmanlike tactics, and whether or not he escapes being penalized, he brings discredit to the good name of the game, which it is his duty as a player to uphold.

Thus in respect of certain phases of university athletics, Canada bears many resemblances to England. Although the Canadian definition of the amateur status has not passed entirely beyond the prohibitory and negative stage, nevertheless in its positive insistence upon personal integrity as affecting amateurism, and in some other respects as well, the attitude of the sportsman is less legalistic and less involved with the letter of rules than it tends to be in the United States.

C. INTERNATIONAL AMATEUR RELATIONSHIPS

Those who look upon the amateur definition in international sport as an offshoot of the British sports tradition may be astonished to learn that it is principally American in origin. The amateur definition of the International Amateur Athletic Federation was adopted at a meeting held in Berlin, Germany, August 20–23, 1913, after the report of a special committee on the amateur status of contestants, which was presided over by an American. The Federation defines an amateur as "one who competes only for the love of the sport." Of the provisions that follow, one states that "competing for money or any other pecuniary reward in any sport makes the competitor a professional in all sports." The fifth has special interest for the United States :

5. One who teaches, trains, or coaches in any sport for money or other pecuniary considerations is a professional, except, however, that so far as competition in his own country, and there only, is concerned, an employee or representative of the state or school or other educational institution, who teaches, trains, or coaches as an incident to his main vocation or employment, may, or may not, be a professional, as the Association of the country of such a person shall decide.

Altogether the interpretations of the definitions in terms of permissible and prohibited practices occupy nearly three quarto pages of small type. Incidentally, the Federation does not prohibit competition between amateurs and professionals, although it stipulates that such contests shall be regulated with stringency.

The definition of the International Olympic Committee is identical with that of the Federation; an attempt at Prague in 1925 to supplement it with the phrase "without any direct or indirect financial gain therefrom" proved unsuccessful. The conception of the amateur in international sport thus clearly owes its definition to amateurism in the United States.

Conclusion

The convention of the amateur status has gained much strength from the adherence of schools, colleges, and universities. In the United States, as well as in Great Britain and Canada, most of its strongest supporters have been university men. It has motivated participation in all forms of college athletics, because, more than any other force, it encourages the individual to develop his own athletic skill in competition with others who, like himself, are protected against the inequalities of opportunity that professionalism brings. Moreover, in the United States the first definition of an amateur to be phrased in the affirmative was the work of men associated with higher education. From that definition as it stands to-day there can be little dissent; of late years the chief disputes involving amateurism have arisen over the application or interpretation of the convention. Two causes of these differences of opinion are worthy of attention.

In the first place, unanimity in defining the amateur status in America was not reached until 1916. For at least thirty years, organized intercollegiate athletic competition had been conducted under an amateur rule phrased in the negative and accompanied and interpreted by long lists of prohibited acts, any one of which made an athlete a professional. The fact that each of these negative injunctions had its origin in a corrupt or questionable practice may explain their constantly increasing number, but it also has served to remind the amateur athlete that he might not do certain things which his own monetary or material advantage made very desirable. In such circumstances it is too much to expect that human nature should not seek to evade detailed regulations, especially when these regulations appear in certain cases to place a premium upon their evasion. With the rise of commercialism in college athletics, its temptations became in many instances too strong to be resisted. The result has been a great increase in the number of ways by which, sometimes even under the guise of philanthropy, the amateur convention is set at naught.

In the second place, a legalistic, rationalizing attitude of mind has contributed to evasions of the convention. There can be little doubt that the multiplicity of rules against professionalism has bred in many athletes, present and past, a strong predilection to satisfy the letter of the amateur rule while knowing well that even in the act of satisfaction they were contravening its spirit. In England, the sportsman's code of "playing the game" has served somewhat to mitigate this influence. In Canada, a similar code of honor has wrought a similar result. In the United States, all too few influences have hitherto been strongly exerted in affirmation of the doctrine of amateurism. Meanwhile, the material rewards of covert professionalism, which have incited to evasion of the amateur convention, and a desire to reap the benefits of amateurism without paying its price, have led to much hair-splitting and the drawing of many fine distinctions. To the individual conscience of the honorable sportsman, there is no middle ground between amateurism and professionalism.

CHAPTER IV

ATHLETICS IN AMERICAN SCHOOLS

ALTHOUGH the groundwork of American college athletics is laid in the secondary school, the present study concerns itself much less extensively with school than with college athletics. The purpose of our secondary school is and must remain two-fold: to prepare for college, but primarily to prepare for life. By assigning this double function to the high school we increase incalculably its burden of responsibility, not alone in academic instruction but also in athletics.

For some time the adjustment between secondary and higher education has been far from satisfactory. The concern that this has caused teachers in schools has led them to attempt by reaching upward to anticipate many of the instructional difficulties that pupils who are to enter college will there encounter. Although the college teacher has at times complained that the school teacher has deprived college instruction of its novelty and interest by attempts to introduce college methods and materials into secondary schools, he has nevertheless continued to employ in his own teaching a pedagogical procedure which many regard as a borrowing from secondary work. Thus, both school and college have adapted one from the other, albeit for purposes alien to the attempt to relate the college more closely to the school. In spite of these measures the instructional gulf between the two institutions has remained wide.

On the score of school activities, however, the pupil enters a current that sweeps him forward into the full tide of college life. Although mainly borrowed from the college, often without due regard to their ultimate effect upon school life, school activities, especially athletics, provide a substantial connection between the college and the school. As a result many of the supposedly new conditions outside of the classroom which students meet on entering college have already formed a part of their school experience.

I. The Bearings of Physical Education in Schools

No country is so rich in educational theory as the United States, especially as regards the secondary school. Whereas in England, practice precedes theory and theory serves to codify practice, the American, like the German, announces his intention to base his practical procedure on the results of psychological and pedagogical experiment. Partly from this cause and partly from others, there is great danger lest the individual relationships between pupil and teacher be ignored. Under pressure of numbers the needs and the initiative of the individual are often sacrificed to the requirements of the group or mass. Enlightened supervisors and teachers of physical education, recognizing this danger, have been among the first to attempt to safeguard the individual relationship.

A. Theoretical Relationships

A recent theory of physical education[1] relates this phase of instruction to the very widespread doctrine of "activity" in educational philosophy, and defines physical education as "education by means of or through large-muscle activities." Whatever we may think of the "activity theory" of education, we can agree that the three general ideals proposed for physical education, — (1) differentiation of program to meet individual needs as determined by a physician's examination, (2) equalization of ability so that a pupil shall compete in athletics with those of his fellows possessing abilities similar to his own, and (3) freedom of choice in the selection of physical activities with consequent full responsibility for behavior, — are important in the development of any individual boy or girl from the points of view of physical health, of ethics, and even of morals. Whatever rational aim may be accepted as the end of education, they may be adapted to serve it. They presuppose, first, a recognition of the individual pupil as the unit of physical education; secondly, a relation between physical activities and athletics on the one hand and more formal classroom instruction on the other; and thirdly, a common ground of moral and ethical relationships upon which impinges every element, small or great, that goes to make up the pupil's life.

B. School Athletics as a Part of the School Curriculum

Although steps have recently been taken toward fulfilling these ideals, few programs

---

[1] By Dr. Frederick Rand Rogers, chief of the Bureau of Physical Education, New York State, *Physical Education : A Résumé for the Educational Administrator*, 1927. The extension of the theory in the same author's *Amateur Spirit in Scholastic Games and Sports*, to praise "contests without victory," is not so successful.

of physical education in America approximate them as a whole. Furthermore, these ideals, however worthy in themselves, like all other phases of education fail of good results when the teachers to whose hands they are entrusted are reluctant or not qualified to receive and apply them. Here, as elsewhere, the problem is a problem of personnel. None the less, in spite of the shortcomings of our practice, our school athletics are much more nearly an integral part of the educational process than college athletics.

This statement must not be construed as a valid argument for the "faculty control" of athletics in colleges and universities. The school and the college years witness in the life of the individual a growth and a maturing that proceeds quite independently of formal education. Unless school athletics and college athletics be seen as inter-acting but separate parts in a single consistent process integrally related to a student's mature growth, neither serves its best purpose and both are in danger of impairment through unconsidered imitation.

II. Organization for Athletics in Schools

A part of the effectiveness of the public school consists in bringing school and home environment into a measure of consonance. This principle applies especially to physical education.

Here the private boarding school, which in a measure can create its own home environment, has an advantage. At a boarding school the loyalties that spring from physical and social groupings tend of themselves to breed a certain homogeneity which can be employed without intermission in shaping the habits of the boy or girl. One result is that organization for athletics is more easily effected and guided in private schools than in public schools.

A. In Public Schools

The place of athletics in the public school and the regard in which they are held may be measured by the fact that forty-seven of the forty-eight states of the Union have their own interscholastic athletic associations. Nevada alone has none. On the other hand, only seventeen states have directors or departments of physical education: Alabama, California, Delaware, Florida, Louisiana, Maryland, Massachusetts, Michigan, Minnesota, Missouri, New Jersey, New York, Ohio, Pennsylvania, Virginia, and West Virginia. Maine, at the time of writing, has an "acting director." If public recognition be a criterion of judgment, physical education is considered to be far less important than inter-school athletics; the part is emphasized at the expense of the whole. In Delaware, the State Department of Physical Education came to be constituted because the importance and usefulness of the Delaware Interscholastic Athletic Association were recognized. A similar development which entails the subordination of the interscholastic athletic association to the department of physical education has occurred or is now under way in a number of other states.

1. Interscholastic Athletic Associations

The membership of a state interscholastic athletic association is typically composed of high schools, small and large schools standing on an equal footing through the votes of their teacher delegates. The meetings, usually held annually, sometimes more frequently, are devoted to discussions bearing upon athletic relationships between the schools, which in some instances may be adjusted *ad interim* by an officer or an executive committee with or without confirmation by the association. Among the chief problems with which such associations deal are eligibility, finance, the arranging of schedules for contests and meets, and the choosing of officials. Of these subjects, eligibility appears to be the most crucial. The pains and consideration which delegates lavish on any phase of eligibility that threatens to deprive their school of the services of one of its skilled athletes, and thereby impair its chances of victory, are astonishing. This single motive appears to control most of the association's deliberations. Usually some form of disciplinary action can be taken against schools or their associations whose athletes violate regulations. Among the interscholastic athletic associations that issue handbooks or yearbooks are those of Indiana, Maryland, Minnesota, New York, Ohio, and Texas. Notice may be taken also of *The Diamond*, the periodical of the Delaware athletic association, and the *Bulletin* of the New York State Public High School Athletic Association, which have done much to emphasize the ethical aspects of games and contests. Continuous use of a publication for this purpose is exceptional.

The interscholastic athletic association is much given to the same kind of debate and controversy as the college conference and is therefore subject to the same or analogous limitations, especially in its dealings with problems of eligibility. Not a few victories in the playing field are made inevitable through the interpretation of eligibility requirements on the floor of the association. In short, the concern of the interscholastic body is mainly with the practical business of school athletics and athletic relationships.

The statewide interscholastic athletic association in most instances is supplemented by district or local leagues for the conduct of contests in the various branches of athletics. Mention should also be made of the National Interscholastic Athletic Association, which is composed on a basis of representation for schools, leagues, and state organizations.

2. Athletic Associations in Individual Schools

With the statewide body the local high school athletic association has much in common. Here the pupils have a part, however nominal it may be. But important decisions and actions are either taken by the teacher members or dictated by them. Town interests beyond school walls are making their influence increasingly felt in financial support to the association or to individual athletes, in procuring expert players, and in providing coaches, especially for football and basketball. In not a few towns, cities, and even states, school athletics have become less an affair of the school than an amusement for the community.

This situation, against which many principals and teachers are contending, has distorted the fundamental purposes and relationships of school athletics and enforced a separation of athletics from physical education for boys and girls at an age when much could be gained by a union of the two. The matter will be discussed in the section that follows. Secondarily, it has exerted a profoundly deleterious influence upon college athletics.

3. Physical Education in Public Schools

Even in the schools of those states which possess departments of physical education, the outdoor exercise under supervision which is the backbone of physical education is in need of all the support, both financial and moral, that can be accorded. It has been estimated by excellent authority[2] that children in at least half of our rural schools have the benefit of experienced direction in physical education. It has also been estimated that three-fourths of the teachers concerned in this task have received some special preparation for it. In states that have departments of physical education, much is being done to correlate athletic contests with this work, but, remarks Dr. L. H. Wagenhorst, in his monograph on the *Administration and Cost of High School Athletics* (1926), "It is inconceivable that fair-minded people will subscribe to the rank injustice of the relatively large outlay for the physical training of those who need it least," namely, the athletes.

Meanwhile, a new conception of the whole situation as it affects public school life and relations is gaining ground. Briefly, it is to the effect that physical training and athletics are parts of physical education and that physical education is, in turn, a component of a larger field of school hygiene, which includes nutrition, medical and dental supervision, posture, and education in human reproduction and development. Indeed, the normal child presents few problems that have not yet been attacked, while some of the needs of the abnormal or the subnormal are being met in a variety of ways. From the point of view of the curriculum, the present tendency is to conceive of the theory and practice of school hygiene as complementary aspects of a larger whole, which includes supervised play for developing capacities and aptitudes.

It must not, however, be supposed that our public schools have as yet generally arrived at a stage in which the welfare of the individual pupil outweighs certain other considerations. This highly important matter will be discussed later.

[2] James Frederick Rogers, M.D., *School Hygiene and Physical Education*, Department of the Interior, Bureau of Education, Bulletin 1927, No. 3, page 11.

B. In Private Schools

Whereas the state department of education or of public instruction has the function of coördinating and suggesting methods and standards in the public schools that it serves, no such public body operates to bring together the private schools of the country. Various organizations have, however, been formed, in some of which membership is divided between public and private schools, and these bodies accomplish much on a basis of voluntary coöperation and interchange of information. Private schools as a group, therefore, may vary one from another over a single state to an even greater degree than city and rural public schools, and therein lie both their strength and their weakness. These observations apply equally to the academic aspects of instruction and to physical education.

From the many phases of athletics at private schools, four only will be selected for preliminary discussion : inter-school pacts, school athletic associations, accommodations for games, and medical supervision.

1. Inter-school Pacts

Whatever the value and importance of the interscholastic athletic association or conference, which includes or is composed of private schools, spontaneous agreements concerning athletic contests may be far more fruitful. One of the most important was concluded on October 14, 1927, between the Choate School at Wallingford, the Loomis Institute at Windsor, and the Taft School at Watertown, Connecticut. It should be noted that the three schools are similar in size, ideals, and clientele, that they are situated near one another, and that their rivalry is friendly and mutually respecting. These considerations are fundamental to any such athletic understanding.

The first provision of this agreement limits the number of contests to six in football, nine each in basketball, hockey, and baseball, seven each in tennis and golf, four in track and field events, and five each in wrestling and association football; defines a "game"; and imposes a definite limit upon outside competition. After a contest starts, a coach will give no instructions during play or intermissions and will make no suggestions regarding strategy, method, or spirit. In short, the function of a coach during a contest is to safeguard the physical condition of the players and, presumably upon this basis, to effect substitutions. The pact limits football practice to the time the school is in session, restricts boys to candidacy for one team only, and makes ineligible for competition during the preceding scholastic year any boy who will become twenty-one years of age before the first of July. Choate School does not subscribe to the non-coaching agreement as it affects football. This provision governs the football games between Loomis and Deerfield Academy.

The agreement has been adversely criticized on the one ground that the non-coaching provision must breed suspicion and distrust ; but until such distrust is actually bred by the agreement in a degree that proves ineradicable or threatens its operation, the eventuality may be regarded as possible rather than as inevitable. An objection which savors of elder prompting is the notion of some of the boys at one school that the elimination of the coach from the contest imposes too much responsibility upon the captain during the match. This attitude can doubtless be modified under the guidance of masters who are determined to train their boys in meeting responsibilities. It reflects one of the most serious objections that can be raised against private school athletics as now conducted.

A similar provision was adopted by the Central Committee of the New York State Public High School Athletic Association on October 20, 1927, as "General Regulation No. 1," and recommended for all interscholastic contests in local leagues.

The fruitfulness of such pacts or regulations depends, of course, upon their fair trial. When those charged with the preparation of school teams conceive their functions as a part of the educational process and not as a means to athletic victory, prefer the training of youth for the bearing of responsibility to the development of winning teams, and act upon these principles with full sincerity, the complexion of school athletics will change.

2. Athletic Associations

The local athletic association of the private school exhibits little variation in principle from the local public school organization. A limited observation indicates that masters in private schools are expected to take a somewhat greater interest and to exercise more active guidance in athletic affairs than the public school teacher. This observation, however, does not apply to the recently inaugurated coaching system in New York City high schools. The private boarding school, with its dormitories or halls of residence, provides a fertile field for the development of those loyalties which beget and strengthen intramural contests and in time grow into a school loyalty, tone, or "spirit," which is accounted to be one of the great advantages of the private institution. To the propagation of school loyalty the athletic association is frequently made to contribute its share, — and perhaps in some instances more than its share, — through its selection of cheer leaders, its management of trips to games away from the school, the award of school letters and class numerals, not to mention cups and other even more personal trophies, and its sponsorship of football dinners and rallies. Many of these practices represent direct borrowings from the university or the college.

3. Accommodations for Games at Private Schools

It is the exceptional public school that provides playing fields and a gymnasium comparable in size, equipment, or care with that of the more favored private school. An explanation is to be sought in the amount of money available for such purposes at the two types of institutions, and especially in the monetary aspects of alumni loyalty. Public school alumni frequently lack the leisure, interest, and financial means that the graduates of private schools almost as a matter of course dedicate to them. Hence it is not astonishing to find the gymnasiums and the playing fields of certain private schools rivaling and even surpassing similar provisions at the most fortunate universities and colleges, if not in size, at least in luxury and architectural fitness.

The supervision of games, practice, and play by masters is rapidly gaining ground in the Eastern States. Deerfield Academy is one of several schools at which a major part of the instructors' athletic supervision is given to less skilled players. The conviction is growing that the more expert the boy at games, the less is his need of personal direction. In other words, the coaching and supervision of private school athletics appears to be entering a phase in which instruction is given to those who need it most.

One aspect of inter-private school relations calls for a word of emphatic commendation, the tradition of hospitality in the entertainment of visiting teams. Some of the examples that have come to the notice of this enquiry have been so outstanding and so pleasant in their results that it is impossible to ignore them. Although in according such entertainment the buildings and grounds of the private school offer opportunities that may be wholly or nearly absent from the public school, yet instances of public school hospitality are equally noteworthy. It were well if a tradition of practical and sincere inter-school hospitality became even more generally established.

4. Medical Supervision

With more money at its disposal the private school has, speaking generally, outdistanced the public school in the use of physical examinations to determine fitness for athletic competition and to assist pupils to enter branches of athletics suited to their tastes and powers. On the other hand, few private schools avail themselves of the full time of a practicing physician. The general rule for schools of moderate size appears to be to enlist the services of a general practitioner in the town, who is summoned as need arises or is expected to devote a part of his time to the school. Boys taken ill or injured in games are sent to the school infirmary, where a nurse looks after them pending the arrival of the school physician on special call or on his round of periodical visits. The plan has many advantages, not the least of which are its economy and its practicability. From the point of view of schoolboy welfare, it may imply, — and in some cases apparently has implied,— that the expertness and knowledge necessary to the satisfactory treatment of athletic injuries is gained from experience with individual cases and at the expense of the victims. The condition, having been much ameliorated over the past decade, need cause little anxiety to the parents of schoolboys, especially since the needs of boys at the best schools are being met with an increasing wisdom on the part of the authorities, and improvements in infirmaries and other provisions, if gradual, are nevertheless constant. The danger lies, of course, in weak or inferior schools, the implications of whose programs and advertising far outrun their capacities or real intentions.

III. The Separation of Physical Education and Athletics in Public Schools

Perhaps the most significant single phase of "large-muscle activities" in the public high school is the gap between physical education and athletics which has been mentioned in preceding pages. A number of states, especially those which possess enlightened departments or directors of physical education, have recognized the breach. Of these states, many have gone little farther than a general lament over existing conditions and a preliminary appraisal of the situation. Some, however, are attempting to weld athletics and physical education into a single active unit by means of regulations imposed from above. Few of the eighteen states that have qualified directors of physical education have as yet reached the point at which the unification of physical education and athletics has become an accomplished fact. Although here, as always, it is extremely difficult to set practice in accord with theory, progress toward this end is clearly discernible. In the long run, it is likely that a somewhat more persuasive course of action, which in time will lead physical directors to practice what so many of them preach, will provide better results. The following sections set forth a very few of the undesirable consequences of the separation.

A. The Impoverishment of Physical Education and Hygiene

It may be taken as axiomatic that high school athletics are no better than the schools that conduct them. Usually they are made to serve the interests of the group in whose hands rests the actual, as distinguished from the intended, control of the school. Usually, also, they reflect very quickly the policies and activities of the principal, the teachers, the political groups, or the townspeople, whichever may be in command of the local school system. Thus, it follows that in communities where wise and adequate direction is not accorded to the educational processes, athletics tend to become corrupted and generally debased. Around high school football, or basketball, or baseball there may cluster abuses that are traceable to the debauching of school athletics through attempts to make them contribute to the financial profit of interested parties. In the words of Dr. James Frederick Rogers, "Since high-school attendance has been made compulsory interschool athletics have been a prominent feature of high-school life; and, following closely the lead of the colleges, the athletics of high schools have developed all the faults and failings found in higher institutions. But these are minor matters compared to the favors shown to these notoriety-and-excitement-furnishing sports at the expense or neglect of normal, healthful activities for all students." A community that finances the construction of a fine high school building out of the profits of basketball is in danger of capitalizing the excitement of the spectators and the notoriety of the players.[3] No amount of capable direction and control can eliminate the potential bad results of such measures.

3 Some cases of "high schools built around basketball courts" may be found in Indiana communities, like, for example, Flora,

The reason is somewhat as follows: The physical care and welfare of a group of schoolboys and schoolgirls contribute little to the entertainment and relaxation of the average community. These involve slow and laborious processes that may utterly lack the spectacular or the sensational. On the other hand, a series of fast, hard games at basketball or football, forming a season that culminates in a championship match, whether lost or won, leads to much excitement, town pride, and ultimate profits in sales of goods by local merchants. Superficially the arguments are all in favor of the immediate financial prosperity and the entertainment of the community, especially when gate receipts bring profits that can be devoted to the erection of school buildings, the centres of which are auditoriums useful as basketball courts. The boys and girls are likely to suffer in two ways, neither of which may be immediately apparent. In the first place, their sense of values will be grossly distorted by the commercialization of school sports. In the second place, their physical well-being is almost certain to be impaired by too frequent or too hard games and long trips. The children of the community are sacrificed to the entertainment of the adults and the easing of the tax burden. The township that deliberately embarks upon such a program of exploitation cannot have wisely counted the costs. That athletics need not impoverish physical education is proved in instances where the processes go forward as one to the ultimate benefit of the communities that have the foresight to regard them in their true relationships.

B. The Prominence of Interscholastic Championships

In June, 1927, the New Jersey State Department of Public Instruction printed the results of a study of the status of athletics in New Jersey high schools. Among the conclusions stand these sentences: "When the majority of the schools which belong to the N.J.I.A.A. are opposed to State championships the consensus of school opinion is evidently in favor of more interclass and neighborhood contests among friendly rivals as opposed to State-wide championships. It is significant that some of the leading schools which have won championships are most eloquent in favor of a new emphasis." "Schools which claim benefit from the enthusiasm, pride, and loyalty generated by championship participation admit that this is often offset by the accompanying distraction of the student group, the physical injury to certain individuals, and the exploitation of school pupils by the 'sporting fraternity.'"

In many instances the regard paid to championships and championship teams is carried to the point of unwholesomeness. Certainly no school athlete is benefited by the sycophantic adulation of his fellow pupils, boys or girls. Such distortion is due less to

with a population of 1,441, a high school enrollment of 90, and a gymnasium seating capacity of 1,200; Martinsville, population 4,895, enrollment 500, seating capacity 5,000; Raub, population 258, enrollment 26, seating capacity 1,000; Veedersburg, population 1,580, enrollment 126, seating capacity 1,200. It is said that basketball is nearly as popular in rural Illinois, Ohio, and Utah as in Indiana.

those coaches and teachers who hold teaching certificates and whose task as instructors is constantly embarrassed by it, than to the influence of townspeople and the part-time coaches whom in some instances they provide.

Of themselves, championships may be a comparatively innocuous phase of interschool rivalry. Certainly they provide an incentive to competition, unify effort, and stimulate one kind of school loyalty, but when they are carried on long after the normal season, when preparation for them is permitted to deprive students not so engaged of the attention that the man or woman in charge of physical education would otherwise accord, and when they absorb so much of the interest of the community that the program of physical education is subordinated to them, their value is at least dubious. It is small wonder that New Jersey schools in a ratio of five to four have declared against them, and four to one against post-season games. It is a pleasure to note the abandonment of the so-called National Interscholastic Basketball Tournament that was to have been held at Wichita, Kansas.

C. The Influence of the Townsman

The townsman who interests himself spontaneously and actively in school athletics is potentially one of the most salutary influences in school life. With an understanding or a sense of the appropriate place and function of athletics in the educational process, a conviction of values that inhere in outdoor life and games, and a regard for good sportsmanship and honor, he may be, and sometimes is, one of the blessings of a high school or a group of schools. It is unfortunate that not all citizens who interest themselves in school athletics are actuated by such standards or informed concerning them. Moreover, it is perhaps natural that the doings of individuals whose influence is baneful should seem to penetrate deeper and last longer than those of their more upright and modest neighbors. It will be as well to consider the adverse results of doubtless well-intentioned activities.

1. The Desire for the Spectacular

An excessive desire for the spectacular and the sensational lies at the root of most of the townsman's harmful influence. The first manifestations of such a spirit usually take the form of pressure from one source or another upon school authorities, including teachers, principals, and boards of education, to authorize practices which, at first glance comparatively innocuous, may develop almost overnight into virulent abuses. The worst influence of such a person upon high school students is probably exerted through suggestions and offers of money for coaches, equipment, extra or post-seasonal games and trips, personal trophies and rewards, and extra prizes. His machinations lead readily to the use of unsuitable events in meets, heavy schedules, series of post-season games, especially the over-valuing of championships, and to ignoring the effects of especially trying contests upon the physical well-being of athletes. Mr. William F. Garcelon speaks from long observation and experience when he says, "Many of the boys come to college broken down and spoiled from the athletic standpoint because of over-training in school athletics." This matter is discussed further in Chapter VII.

In combating these tendencies the influence of certain state departments of physical education, the New England College Conference, the Public Schools Athletic League of the City of New York, and the Women's Division of the National Amateur Athletic Federation, together with such individuals as Dean Briggs, Mr. Garcelon, Mr. Gustavus T. Kirby, Mr. John F. McHugh of the New York City Public Schools, Dr. J. Anna Norris, of the University of Minnesota, and Dr. Allan Winter Rowe, is commendable. It is a pity that such college influences as are embodied in the championship tournaments and meets conducted in the name of the Intercollegiate Conference, the University of Chicago, the University of Pennsylvania, and many other colleges and universities, should not be directed wholly to similar ends. The doubtful value of spying out promising schoolboy athletes is scarcely a legitimate excuse for the excessive devotion to the spectacular to which many such meets and tournaments contribute.

2. The Providing of Special Coaches

It is normal for teachers of academic subjects to manifest active interest in the games and contests of their pupils and to serve as coaches or advisers of teams. Indeed, this practice receives official recognition and sanction in the public schools of New York City. A similar interest is normal to the teachers of physical education. But not infrequently it happens that the proportion of victories won under such auspices does not satisfy the townsman whose interest is shown in selecting and paying a professional coach or trainer and donating his services to the school or its athletic association. Sometimes the professional coach is engaged by school authorities themselves because of the pressure exerted by town enthusiasts who desire winning teams, no matter what the cost. Even the openly professional coach is a more honest influence than the professional or semi-professional athlete hired covertly and given a position in a local store or factory in order to disguise his true relation to school athletics. The New Jersey report, already cited, indicates that in that state nine-tenths of the coaches are paid regular salaries by local boards of education and that only eight schools have coaches "furnished by private arrangement not connected with school moneys." In the West and Southwest several instances were encountered of coaches provided by private arrangement of this nature.

If principals are to be held responsible for athletics in their schools, certainly one of the surest ways to deprive them of the control which is a corollary to that responsibility, is to permit the hiring of an alien mercenary to perform the duties of an appointee of the local school system.

3. The Money Appraisal of Games

It is highly improbable that many schoolboys or schoolgirls who have not been subject to older influences would spontaneously appraise athletic contests in terms of their return in dollars. Those cases in which the financial profits from athletics have been used in materially enriching organizations or in providing buildings and playing fields, with the consequent easing of the taxpayers' burden, reveal the tampering of older persons. In many such instances school officials, be it said to their very great credit, have been reluctant to further such expedients and dubious of their results. More than one principal, while crediting the sponsors of financial profits from games with the best intentions, has remained skeptical as to the wisdom of providing material facilities at the expense of possible harm to boys and girls from heavy schedules, unsupervised journeys of teams and supporters to distant points, injuries in games played during over-strain or over-fatigue, and the other innumerable adverse conditions that follow the frank commercializing of high school athletics.

In such conditions the money value of the trophy or the prize is always more important than the honor which it confers.[4] The local merchant who wishes to present sweaters to the high school team will naturally find his altruistic advertisement scorned unless his sweaters are of a grade that flatters the self-esteem of the recipients. The cup or the plaque must be of sterling silver. The group of business men who tender a complimentary dinner to a championship team must look to it that their viands are as choice as their good wishes. Commercialism cuts both ways. It destroys youth's discernment of true values and intentions, and it depreciates the worth of the very device that engendered it. Continually appraise athletic performance at a price, and all that contributes to it and honors it has also its price.

D. Scholastic Abuses and Athletics

During the course of our study, a number of college officers have pointed out that however strictly a college may try to administer its requirements with the intention of admitting only candidates with the requisite credits or points, a few school principals and headmasters in letters of recommendation customarily stress not alone desirable traits of character but also athletic success as qualifications entitling boys to special consideration. In response to a request for appraisal of a candidate's character as a guide to the admissions body, a principal may go out of his way to extol the athletic ability of boys whose class records and standing leave much to be desired. Perhaps in some cases principals and headmasters are forced to praise athletic skill because of a

---

[4] We are told on good authority that in the settlement houses of a great Eastern city it is common practice for boys of from twelve to eighteen years of age to offer their services in athletics to the settlement that offers the most desirable rewards in the way of prizes, trophies, and refreshments, and even to refuse to play for a given house unless the rewards are satisfactory. Of all the boys who are members of these houses, about one-third plan to attend college. Some have very definitely expressed their intention to attend that college at which they can obtain most assistance in exchange for their participation in intercollegiate athletics.

lack of other qualities and characteristics that are commendable from the supposed point of view of the colleges. Another factor in such commendation may be direct or implied promises to schoolboys that they will be financed in college provided they enroll in a particular secondary school. Of such promises principals may have an inkling. Grades assigned by school teachers for particular courses are known to have been raised by certifying officers on solicitation of college coaches or alumni in order to enable boys to slip easily into college. The complaints of not a few college officials, verified by field agents of this study, indicate that these dishonest practices are far more extensive than is generally realized. The claim is not advanced that such practices are automatically eliminated by the union of physical education and athletics. On the other hand, it appears certain that in state school systems and in preparatory schools in which athletics are made a part of a program of physical education, absence of a mercenary motive helps to minimize these dangers.

E. The Effects upon the Schoolboy

The principal sufferers from the policy of separating athletics and physical education in many public schools are the body of youth whom it touches. If it were necessary to sum up in a single phrase the worst results of that separation, probably that phrase would be the impairment of ethical and moral standards of schoolboys through the commercialization of athletics. Although it is true that merely advertising school athletics to be a phase of physical education guarantees no lasting good, on the other hand it provides an approach to a difficult problem from the solution of which, under qualified teachers and competent directors, much benefit may ultimately result to the individual pupil.

Of a number of cases that have been collected, one will illustrate almost all of the abuses to which the divorce of athletics from physical education in schools can lead: the secret payment of money for athletic participation, physical violence, and dishonesty.

In a large Eastern city there recently arose an angry controversy over the eligibility of a school athlete on the ground of age. Although the athlete, his father, and a clergyman all maintained that the boy was eligible, a public school official, being led by virtue of his office to investigate, concluded from records of the athlete in a neighboring state, as well as from local documents, that the boy's age was being misrepresented and that he was too old to participate under the rules. The official presented these facts to a meeting of the local athletic committee and the boy was declared ineligible.

On leaving this meeting the school official was confronted by the young man's father, who demanded, "Why have you interfered with my boy's education?" The official replied that he was merely carrying out regulations. Without warning the parent struck the official. Just then the boy appeared and expressed his desire to "take a crack" at the official, too. Thereupon the official threw down his armful of books, his overcoat, and various other encumbrances, seized a chair, and stood his ground. Later in the day the boy's school fellows held hostile demonstrations before the official's office and also at the office of the high school principal, but nothing came of either disorder.

Weeks afterward, however, because of the athletic reputation of the boy, a committee was appointed to enquire into the case. It ascertained the facts set down above and also the additional facts that a teacher in the school, who had received extra pay for coaching at football and basketball, had entertained the boy at his home before the boy had transferred to the school, and that at that time $75 had been given to the athlete.

The results of the committee's findings were salutary: the teacher-coach resigned from all connection with school athletics; the boy first was removed from school, then was expelled permanently, and finally left the city; a new eligibility code was adopted by the city high schools; a supervisor of secondary school athletics was appointed; and the particular school has a new director of athletics. "In general," writes a gentleman who was much involved in the case, "I believe athletics have been benefited by this straightening out of affairs."

IV. Some Deficiencies of Athletics in Private Schools

Most of the deficiencies of athletics as they are conducted in American private schools are to be referred to shortcomings in the life or the management of particular schools. Thus, the school that neglects to guard adequately the health of its pupils is likely to neglect also the supervision of the physical welfare of its athletes. The school that is operated primarily for profit to its owners and secondarily for the good of its pupils usually exhibits commercialism in its athletics. Let a school be bent upon inflating its reputation through newspaper accounts of its games, and it can generally attain to its desire. The best private schools do none of these things; the least satisfactory usually do all.

It has already been pointed out that many private schools might well devote attention to improving the conditions that surround the physical welfare of their athletes and also that much is being done in this direction. Among the deficiencies in athletics which are known to many headmasters and which the most enlightened are attempting to correct, two deserve special emphasis: the development of undesirable attitudes towards athletics in schoolboys, and the unwarrantable assistance given to athletes. The results of the practices that these two factors imply unite to impair both school and college athletics at their core. Parenthetically, it may be said that ample evidence shows certain public schools to be as guilty of these abuses as any private school.

A. The Cultivation of an Undesirable Schoolboy Attitude towards Athletics

The undue publicity lavished upon certain private preparatory schools leads inevitably to developing undesirable attitudes towards athletics among their boys. As a result, not alone from schoolboys and masters, but from graduates who have finished their schooling or have gone on into college, comes evidence that certain individuals have encouraged boys to set a price upon their athletic ability: sometimes hired coaches have been guilty of this practice, sometimes graduates whose way to college has been made easy because of their skill at games. One well-substantiated case involves a college undergraduate, himself heavily subsidized, who in effect offered to deliver to a college coach athletes from his old school, whose services he had pledged after the methods of the professional baseball scout.

Nor are some private schools above capitalizing athletic ability for their own supposed benefit at the expense of the boy. A pupil may be officially advised to drop certain courses of instruction that conflict with football practice. Others — and this has occurred in cases of athletes who have transferred from public to private schools — are kept at the school a year longer than is necessary for them to complete the work, simply because of their skill at football. One Pennsylvania school sent its football team to play games in Texas and charged their expenses to school advertising. Another, whose football teams win many games, appears to have solicited athletes from public schools by promising not only a school but a college education with all expenses paid. When such practices are current, as they seem to be in certain Eastern and Southern states, the Sunday newspaper that prints a photograph of a school baseball player with the caption "His Athletic Prowess Wins Him a Scholarship," specifically naming player, school, and college, is only recording information which is already widespread. Such a picture and caption are reprehensible in that they inculcate in many athletes at public and private schools a notion that they can sell their athletic services. From all of these practices it is only a step to "shopping-round."

1. "Shopping-Round"

"Shopping-round" is the soliciting by a prospective college athlete of financial assistance in the form of a scholarship or other aid at a college or a private school in exchange for athletic participation, in such a fashion that the offers, real or imagined, from one institution are used to procure offers or overtures from another. The causes and results of this process, as regards the college or university, will be discussed in their appropriate connections. For the moment we are concerned only with its effect upon the schoolboy.

Perhaps the most important single result of "shopping-round" upon the schoolboy's character is the engendering of a purely materialistic attitude at an age when his outlook upon life is naturally quite the opposite. A lad hears tales of "easy money" made by his fellows merely from a game that he plays for fun. Some of these other boys he knows to be less expert than he. Now, a youth of college or school age is rarely supplied so generously with money that he cannot use more, and so, when a means of capitalizing athletic ability presents itself, its temptations are likely to be too strong to be resisted. Not infrequently the reasoning runs thus: Others get subsidies through "shopping-round." Why should n't I? I can use the money as well as anyone else. If money is to be had, I am a fool not to get my share. The boy puts out feelers in the form of letters to coaches or alumni of a few colleges. Much of the lad's character and future career depends upon the replies which he receives to those first communications. If his correspondents answer him sharply and wisely that they and their institutions do not countenance athletic subsidies, he may be brought to realize the implications of his course in time to abandon it. If, on the other hand, a correspondent indicates a willingness to go deeper into the boy's case, the way is open to striking a secret bargain which in time may convert that boy into an athletic impostor, and place the university or college in a position of deceit with relation to other institutions. These remarks are not theoretical. They are grounded in the history of many cases in which precisely these debasing things have happened to scores of youths, schools, and colleges.

The process of corrupting a boy's ideals, as just outlined, is not confined to the private schoolboy and the college. It exists between the public schoolboy and the private school, and the public schoolboy and the college. One of its most astonishing results was the "Intercollegiate Athletic Bureau."

2. The Intercollegiate Athletic Bureau

During the autumn of 1927, not a few school athletes received circular letters to the effect that "The Intercollegiate Athletic Bureau, Eastern Division" was prepared, on payment of a fee, to bring their names to the attention of nearly one hundred universities and colleges so that registrants might reap the advantages of whatever aid should be forthcoming in exchange for their services as athletes. The young men who had organized the Bureau appear to have regarded their enterprise as a commendable attempt to bring goods to market. Fortunately, the chairman of the athletic committee at a large Eastern university had a different view. The rapid steps that he initiated showed the entrepreneurs that their work had fewer merits than they thought and the Bureau voluntarily ceased to operate. Since only six athletes had paid a total of twelve dollars in registration fees, on the financial side little damage was done. But it is regrettable that between the schools and the colleges of the United States there should exist even the shadow of a relation that should seem to provide a field of operations for such an undertaking.

B. ASSISTANCE TO SCHOOL ATHLETES

As a rule, American public schools have little to offer the schoolboy athlete in money or in kind. Their clientele is limited geographically to the communities or districts in which they are situated and their alumni rarely proselyte from other schools. It were well if this last statement could be made of all private institutions. Certain Eastern private schools have received boys supported not by their parents but by college alumni, and prepared them for passing university entrance requirements for particular institutions, where also they were to be financed in order to participate in athletics. The headmaster of one such school sought to justify his course on the ground that he believed his school was the better for admitting poor boys to fellowship with the well-to-do, even upon an equivocal status. More than one headmaster appears to tolerate the subsidizing activities of college alumni on the pretext that no discrimination must be exercised against the athlete. Few school alumni to-day are active to the same degree as college alumni. It is generally the college alumnus with a distorted sense of values who recruits public high school boys for preparatory schools with a view to getting them ultimately to play upon university teams. Our study has revealed arrangements between college coaches on the one hand and high school and academy coaches on the other, whereby, all unknown to the authorities of either school or college, promising athletic material is passed on from one to the other (Dean Academy, Bellefonte Academy,[5] Kiskiminetas Springs School; Carnegie Institute of Technology, New York University).

The number of coaches who understand and resent these practices is fortunately increasing. One such instance concerns the track coach of a New York City high school, whose salary is paid for teaching an academic subject and whose coaching is a labor of love.

Hearing that one of his team had received offers from the alumni of an Eastern university, the coach attempted to dissuade the boy from accepting the proposal that he should enter a preparatory school and later a university without cost to himself. Soon the coach was called on the telephone by a man who gave the name of an alumnus of the university, now practicing law, and demanded what business it was of the coach where the boy went to college or what he did, and warned the coach to keep his hands off the matter. The coach insisted that it was his affair, inasmuch as the boy had developed under his tutelage and responsibility. The alumnus scoffed at this attitude. The boy entered the preparatory school and at this writing is registered at the university and participating in intercollegiate athletics.

As a matter of fact, the headmaster of any preparatory school can encourage or terminate such practices at will, but ending them is far easier at their inception than afterward. A famous headmaster of a famous school, on being asked for his views upon what assistance might justifiably be given to an athlete found it

difficult to frame a satisfactory answer which can be regarded as applicable in all cases and fair to all concerned. The matter is one to which I have given many years of careful thought, however, and my conclusions are pretty definite. Further, the fact that I have participated vigorously in athletics in

[5] *Bellefonte*, Headmaster J. R. Hughes, letter of May 14, 1929: The Academy has "abolished the practice of giving full scholarships. Very few athletic officials are paying the expenses of needy athletes in schools like Bellefonte."

my undergraduate days, have served as coach for the first few years of my teaching experience, and have always kept in intimate touch with this phase of school and college life ever since should at least furnish me fairly good grounds on which to base my judgment.

Let me say frankly that I do not believe that an athlete should be treated to any degree in any way different from that which applies to one with no athletic ability whatever. Not only does the institution which offers inducements to an athlete suffer, but the effect on the boy himself is generally serious and frequently disastrous. It is grossly unfair to exploit a boy's athletic abilities in connection with the so-called education which an institution offers in return. I am confident that there is a growing reaction in high-grade institutions against this practice, a reaction which, it seems to me, is likely to spread. Where a boy has athletic ability and limited material resources, he should be treated exactly as any other boy with limited means. Certainly he should have no special inducements offered him. I have come to feel so strongly on this point that I have sometimes wondered if I did not unconsciously lean over backwards in dealing with boys applying for admission who are known in advance to possess ability in athletic lines. In past years we were not so particular, and, looking back over those years, it is clear enough that neither the school nor the boys concerned were helped by the more generous policy which prevailed in those earlier days.

I realize that it is utterly impossible for any institution to prevent its alumni and friends from the outside from encouraging, even to the extent of aiding, promising athletes to gain admission. The situation can only be corrected when a stronger public sentiment is created against what those on the inside know to be a manifest unfairness to the institution concerned and to the boys who, contrary to a carelessly formed judgment, do not profit but are actually injured by accepting inducements of this kind.

It is certain that the subsidizing of athletes in preparatory schools leads to jealousies among the student body, discourages honest boys from competing for teams, ruins in time the tone of the school, destroys the honor of the mercenary, and brings discredit upon athletics. Subsidies for athletic participation are among the first fruits of commercialism. As one bad apple will rot a barrel, so one subsidized athlete will corrupt a school.

C. Summary: Athletics as a Factor in School Tone

However well American school men have understood the uses of athletics in creating for a school, especially a private school, a satisfactory tone, it has been not they but English schoolmasters who have used games most successfully for this purpose.[6] In attempting to estimate the values of athletics to a school, a few critics have gone so far as to put to one side their influence upon the schoolboy's health and more have merely taken this result for granted. It is obvious that games which fetch boys out of

---

[6] See *Games and Sports in British Schools and Universities*, Bulletin Number Eighteen of the Carnegie Foundation, 1927, pages 26 ff.

doors into the sunshine for an hour or two of each day tend to exert a beneficial effect upon those who play them, whether or not these boys are periodically measured and tested to determine precisely the extent of their physical improvement. Besides such effects, athletics may be, and at many schools are, so conducted that under wise guidance they give opportunity for exercising the schoolboy's capacity for responsibility, his initiative, and his trustworthiness. For the present, the claims of some moralists that athletics engender courage, perseverance, coöperation, and other such traits may be omitted. A diversity of games and contests is clearly beneficial. More than one critic has indicated that the evils of subsidizing and recruiting, which demonstrably impair the tone of any school, would be abated if less attention were given to the American form of football and the development of football material for college consumption, and if more encouragement were bestowed upon soccer and touch football. Be this as it may, the observation is sound that body-contact games tend to diminish among their participants the repugnance that many boys feel to physical impact with their fellows. Furthermore, when most of the boys of a given school play games with a measure of interest and spontaneity, there is less tendency to lionize unduly the football or baseball hero. Athletics, well-guided and supervised, contribute to a genuine and fine school loyalty, which is to be contrasted in all its works with the factitious loyalty that sets victory above honesty and manliness. On all of these grounds, then, well-diversified and well-conducted games may exert, through their effect upon the individual schoolboy or schoolgirl, a beneficial effect upon the group that is the school.

V. SOUND FEATURES OF PRESENT-DAY SCHOOL ATHLETICS

It would be unfortunate if from parts of the preceding discussion any reader were led to infer that athletics in American schools exhibit few commendable features. The fact is quite to the contrary. Aside from the material aspects of the matter, such as the acquisition of playing fields and the erection of fine gymnasiums and swimming pools, which any school board or group of trustees may compass by the expenditure of sufficient money, a feeling is growing that physical education and its component, athletics, have an important even though a subordinate function in the schooling of youth. In securing their benefits to boys and girls less depends upon material facilities than upon competent, acute, and sympathetic teachers. Such teachers have made their work notable in a variety of ways, only a few of which may be here particularized.

A. INCREASED PARTICIPATION

Some time ago the United States Bureau of Education wisely suggested that every school child should enjoy an "ideal minimum" of two hours a day in out-of-doors activity. A few English "public schools" have exceeded this allotment. No case is known in which an English secondary school has equalled it.[7] During some parts of the year certain Canadian schools probably achieve it, and although, according to Dr. James Frederick Rogers,[8] it is "seldom attained" by schools in the United States, yet through school supervision of after-school play periods it has been "more nearly approached." If American public schools and English secondary schools were compared, it would probably be found that certain American schools give to physical education through supervised play at recess periods, well-directed athletics, and after-school physical activities under competent teachers, a proportion of each school week about equal to that devoted in many English secondary schools to physical training and sports and games as conducted by masters. Indeed, in England the tendency appears to be for the school to increase the time and the amount of supervision of "large-muscle activities," to the end that more boys and girls may participate in their benefits. It does not appear that to such a program superlative playing fields and equipment are so essential as competent personnel. Given fairly adequate playing space, when well-qualified men and women are placed in charge of the work, school pupils are quick to increase their participation. Although regulations requiring pupils to take part have their value, especially in initiating a program, they appear not to be so important as sympathetic and capable teachers, whose work arouses their pupils to use well the regular school periods devoted to games, and also to take a spontaneous, interested part in after-school athletic activities. By these means "athletics for all," a slogan expressing merely a hope, has become in some schools a reality.

B. THE FINANCING OF SCHOOL ATHLETICS

There is a strong contrast between the days when a high school athletic association, with weak or comparatively little guidance from teachers, controlled the athletic finances of the school, and the present, with its emphasis upon teacher interest and guidance and its tendency on the part of boards of education to provide both money and personnel for games. The difficulty that besets the change from the old to the new condition is well presented in the New Jersey report:[9]

> The problem of financing athletics without gate receipts is easily answered theoretically; namely, make athletics a part of the school program for all pupils and finance these activities through funds of the board of education. But until this is done the schools are obliged to obtain the money from gate receipts, or such part of it as is not obtained from athletic association dues and supplementary entertainments.

---

[7] "The public schools of England correspond roughly to the American private preparatory schools . . . and the secondary schools to the American public schools." *Games and Sports in British Schools and Universities*, 1927, page 24.

[8] *School Hygiene and Physical Education*, Bureau of Education, Bulletin 1927, No. 3, page 11.

[9] "The Status of Athletics in New Jersey High Schools," in the *Education Bulletin*, June, 1927, page 420.

The returns from New Jersey high schools indicated that in sixty schools the chief source of athletic revenue was admissions to competitive games, that in thirteen entertainments supplemented these funds, and that in six the sole support is derived from dues paid to the school athletic association, but that in nine cases athletic support was provided by local boards of education presumably out of school funds. The significance of these figures lies, not in the fact that only nine schools receive their athletic support from their boards, but that any school should. These figures probably reflect a condition that is spreading throughout the Eastern states.

C. Physiological Considerations in School Athletics

Two important recent steps in school athletics are praiseworthy as modifying their physiological effects: the growing restriction of kinds of events for competition, and the use of medical examinations and physical fitness indexes.

1. The Restriction of Events

The physiological bearings of various athletic practices as they affect boys and girls of high school age are discussed in connection with the hygiene of athletic training in Chapter VII. For the present, attention may be drawn to only one phase of the matter, the possible physiological effect of various branches of athletics. The spirit of competition is never stronger than among boys and girls of high school age. For this reason pupils need the more rigorous protection against the possible ill effects of following their own athletic inclinations, always, however, with the ultimate object of creating independence of judgment and capacity to weigh advantages against dangers. Perhaps it is too much to expect that an athletic boy of twelve or thirteen should forego championship races or abstain from possibly harmful forms of activity of his own accord, especially when the pressure of school opinion, his own loyalty, and his parents' probable lack of information are considered. It is coming to be generally agreed that up to the age of, say, sixteen, such a boy must be protected by the school through a discriminating choice of events and games for various ages, improved physical examinations, the use of their results in determining qualifications to compete, and careful, qualified supervision. After that age a greater latitude may be desirable, but never to a degree in which championships and records take a more important position than the well-being of the pupil. In the guidance of school athletics, final responsibility and authority must reside in the principal.

Such considerations as these are actuating the most enlightened state departments of physical education, interscholastic athletic associations, school boards, principals, and teachers. They have received wide attention through the efforts of the Playground and Recreation Association of America, the Public Schools Athletic League of New York City, and, with special reference to girls, the Women's Division of the National

Amateur Athletic Federation. When all parents, whether through the work of parent-teacher associations, or through their own initiative, understand the implications of undue or unsuitable athletic competition and participation, the dangers will be much curtailed. To this end, many men and women who are concerned with physical education in our secondary and private schools are contributing their share of effort.

2. The Use of Medical Examinations

The work of the school medical officer and the school nurse can be so planned and performed, especially as regards the examinations which they give, as to exert a powerful influence upon physical education and athletics. In a number of cities, this factor is already relatively successful. From the point of view of theory it matters little whether the "thorough overhauling for purposes of all around improvement" of the pupil, be the responsibility of the educational authorities, as it is in Boston and New York, or of the department of health, as in Providence. The essential features are that it shall be thorough and periodic, and that its results be utilized by all of the agencies concerned in fostering the pupil's physical welfare.

D. The Discernment and Use of Ethical Values in Athletics

For a long time Americans have been content to reap the ethical advantages from school athletics without much attention to cultivating those advantages. Not so the Englishman. His "cult of games" has made constant use of such expressions as "It isn't cricket," and "The game for the game's sake," whereby boys and girls of school age have for years been deliberately inoculated with the ethical and moral values that flow from athletics. Owing partly to this effort, Englishmen have come to follow in certain personal and even official relationships an unwritten code. This code may be traditional and irrational, but it is powerful and fruitful, not alone in a single stratum of society but throughout the nation. As an American school principal who has done much for the ethics of interscholastic athletics has indicated, until recently we have been too much concerned with the business and technique of our school athletics to pay much conscious attention to their effects upon the character of the schoolboy and the schoolgirl. Many signs show that this state of affairs is changing. The work of the Sportsmanship Brotherhood is one of a number of forces that are exerted to a single end. Yet the Brotherhood appears to be the only organization whose chief emphasis is laid upon the moral and ethical values that athletics can be made to yield.

Conclusion

The ultimate justification for athletics in secondary schools, public or private, is the welfare of the individual boy or girl. Any contribution that athletics can make to his welfare should be fostered; all that tends to impair it should be discouraged and, if possible, abolished. Needless to say, the capitalizing of the athletic skill of a group of players to obtain funds for school buildings or equipment is of less benefit to school children than to the purses of their parents. This phase of commercialism in school athletics may be no less vicious than the secret and dishonest capitalizing of individual athletic skill to obtain a college education. No school or college course is worth purchasing by a living lie. Probably those who have covertly bought for money or procured by underhand methods the services of athletes for college or school teams have never paused to consider thoroughly the implications of their conduct from the point of view of truth. They have not realized that their machinations have impaired the potential benefits of their cause and operated to corrupt the moral fibre of the schoolboys they have suborned.

Responsibilities in school athletics may be briefly summarized from three different points of view.

A. The Responsibility of the Schools

The responsibility of the school for its athletics resides, like all other matters touching pupil welfare, in the governing body, whether trustees or school committee. This body may delegate its responsibility, and so much of its authority as may be necessary to validate it, to a headmaster or a principal, who in turn must be the judge of the benefits to the pupils obtainable from the equipment, methods, and personnel employed in the task. Here, as in other aspects of education, the choice must be made between the apparent benefit to the group of pupils and the genuine benefit to the individual.

B. The Responsibility of the Parent

The parent who justifies the relationship is increasingly insistent that his child be dealt with as an individual. Nowhere is this more essential than in the relation of the child to school athletics. Some of the corruption that has crept into school athletics has come from unwise parenthood. The father who would be horrified to find that he was forfeiting his own amateur standing at golf, or that his behavior on the tennis court was regarded by others as bad sportsmanship, is not always prompt to reprimand and stop a boy's "shopping-round" for athletic inducements or resenting or whining over defeat.

C. Responsibility and the Pupil

As matters now stand the American schoolboy bears comparatively little of the responsibility for his athletics. His elders organize and coach his teams, devise his plays, arrange his schedules, finance his contests, and in general perform the great bulk of his work. Between the first and the last years of the secondary schools there appears to be little difference in the treatment of pupils with respect to the responsibilities of athletics. Fortunately, to this generalization there exist important exceptions; but the fact remains that we tend to neglect what might be made one of the most advantageous factors in the growth of the school pupil as an individual, — maturing under responsibility. The consideration so often urged to the effect that school athletics have become too complex and exacting to trust any of their essentials to boys and girls is a commentary not only upon athletics but upon the quality and results of our educational processes. In this respect, Canadian schools, whether or not from their closer relation to England, appear to have advanced beyond the schools of the United States, or perhaps rather to have clung to an educational tradition which in the mother country bears much good fruit. If it be true that our school athletics have grown too complicated to be dealt with by boys and girls, it would appear to be high time that they were modified from this point of view. Granted that the high school freshman can be expected to sustain little if any responsibility for his sports, nevertheless the older boy or girl, under wise guidance, might bear much. The best ideals and practices of physical education in high schools recognize a rising scale of maturity and provide means for its eventual use. Its neglect when school athletics are divorced from physical education only makes their union the more necessary to the welfare of the individual pupil.

CHAPTER V

THE ADMINISTRATIVE CONTROL OF
AMERICAN COLLEGE ATHLETICS

I. THEORETICAL AND ACTUAL CONTROL
II. THE IMPLICATIONS OF CONTROL
    A. Connotations of the Term *Control*
    B. Administrative Controversies
III. ATHLETIC POLICIES AND PRACTICAL AIMS
    A. The Shaping of Athletic Policies
    B. The Interests that Athletic Administration
        Must Serve
IV. THE ADMINISTRATION OF ATHLETIC POLICIES

A. Finance and Accounting
B. Gymnasiums, Playing Fields, and Equipment
C. Eligibility
D. Schedules
V. "FACULTY CONTROL" AND ITS RESULTS
    A. Pseudo-Faculty Control
    B. Faculty Guidance
    C. True Faculty Control
    D. The Tests and the Application of Faculty
        Control

HOWEVER the academic aspects of the American college may have changed during the past thirty-five years, the changes in college athletics have been far greater. A growing recognition of the educational bearings of athletics, a flood of new students, the enormously rapid increase of material facilities, and the increasing influence of conferences and associations have united with a quickened public interest in college games to force a revision of athletic administration, while the theory of "faculty control" has been extended by the development of departments of physical education. For the most part, the general movement of change has been imitative in character; rarely have the results of the innovations been foreseen from their inception. Apparently, the conviction has been that one best method of controlling college athletics must exist, if only the formula could be discovered. The quest has proved, and is likely to prove, as elusive as the search for the philosopher's stone. No such formula has been found.

I. THEORETICAL AND ACTUAL CONTROL

Between the control that any system is supposed to exert over athletics in a college and the control which it actually exerts, a wide divergence may, and indeed often does, exist. If it is one thing to announce a program of athletic administration and another to effectuate it, it is a third and entirely different matter to maintain in its practical application the balance of powers which any such system is designed to guarantee. A writer who recently studied control in some one hundred and fifty-one universities and colleges concluded that in all but one, control was exercised through committees, that in 56 per cent of the cases these committees included faculty representatives, students, and alumni, and that 16 per cent of the institutions studied have their intercollegiate athletics directed by a faculty committee, and "it is likely their athletics are directed from the faculty view-point." It is perhaps pardonable to suggest that in the last clause the wish is father to the thought. Certainly our enquiry has convinced us that in a large number of institutions the actual weight of authority and control rests upon quite other shoulders than those intended by the framers of the systems.

Such a result should cause no astonishment. The administration of American college athletics is in reality a problem in the adjustment of human relationships, and its solution depends upon a compromise and coöperation which some of those concerned appear unable or unwilling to accord. Yet few college administrative officers appear to have attended sufficiently to the fact that the devising of a logically complete system for the control of athletics has little relation to the way in which that system may operate over a period of years.

II. The Implications of Control

Before going further into the practical aspects of control and the interests that it serves, we shall do well to examine some of the functions which the administration of college athletics discharges.

A. Connotations of the Term "Control"

It is a commentary upon the nature and the functions of most of the bodies charged with the administration of athletics that the term most used in referring to it is "control." This term connotes the curbing of a force which is or may be dangerous, or which may get out of hand if not treated firmly. No one talks of controlling the academic aspects of college life; most men speak of controlling athletics. If the least controversial aspects of the control of athletics be regarded, the term implies the conduct of games and contests through the definite delegation of authority and responsibility touching a vast number of phases of college life, including a clear assessment of purposes both actual and theoretical, the framing and execution of a policy that takes account of the interests, whether practical or sentimental, of various groups, the provision and care of suitable accommodations, medical attention, finance, including auditing and bookkeeping, the preparation and the holding of contests, their schedules, and external relationships in competition. At some institutions separate regulation may be exerted over intercollegiate athletics and intramural athletics, for men and for women. All of these functions have come to be theoretically included in the whole duty of an institution of higher learning.

B. Administrative Controversies

Most Americans who are concerned with the educational process agree that the unit which it must serve is the individual boy or girl, young man or young woman.

With athletics, however, the case is different. Their financial and public aspects, the reputation which they confer upon the institution, and a thousand other forces have united to make them not so much activities of undergraduate life as joint coöperative enterprises involving presidents, trustees, faculties, alumni, and townsmen, and the vast publics of the radio and the press; they are undertaken less for the diversion of the schoolboy or the undergraduate than for the amusement of others. Thus, their "educational values" have frequently to be rediscovered and proclaimed in order that the hospitality of the college toward commercialized athletics may be justified. Naturally, then, the desire for power and influence is the source of most controversies over athletic administration and control.

III. Athletic Policies and Practical Aims

No one who is familiar with the history and aspirations of higher education expects that the administration of college athletics should be entirely logical, or that it should wholly serve the ideals to which so much lip service is rendered. We talk much of sportsmanship, fair play, and the moral values inherent in games, but we act as if we believed that an ornamental gateway to these ends must be provided before the ends themselves can be served. Much of the work of administering our college games, therefore, rests upon expediency. The notion is that the first essential to the execution of any athletic policy is money, and plenty of it. This attitude is accounted to be hard-headed and practical, and such it is, but it is also short-sighted in that it leaves out of consideration the fact that athletics are grounded in human relationships that are at least as much spiritual as physical or financial.

A. The Shaping of Athletic Policies

Of the institutions visited, very few appear to operate upon a consistent or complete educational policy that includes athletics. The attitude of administrative officers, like presidents, assistants, and deans, ranges from attempts to justify, upon various grounds, an apparently deliberate unconcern with athletics (Dickinson formerly, Wisconsin), to active participation in even their most minute phases (Allegheny, Oglethorpe, Wesleyan). As regards the weight of control exercised by administrative officers, most institutions occupy a mid-ground. The result is a delegation of authority and function, usually tacit, that may be characterized as pragmatical. Although the control of athletics in most institutions probably derives from the charter or act of incorporation, nowadays custom at the great majority vests it in committees whose membership represents a variety of interests, professional and sentimental.

In the resulting confusion of functional powers it is not astonishing to find that many institutions have no settled athletic policy. A number (Georgetown and other

Catholic universities, Harvard, University of Iowa, Lehigh, Massachusetts Institute of Technology, Michigan, Pennsylvania, Princeton, Reed, Toronto, Trinity) have considered the matter thoroughly and have adopted courses of action that will probably influence future events. Many of the rest have presidents too much occupied with the daily duties of their offices, or graduate managers or directors whose powers have come to them too much through a process of unregarded accretion, to have bestowed upon athletic policy the consideration which it merits. Aside from the hurried, imitative adoption of a few catchwords and clichés, like "Athletics for all," or "Every student a player," and a very high regard for material equipment, the shaping of a comprehensive administrative policy for athletics has very generally been neglected.

It is far from our intention to imply that no American college or university possesses a well-reasoned athletic policy in the molding of which all of the needs and responsibilities of the institution have been considered. The Massachusetts Institute of Technology, Oberlin, Reed College, the United States Military Academy, the United States Naval Academy, and the University of Toronto may be taken as examples in which the administration of athletics has been bent to serve first the interests of the undergraduate and the educational program as a whole. To this brief list other names might be added, but not those of institutions at which slogans have been permitted to take the place of sincere and genuine consideration. At some institutions the shaping of a new athletic policy has required a complete reëmphasis and reorganization. At others, new uses have been brought out of old instrumentalities, new functions have been allotted to old officers and committees, or reapportioned among them, and new and sharper meanings have been given to old pursuits without changes in the fundamental elements of control. In short, the process has entailed readjustment to accord with changing conceptions and purposes, or, in some instances, a return to older standards.

It is, however, our intention to suggest that many university or college presidents have left the shaping of athletic policies to conferences, committees, or specialists in physical education, who represent not so much the welfare of the institution and its undergraduates as special interests of one sort or another, all of which apparently feel that material prosperity, their own prestige, or professional standing must be served before other ends can be considered.

B. The Interests That Athletic Administration Must Serve

It would not be difficult to defend the theory that the only persons who ought to be intimately concerned with college athletics are the undergraduates, but the theory would not represent the facts of academic life, past or present. Even at those institutions at which undergraduates have achieved most nearly complete direction of their own athletic affairs (Amherst, Massachusetts Institute of Technology, Reed, Wyoming), their policies and decisions, in the making or in final form, are subject to the guidance of older persons. In reality, athletics involve several groups, many of which have come to feel in them an interest which savors of the proprietary.

An enumeration of these special interests will illustrate the resulting confusion of aims to which athletics at present are subject. First, then, university presidents must be considered by virtue of their responsibilities and functions as coördinators of general policy. Faculties must be considered for disciplinary and educational reasons, although few persons have taken the trouble to analyze precisely what those educational reasons are or may be. Moreover, the profits from athletics, and especially from football, may be put to academic uses in the form of new buildings and increased equipment. It is held by many that this use of such profits removes from athletics much of the opprobrium that is felt to attach to them. Directors and departments of physical education must be considered because of their convictions concerning the values inherent in athletics as well as because of more personal ambitions and reasons. Alumni must be considered ostensibly on account of their loyalty to Alma Mater, less often or less admittedly because, now that their financial support to the institution is an established fact of university policy, they are held to have in justice a right to a voice in the conduct of those of its activities which afford the most spectacular and concentrated diversion. One avenue to such service is the appointment of alumni advisory committees (Brown, Columbia, University of Pennsylvania) to various branches of athletics, a practice dangerous in some of its aspects, because it is likely to result sooner or later in alumni domination. This practice has been abandoned at Harvard. Trustees in some institutions must be considered, because, as in the case of faculties, the profits from intercollegiate contests represent increases in college or university wealth; it is comforting to find one source of funds that gushes without the use of a rod. Townsmen must be considered because of the financial returns from the crowds of people who attend games, not to mention the active civic pride of trade and welfare organizations. Undergraduates must be considered, not because athletics necessarily fire them with a spontaneous loyal enthusiasm but because it is nowadays assumed that athletics benefit the institution; because athletic contests sometimes resuscitate a waning interest in calisthenics or gymnastic drills which long ago came to be regarded as "good for" undergraduates and required for their degrees; and, finally, because teams that "represent" a university are traditionally composed of student members of the university.

Many of the motives actuating the groups that embody these special interests are unselfish. Because those motives spring from the idealism and the loyalties which characterize men, and especially youths, the world over and which smolder but are not quenched under the advance of years, we should be the poorer without them. For one New England college Daniel Webster set them forth in enduring words. With Americans a passive college loyalty is not enough. True loyalty to a university must actuate to pride, and pride to activity. Nor must that activity be merely nominal. It must not stop with polite unessentials; it must dominate and control. Once the seeming necessity to control emerges, the conflict of the interests begins. Trustees, faculties, directors, alumni, townspeople, all, indeed, except the undergraduates, who might profit most by athletics, have expected, and in some instances demanded, that the shaping of athletic policies be entrusted at least in part to them.

These facts are reflected in the various forms of athletic control which exist in the colleges and universities of the study. The most popular single type of board embodies a balanced representation of various groups, for example, the faculty, alumni, and undergraduates, each equally, to the number of two, three, or four members. It is, of course, obvious that in such a body the persistence or the strength of character of an older or more expert member may easily dominate. Several instances (Allegheny, Dartmouth, Pennsylvania State College, University of Pennsylvania) illustrate absolute alumni control. Sometimes alumni control in one or more phases is indirectly gained or increased through the personal power and influence of a single alumnus (Amherst, Brown, Colgate, probably Fordham, University of Georgia, Lehigh, Purdue, Western Maryland). Local business men have formal representation at three institutions (Denver, Grove City, Southern Methodist). Finally, the agitation for faculty shaping and execution of athletic policy has led to results which will be specially discussed in later pages.

In a word, the athletic situation in most American colleges and universities has been met by a compromise that involves the yielding of the less vocal interests. Often, however, the shaping of policy has depended upon satisfying as many special claims as possible without due regard to the best interests of the undergraduates, and especially to the diversification of those interests. The serving of the special groups that have been particularized has led to a confusion of the aims and purposes of athletics which has obscured not only the benefits to be derived from them and the values they contain, but even the means, financial and otherwise, by which they may be honestly fostered.

One key to the legitimate aims of athletics may be derived from a frank consideration of the purposes of intercollegiate contests and intramural contests, both of which, needless to say, are included in a reasoned athletic policy.

1. Fundamental Considerations in Intercollegiate Contests

When two institutions compete in athletics the ends involved belong less to the fields usually labeled "educational" than to what one university president has called "the pageantry of college life." There probably are moral values to be developed from a game well played or a race well run, but they accrue less from the final contest than from the period of preparation and training. Partly for this reason, the fundamental purpose of intercollegiate contests ought to be the diversion or development of undergraduates, alumni, other members of the college family, and their guests. As matters now stand, their fundamental purpose is financial and commercial. The monetary and material returns from intercollegiate athletics are valued far more highly than their returns in play, sport, and bodily and moral well-being.

The observation is especially true of football, but it holds good for other branches of athletics as well, except rowing and fencing and, perhaps, squash racquets. Football carries the bulk of the monetary burden. Any other branch that can be so administered as to leave untouched some of the profits from football thereby augments the sums that can be expended on improving athletic facilities and university buildings. This commercial aspect is illustrated in the making of football schedules, especially when they include games to be played on "neutral" grounds. It is almost universal. In New England, traditional rivalry may outweigh it (Amherst, Bowdoin, Wesleyan, Williams), and in some other parts of the East as well. But in Pennsylvania two universities (Pennsylvania, Pittsburgh) reshaped their athletic policies with a view to higher profits from contests. Even in instances where football receipts have reached hundreds of thousands of dollars, games with well-established rivals have been abandoned if they have involved financial loss (New York University and Syracuse; Ohio State and University of Iowa). The Missouri Valley Conference was reorganized to eliminate four financially unprofitable institutions. In the Intercollegiate Conference, the cry is "We've got to have money." The fundamental principles of athletic profits are so well known that the losses occasioned by the Carnegie Institute of Technology-Georgetown football game in 1928 occasioned much newspaper comment. In short, the commercialization of intercollegiate athletic policy in the United States is undeniable. In Canada, university rivalry is no less keen, games are no less enjoyable, and sport is not less well served because its monetary aspects are less magnified. Other powerful materialistic considerations enter into the shaping of athletic policy. The supposed advertising values of success at football and a few other branches has led some institutions to charge certain athletic expenses to advertising, and others to render a naïve and undue regard to the notice which a victorious team or an athletic event attracts (Bellefonte Academy, Centre, Drake, Notre Dame, Southern California). Rowing appears to be the only major branch of intercollegiate athletics from which commercialism is absent. Even in cases where the formalities of bookkeeping do not involve charging expenses of a team to college advertising, the motive of advertising and publicity is often discernible. On the other hand, a college may become self-conscious with respect to losing teams and a defeat at football is regarded as a major tragedy. Alumni testify to great embarrassment because their football team does not win from their dearest rival or is not numbered by sports writers and enthusiasts among the outstanding teams of the section (Brigham Young, Columbia, Cornell, Tufts). The exaggeration of values occurs as frequently, if not more often, in institutions where intercollegiate contests are very much curtailed (Emory, Reed). The inroads of money have been gradual and they have increased with the rise of costs in general, on the one hand, and with the seeming necessity of augmenting facilities and the luxuries of athletics, on the other, until they have dominated intercollegiate competition, especially, and unfortunately, in football.

2. The Purposes and Results of Intramural Athletics

It is generally agreed, if only in principle, that deep and probably lasting benefits are to be gained from well-administered intramural athletics. American intramural contests are even more characteristic of the American college than the American college is of the land which gave it birth. Intramural athletics stand among the natural phenomena of adolescence. The formalizing recognition of what we now call "intramural programs" only set a seal upon the dormitory and fraternity leagues, especially in baseball, which in an earlier day afforded part of that bodily relaxation and recreative exercise which every young man needs and will secure, whether under supervision or not. On the whole, American intramural athletics represent a sounder process of development and sounder aims and purposes than intercollegiate contests.

Yet intramural athletics of to-day manifest a few tendencies which impair somewhat their potential worth : First, there is much readiness to set on paper ambitious programs which are not put into practice and, indeed, cannot be for some time to come. Such a program is well enough if it be regarded as an ideal toward which the university or college is genuinely striving, but the best purposes of intramural athletics are not served by the acceptance of promises in lieu of performance. Another negative tendency is the intimate connection of intramural athletics with intercollegiate athletics under personnel that is interested primarily or exclusively in intercollegiate contests. Adequate facilities for excellent intramural programs may be available, but they lie comparatively idle except when intercollegiate schedules bring them into full use. Even more unfortunately, the time of an athletic staff may also be comparatively unoccupied except during the seasons of the branches in which they are particularly interested (Alabama, Coe, Dartmouth, Drake, Yale, various Southern universities). Finally, it is common to withhold the best athletes from intramural contests or segregate them into freshman squads which become mere nurseries for 'varsity groups. At those institutions, later to be discussed, which possess organized systems of recruiting, the men thus obtained are held so definitely segregated from the rest of the participants in general athletics that it is difficult to understand how coaches, directors, and others can be ignorant of their special status. Incidentally, in this sort of esoteric information resides much of the power of the commercially-minded director or coach. It is paradoxical that the "freshman rule" should have been instituted primarily to protect first-year athletes against too heavy encroachments upon their time and energy during those initial months of a college course which should be devoted to winning a place in the institution and laying a firm foundation in academic work. In the special training regimen that to-day exists for freshman squads, it is common for these young athletes to undergo as great a strain as they would in competing for university teams.

In spite of these defects, the general developments and purposes of American intramural athletics are more salutary than those which motivate intercollegiate contests. Especially worthy of praise in this particular are institutions (Amherst, California, Cornell, Harvard, McGill, Oberlin, Princeton, Stanford, Toronto, Wesleyan, Williams) at which the athletic needs and capabilities of entering students are determined by analysis of individual cases through physical examinations and tactful interviews, and advice is given as to which branches of athletics offer most opportunities for future success, often as a welcome substitute for the physical training required for a degree. Once enlisted in the branch of athletic exercise appropriate to personal needs, the undergraduate finds his participation enlivened by the hope that he may some day represent the university. His youthful ambitions are stimulated and he is led at all times to do his best. The result is an attempt to enrich his own experience of athletics in a way that can yield much good.

Conversations with many athletes, as well as independent observation, prompts to the belief that, aside from academic requirements, the most common stimuli to competition in intramural sports are, first, loyalty to a group or organization, such as a fraternity or club, and, secondly, a desire for relaxation from the rigorous training for intercollegiate contests, coupled with the "instinct" for play. Although expert 'varsity players choose to compete for intercollegiate teams in preference to participating in intramural contests, it appears probable that in most cases their motive is not so much the pleasure of the game as their connection with the larger group, — tinctured in many cases by a craving for publicity. Those who have been questioned in this particular were almost unanimous in their preference for inter-fraternity or other intramural contests. If enjoyment and recreation are to be sought, it is significant that, with the exception of larger institutions, few of the better intramural teams possess the ability to compete with representatives of other colleges. Occasionally, where an intramural team has displayed unusual talent and has won all or most of its games, efforts are made to arrange contests with extramural rivals.

The tests of a beneficial intramural program can be derived from close scrutiny of experience : the sincerity of the contests and the participants, their spontaneity and voluntary nature, and their persistence, or even their development, from year to year. The great adverse influence is perfunctoriness in administration or in play. Owing to the fact that not a few intramural programs have grown out of the prescription of physical training for a degree, participation easily becomes mere lax credit-seeking on the part of the student, or involves on the part of the director, a bewildered attempt to keep large numbers of men and women occupied.

At a number of institutions, however, it is not so much compulsion as guidance that undergraduate participants in intramural contests need and receive (Amherst, California, Dartmouth in winter sports, Harvard, Oklahoma, Princeton, Toronto, Wisconsin certainly in football). In such instances, and especially at institutions (Emory, Massachusetts Institute of Technology, Reed, Stevens Institute) where intercollegiate games are curtailed or lacking altogether, the competitive tendency and the "instinct" for play have developed and enhanced each other. To achieve such a result at any college, the man or woman responsible for intramural contests needs certain qualities of the good teacher that are rare in their best manifestations: tact, enthusiasm, ingenuity, resourcefulness, and sympathetic understanding of youth. That intramural programs are in the best sense successful at so many universities and colleges should lead the most discouraged critics of intercollegiate athletics to take heart. The pity is that such beneficial results as are now being achieved are allowed to depend universally upon the financial prosperity of football.

Because of the development of intercollegiate competition, not so much in games as in its material and especially in its monetary aspects, its bearings as play have fallen largely into a subordinate position. The task confronting those concerned with the development of intramural athletics involves the restoration of play as recreation and diversion to its appropriate place in college life.

IV. The Administration of Athletic Policies

It would be a hopeless task to attempt to deal with all of the details of administration of American college athletic policies. Nor would it be desirable. For the moment it will suffice to select a few topics, such as finance and accounting; playing fields, stadiums, and athletic buildings; schedules; and eligibility in its home aspects; leaving to succeeding chapters the discussion of wider relationships. We turn, therefore, directly to the manner in which athletics are financed and accounts are kept.

A. Finance and Accounting

The financing of athletics includes provision of the sums of money necessary to put into effect year after year the various forms of athletic enterprise to which the university or college from time to time commits itself. Accounting concerns the keeping of financial records and making them available to the friends of the institution or to the public.

1. Financing

The sources of athletic receipts in the main are two: paid admissions to games, including guarantees on account of trips away from home, and fees collected from students. Many, but not by any means all, institutions provide athletic budgets for the entire program or for its component parts or branches, by which the amounts of money expected to be available are allocated to each branch or team. Usually, general managers — that is, older paid employees, often graduates of the university — or athletic directors responsible to a representative body, expend the sums thus allocated, and usually careful accounts are kept. The details of the process thus summarily outlined are often extremely complicated.

Of these receipts, admissions to football games provide by far the major portion. Examples chosen from different parts of the country for recent years establish this fact in striking fashion. Although in most instances the sums are stated in round numbers, the data on which they are based were furnished in detail by responsible university or college officers at the time of the respective field visits or later. Since that time the sums have generally increased rather than diminished. At the University of Alabama one year's total receipts were $150,000, of which nearly $72,000 came from football, and over $60,000 from a single post-season game played in California; expenditures totaled $79,000, of which $19,500 were expended on football exclusive of the California game. Exceptionally, at the University of Arizona football is the least profitable branch; its receipts were $8,700 and its expenses $12,800. Athletics at Bates College in a recent year profited by about $1,090 from football, total football receipts being $9,160 and expenses $8,070, although Bates has access to large groups of spectators only through travel. Baylor University, where athletic funds are kept as a part of university funds, profits by about $10,000 a year from its athletics. There football gate receipts are handled through a business firm which owns the grandstand. At the University of California, of total athletic receipts of $486,162, football contributed $457,016 and expended $239,640; the net gain for all branches was $173,891. Net earnings for football at Colgate totaled $11,400. By gains of more than $98,000 in football Cornell University turned a deficit of $26,000 into a surplus of $19,000, although rowing cost more than $25,000. Geneva College with athletic expenses of $21,000 had receipts of about $17,600, which left a deficit of $3,400. Harvard gained more than $131,000; receipts from football totaled $429,000. At Princeton football receipts totaled $244,000, with an unexpended balance of $152,000; total receipts for all branches were $357,500, but the year's deficit was $13,500 because of resurfacing the football field in Palmer Stadium. The University of Southern California showed gross football receipts of $426,500, with disbursements of $331,500, which netted $95,000; total gross receipts from all branches were $478,000, of which football provided nearly eight-ninths. At Southern Methodist University receipts totaled $117,000, of which football, with expense of $54,000, provided $93,000 and contributed all of the total profit of about $27,000. With receipts of $230,000 and expenditures of $192,000 athletics at the University of Washington showed gains of only $38,000, largely from games played away from home. The Yale University Athletic Association, for the year ended June 30, 1928, reported a gross revenue of more than $1,119,000, and its excess of revenue over expenses at $348,500 and more.

Many of these figures represent large sums of money irrespective of the purposes for which they may be expended. In most instances receipts from student fees, whether paid for athletics, sometimes in purchasing season tickets, or generally for the support of student activities, athletics receiving their proportion, provide not a tithe of the receipts from admissions or guarantees. It may appear unjust to criticize adversely the mere size of the amounts of money involved in a year's athletics at any institution, but it is unfortunate that modern college athletics cannot be more simply and modestly conducted. High gate receipts inevitably reflect commercialism and all the evils that follow in its train. The availability of such resources stimulates from year to year the desire for steadily mounting sums that athletics, and especially athletic success, will bring.

Moreover, from the hugeness of athletic receipts, there flow certain results which have not yet received the scrutiny that is their due. Of these results, first stand the luxuries which nowadays are lavished upon players in the continuous supply of new personal equipment and in traveling accommodations. Secondly, a great extravagance is apparent in the special personnel, including advertising agents and publicity men, employed by athletic associations or paid for by them. Annual expenditures in this direction may run as high as $10,000 or $15,000, sums which contrast discreditably with the miserable $300 or $400 paid out for medical advice and care. Some institutions are prodigal with free passes to games (California, Southern California, Wisconsin); one (Alabama) paid the expenses of newspaper men who accompanied its football team across the continent; and others have gone to comparable extremes on a smaller scale. Thirdly, with such large receipts there is a tendency to charge against athletics the salaries of certain officers or the services of employees which should be paid from university funds (Dartmouth, Ohio State). Fourthly, and generally, from the size of athletic accounts there grows a fictitious exaggeration of the importance of athletics and especially of football in American college life. The regard of youth for physical strength and expertness is natural and, mainly, wholesome. It needs no colossal financial program to heighten its force or its sincerity. When, however, football supports not alone itself but all or nearly all other forms of athletics as well, and when it is so managed as to provide college buildings and equipment, and to pay inflated salaries, its rational functions in athletics and in college life are grievously distorted, first, in the minds of those actively concerned with its direction and management, and secondly, throughout the clientele of the institution. The result is a general increase in the material emphasis of university life and consequent neglect of teaching and research, especially as regards salaries and grants of money. A genuine interest in academic pursuits and the things of the mind and of the spirit becomes secondary to material development. In the circumstances, it is small wonder that occasionally the college teacher of academic subjects exhibits envy of the material successes of the athletic director, the graduate manager, or the football coach. The question whether profits from football are rightly used in the erection of college buildings is reserved for later discussion.

The increasing amounts of money that flow through the athletic treasury have led as a natural consequence to the transfer of the financial aspects of college athletics from the hands of the undergraduates to those of older and, presumably, wiser men. At about half of the colleges and universities visited, the control and management of athletic funds are in the hands of the secretary or treasurer of the institution, the general manager, a dean, or a member of the faculty. Their handling of funds and accounts will be discussed in somewhat more detail in the following section. At two institutions (University of Pennsylvania, Ursinus) the undergraduate members of the athletic committee do not vote on matters of finance lest their votes, being the votes of minors, invalidate contracts. The size of the American college's athletic budget has deprived the undergraduate of most of his share of responsibility for its handling. Yet at the University of Wyoming, where undergraduate officers of the student body are charged with the shaping of financial policies and with expenditures, although the university treasurer cares for the funds, the arrangement has resulted in significant economies.

2. Accounting

The country over, athletic accounts are well kept. Usually they are audited by an accounting firm of recognized standing. Approximately one-half of the institutions visited require a bond or surety from the custodian of the funds. All this is quite as it should be.

In respect to the practice of placing the funds and accounts in the hands of the secretary or treasurer of the institution, an official charged with other responsibilities, a dean, or a faculty member, there is little uniformity. At a number of colleges and universities the athletic director or athletic manager has charge. At others (California, Colgate, Dartmouth, Harvard, Southern California, University of Washington, Yale) a general or graduate manager controls the funds or actually disburses them. The proportion of institutions at which an academic teacher — in each instance the chairman of the athletic committee, with functions corresponding to a director of athletics — is responsible for both the keeping of accounts and the management and custody of funds is not large (Amherst, Franklin and Marshall, University of Georgia, Tennessee), but the results appear to be excellent when the custodian has organized his work well and does not permit details of bookkeeping, requisitioning, and similar matters to overwhelm him. The systems of accounting kept in the athletic departments might be characterized generally as good or fair. Some, however, are superior (California, Colgate, Cornell, Dartmouth, Southern California, Stanford, University of Washington, and a number of other institutions). It is of some interest that where graduates or undergraduates are in complete or nearly complete control of accounts, they are well kept. At a few institutions (Alabama, Allegheny, Oberlin, South Dakota), the systems appeared, at the time of the field visits, to be susceptible of improvement.

The attempt strictly to classify systems of athletic accounting encounters exceptions. For instance, as has already been hinted, Baylor University sets up no books for athletics; all items of income and expense are entered in the books of the University and no segregation takes place at any time. At Grove City College two sets of accounts are kept by two different individuals: the one shows expenses incurred in regularized athletic competition; the other contains items bearing on coaches' salaries and the subsidies paid to athletes. The head football coach at Ohio Wesleyan keeps all accounts. Duplicate systems of accounting are maintained at Ohio State, Purdue, and Wisconsin, one in the athletic offices and one in the university business office. Whatever value may result in accuracy and checks, it is impossible to refrain from suggesting that such a system is not so economical as a single set of books well kept and well audited.

In general, then, it may be said that in American university athletics accounting has been developed to keep pace with increases in athletic receipts and disbursements. Some methods might be simplified, others improved, and changes in the manner of classifying items and reporting conditions inaugurated here and there to the advantage of particular institutions, but these are to be expected as parts of a fairly natural process of growth and adjustment.

Without exception, it has proved more satisfactory to have the university treasurer or the university business officer in actual control of the care and distribution of athletic funds. University officers apparently possess a better appreciation of the value of money in an educational institution. Praiseworthy economies have resulted in instances in which the university treasurer with the power to reach decisions on expenditures and curtail requisitions has handled athletic funds. On the other hand, it is natural that athletic officers and graduate managers should feel that inasmuch as their efforts bring money to the athletic treasury, they themselves should have the power of disbursement according to their judgment concerning needs. The control of athletic moneys by university officers eliminates slush funds that official scrutiny would scarcely tolerate. A case in point is to be found at the University of Wisconsin, where certain unpermissible trips of freshman squads and the entertainment of athletes have been paid for out of athletic revenues.

B. Gymnasiums, Playing Fields, and Equipment

Besides matters of finance and accounting, the executing of athletic policy involves the provision and care of playing fields and equipment.

Recent increases in the amount and extent of equipment used in college athletics appear to be a natural result of policies consciously adopted to meet changing conditions. After the war much of the required work in physical education was transferred from indoors to out-of-doors. Although the post-war growth in registration found some institutions unprepared to meet the new conditions with the needed physical equipment, it was quickly perceived that many college and university gymnasiums were inadequate and that not a few athletic fields were too small for the increased numbers of participants thrown upon them by requirements for the degree. For the most part, the gymnasiums of Eastern institutions had — and indeed still have — capacities far below the needs of their undergraduates.

1. Gymnasiums

From the point of view of beauty, the older type of university gymnasium had little to commend it. Often it resembled nothing so much as an obsolete fortress,— doubtless because in some instances it combined the functions of a gymnasium and a drill shed for military units. The newer structures, however, are attractive, even imposing in design, and the decoration of many, if elaborate, is architecturally justifiable. Among the institutions which in recent years have built new gymnasiums are Arizona, California, Carleton, Colgate, Colorado, Des Moines, Dickinson, Drake, Montana State, Oregon Agricultural College, and Wyoming. At Minnesota, Ohio State, and Wisconsin old buildings combine the functions of both armory and gymnasium. A few gymnasiums, like that of the University of Iowa, where the armory is a part of the field house, although strictly utilitarian, forfeit none of their usefulness on this account. At certain institutions (Cornell, Illinois, Purdue) it was stated that little gymnasium use has been made of the armory accommodations owing to the objections of the military instructors.

In comparison with the facilities lavished upon men students, the gymnasium provisions for women usually leave much to be desired. When a new gymnasium is erected for the men, the older, disused structure is generally turned over to the women (Alabama, Northwestern, University of Washington). Sometimes (Tufts and Jackson) a temporary wooden frame structure, partly given over to other uses, is built for the women. Of the institutions visited, California, Coe, University of Iowa, Ohio State, and the Oregon Agricultural College have excellent gymnasiums for their women students.

The universities that lie west of the Alleghenies and in the Southwest have been especially alert to provide new gymnasium facilities. It is, however, to be regretted that institutions sponsored or controlled by religious denominations, however keenly and profitably they may have developed intercollegiate athletics, have been among the slowest to provide indoor playing space and make it available for general student use (Baylor, Brigham Young, Coe, Southern Methodist, various Catholic institutions; Denver, Southern California). A number of other universities which needed larger gymnasiums elected, in some cases after much consideration, to erect stadiums for football and other branches before providing adequate indoor facilities (California, Cornell, Denver, Harvard, Ohio State, Oklahoma, Texas, Tulane). On the whole, this choice is not to be regretted when it has been accompanied by a thoroughgoing effort to bring as many branches of athletics as possible into the open air. The institutions that erect stadiums with the single motive of increasing athletic receipts and manifest no concern to get their undergraduates out-of-doors, display an unfortunate purpose in what ultimately may develop into good works. During our visits to five institutions (Bates, Brown, Michigan, Oklahoma, Yale) construction of new and more nearly adequate indoor facilities was under way.

Thus, although Western and some Southern institutions have been somewhat slow in acquiring playing fields and providing gymnasiums, the change from indoor to outdoor work, a rapid growth in registration, and the prosperity of football have operated together both to reveal needs and to provide a ready means for the acquisition of new facilities. The best criterion of judgment is not the size or the quality of the plant, but the purpose for which it is provided and the use that is made of it.

2. Fields, Football Stadiums

Two forces, namely, the insistence of alumni and townspeople upon accommodations at intercollegiate contests and the profits to be reaped from vast crowds in attendance at football games, have pressed to increase the size of stadiums. It is true that some institutions appear to have over-built, although as yet it is too early for judgment upon this matter. The general practice has been to erect stadiums from bond issues, and many also have thus been materially enlarged after building. Strength of construction, visibility from all seats, the economical use of terrain, and other considerations have contributed to set aside stadium building as almost a special branch of the architectural profession. Unfortunate accidents, like the falling of a stand at Washington and Jefferson, have served only to emphasize the importance of sound construction and to increase the amounts of money expended upon the security of spectators.

Although a single structure may accommodate as many as 74,000 (Yale) or even 88,000 (Stanford) spectators, or cost as much as $1,700,000 (Illinois), it is not our purpose to lament the size or the cost of stadiums. Here again doubtless a more modest intercollegiate athletic program would render unnecessary the building of such structures, however beautiful or impressive their architecture may be. But it is unfortunate that it should appear necessary to increase so much the accommodations for intercollegiate competition before facilities for intramural athletics are provided. The reason, of course, lies in the opinion that much money must be found before intramural athletics can be developed. Moreover, the seeming importance of intercollegiate competition has led to reserving for it the best and largest athletic facilities of universities, with the consequent impoverishment and, in many cases, a consequent inadequacy in the facilities provided for intramural athletics.

3. Field Houses

Whereas in the East a field house is generally taken to be a building or a group of buildings containing dressing-rooms and other accommodations for coaches, physicians, and players, in the West the term implies a large structure, resembling an aviation hangar or a military drill-shed, used for various athletic purposes. Construction of field houses of this sort was initiated by the University of Michigan. Other institutions have rapidly followed her lead.

The field house at the University of Iowa with accommodations for many forms of athletics, including jumping pits, baseball cages, and football practice space, and for military drill, has become a kind of athletic centre in which all types of activity may find place. One wing contains a large gymnasium, the other a swimming pool. The Yale field house presents many similarities to the Iowa building. One great difficulty in constructing a field house lies in acquiring a suitable location. The Amherst field house stands at some distance from the campus proper. Parenthetically, the Brown University gymnasium is situated far from the campus. At Yale, buses transport men from the University to the house at a cost to the athletic association of about $25,000 a year. The University of Michigan has plans that will in a measure obviate this difficulty; smaller gymnasiums and swimming pools in the midst of the campus are expected to attract undergraduates during their leisure hours. Field houses are popular, and it is likely that coming years will see similar structures erected at many large universities.

4. Dressing-Rooms, Lockers, and Showers

Usually the best of the shower baths, lockers, and dressing-rooms are reserved for teams and squads engaged in intercollegiate competition. Usually, also, the accommodations so reserved are adequate, not to say luxurious. The provisions for participants in intramural athletics are generally inferior. The situation resembles that which would exist at a country club if the best accommodations were reserved only for the golf team and were not distributed with at least a show of justice among the other members of the club. Generally, the provisions for bathing and sanitation are adequate. In some instances, however (Massachusetts Agricultural College, some denominational institutions), this is far from the case.

5. Swimming Pools

Strangely enough, the importance of swimming as an exercise and as a measure of personal safety is far from universally recognized. For instance, Harvard has only recently given practical testimony to the value of a swimming pool. Among the universities of the Intercollegiate or Western Conference, pools are not common, although most gymnasiums of newer design include them. Among the most inviting may be mentioned those of Colgate, Illinois, University of Iowa, Massachusetts Institute of

Technology, Michigan, Northwestern, Oregon Agricultural College, and the University of Pennsylvania.

6. Offices for Medical and Other Services

It is a pleasure to record that a number of colleges and universities have made for the physicians and others charged with the physical welfare of undergraduates a provision that seems to be adequate. At Chicago, Dartmouth, Oberlin, University of Pennsylvania, and Yale the doctors' offices and equipment appear to be of the best. At Harvard, ingenuity, resourcefulness, and a leaning toward scientific research have combined to place the accommodations provided for the field physician and the medical adviser among those most productive of good, not alone for 'varsity contestants but also for all men engaged in athletics. At a number of other institutions (Amherst, McGill, Toronto), although facilities for medical departments cannot be regarded as of the first class, yet the attention given to the needs and physical condition of students indicates that much is being made of only fair or even mediocre equipment.

7. Athletes' Clubs

Somewhat like the Gridiron and Vincent's at Oxford and the Pitt Club at Cambridge, 'varsity clubs at Harvard, Pennsylvania State College, and the University of Pennsylvania provide special accommodations for coaches and members of university teams and squads. The disadvantages of such a club include the segregation of the athletes of the university from other students, and the employment of athletes in the capacity of waiters and door-keepers and otherwise. The advantages are to be seen in the assurance afforded that the food of the athlete is wholesome, well prepared, and suited to his needs. There are signs that the general run of undergraduates, both athletes and non-athletes, are better served by college unions which (Michigan, Purdue, Toronto) are designed to be social, recreational, and, in some cases, athletic centres of student life. In contrast to the segregation of athletes at Harvard, Dick Hall's House at Dartmouth, erected by a great sportsman in memory of a son of rare promise, provides a place of rest and recreation for all undergraduates.

8. Personal Equipment and Its Uses

It has long been observed that the American college athletic association lavishes upon participants in 'varsity athletics a wealth of personal equipment which finds no counterpart in other American college activities or in the university athletics of other countries. Only within comparatively recent days have economies been effectuated in the issuing of athletic uniforms and in the salvaging of athletic equipment. This liberality in providing equipment for 'varsity players has had its roots in the notion that an attempt to get full value from the personal equipment issued reflects niggardliness. Among players there has grown up an attitude which at one Western institution was interpreted in the sentence, "Get all you can; Dad's rich." The result has been a lack of appreciation on the part of undergraduates and a growing notion that a boy who represents a college in athletics thereby confers a favor upon the institution.

Another phase of this general matter bears very directly upon commercialism and its results. With the intensity of modern competition in football, personal equipment has taken on an importance that far transcends its true value. An institution (for example, Notre Dame) that can pay from seventeen to twenty-five dollars a pair for the lightest weight, best-made football shoes and purchase for its squad pants made of aeroplane silk has an obvious advantage over the college that cannot or does not spend its money upon such luxuries. But the young man who, as an undergraduate, is provided with luxurious personal equipment will not be inclined to purchase less refined and costly equipment out of his own pocket when he begins to earn his living, and thereby his inclination to participate in sport after graduation will be considerably dulled. Many universities and colleges, instead of continuing the lavishness of their provision, would do well to give more attention to increasing the use to which athletic equipment is put, provided always that the health of the participants is adequately guarded.

It is safe to say that in no country of the world are the buildings and stationary equipment devoted to the athletic activities of the college or university student so costly or so extensive as in the United States. On the other hand, no American institution of from three to five thousand undergraduates devotes to out-of-door athletics the acreage occupied by the thirty-odd playing fields at Oxford, or even the twenty or more grounds at Cambridge. Many American universities find themselves in a situation comparable to that which exists at a number of the newer universities of England. Urban sites and the impossibility of devoting to the purchase of quickly accessible city land sums of money sufficient to provide every student with an opportunity to participate in games at convenient hours, are factors which defer the full development of intramural athletics on both sides of the water.

C. ELIGIBILITY

The third responsibility in the execution of athletic policies is the determination of eligibility. In general, eligibility confers upon undergraduates the permission and privilege of representing the university or college beyond college walls in such extra-curricular activities as dramatics, athletics, debating, and singing. Specifically, for present purposes, eligibility is considered only as it concerns participation in inter-collegiate athletics. These somewhat obvious facts are stated at the beginning of the discussion because it is essential to recall that considerations of eligibility affect not only the various branches of athletics, but also all extra-curricular activities in which undergraduates may be concerned.

The standards of athletic eligibility are dual, in that one group is set by the athletic conference of which, in the majority of cases, the institution is a member, while the other group is imposed at the individual institution. With respect to this second group, it is almost universal practice to place the formulation of such standards in the hands of faculties. A faculty, however, may delegate its responsibility to a committee of its own, to a dean, to a registrar, or to some other officer. At one institution that did not coöperate in the enquiry (Oglethorpe), matters of eligibility are handled by a baseball coach who works also as registrar. At New York University the faculty member charged with the checking of eligibility was guided by the advice of the head football coach and the graduate manager. In a very few instances eligibility is determined by a body upon which alumni have majority representation (Allegheny, Dartmouth). It is never entirely in the hands of undergraduates.

Questions raised by the standards of eligibility imposed by athletic conferences are deferred for later discussion. At present our concern is with those criteria involved in the carrying out of athletic policies by individual colleges and universities.

In these criteria two groups of factors are discernible: the scholastic factors, and those factors of a somewhat miscellaneous nature which may be grouped together under the general term "status." The scholastic aspects of the matter depend essentially, first, upon the administration of admission requirements, and secondly, upon the quantity and the quality of academic work performed by the student after admission. Entrance credits, the amount of work required in course, transfer rules, and other matters of eligibility as treated by the leading athletic conferences are discussed elsewhere. Over the United States as a whole the amount of the academic requirement appears to be growing in importance, whether from the point of view of the conference or from that of the individual institution. On the other hand, for purposes of athletics, the quantity of the undergraduate's performance is receiving more attention than the quality. The reason for this emphasis, which many will regard as mistaken, lies in the necessity of translating into comparable units the academic record of those undergraduates who participate in intercollegiate contests.

The most important single phase of scholastic eligibility is "probation." A student incurs probation when the quantity or quality of his college work runs below the standard imposed by the institution, as reflected in the grades that he achieves in daily work or periodical tests given to determine his progress. It is the general rule that the student who suffers probation must relinquish for a time the privilege of "representing" the university. With one exception, institutions regard the imposing of a probation as a function of their faculties; only at Wisconsin do deans and faculty representatives prefer not to be involved in any question touching the eligibility of an athlete.

The miscellaneous criteria of status, which supplement and, in part, duplicate the scholastic standards, are imposed partly by conferences and partly by individual institutions. They include the age of a student, the character and length of his previous participation, the time he has attended college, and the sources of his support; in some instances they involve even the definition of a college. Consideration of these matters belongs appropriately in subsequent chapters of this study.

It is important to recall that the admission requirements for eligibility rest upon a delegation of authority by the faculties to representative officers or committees. In practice, it is customary for an officer, such as a dean or a director of athletics, to prepare for coaches, managers, and others at the institution, and for opponents or extramural bodies concerned with eligibility, lists of students eligible for participation in such contests as the institution is preparing to undertake. The process is really one of certification to the effect that each student whose name appears upon such a list has complied with both the scholastic and the status requirements concerning eligibility, whether they be imposed by the conference, or by mutual agreement between opponents, or by the faculties of the university.

In general, the problem of scholastic eligibility is attacked with something more than a mere show of conscientiousness. That the operation of the American method of determining and enforcing standards of eligibility is not more effectual is due to inherent weaknesses as regards the quality of academic work, the delegation of responsibility, and the keeping and use of certain records.

1. Weakness in Quality of Academic Work

It has sometimes happened that a conference will set a lower standard of eligibility as regards quality of scholastic achievement than its component institutions impose individually. In one or two instances where this has occurred an institution has adhered to the standard set by the conference and thereby has lowered its own scholastic requirements. In at least one case, however, the reverse is true.

2. Eligibility and the Delegation of Authority

A second administrative weakness involves not alone a tendency to delegate authority in too great a degree but also the delegation of authority to a personnel that may not be fitted to receive the responsibility. Two such cases came to the attention of the enquiry. At one institution the task of passing upon the academic records of undergraduates as affecting their eligibility was taken from the hands of the registrar and given to a faculty representative who happened to be an active proponent of athletics. Thereby the function of the registrar changed from critical scrutiny of evidence to mere certification of his records. At another institution both the registrar and the faculty chairman signed a misleading statement of eligibility that had been prepared by a third party, the football coach. On a number of occasions registrars or other signers of eligibility certificates stated that they would not be willing to vouch for the truth of their information under oath. In at least two instances, officials suggested that students establish their eligibility by statements which both knew to be false.

On the other hand, at the University of Denver the faculty chairman accepts no information concerning eligibility for certification over his own signature without personal investigation and access to original sources, such as official documents and persons having knowledge of the facts. As a rule, the chief difficulty in present methods of certification for eligibility lies in the passing of judgment by men who lack understanding of the implications of the documents to which they affix their signatures.

A further operation of this tendency is discernible at institutions in which the responsibility for certification as regards eligibility is divided, the registrar being held responsible for the scholastic record and a faculty chairman of athletics or a dean being concerned with the amateur and general status of the students. Because the blanks upon which certification is made are faulty in their construction, as they are, for example, in the Pacific Coast Conference and, especially, at Oregon Agricultural College, a registrar may be forced by circumstances to vouch not alone for the scholastic standing of the student, a field with which his duties should make him thoroughly conversant, but also for the less specific aspects of eligibility, the signature of the second officer being attached as a matter of form.

3. Validity of Registrars' Records

Although excellent progress toward trustworthy accuracy in the records kept by registrars' offices in the United States has been made during the past two decades, our observations and examinations of individual documents and correspondence lead us to conclude that they are far from infallible. A very large proportion of the institutions visited has displayed in registrars' offices weaknesses either of system or of personnel. Not all college and university presidents and their registrars appear to have realized to the full the duty of the registrar in protecting the honor of the university rather than in rendering as many expert players as possible eligible for intercollegiate participation. In part, this situation has arisen out of personal solicitation of registrars and other responsible officers by members of athletic staffs and by alumni who urge that young athletes, for one reason or another, be accorded special consideration or privileges. Personal solicitude on the part of administrative officers (California, Southern California) is not so uncommon as it should be. Detailed examination of files and the estimates of several registrars indicate that correspondence relating to the scholastic and academic standing of athletes is ten times as great as that which deals with the standing of other students, whether or not they are engaged in non-athletic extracurricular activities. Nor are undergraduates reluctant to offer special pleading for their fellows. The result has been that some registrars have become the victims of a situation which it should be the function of their offices to mitigate or to prevent entirely. Nor have all registrars succeeded in impressing upon their subordinates their own desire to eliminate errors and to protect the honor of the institution. Too often crucial interpretations of rulings must be left to assistants, with the apparent result that the wishes of the student are served rather than the interests of both undergraduate and university, which are, after all, identical. On the other hand, certain institutions (Chicago, Georgia School of Technology, Harvard, Yale), in choosing officers who have interpreted eligibility requirements conservatively, have gained through these interpretations the respect and confidence of fellow institutions in matters both scholastic and athletic.

In spite of recent progress in such matters, the practice of accepting credentials directly from the potential participant rather than writing to the institution from which he has just come still exists. This fact is known to have led to the use of forged or fraudulent credentials at Lehigh University and Milligan College. The fraud was detected.

Incidentally, masters of schools have exhibited much astuteness when writing recommendations for athletes who are candidates for college admission. Not infrequently their comments are especially guarded in references to scholastic capabilities of candidates, while lauding those qualities of character which are most easily interpreted in terms of athletic prowess. These evasions harm both the college and the school. They tend to impair the confidence which college officials, especially deans, registrars, and admissions officers, feel respecting all such estimates.

D. Schedules

It has already been pointed out that monetary profits from intercollegiate contests are the prime consideration in the making of athletic schedules. Second to this aspect, and closely allied with it, stands the desirability of pleasing alumni, often in distant regions. Occasionally, as in Pennsylvania, the possibility of securing legislative appropriations has influenced schedules. A fourth strong consideration in schedule-making is in many instances the conference, which may dominate the selection of opponents, restrict a university's contests to its own fellow members, endanger its athletic autonomy, and greatly increase the commercializing tendency. Justly or unjustly, it has been urged that the principal motive that leads directors to favor simultaneous dual football contests between universities is a desire to double football receipts. With the making of intercollegiate schedules, academic engagements are seldom permitted to interfere. In intramural schedules, however, the class appointments of participants often present serious difficulties. Here commercial considerations are almost wholly absent.

V. Faculty Control of Athletics and its Results

Among recent measures of athletic administration, none has received more favorable notice or spread more widely than the system that goes by the name of "faculty control." The term itself is not clear in many minds, nor has it been considered with a care sufficient to bring out its full implications.

A. Pseudo-Faculty Control

On earlier pages it was indicated that the mere setting up of a method of administering college athletics provides no inherent guarantee that the principles of the system will be carried out in practice. Certainly no more illuminating illustration of this statement could be found than exists in those institutions where "faculty control," although assumed to be absolute, is restricted to the responsibility of passing upon the scholastic eligibility of participants. Actual practices in faculty control range from this condition on the one hand, to a situation on the other in which a single member of the faculty participates and even dominates in the financial management, the provision of facilities, the making of schedules, and the hiring and the discharge of coaches.

One or two cases that lie midway between these extremes are not without interest. Geneva College athletics are in the hands of a graduate-manager-director who teaches engineering, supplemented by an advisory council. At Lafayette College matters concerning schedules and eligibility are dealt with by a faculty committee, while a committee appointed by the trustees acts upon budgetary matters and appointments. A more complex arrangement is in force at the University of Southern California. There, a general athletic council consists of two alumni, five members of the faculty, and two undergraduates, all chosen by their respective groups, supplemented by the director of physical education, the publicity manager, the general manager, and the coach of each branch of athletics in season, all ex officio and all without vote. The functions of this body overlap those of the faculty athletic committee of five members which deals with eligibility, absences, the budget, and kindred matters.

Not infrequently "faculty control" exists in name but scarcely in fact. Although the regulations of the Intercollegiate Conference stipulate for complete faculty control and provide for an operating body of faculty representatives, the actual control often appears to rest with the directors or the coaches. Presumably the fact that such officers hold their appointments from university trustees is felt to make them thoroughgoing faculty members. One or two universities (Iowa, Minnesota) fix such authority in their presidents; in final decisions and in the execution of policies little regard appears to be paid to representatives of the faculty. This condition prevails to an even greater extent in the Missouri Valley Conference. Apparently, the ethical bearing of intercollegiate football contests and their scholastic aspects are of secondary importance to the winning of victories and financial success.

The compensation paid to certain faculty representatives increases the weakness of this situation. The receipt of an honorarium of, say, $600 from athletic funds and various favors and honors may easily tend to obligate certain of these faculty representatives to defend not alone athletes and athletics but also existing conditions. It is, therefore, not necessary that the actual control shall lie with others than academic teachers if deficiencies in faculty dominance are to be sought.

B. Faculty Guidance

In the far Western universities organizations known as the "Associated Students" are responsible for athletics. Usually about four-fifths of the controlling body are undergraduates, to whom are added as advisers one alumnus and one faculty representative. The weakness of such an organization is its liability to lack of continuity in experience and policy because of changes in the controlling body from year to year. At the University of Wyoming, where a member of the faculty unobtrusively guides affairs, the arrangement is also successful

C. True Faculty Control

It must not be inferred that genuine faculty control, that is, the actual regulation of college athletics by the academic members of faculties, does not at present exist. On the contrary, it is found at a number of institutions where its operations appear to be salutary. At least five members of the Southern Conference (Georgia, Georgia School of Technology, North Carolina, Tennessee, Tulane) have established a practice which, less in its formal aspects than in its results, resembles the methods of control in English universities, both older and newer.[1] The regulation of athletics rests in the hands of faculty members, whose principal duties and interests lie in teaching and research. The teaching programs of these men are somewhat abated to enable them to give the requisite time to athletics. Outside of the Southern Conference, similar conditions exist at New York University, Princeton, and Yale, and at three Canadian universities (Dalhousie, Queen's, Toronto).

The application of true faculty control not only makes heavy demands upon the time and energy of the responsible individual, but also requires a point of view sympathetic with the interests of young men. Many of the directors of athletics who perform their functions on the basis of genuine control by faculty representatives are held, as a matter of fact, in high regard by students. This, however, cannot safely be ascribed exclusively to the successful conduct of their office, for the qualities of character which an ideal director should possess, would make him also an ideal teacher.

D. The Tests and the Application of Faculty Control

The final tests for the presence or absence of true faculty control would seem to be

---

[1] For description and discussion of this matter see *Games and Sports in British Schools and Universities*, Bulletin Number Eighteen of this Foundation, pages 75, 132, and 166.

these : First, is the guiding influence that of a man whose chief activities and interests lie in academic fields, or of one to whose income athletics contribute directly or indirectly ? Secondly, are the coaches immediately responsible to a faculty representative whose principal concerns are academic, or are they subordinate to another or former coach now elevated to faculty status, or of a former business manager or an alumni secretary who is under academic appointment for the sake of the good that may accrue to athletics from his connection with them ? Certainly, in the institutions where faculty control exists at its best there appears to be little truckling to special interests or privileged groups, because the director is not in any way dependent upon athletics for success in his professional career.

The present tendency is to look upon "faculty control," whether genuine or not, as the panacea of all the ills of athletics. When the criteria which have just been set down lend reality to what is so often a mere subterfuge, certainly true faculty control at its best is to be preferred to control by graduates or coaches.

Conclusion

From the point of view of education, the most regrettable aspect of the control of college athletics in the United States to-day is the meagreness of the responsibility that is entrusted to the undergraduate. Although some institutions, especially in Canada, present exceptions to the general rule, the composite of our practice exhibits a uniformity that is the result by no means of accident, but of deliberate calculation. Bearing in mind the enormous increases in gate receipts and expenditures that have taken place since, say, 1875, he would exhibit the boldness of ignorance who should contend that all of the weight and the complexity of the financial burden should fall upon undergraduate shoulders.

There is, however, a middle course ; namely, to entrust the young men of our colleges over a period of years with an increasing proportion of this responsibility. If it be urged that such a course would interfere seriously with academic work and provide an overwhelming interest that would rob study of all attention, the answer is to be found in a thoroughgoing change of methods and aims in college instruction. A change of emphasis in undergraduate life would follow naturally and almost immediately.

Moreover, the administration and control of college athletics are composed of numerous phases of which finance, although it bears upon and penetrates all, is only one. It is not our notion that changes in the distribution of responsibility could or should be made in haste or without extended consideration. Our concern is to the following effect : The management of athletics, both intercollegiate and intramural, entails an apportionment of valid responsibilities, few of which are at present borne by undergraduates. Now, the bearing of responsibilities presents one of the most important means by which youth may be matured into manhood and certain qualities that are desirable in any citizen may be developed and strengthened. Yet, for one reason or another — the large amounts of money received or expended, the fear lest habits of study may be impaired, or a general feeling that young men of college age are not old enough for the tasks involved — more and more of the responsibilities that athletics imply have been progressively shifted from younger shoulders to older. The reproach of "Roman holiday" that occasionally breaks forth is not without justification, and one of its justifications is precisely this: Much of the genuine educational benefit that responsibility in the administrative control of college athletics might bring is reaped to-day by men whose formal education has ended.

CHAPTER VI
ATHLETIC PARTICIPATION AND ITS RESULTS

IN the chapter devoted to the control of athletics many matters bearing upon participation inevitably found place. The subject of the present discussion interweaves itself also with the hygiene of training, and indeed with many other topics of the study. In considering it, we shall find the most convenient order of topics to be, first, the forces and motives which lead men and women to engage in college athletics; secondly, the characteristics of these participants; thirdly, an enumeration of the branches of athletics now prevalent in colleges and universities; fourthly, the conditions under which students take part; and, finally, the immediate and the ultimate or deferred results of their participation.

I. What Leads Undergraduates to Participate in Athletics?

Although the reasons for participation in intercollegiate athletics differ somewhat from those that prompt participation in intramural games, these differences are more or less incidental to general underlying causes.

A. The Inherited Characteristics of Athletes

In a special study of the inheritance of athletes made for the present enquiry, Mr. Richard H. Post and Dr. Charles B. Davenport, Director of the Laboratory of Experimental Evolution of the Carnegie Institution of Washington, at Cold Spring Harbor, Long Island, considered the inherited characteristics of some 587 athletes, belonging to fifty-four American families. Studies in this or related fields had already been made by, among others, Dr. Davenport, Sir Francis Galton in 1869, Dr. F. Bach in connection with 3,457 participants in the Munich Turnfest of 1923, and Dr. O. Schlaginhaufen in 1927. From these previous enquiries and from the newer data of Mr. Post and Dr. Davenport, a few fundamental inferences may be drawn respecting the inherited characteristics of athletes as contributory to their participation in athletics.

Sixty years ago, Sir Francis Galton [1] showed that unusual ability in rowing and wrestling may "run in the family." By anthropometric measurements, Dr. Davenport [2] fifty years later demonstrated that both stature and body-build are family traits. Dr. Bach [3] concluded substantially that "it seems impossible that the sport-types have been formed exclusively by environmental influences. We must rather assume a genotype which directs its possessor to certain bodily exercises." In other words, the athlete's inheritance of physique not only predisposes him to athletics in general, but may even tend to direct him in his choice of branches for participation without his being fully aware of its influence. Thus a long-legged youth becomes a sprinter primarily because of his long legs. A short, stocky, powerful-shouldered man becomes a wrestler partly because of his build. The influences of initial success at some branch or the urgings of a trainer or a fellow-athlete are, from the point of view of genetics, secondary to the initial promptings of inherited physical characteristics. On the other hand, other environmental forces may inhibit or modify this native predisposition, and so not all long-legged boys become sprinters nor do all heavily built men become wrestlers.

The inheritance of traits of character is far less easily demonstrable. The studies of Dr. Davenport and Mr. Post have indicated a probability that a father's interest in athletics may result in a son's becoming an athlete, perhaps through the influence of home or other environmental conditions or the removal of prohibitions. Certainly, such qualities as self-assertion, physical energy, control of temper, coolness, fondness for publicity, persistence, and many more besides, are common in varying degree to all men. Some may be inherited in a higher degree than others. Apparently, participation in athletics develops, rather than implants, certain traits of character. After

---

[1] *Hereditary Genius,* 1869.

[2] C. B. Davenport, "Inheritance of Stature," *Genetics,* Vol. II, 1917, pages 313–89; *Body-build and its Inheritance,* Carnegie Institution of Washington Publication No. 329, 1923.

[3] F. Bach, "Körperproportionen und Leibesübungen, u.s.w." *Zeitschrift fur Konstitutionslehr,* Vol. XII, 1926, page 522. His conclusions are developed by O. Schlaginhaufen, "Anthropologie und Sport," Die Körpererziehung, Vol. V, 1927, pages 3–14.

inherited physical conformation has predisposed some persons to athletic exercise, habituation emphasizes and heightens certain characteristics already present.

We turn now to the results of environment, which, Professor Elmer D. Mitchell says,[4] "is a more potent factor than heredity in the playing of athletic games." Given an inherited tendency to athletics, what conditions encourage the fulfilling of that tendency?

B. REQUIREMENTS IN PHYSICAL EDUCATION

Among such conditions, the requirements for physical education in secondary schools and in colleges stand out as preëminent. Each of the seventeen states which have departments of physical education requires that boys and girls of school age shall take part in games and contests of some sort. In the other states, high school athletics play a prominent rôle, although in some instances they may not be dignified by the term "physical education." No private preparatory school is known in which athletics or physical education does not now find its place in school life. Finally, all American colleges or universities appear to countenance athletics, intramural or intercollegiate, or both, — indeed, the great majority insist upon the satisfactory completion of a course in physical education for graduation, require that it be taken early in the college course, and count the time spent upon athletics, formal or informal, toward its completion. Thus, curricular requirements serve college athletics. A requirement to the effect that each college or school student shall take physical or athletic exercise according to his capabilities and inclinations is commendable, once his condition and needs are determined through adequate physical or medical examination by a competent examiner.

C. ENJOYMENT OF ATHLETICS

During the past few years, a number of "confessions," written by former college athletes and published in periodicals, have contributed to a widespread notion that participants in college athletics get little pleasure from them. Consequently, in the course of our enquiry, numbers of athletes at many institutions have been asked, "Do you enjoy playing?" The replies may be summarized as follows:

By and large, undergraduates enjoy participating in athletics. But one whose principal interest is his academic work tends to be irked by the intensity of modern training, especially at football. When in such circumstances a choice must be made between academic work and intercollegiate athletics, the decision is doubly irksome and may lead to protests against the stringency of training. A majority of the intercollegiate football players questioned appear to enjoy playing football, but not to regard it as fun or recreation; their enjoyment seems to arise from more intangible rewards, — the atmosphere surrounding competition, the notoriety that success

[4] "Racial Traits in Athletics," *American Physical Education Review*, May, 1922, page 206.

brings, and the like. A great many football players volunteered the information that for actual fun, they prefer the less formal intramural games to intercollegiate. The indulgence of the "play instinct" is rarely possible in modern intercollegiate athletics, especially football.[5]

D. COLLEGE OPINION

The American undergraduate is less individualistic than the undergraduate of Oxford or Cambridge in deciding whether he shall take part in athletics. College opinion in the United States is apt to be stronger than the individual's personal inclinations. A skilled runner or football player or skater who decides to abandon intercollegiate competition and to devote more time to his studies is confronted by pleading fellow students and friends, coaches, alumni, and even, in some instances, officers of the university, who endeavor to rouse his conscience and sense of "duty" to Alma Mater. Few young men can resist this pressure, especially in view of the social stigma attached to the "quitter" and the fact that they are "getting by" in their academic work. This tendency to bow to convention and unreasoning college opinion is one of the least admirable qualities of American university life. Our athletics increase it by insistence upon the values of team play at the expense of independence in judgment. The man's final decision is of secondary import compared with the mental processes and the reactions to outside stimuli that lead to it. When the academic aspects of American college life command the best interest and endeavors of a student body, this particular phase of what is commonly termed the "over-emphasis" of athletics considerably subsides.

E. THE FUTURE CAREER AS A MOTIVE

In numbers of instances, voluntary participation in college athletics is prompted by considerations respecting the life career that the participant intends to enter. To the successful athlete who decides to capitalize his reputation, three roads are open: playing as a professional, coaching or work as director of physical education, and certain kinds of business.

1. Professional Athletics

Sharp competition for expert players has enhanced the value of the college athlete as a recruit to professional teams in football, baseball, hockey, basketball, and, in a very few instances, soccer. The influence of such overtures, even when the athlete is supposedly safeguarded from professional inducements and left to complete his college course, is overwhelmingly in the direction of commercializing college athletics. For example, during college games which "scouts" or promoters of professional teams

---

[5] For some of the more technically psychological aspects of athletics and participation, see Professor Clark W. Hetherington's discussion in the *Cyclopedia of Education*, 1911, s.v. *Athletics*.

attend in order to discover promising material, the players tend to become self-conscious, and if they make errors of play, they are commonly chided with such jibes as "That will cost you a job for next year," or "That will cost you money." In the South and Mid-West, the professionalizing motive apparently becomes strong in many athletes as early as their high school days, with the result that not a few players of baseball at school enter college merely to play on college teams in hopes of establishing reputations that will attract substantial offers from "scouts" and professional leagues. In such instances, the academic aspects of college or university life are naturally of comparatively minor importance. The awarding of scholarships or other aids to college athletes whose intentions to enter professional athletics as a career are known, is difficult to justify. On the other hand, not a few undergraduates who have received offers from professional teams after graduation have refused them from a variety of motives : previous selection of a different career, the fear of losing social position, parental objection, contrary advice from college officers and coaches, and other reasons. A further motive for professionalizing one's athletic career is discernible in cases of athletes who have entered professional athletics after graduation in order to earn, readily and pleasantly, money to start themselves in business or in training for a profession. Certainly, to all forms of professional athletics, successful participation in college athletics affords a comparatively easy and enjoyable approach.

2. Coaching and Director's Work

The schoolboy whose athletic success or related interests have led him to look forward to work as coach or as director of physical education will generally enter a school or department of physical education. So far as can be ascertained, no university or college segregates for athletics students of physical education from students whose principal academic interests lie in other fields. At a few universities (Illinois, Michigan, Wisconsin), the presence of such men appears to have greatly strengthened football or other teams. These expert athletes, spurred on by the possibilities of employment as coach or director after graduation, give an unfair advantage to any team of which they are members. However this may be, at a number of Western and Mid-Western universities, the intention to enter coaching or teaching of physical education has undoubtedly provided a powerful incentive to take part in athletics, first, because of the knowledge and skill to be gained therefrom, and secondly, because of the value of the reputation that success as an athlete brings to the man who intends to coach, teach, or direct athletics.

3. Business and the Athlete

In the past, business men have set much store by some of the qualities that athletic participation is commonly supposed to engender, — the ability to approach other men, quickness of decision, social ease in meeting people, and so on. While it is undeniable that these qualities are seldom to be found in the "grind," who has paid attention only to his books and to none of the socializing aspects of college life, the influence of these motives upon the athletic participation of individuals has probably been negligible. Nevertheless, the undergraduate's vague notion that athletics are a good preparation for business is explicable through one or both of two more general convictions: (1) College athletics are a socializing force. (2) Men of social leanings tend to take part in college athletics. It is to these truisms that the alumnus refers when he says, "Of all my school course I got the most out of athletics." [6]

F. PAYMENT FOR PARTICIPATION IN INTERCOLLEGIATE ATHLETICS

Because the matter of compensation to college athletes receives detailed discussion elsewhere in this study, it is sufficient to note here that the threat, expressed or implied, that a scholarship or subsidy may be withdrawn if the recipient athlete fails in athletic performance is a powerful compulsion to participation. The importance of athletics in the mind of the subsidized athlete necessarily dwarfs the importance of maintaining satisfactory academic standing.

A curious instance of the prevalence of this feeling occurred at a college where no athletic subsidies are in use. An athlete who had been awarded a scholarship on the grounds of his financial need and adequate academic standing, called upon the president and offered to resign his scholarship because, not having been selected as a member of the football team, he was not earning his stipend. Upon the president's asking what that had to do with the matter, the young man replied that it was his understanding that he had been receiving a football scholarship and that he could not continue to accept money that he did not deserve. It took the president longer than a few minutes to set matters straight in the athlete's mind.

G. SUMMARY

Of all the foregoing incentives to take part in athletics, the most powerful of all is enjoyment. In cases in which subsidies are paid, the pleasure of notoriety persists as a secondary motive. Requirements for graduation doubtless direct toward athletics many students who might not otherwise participate in team games. But it is only when an athlete begins to capitalize his athletic ability, whether through covert subsidies or through overt acts, that cupidity or financial need tends to become the most powerful single motive in his participation.

II. THE BRANCHES OF COLLEGE ATHLETICS

For some years it has been customary in the United States to regard the branches of college athletics as divided into two categories: "major sports" and "minor

---

[6] For the point of view compare Thomas W. Slocum, "Fools Trespass When Angels Keep off the Grass," *Harvard Advocate.* Vol. CXIV, Number 8, May, 1928, page 49 f.

sports." Strictly speaking, this classification, which is in the nature of a rating, applies only to extramural athletics. To the American college man or woman, the terms "major sports" and "minor sports" carry very definite connotations, but they are difficult to define in universal terms, and the distinction is probably breaking down.

A. MAJOR AND MINOR SPORTS

The implication of rating contained in the terms "major sports" and "minor sports" is to the effect that some branches of athletics are more important to a college or university public than others. Formerly, the right to wear, usually upon athletic clothing, the initial letter of the institution was enjoyed by those who represented the institution in a major sport. The award was made on recommendation of due authority such as a coach, director, or captain, and was formally conferred by vote of the athletic board or association. Nowadays, practice in this matter appears to be changing rather rapidly. It is becoming more usual for conferences to prescribe the details of award of insignia. At some institutions distinction between major and minor sports has been abolished altogether, while at others continued success of teams in a minor sport has led to the elevation of that sport to major status. Members of second or junior 'varsity teams in major sports are rewarded by lesser but similar distinctions and privileges, usually carefully distinguished from those awarded for minor sports.

Nearly all American colleges regard football, baseball, basketball, and track and field athletics as major sports, and award "major" insignia or "letters" for distinguished participation therein. Colleges and universities that support intercollegiate competition in certain of the other branches of athletics regard them also as major sports: rowing, cross-country running, and ice hockey. Exceptionally, Columbia includes fencing as a major sport, while Yale so rates swimming, and Pennsylvania, soccer.

A "minor" sport is a branch of athletics, generally intercollegiate or extramural, in which distinguished participation and representation of the university is rewarded by the right to wear some insignia other than the major-sports letter. Minor sports include association football, boxing, fencing, golf, lacrosse, polo, swimming, tennis, wrestling, and occasionally gymnastics on intercollegiate teams, rifle shooting, trap shooting, water polo, and, on the Pacific Coast, English "rugger."

Dartmouth College and, even more emphatically, the University of Iowa, have abolished the distinction between major and minor sports, so far as awards are concerned. One of the notions behind this action appears to be the feeling that men who worthily represent the university in intercollegiate competition should have the same, or essentially the same, honor.

The distinction in awards for major and minor sports is comparable to the distinction between the blue and the half-blue at Oxford, Cambridge, and most of the newer

English universities. The American "letter man" corresponds roughly to the Oxford or Cambridge "blue," and the American member of the second string or second team to the Oxford or Cambridge "half-blue."

B. Intramural Sports

Intramural sports are those branches of athletics in which competition takes place between teams representing different groups within the student body of the institution, organized usually upon the basis of daily associations and loyalties. All of the major and minor sports find places upon schedules of intramural contests, although basketball is more nearly universal than American football, which in a few institutions has been stricken from the intramural program. In addition to the usual major and minor branches already enumerated, speedball, volley ball, handball, playground ball, soft ball, touch football, any of the six varieties of indoor baseball, foul throwing or shooting, as adapted from basketball, horseshoe pitching, and occasionally squash, bowling, and hiking, are included in intramural athletics. At universities and colleges where physical education and credit requirements have not led to the extension of intramural programs, class teams and contests in both major and minor sports are usual. Membership in an American class team and the award of "numerals" may be regarded as analogous to playing on an Oxford or Cambridge college team, which is rewarded by the college colors. The English college blazer, which all members of a college amalgamated club are entitled to wear, has no close American counterpart, except possibly in the baseball, track, or football uniform; the use of American college colors is not entirely similar.

C. Women's Sports

Sports for women, played under women's rules, are usually organized on an intramural basis. Most of the women's colleges, however, permit contests with other institutions of their kind, and some (Bryn Mawr, Wellesley) allow teams of undergraduates to meet teams representing approved women's amateur clubs. Branches of women's athletics include field hockey and basketball, which are the most popular, swimming, running, jumping, gymnastics, volley ball, and more rarely, rowing, golf, and tennis.

D. Summary

The most notable characteristic of the lists of major, minor, and intramural branches of athletics is the greater catholicity of the intramural schedules. Intercollegiate branches are traditional as regards the divisions into major and minor sports. The intramural program, on the other hand, has had to form its own athletic traditions. Its problems have been to schedule contests in as many branches as may interest and suit the needs of undergraduate participants, and to develop skill upon a less specialized basis of expertness. Hence the wider range of intramural as compared with intercollegiate athletics.

III. The Participants in College Athletics

Data concerning participation in college athletics are likely to be unsatisfactory for several reasons. College athletics cannot be subjected to the same statistical treatment as a military unit. Not a few institutions keep only approximate records of participation. Many keep none at all. These conditions are seldom due to lack of good intentions. The principal causes are deficient training of the staff in statistical method, meagre office space and equipment, and emphasis upon activity rather than upon research. It must not be supposed, however, that the athletic records of all institutions are faulty. Generally, state universities appear to keep excellent account of all student athletic activities (California, Illinois, Indiana, Iowa, Michigan, Minnesota, North Carolina, Ohio State). The same is true of a number of privately endowed universities (Brown, Cornell, Lehigh, Notre Dame, Oberlin, Ohio Wesleyan, Princeton, Toronto). Certain colleges, also, are so fortunate as to possess serviceable data (Amherst, Bowdoin, Reed, Wesleyan, Williams). As might be expected, the records of the United States Military Academy respecting participation are exceptionally complete.

The chief obstacle to arriving at a trustworthy estimate concerning the numbers and proportions of men engaged in the various branches of athletics, intercollegiate or intramural, is the duplication of names. In required courses in physical education, in which participation in athletics is counted for credit, a man may "sign up" for several branches, and may actually play a number of games; thus his name will appear in lists of players at touch football, basketball, tennis, and baseball. A card register of students with a clear indication of the branches in which they have engaged and their proficiency or improvement in health is comparatively rare. Still rarer is the attempt to study such records scientifically. After all, it is far more important, — and it will be for at least the next decade, — that undergraduates should be led to participate more and more generally in wholesome and well-managed athletics and should receive the attendant benefits, immediate and ultimate, that inhere therein, than that statistical counts should be meticulous.

A. Previous Estimates of Athletic Participation

Before the present study, three outstanding estimates of the proportion of undergraduates participating in athletics had been made: by Professor Henry M. Sheldon, of the University of Oregon, in 1901; by Professor George L. Meylan, of Columbia, in 1911; and by Professor Thomas A. Storey, of Stanford, in 1927.

1. Professor Sheldon's Estimates

About 1900 Professor Sheldon sent to directors of physical education in twenty large and twenty small colleges a circular letter, to which thirty institutions responded. "Seven reported less than 20 per cent of students taking part in athletics, twelve reported that from 20 per cent to 25 per cent participated, six placed the estimate between 25 per cent and 50 per cent, with three above the 50 per cent line." Professor Sheldon concludes: "When allowance is made for the tendency on the part of the physical directors to have their institution stand well, and consequently to give themselves the benefit of all doubts, it will be seen that 20 per cent is probably a fair average." [7] This figure applies principally to intercollegiate competition.

2. Professor Meylan's Estimates

In 1911 Professor Meylan stated that "out of about 80,000 male students ... 32 per cent are engaged in some form of athletics. Out of 26,000 female students, 18 per cent are engaged in some form of athletics." [8] By this time intramural contests had attained a certain popularity, and these figures reflect the increased participation that they called forth.

3. Professor Storey's Estimates

Professor Storey's figures concerning participation, gathered in 1923 and verified in 1925, deal with a total of 442 institutions.[9] Among these, one hundred and six colleges and universities had voluntary programs for men, and of these, sixty-seven gave percentages of participation. "Forty-two (more than half) of the sixty-seven report percentages that range from 10 per cent to less in three institutions to from 50 per cent to 60 per cent in fourteen. Twenty of the forty-two report less than 40 per cent; only sixteen of the sixty-seven report more than 60 per cent." Twenty-nine colleges and universities reported the proportion of their upper classmen taking part in voluntary and intramural athletics. All told, sixteen indicated fewer than 60 per cent, and of these sixteen, ten reported less than 50 per cent. "Only six of the twenty-nine colleges and universities reporting on the participation of their upper classmen students ... record them as participating in percentages above 80."

In analyzing these figures, Professor Storey concludes that participation in intramural athletics as part of courses in physical education required regularly of underclassmen does not lead to voluntary athletic activity, and that "at least half of the

[7] Henry D. Sheldon, *Student Life and Customs*, 1901, pages 533–34. Some of the proportions of athletic participants at individual institutions have interest: "Amherst, about one-fourth, Bowdoin fully fifty per cent, Cornell ... from ten to fifteen per cent, Wesleyan at least twenty-five per cent, California twenty-five per cent, Columbia twenty-five per cent, Pennsylvania from one-third to one-fourth, Vanderbilt thirty per cent." The Report of the president of Harvard College for 1897 showed that 21 per cent of the undergraduates passed in that year the examinations prerequisite for participation in athletics.

[8] "Athletics" in *A Cyclopedia of Education*, Ed. Monroe, 1911, Vol. I, page 276.

[9] Thomas A. Storey, M.D., *The Status of Hygiene Programs in Institutions of Higher Education in the United States*, 1927, pages 87, 92.

students in colleges and universities . . . are failing to practice or establish regular habits of recreation. This indifference is indicative of a failure of the programs of required physical training in the institutions concerned." And yet, with due regard to all the doubtful factors involved in such estimates, it would appear that between about 1900 and 1925 the proportion of American men undergraduates participating in voluntary athletics, both intercollegiate and intramural, more than doubled, and that the actual numbers increased at least five-fold. It is true that in comparison with the extravagant claims to success made for programs of physical education in speeches, printed discussions, and college catalogues, these figures are disillusioning. On the other hand, as a measure of progress they are distinctly heartening.

B. Estimates from the Present Study

The figures collected in the course of the present enquiry do not lend themselves to very extended statistical treatment. In the first place, the numbers of men engaged in athletics, whether taken as a whole, divided into intercollegiate or intramural activities, or considered by branches, were not available at a considerable number of institutions. Other colleges had records for intramural teams or squads, but not for intercollegiate, and vice versa. Very few institutions place the same branches of athletics on both intercollegiate and intramural schedules, and probably at no two colleges are the same groupings used. Finally, there is always the problem of duplication of names.

If, however, from the institutions possessing comparable figures for various branches of athletics, we consider the numbers of undergraduates presumably eligible and the total numbers of known participants, we may proceed to a few rough estimates concerning numbers and proportions engaged.

We estimate that about 63 per cent of all undergraduates in the one hundred and twelve colleges and universities of the study, taken together, take part in athletics regularly or intermittently. Of these undergraduates, from 18 per cent to 25 per cent, as compared to Professor Sheldon's earlier estimate of 20 per cent, engage in intercollegiate athletics, while from 50 per cent to 63 per cent on the average take part in intramural athletics, voluntary or compulsory. The requirement of physical education for a degree, and the counting of satisfactory participation in intramural and other forms of athletics to satisfy this prescription, introduce an element of compulsion that obscures all questions of voluntary participation.

Our estimate in general is that basketball engages the greatest proportion of undergraduates at the institutions where it is played, namely, about 21 per cent; that football comes next with about 12 per cent, and tennis and baseball next with some 10 per cent each.

Respecting intercollegiate competition only, we estimate that football includes between five and six per cent of registrants, track and field athletics about five per cent, lacrosse, where it is played, about four per cent, and rowing and baseball on the average about 3.5 per cent each.

As regards intramural athletics, we estimate that baseball is played by about ten per cent of the undergraduates whose institutions schedule it, basketball by between eight and nine per cent, and soccer by about four per cent, or about double the proportion of those who participate in it as an intercollegiate branch. At two institutions where indoor baseball is much emphasized, it appears to engage well over 20 per cent of the undergraduates. It should be repeated that the foregoing figures are rough, general estimates only.

C. SUMMARY

In a comparative view of the foregoing four sets of statistics respecting athletic participation a few inferences stand out plainly.

First, from Professor Sheldon's estimate of 20 per cent participation nearly thirty years ago and the figures collected for the present study, it is apparent that no great increase has taken place over the past thirty years in the proportion of undergraduates participating in intercollegiate athletics. Over the period, however, participation in some form of athletic activity among undergraduates has more than doubled, and probably trebled.

Secondly, in view of the effort that has been made during the past six or seven years to bring athletics and their benefits to the attention of the individual undergraduate and to enlist his interest in them, the increases in proportions of participants to registrants, as indicated by Professor Storey's figures on a basis of voluntary participation, and by the figures of the present study on a basis both voluntary and compulsory, are not abnormal. Professor Storey's inference that almost half of the eligible undergraduates in American universities and colleges are not availing themselves of the advantages that voluntary participation in athletics might bring, is justified.

Thirdly, with an average of only 50 per cent or 60 per cent of undergraduates participating in college athletics, much remains to be done in tactfully enlisting the interest of students in intramural contests. Certain of the larger universities (California, Michigan, Toronto) have shown the way to approach students on the basis of their individual needs as determined by physical examinations and their own private interests. Doubtless, administrative officers of such institutions have been stimulated in this task by the larger numbers of undergraduates with whom they must deal and by the difficulty of solving the problem of approaching the tastes of the individual student. Only a few outstanding smaller colleges (Amherst, Bowdoin, Middlebury, Reed) have succeeded so well.

IV. A Few of the Conditions of Participation

Of the conditions that must be met before a college man may participate in athletics, some are discussed in other parts of this study. For example, the provision of playing fields and personal equipment and their care were dealt with in Chapter V. The uses of the medical examination find place in Chapter VII on the Hygiene of Athletic Training. The general tendencies of the eligibility rules of conferences are a part of the extramural relationships of colleges. The present discussion is concerned with a few of the other aspects of participation, some of which are related directly to college discipline and standards.

A. Conditions of Participation in Intramural Athletics

Aside from the provision of facilities, the conditions which must be satisfied before a student may take part in intramural athletics, whether the basis of such participation be "credit" requirements in physical education or the individual's own volition, are comparatively few. Those which refer to medical examination and physical fitness are, at most colleges, less strict than they should, and doubtless in time will, be.

A second weak point is supervision. Here difficulties arise from the fact that owing to the intensity of intercollegiate rivalry, especially in football, coaching staffs have been strengthened out of all just proportion to their importance in the welfare of undergraduates. In the past half dozen years, however, some college administrators have come to see the matter in a different light, with a consequent perceptible improvement in the amount and character of the attention devoted by certain coaching specialists to intramural athletics (Michigan, Notre Dame, Oberlin, Stanford), whether in their particular fields or in others. Even so, far less attention is given to college intramural programs than is bestowed upon similar enterprises at the best schools, both public and private. Until the welfare of all undergraduates, both general and individual, comes to be regarded as more important, in practice as well as in theory, than institutional success at intercollegiate athletics, especially at football, the supervision of intramural athletics will continue to lag.

Thirdly, to assure the success of intramural athletics and a widespread participation in them, it is not enough to provide playing fields and a program of practice hours and contests. Intramural athletics must be brought home to the individual student. Here arise some of the most difficult problems. So long as the requirements for degrees can be made to feed participants into the intramural machine, all that is needed is to care for the raw material. After this requirement has been satisfied, the test comes, and that test is, roughly, this: Do the habits and the interest that compulsory intramural athletics have aroused lead to voluntary participation in games, during subsequent years of the college course, and in after life? Thus far in the history of organized intramural athletics, whether required or voluntary, there are no clear signs that they do. But there are slight indications of improvement in this respect, and it should be noted that one college generation does not afford sufficient time to test the interest engendered by an intramural program; a decade is probably too short.

B. Conditions of Participation in Intercollegiate Athletics

Some of the special regulations made by individual institutions for participation in intercollegiate athletics are the result of the standards set by conferences or associations of colleges; others have been individually evolved.

1. Daily Programs and Time-Tables

The amount of time devoted to practice for intercollegiate matches is generally the result of compromise between their proponents and those whose interests lie primarily in other fields. As soon as required courses in physical education include intramural contests, this problem with respect to intramural athletics is solved. Not so with intercollegiate athletics. It would be possible, if it were worth the effort, to construct a scale in which universities and colleges should find their places on the basis of the hours that are daily allotted to preparation for intercollegiate athletics. In such a scale, if constructed with special reference to football, at one end might stand such institutions as Colgate [10] and New York University, where at the time of the field visits candidates for the team appeared to spend most of their afternoons and evenings at practice; and at the other end, the Cornell of 1927, where, because of laboratory and shop requirements, candidates had few daylight hours to devote to practice. Many college football fields are equipped with electric lights for night practice. Either of these extremes is unwholesome. If intercollegiate athletics are to be permitted at all, they should be accorded a just proportion of the daylight hours; but that they should absorb an undue amount of time points to a condition which is to be remedied only by the sincere coöperation of college administrators on the one hand and coaches, captains, and managers on the other. Much of the same might be said of early autumn football practice.

2. Scholastic Requirements and their Administration

In the course of the study much attention has been paid to scholastic requirements for participation in intercollegiate athletics and the strictness or laxity with which they are administered. Some hundreds of academic records of athletes and non-athletes have been examined, transcripts have been freely furnished by university officers upon request, the attendant circumstances surrounding many records have been canvassed, and even preparatory and high school records have been studied. The importance of the matter lies in its bearing upon the standing of the institution and its attitude toward the problems of eligibility and status.

[10] Mr. W. A. Reid, Graduate Manager, April 23, 1929: "Daily football practice not in excess of four hours on any given day."

It is possible to say, first, that over the past twenty years American scholastic standards for participation have risen, and, secondly, that there is still room for their improvement. Probably at no other point in the administration of athletics is imitation of good practice so salutary. Yet the mere announcing of standards is not enough. It is their application that matters.

Not a few universities possess scholastic requirements higher than those of the intercollegiate conferences or agreements to which they subscribe (Chicago, Cornell, Harvard, Princeton, Yale), and their enforcement of these standards respecting both admission and collegiate standing is honest, willing, and sportsmanlike. Other institutions (Columbia, Georgia School of Technology, Tulane) possess equally high requirements, which are rather frequently met through tutoring. Although certain Canadian universities have been accused by sister institutions of relaxing requirements for participation (Dalhousie, Queen's, Toronto), we have not found the charge to be justified. Not so, however, in the case of many other institutions.

All such matters are in the hands of faculties. They are not the concern of alumni or of friends of a college. When, therefore, standards are relaxed to permit skilled athletes either to enter a college without due qualifications or to compete in intercollegiate athletics without satisfying academic requirements, these matters also are the affair of faculties. But when the faculty officers concerned with eligibility happen to be athletic enthusiasts as well, the resulting division of responsibility has worked, in an appreciable number of cases, to the impairment of the standards and standing of the institutions.

A collection of examples (Alabama, Boston College, Fordham, Grinnell, Iowa, New York University, Northwestern, Notre Dame, Southern California, Stanford, Wisconsin) drawn from many parts of the United States will illustrate some of the results of conflicts between athletic ambitions and academic standards. The decision of one university faculty in a matter of participation and eligibility was overruled by the president. A trustee of another institution endeavored to persuade a college president to admit a young athlete whose credentials were not sufficient to justify this course. Prominent alumni of a third were embarrassingly insistent in their demand that a scholastically unqualified athlete should be admitted. The double standard that results from different university and conference requirements, non-athletes meeting the higher university requirements and athletes being held to meeting the lower conference requirements, not to mention a tradition of *laissez-faire* respecting a dean's office, results in immediate injustice to non-athletes and lasting injustice to athletes. At certain Southern institutions the practice of checking of players' scholastic records in mid-season has not been followed by the strictest adherence to requirements. At another university an athlete attained scholastic eligibility through the passing of an examination under circumstances that were, to say the least, unusual. The registrar of this same university has in at least three instances received instructions to admit candidates whose records were defective because of "the unusual conditions surrounding the case." The rulings concerning scholastic eligibility at certain Catholic institutions have been widely questioned. It is a pleasure to note that at another Catholic university (George-town) a strengthening of eligibility requirements is said to be in process. In two care-fully studied cases, one of which is typical of a very large majority of institutions that are members of highly respected conferences, the functions of the university reg-istrar are debased to those of a clerk, with the result that questionable rulings are re-flected in questionable practices.

In short, high though the academic standards of participation maintained at certain institutions may be, they represent no universal condition. Faculties, trustees, and even college or university presidents are not as yet united as respects the maintenance of strict requirements in the face of the supposed benefits that can be wrung from winning teams. The fact that all of these supposed advantages are tinged at one point or another with the color of money casts over every relaxation of standards a mer-cenary shadow. The good repute which a university attains through high academic standards and their honest enforcement is priceless, and it is not to be compared with the cheap and ephemeral notoriety that winning teams may bring.

3. Limitations upon the Period of Participation

The past five years have brought forth a number of proposals to limit the participa-tion of individual students in intercollegiate athletics.[11] In only one instance have undergraduates had a hand in shaping the suggestions.

Some of these proposals contain much that is of interest. One of the earliest was the so-called Fauver Plan, set forth by Professor Edgar Fauver, of Wesleyan University, to the effect that no man should be allowed to engage in intercollegiate competition in any branch of athletics for more than one season. In connection with this suggestion, a well-known authority on rowing, who has long interested himself in the crews of an Eastern university, has indicated that he should not object to seeing the principal 'varsity race of the season rowed by novices, although he realizes that to bring this about it would probably be better first to place a limitation of, say, two years for men on a 'varsity crew than to make the complete change at once. This matter came before the Wesleyan Parley of December, 1926, which in the previous year had discussed a "four-game plan" for football. Extensions of the one-year plan have been proposed in two forms, both implying two years of intercollegiate competition. One, set forth by Dr. John W. Wilce, then of Ohio State University, would limit such competition to the junior and senior years. The other, submitted by Mr. Arthur Howe to the Ohio College Association, would restrict intercollegiate competition to the sophomore and junior years. To this proposal President Ernest M. Hopkins, of Dartmouth College, would add two further limitations respecting football: "The development of two 'varsity elevens, the one to play at home and the other away on the same days," and the abolition of paid coaching, "the coaching to be done by undergraduates, preferably seniors." Early in 1928, the Advisory Committee on Athletics at Oberlin College, con-sisting of three members of the faculty, three alumni, and three undergraduates, expressed itself as "unanimously in favor of limiting participation in intercollegiate

[11] For a discussion of some of these plans, see the remarks of Professor Ernest H. Wilkins, now president of Oberlin College, Proceedings of the Twenty-first Annual Convention of the National Collegiate Athletic Association (1926), pages 81 ff.

athletics to two years in any one sport"; with choice by the individual as to which two of the sophomore, junior, and senior years should be selected, and permission to participate in intercollegiate athletics during those years, but not in any one branch for more than two of the three. These proposals were approved in principle by the faculty at Oberlin, and the next stages in their development were entrusted to President Wilkins.

In addition to these formal proposals, two other suggestions have gained many adherents. First, it is asserted that all or most of the difficulties that beset intercollegiate athletics would disappear if standards of scholarship were strictly enforced without exception. Secondly, it is claimed that all that is needed to improve intercollegiate athletics is an age limit upon participants, similar to that adopted in 1928 for Oxford-Cambridge matches.

Against most such proposals, the following arguments have been advanced: They are the work of theorists. They would deprive the skilled athlete of privileges which are really his by right. They must decrease the precision of performance. Novice teams and crews would lessen the interest of alumni and friends of universities in college athletics. Coaching by undergraduates will increase the dangers not alone of football but of all games. In short, all such suggestions are termed impracticable, — they are the work of men who, to quote one newspaper writer, "would take the joy out of college life."

In considering these suggestions and the arguments that have been advanced both pro and con, it is pertinent to observe that at this writing not one of these proposed "reforms" has even entered the experimental stage. The opponents have won by default, and this comparatively easy victory has much strengthened their position. Only one objection is really worth taking seriously, namely, the possible dangers to players that might arise from the abandonment of paid coaches. If it be urged that American football is not a game that can be safely coached by undergraduates, one answer is that it might be made such; certainly there has been nothing sacrosanct about the football rules.

As a matter of fact, one of the most interesting tendencies in American college athletics of recent years is the increasing number of limitations that have been placed upon them. The practically universal rule which prohibits freshmen's playing on 'varsity teams has proved beneficial, in protecting the newcomer from the distractions incident to intercollegiate competition and enabling him to orientate himself before entering upon it. Certain benefits of the rule, however, are forfeited when freshman teams are permitted to undertake long schedules, and when expert coaching is lavished upon such teams in order to develop 'varsity material. It is common experience the country over that freshman members of major-sports teams are distracted to a much greater extent than 'varsity athletes for several reasons. In the first place, athletic success during a first year means more to a freshman than success in any subsequent year. Again, freshman competition is keener and apparently somewhat more spontaneous; men throw themselves into it with the abandon of inexperience, especially because success or failure as a first-year athlete may have important bearing upon the status of a candidate for a 'varsity team in later competition. All of these considerations impart to freshman participation a tenseness and a strain that may be present among contestants for 'varsity positions, but rarely to the same degree.

The restriction upon the playing of students who have transferred from one institution to another has operated greatly to diminish the number of tramp athletes. In at least one notorious instance of recent years the operation of the rule has provided a valid test of the honesty and good faith of a player, who wavered in his declarations concerning his participation before transferring. Incidentally, in this case supporters of athletics at the university in question, who clamored for a modification of the transfer rule, completely ignored its beneficial aspects. The athletic authorities who debarred the transferred player took therein the only course consistent with honor. Committees at other institutions have not always been so mindful of this consideration. The period during which a transferred student must wait before he may enter intercollegiate athletics is variously set as a season, a term, a semester, or a full academic year. Those institutions which permit a man to transfer to the college in, say, February, and to participate in intercollegiate football during the following autumn after a summer-school course are at fault if they advertise this provision as a one-year rule. The two- or three-sport rule, which prevents an athlete's competing in more than two or three branches of intercollegiate athletics has done much, when related to local conditions, to diminish certain phases of athletic over-indulgence.

All such limitations have proceeded, sometimes indirectly, from the work of conferences and associations, and are to be regarded as among their best fruits. Their chief benefit is the protection they afford the too ambitious undergraduate from the pressure of partisans and disciples of victory. The limitations that have been imposed upon intercollegiate competition are the products of courage and a spirit of experiment. There is no reason to suppose that either quality will be lacking in American college athletics of the future.

4. Participation and the Coaching School

Apparently, to become a successful teacher of physical education, in high school or college, demands an intensive, year-round study of football. Whatever other instruction candidates for degrees in physical education from schools, colleges, and universities receive, in the autumn they practice football, in the early winter they study the theory of football, in the later winter they deal with the coaching of football, and in the spring they again practice football. Some sort of practice or instruction may continue during the summer. It is doubtful if in any other department of the American college curriculum a single subject receives more thoroughgoing attention. Students in such courses are welcomed to 'varsity squads and teams; and coaching courses and schools, baited with elegant descriptive pamphlets and other expedients, are the tackle that has landed many a prominent schoolboy athlete for the creel of college athletics. The ethical aspects of using on supposedly amateur college teams men who are essentially professional in their attitude towards the game, not to mention men who, however "legitimately," receive university scholarships for studying football as a part of the college curriculum, do not appear to have been seriously scrutinized.

C. Summary

The conditions of participation in college athletics are, from the undergraduate point of view, neither onerous nor uninviting. Although in certain schools, where interscholastic contests have been abandoned and increased attention paid to intramural athletics, a greatly enlivened interest has been stimulated, it is not necessary for colleges and universities to go, as some have done (Emory, Reed), to a similar extreme in order to benefit an increased proportion of their student body through intramural athletics. What is most needed for the development of an intramural program is fertility of resource and a persuasive attitude on the part of those in charge, material facilities not necessarily luxurious but adequate as compared with those allotted to intercollegiate athletics, and a staff for intramural contests that equals the intercollegiate coaching staff in character, ability, and skill.

V. The Immediate Results of Participation in College Athletics

We turn now to a few of the results, such as improved physical health and fitness, honors and awards, social advantages, and moral qualities, which participation in college athletics may or do bring to the undergraduate.

A. Physical Results

The effect of participation in college athletics upon the physical condition of undergraduates as individuals, which is discussed at some length in connection with the hygiene of athletic training, is measurable in terms of weight, height, and strength, and at some institutions has indeed been measured by means of successive periodic medical examinations. These measurable characteristics may be regarded provisionally as indications of physical health as determined by the vigor and regularity of the functions of the vital organs. No one will dispute the values of such results as these. But athletic injuries are far more frequent and more serious than they should be. Apparently the high incidence of such injuries and accidents is part of the price paid by certain individuals for the benefits received by themselves and their more fortunate colleagues, although this is no reason for neglecting any means whereby the incidence of such injuries may be lowered.

B. ATHLETICS AND SCHOLARSHIP

It has become a commonplace of the adverse criticism passed upon American college athletics that they weaken the intellectual spirit and lower the academic standing of undergraduates. Likewise there has developed a series of defensive sallies, designed to establish the claim that athletics do not weaken the scholarly tendencies. For the present enquiry two approaches to this question have been devised. The results are set forth at this point.

1. The Academic Records of Athletes

In accordance with a plan outlined in the Twenty-Second [12] Annual Report of the Carnegie Foundation for the Advancement of Teaching, 1927, detailed studies of the academic records of 2,787 athletes and 11,480 non-athletes in fifty-two representative colleges and universities of the United States were made at the institutions by registrars, deans, professors, and others. These results, assembled in the offices of the Foundation, are of sufficient accuracy to be interpreted as follows, due allowances being made for deviations in methods of grading and differences in type and procedure regarding intelligence tests and scores:

a. *Program Hours Carried*

Although athletes tend to carry a slightly greater number of program hours than non-athletes, this difference between the two groups is so slight as to be insignificant. During the first college year, and during a fifth year, if required for graduation, athletes carry slightly heavier programs than non-athletes; the reverse is true in the second, third, and fourth college years. The third-year program of athletes is the heaviest, as contrasted with the second-year program of the non-athletes.

---

[12] Pages 49–65. The method there set forth is too detailed for the present discussion, which deals only with its results, when applied to athletes and non-athletes in the fifty-two institutions listed below. Although not complicated, its use is somewhat arduous, and the thanks of the Foundation are extended to those men and women who contributed generously of time and effort to make the study.

The reasons given for twelve refusals to undertake the work are of interest: lack of time prevented in six cases, lack of information in three, while lack of funds, disapproval of the method proposed, and the sending of a brief previous report led to non-coöperation in the remaining three cases of refusal. Yale University is not included in the material. On February 25, 1928, President Angell wrote "that the expense involved will be more than, at the moment, we can properly undertake. Moreover, I think there would be some rather grave objections to that part of your request which relates to a classification of courses from the point of view of their severity." The offer, on March 7, 1928, of a subsidy suggested by Yale as sufficient to cover the work, did not meet the "rather grave objections" set forth by the president.

The fifty-two institutions that coöperated fully, even to an analysis of "hard" and "easy" courses are Allegheny, Bradley Polytechnic Institute, Butler, California Institute of Technology, Carleton College, Carnegie Institute of Technology, Case School of Applied Science, Colgate, University of Colorado, Colorado College, Columbia University, Cornell University, Dartmouth, Denison, Earlham, Emory, Furman, Georgetown, Harvard, Illinois, Knox, Lafayette, Lehigh, Michigan, Middlebury, Mississippi A. & M., University of Missouri, Muhlenberg, University of New Hampshire, Notre Dame, Oberlin, Occidental, Ohio State University, Oregon Agricultural College, Pennsylvania State College, University of Pittsburgh, Princeton, Rensselaer Polytechnic Institute, Rice Institute, Ripon, University of Rochester, Rutgers, St. Olaf, Southern Methodist, Stanford, Syracuse, Vanderbilt, Virginia Military Institute, Wesleyan, Whitman, College of Wooster, Worcester Polytechnic Institute.

b. *Scholarship Grades*

The scholarship grades of athletes seem to average slightly lower than those of non-athletes, but the ascertainable difference in favor of the non-athletes is probably so slight as not to possess statistical significance. Athletes average higher during the first college year, non-athletes during the remainder of the course. The condition works out much as the number of program hours carried. For both of the groups, grades improve consistently in successive years; the grades of non-athletes are appreciably better in the fourth year than in any previous year for either athletes or non-athletes. For both types and all years grades are better during the second semester than the first.

c. *Time Spent in College for Degrees*

The academic "mortality" of the athletes was lower than that of their fellows; that is, a higher proportion of athletes graduate than non-athletes. But it takes the athlete about half a college year longer, on the whole, to obtain his degree. The figure is probably less serious than at first appears, because in cases where longer than the normal time is required to obtain the credits for a degree, it is the almost universal rule that a semester of attendance is the minimum that can be required. On the average, about 95 per cent of the athletes registered as members of each successive college class returning to college in the following semester, as compared with 90 per cent of the non-athletes.

d. *Probation*

A slightly higher proportion of athletes than non-athletes incurred probation at some time during the college course. The difference is very slight, but it may reflect the general use of probation by faculties and administrative officers as a means of protecting the athlete against a tendency to overdo his sports.

e. *Scholarship Grades by Sports*

Respecting the average comparative scholarship of individual participants in sports by branches, only general tendencies have importance. Wrestlers, cross-country runners, and track men do well, — indeed, far better than the general run of both athletes and non-athletes, especially the wrestlers. Swimmers and oarsmen do better than the average of athletes, but not quite so well as the average of non-athletes. Soccer, lacrosse, and baseball players are below the averages of both athletes and non-athletes. Football and polo players stand at the bottom of the list. Athletes rank below non-athletes in scholarship, but the difference in average grades [13] between the two general groups is statistically negligible. Participants in two or more branches of athletics stand on the average considerably below all athletes, as a group, and nearly as badly as football players.

[13] Non-athletes, 8.25; athletes, 8.18; with an average for all individuals of 8.01.

f. "Hard" and "Easy" Courses

It cannot be justly said that in general athletes are greater idlers than non-athletes. Curiously enough, although a larger proportion of athletes than non-athletes elected "easy" courses, the same is true, in exactly the same proportions, respecting "hard" courses. In every case among the two groups, grades in "hard" courses were higher than those in "easy" courses, and both of these sets of grades were better than the averages for other courses not designated as "hard" or "easy."

g. The Passing Line

A few more athletes than non-athletes received grades near the passing line, but a larger proportion of both groups than might be expected received such grades.

h. Intelligence Scores

An examination of intelligence test scores led to inconclusive results. Of the fifty-two coöperating institutions, only twenty-two examined their class of 1925 in this particular, and of these only three used the same tests. It was possible, however, to consider the results of these tests and of the study of the scholastic records on the basis of institutions rather than by individual scores and grades in the aggregate. The results of these comparisons, although fragmentary, tend to corroborate the conclusions already set forth. Non-athletes, in both cases, did slightly but not materially better than athletes, and the other results are similar.

2. The Pennsylvania Achievement Tests

In May, 1928, under the auspices of the Association of College Presidents of Pennsylvania, the Carnegie Foundation administered a specially devised test of 3,500 questions, which consumed eight working hours of 4,412 seniors at forty-nine colleges, universities, and normal schools. Of these institutions thirteen [14] assisted the Foundation to study the scores of athletes and non-athletes, with the following results:

a. Average Scores by Groups

The highest individual score among the 4,412 students taking the test at forty-nine institutions was 1,583, made by a male non-athlete, the lowest 110, the statewide average 568.9, and the average for all men 577.4. At the thirteen institutions under present consideration, 290 athletes made an average of 636.37, while 1,340 non-athletes scored on the average 615.55 points and both athletes and non-athletes in the thirteen coöperating colleges, 619.25 points. The difference between the average scores of the 290 athletes and the 1,340 non-athletes is 20.82. This difference is not significant from a statistical point of view. The athletes, it is true, did better, but not sufficiently better to make their excellence noteworthy. But when compared with the statewide averages

[14] Albright, Allegheny, Bucknell, Carnegie Institute of Technology, Geneva, Grove City, Haverford, Juniata, Lafayette, Lehigh, University of Pennsylvania, Thiel, Ursinus.

for men, 577.4, and for all students, 568.9, the higher average score of the athletes, 636.37, is important.

b. *Average Scores by Sports*

Altogether, some sixteen branches of athletics are represented in the thirteen Pennsylvania colleges. Those branches include, however, cricket, golf, rowing, and gymnastics, in which the numbers of participants are too small for statistical purposes. With these four branches eliminated, the remaining twelve, with their average scores, may be classified as follows:

The first group comprises wrestling (805.05); soccer (788.14); and boxing (759). The second group includes lacrosse (751.91); rifle-shooting (748.86); and swimming (719.86). The third group is composed of track and field (675.25); cross-country running (654.56); and tennis (621). The fourth is made up of football (609.42); baseball (559.8); and basketball (553.83). The second highest score made by a man among the total of 4,412 students taking the test in the state, and the highest of all athletes' scores, was 1,560, achieved by a track athlete. These scores compare well with the statewide average for all men, 577.4.

Men participating in two or more sports did slightly better in the tests (638.29) than the athletes as a whole (636.37), but for statistical purposes these two groups are practically one, because of the smallness of the mean difference between them (1.92).

c. *Significance of these Results*

If, then, the Pennsylvania tests actually measure intellectual capacity or intelligence in conjunction with a certain amount of accomplishment, as they are intended to do, the list of sports and scores just given represents a rating of the intellectual capacities of athletes who took the tests. On the same basis, we may infer from the comparative scores that these athletes have a better intellectual capacity than the non-athletes among the men, and the general run of undergraduates, both men and women.

3. The Effect of Athletics Upon the Scholarship of Athletes

These two independent sets of information considered together, afford interesting conclusions, if they are premised by the assumption that the data are typical of all American colleges taken together.

First, from the Pennsylvania scores it appears that athletes engaged in intercollegiate competition possess about the same or slightly better intellectual capacity than non-athletes. This is even more to be expected in view of their inheritance of vigor in body and hence in mind. We should therefore expect the scholarship grades of athletes as a whole to be appreciably higher than those of non-athletes. But this is not the case, and we seek a cause. Putting to one side the possibility that the educational aims and processes of the American college are at fault, we are led to the alternative hypothesis that some factor related to intercollegiate competition, — such, for example, as time spent upon practice or games, the fatigue of contests or preparation, injuries, attitude, point of view, or something, — in general holds back the athletes from intellectual performance up to the limits of their capacities.

Second, if this reasoning is justified, from the relative positions of the participants in various sports in the two sets of data, it appears likely that participation has no deleterious effect upon the academic work of men taking part in intercollegiate wrestling, rifle-shooting, swimming, track and field, cross-country running, tennis, baseball, and basketball. It appears, however, to lower the academic achievement of 'varsity participants in soccer, boxing, lacrosse, and football.

Finally, from the lower average grades of participants in two or more branches who seem, from the Pennsylvania data, to be of about the same intellectual promise as other athletes, it would appear that one of the most important functions of the college administrative officer is to continue to protect the skilful athlete from the results of excessive zeal on his own part or too many demands upon his time and energy resulting from over-participation in intercollegiate athletics. The question whether this should be accomplished through restrictions or through setting up a fresh educational goal that will challenge anew the interests and capacities of all undergraduates, need not detain us here.

C. The Rewards of Athletics

Of the awarding of college letters, class numerals, and other symbols for distinguished participation in college athletics little need be said in addition to what has gone before. In such awards the essential factor is the honor which the right to wear the insignia confers. Although at Louisiana College in 1926 football letters were awarded by vote of the 'varsity squad, the fact that at no institution of the study has serious dissatisfaction with the method of award been expressed is valid testimony to its fairness. The ephemeral protests to which college undergraduates seem prone have in no instance reflected deep-seated dissatisfaction.

For women's athletics the system of points awarded for participation, suggested by the Athletic Conference of American College Women, has many advantages. Its administration involves no very onerous undertaking by the department of physical education, and the points won by individual athletes afford a means of comparison and even of competition between separated institutions. The system is in use for women at a number of state universities in the Middle West and the West, but in only a few women's colleges and Eastern co-educational institutions.

All such awards possess no monetary value. The money value of certain testimonials offered rather generally to successful athletes, such as cups, gold footballs for watch chains, sweaters, wrist watches, traveling bags, and other items, is, however, considerable. Again, no instance has come to the attention of this study in which a college athlete has attempted to realize the value of trophies by selling or pawning them. Prizes officially awarded to American undergraduates for participation in college athletics are widely esteemed for the honor which they symbolize.

Concerning unofficial awards the same cannot be said. The local merchant who in a kind of ostentatious competitive generosity offers clothing or jewelry to the player who scores a touchdown or a home run is on the one hand merely exploiting college athletics for his own ends or the ends of trade, and on the other injecting into the individual athlete's attitude toward sport an element which may lead, especially with repetition, to a higher regard for the money value at stake than for the honor which it is intended to manifest (Colgate, Dartmouth, University of Georgia, Lehigh). The utility or the non-utility of such awards is a criterion which might prove serviceable to college administrative officers who desire to end a questionable practice.

D. The Moral Qualities

The moral qualities that participation in college athletics is widely supposed to engender — courage, obedience, unselfishness, persistence, and the rest — have formed the theme of countless eulogies of athletes and athletics. No attempt to measure them has yielded unmistakable results.

The studies conducted by Mr. Post and Dr. Davenport for the present enquiry indicate, however, that to some extent they may be transmitted as hereditary traits. This view is shared by other authorities. Once transmitted, they can be and probably are developed by athletic participation. Thus, for example, an athlete possesses his share of courage when he begins his career at football. From experience of practice and games he gains the power of better controlling his own impulses to fear. As a result, he in time becomes habituated to a series of acts that a non-player might fear to perform altogether or might perform only under the most urgent compulsion or in consequence of an even greater fear. Besides, the athlete's skill increases his self-confidence. At the same time, his development in this particular is furthered by an improved neuro-muscular coördination, until, finding that he can habitually perform certain feats without the disagreeable or painful consequences that he formerly anticipated, he in time becomes a courageous football player. Other moral traits may be similarly developed in other branches of athletics; they may vary from game to game and even as regards different positions in the same game.

A bit of testimony from a director of physical education, who is skeptical concerning the wholesale "inculcation of moral values" through athletics, is pertinent. Long experience has convinced him that a body-contact activity like football, basketball, or boxing, does much to remove from participants the aversion to rough physical contact that young men frequently display. Thus the essential nature of all such activities appears to increase the physical courage of participants.

On the other hand, our study of the recruiting and subsidizing of college athletes affords much direct evidence that college athletics can breed, and, in fact, have bred, among athletes, coaches, directors, and even in some instances among college administrative officers, equivocation and dishonesty, which actual participation has not removed or prevented. The impairment of moral stamina that such practices imply is the darkest blot upon American college athletics.

VI. The Deferred Results of College Athletics

Of the effects of college athletics that persist into life after graduation, the physical benefits or disabilities are the most easily recognizable. These effects are in part reflected in the longevity of athletes as compared with other groups, such as the general male population and college graduates. The influence of athletic participation upon the future career and the persistence of habits of exercise acquired in college days into later life are matters concerning which individual experience has shaped judgment.

A. The Longevity of College Athletes

Before the meeting of the National Collegiate Athletic Association in December, 1928, Dr. Louis I. Dublin, statistician of the Metropolitan Life Insurance Company of New York, presented results of studies [15] in the longevity of college athletes, honor men, and graduates. The conclusions which Dr. Dublin drew from his analysis of the life records of these 38,000 graduates of eight American colleges, in the classes from 1870 to 1905, inclusive, may be set forth with comment as follows:

1. Dr. Dublin's Conclusions

On the whole, college men have an expectation of life appreciably above normal. Compared with recent insurance mortality tables, their mortality is relatively lower at the older ages than in early adult life. Their death rates have been declining regularly from earlier to more recent class groups, and the decline has been greatest at the younger ages. Men who graduate from small colleges show a lower mortality than graduates of large universities.

Athletes, that is, "letter men," have a somewhat higher mortality than other graduates. Although at ages over forty-five the athletes did somewhat better than the

[15] Dr. Dublin's researches may be examined in three phases: (1) A study of the longevity of 4,976 "letter men," members of classes graduated at Amherst, Brown, Cornell, Dartmouth, Harvard, Massachusetts Agricultural College, Tulane, Wesleyan, Wisconsin, and Yale, was undertaken under the auspices of the Presidents' Committee of 50 on College Hygiene and such constituent organizations as the National Collegiate Athletic Association and the Society of Directors of Physical Education. The Carnegie Foundation gave aid and support to the project, and the Statistical Bureau of the Metropolitan Life Insurance Company guided the work and tabulated results, which "were, on the whole, favorable to the prospect of long life for these men. With but few exceptions, they did somewhat better than the carefully selected persons insured by American life insurance companies." The results were published in *Harper's Magazine*, July, 1928. (2) Dr. Dublin, with the coöperation of the Presidents' Committee of 50 and the American Student Health Association, proceeded to a further "study of the mortality and the length of life of the general student body since graduation" from Amherst, Brown, Cornell, Dartmouth, Harvard, Wesleyan, Williams, and Yale, in classes from 1870 to 1905, inclusive, totaling 38,269 men. This research Dr. Dublin discussed before the N.C.A.A. in 1928. (3) It is now proposed to press the matter further by collecting and studying data over a period of future years.

whole group, at ages under forty-five their death rates were distinctly higher than among alumni generally.

But men of high scholarship outlive both athletes and all graduates as a group, and the death rates among them are lower throughout the life span.[16] Dr. Dublin notes the existence of "a large and growing body of data, which tend to show that it is not men or women of the best physique particularly who live longest. . . . It may be that we have expected too much from our athletes. It is, after all, a good deal of an assumption that the athletic type of build and great longevity go hand in hand. . . . Certainly if fine physique was a requisite for long life, we should have found a life expectation of college athletes much in excess of normal and appreciably greater than that of their fellows at college. Our analysis shows, however, that the honor men, the men who spend much of their time in the library and in the laboratory, come out best in the matter of longevity. This result should give us all much to think over."

2. An Extension of Dr. Dublin's Conclusions

As long ago as 1869, Galton noted that a considerable number of eminent men possessed unusual physical vigor. In 1925 Professor Lewis M. Terman's *Genetic Studies of Genius* called attention to the fact that in a majority of cases the intellectual superiority of the gifted was evidenced at an early age and associated with physical vigor. Apparently, then, our college athletics as they have been conducted for a generation and more have not conduced to long life. Nor have they, in their intercollegiate phases, markedly attracted those undergraduates who are the most vigorous mentally or physically.

B. PARTICIPATION IN COLLEGE ATHLETICS AND THE LIFE CAREER

Most of the attempts to account for success in life as a product of college athletics have neglected at least two possible fallacies. First, the measure of success has often been defined badly or not at all. In the second place, it has been unwarrantably assumed that when former athletes achieved success, however defined, such success is necessarily the effect of athletics. More probably a successful career is the product of qualities that lead not alone to success in life but also to athletic prominence, and the underlying causes of later success are the same as those which lead to success in athletics. Athletics may intensify valuable personal characteristics, but it is to be doubted if they create them.

1. The Scholar in Business

So far as is ascertainable, only one statistical study has been made involving the relationship of the academic standing of college undergraduates to business success in

[16] The results of studies of the completed lives of 358 teachers who had received retiring allowances from the Carnegie Foundation, 1906–27 (Twenty-Third Annual Report, 1928, pages 34–37), tend to corroborate this conclusion. Presumably these teachers were, one and all, men of high scholarship.

later life, namely, the analysis of the academic and business records of 4,125 college graduates in the employ of the American Telephone and Telegraph Company.[17] "In this particular study made by the Bell System salary has been used as a measure of success." Although in presenting the results President Gifford states that he does not believe that success in life can be rated by income, he is convinced that "as between one man and another working in the same business organization, success and salary — while not the same thing — will, generally speaking, parallel each other." He points out, furthermore, that success in life for both the individual and the nation depends upon the use of leisure.

Although the inferences of the enquiry are based upon "the averages of the performances of the men in different groups and the records of individuals in each group varying widely from the averages," it is clear that "in the Bell System, on the average, men who were good students have done better than those who were not. There are, of course, exceptions — men who were poor students who are succeeding well and men who were good students succeeding less well — but on the whole the evidence is very striking that there is a direct relation between high marks at college and salaries afterward in the Bell System." President Gifford notes that the undergraduate, if he connects his college course with a business future at all, is likely to think that his athletic and social activities, his work on college papers or in dramatic clubs, or some other extra-curricular efforts are better training for the future than his academic work, "and in taking this attitude the boys reflect fairly accurately the opinion of many of their elders, under whom they are going to begin their working career." Yet, "if studies by others corroborate the results of this study in the Bell System and it becomes clear that the mind well trained in youth has the best chance to succeed in any business it may choose, then scholarship as a measure of mental equipment is of importance both to business and to business men."

These results are, of course, provisional and it will take years of effort to corroborate them with respect to business as a whole. Their value lies, first, in their pointing the way to other enquiries, and secondly, in their indication of the attitude of one of the largest employers in the world. With respect to the question whether the athlete has a better chance of success in business than the scholar they are silent, except for such inferences as may be drawn from them, and yet the argument *ex silentio* is here more powerful than the unsubstantiated assertions which have pleased so many willing hearers in the past.

2. The Athletic Manager and Business

Whatever opinion may be held concerning the value of athletics in general as a preparation for a business career, there appears to be little doubt that the work of the manager of a class or a 'varsity team or crew, through inculcation of habits of accuracy and purposeful activity, is directly related to a business career. Testimony, the country

[17] Walter S. Gifford, "Does Business Want Scholars?" *Harper's Magazine*, May, 1928, pages 669 ff. The study was made by the Personnel Department of the American Telephone and Telegraph Company, under the direction of Mr. E. K. Hall, and the preliminary stages of it consumed about two years. The number of colleges involved was 104.

over, is to the effect that the undergraduate who is concerned with the management of athletics is forced to devote to his task more time and effort on the average than the active participant on the playing field. Moreover, not a few college officers feel that the duties of a manager are more likely to impair academic standing than the training of a participant. In the present study no direct effort has been expended in measuring the effect of the manager's duties upon his academic career, because the number of men involved is comparatively small. It is obvious, however, that habits of application engendered in managing teams and the acquaintance with aspects of business which managership involves, are useful preparation for business and the professions, especially if coupled with intellectual ability and accomplishment.

3. Summary

On these grounds, then, there exists much doubt whether success in athletics should be regarded as an earnest of success in later life. Such statistical studies as have been made lead to the inference that, as an index of future success, academic standing is more trustworthy than performance as an athlete. These conclusions are, of course, provisional. A final summation of the matter must depend upon far more extensive studies than have thus far been made, and may also be postponed until the wave of changes in college curricula and methods of study which is now sweeping over parts of the United States, has subsided into a comparative calm for a length of time sufficient to make possible trustworthy results.

C. EXPERIENTIAL KNOWLEDGE OF GAMES

Although accurate data are lacking concerning the extent to which habits of participation in college athletics persist into graduate life, nevertheless it appears that the American college graduate generally prefers watching many games to playing them. Doubtless this is partly due to the fact that American football is essentially a game of youth. Whether it should or should not be played by men between the ages of twenty-one and thirty-five is beside the point; the fact is that, generally speaking, it is not so played. The rigors of training required for many branches of intercollegiate athletics are impracticable after graduation. Hence it is to the development of intramural or general athletics that, so far as the college man or college woman is concerned, the nation must look for the spread of habits of athletic activity in the individuals who compose it. If it be assumed that the function of collegiate education is to prepare for later life, including the wise use of leisure, then such sports as tennis, golf, handball, and swimming deserve the attention of every teacher of physical education and every undergraduate.[18] Few colleges or universities can give to their students the

---

[18] One reason why athletic activities are so frequently abandoned after graduation is a neglect on the part of those in charge of our physical education of the sports most suited to maturer men and women.

Professor Harry A. Scott, in answering the question " What Should the Department of Physical Education Require of its

experience of games which the United States Military Academy requires of its fourth-class men. But habits of participation in not too strenuous games and contests during undergraduate days provide at least a guide to exercise and to keeping fit in later years.

CONCLUSION

It appears that American college athletics, and in particular intercollegiate athletics, are not contributing to successful undergraduate or postgraduation careers in the extent that they should or could be made to contribute. As regards inheritance, inter-collegiate athletes should be the best endowed of college men. But, although their natural capacities are high and their physical condition is measurably benefited by games, their college and academic records are not especially distinguished above those of their fellows and in some sports are even impaired by their participation. After graduation their span of life has not been lengthened beyond that of their more studious fellows or that of the generality of men, nor do they generally continue the more exacting forms of exercise in which as undergraduates they indulged. Finally, from the point of view of rewards, contentment, and fruitfulness of service in at least one very large industry their success in life depends less upon their standing as athletes than upon their academic achievement. Briefly, then, the situation is this : On the one hand, we have youths well endowed physically and mentally who should outdistance their fellows in the race of life ; on the other, we find no evidence that the best places in this race have been won by these men, whose tastes and training have led them into inter-collegiate athletics. The indicated conclusion is that the American system of inter-collegiate athletics is to blame for this situation rather than the body of youth that is subjected to its workings.

In athletics, as in the academic branches of education, Americans have long since accustomed themselves to regard the individual less than the group, whereas the unit of measure in both fields should be the effect of the respective processes upon the individual. The statistical data assembled in this chapter from many sources point in a single direction, and materials presented in other chapters of our study support

---

Students for Graduation?" (*American Physical Education Review*, March, 1928, pages 142–51), sets forth the recreational activities reported by three age groups:

25–35 years	*36–50 years*	*Over 50 years*
Swimming	Fishing	Gardening
Fishing	Swimming	Hiking
Tennis	Golf	Fishing
Golf	Hiking	Golf
Hiking	Gardening	Calisthenics
Handball	Hunting	Hunting
Calisthenics	Tennis	Swimming
Volley Ball	Calisthenics	Tennis
Gardening	Handball	Rowing
	Rowing	Volley Ball

Aside from the question whether training in athletic sports transfers from undergraduate to postgraduate days, the direct relationship of athletic skills and habits in the two general periods of the life of the college man is worthy of far more attention than has hitherto been vouchsafed to it.

them. To the development of the individual capacities of young men and women, — their appreciation of true values, their powers of decision and choice, their sense of responsibility, and their ability to sustain it when once it comes to them, — to the development of these and of all other best habits of mind and traits of character, college athletics must contribute far more than they have in the past if they are to justify the time and effort that are lavished upon them.

CHAPTER VII
THE HYGIENE OF ATHLETIC TRAINING

THE report which forms the basis for discussion of the hygiene of athletic training was prepared for this enquiry by Dean F. Smiley, M.D., Medical Adviser of Cornell University, and Secretary of the American Student Health Association. Dr. Smiley and the Foundation have been fortunate in enlisting the interested and active coöperation of an advisory group composed of men distinguished in several fields closely related to the hygiene of training: Francis G. Benedict, Ph.D., Director of the Nutrition Laboratory at Boston of the Carnegie Institution of Washington; E. V. MacCollum, Ph.D., Professor of Bio-Chemistry in the School of Public Health, Johns Hopkins University; Livingston Farrand, M.D., President of Cornell University; Joseph E. Raycroft, M.D., Professor of Hygiene at Princeton University; and Thomas K. Richards, M.D., Instructor in Surgery at the Harvard Medical School, and Chief Surgeon of the Harvard Athletic Association. Once the facts of the study had been gathered by Dr. Smiley, the work approached the nature of a coöperative enterprise, to which the members of this advisory group contributed most generously of time and effort. The conclusions and suggestions which grew out of the work therefore represent a composite drawn from fact and foresight which would otherwise have been impossible.

Under these special conditions the present chapter presents recommendations as well as facts and inferences. Inasmuch as the underlying data were collected by a physician from physicians in a confidential relation, the names of the schools, colleges, and universities, although listed at one point together, are represented in discussions of specific cases by letters and numerals.

I. A STUDY OF ATHLETICS IN RELATION TO STUDENT HEALTH

In recent years, numerous attempts have been made to define the bearings of secondary and higher education upon health, and to particularize the terms employed. The definition of the term "health" set forth by the joint committee of the American Medical Association and the National Education Association emphasizes four aspects of health, mental, emotional, moral, and social, that are important in the attainment of physiological health. That the promotion of health, as implied in these terms, is one of the purposes of school and college athletics, is widely accepted; but great diversity of opinion exists as to which of the four aspects should be subserved for the attainment of physiological health. Doubtless part of this uncertainty is due to the fact that no accurate measurement of the results of school and college athletics has ever been made in these terms. Indeed, a trustworthy method of measuring the mental, emotional, moral, and social results of athletics has yet to be formulated. Even without it, a study of one phase of the physiological bearing of our present athletic practices is practicable.

A. PROBLEMS OF THE STUDY

A study of current training practices, so far as they are ascertainable, limited to the physical aspects of health, was clearly indicated. The attempt has been made impartially to apply relevant principles from the fields of physiology, hygiene, medicine, and surgery, to ascertainable facts concerning the steps that are being taken to foster and to safeguard the physical health of participants in our school, college, and university athletics, in the hope of arriving at an approximate evaluation of the efforts that are now being put forth in the limited field of physical health.

B. METHODS OF THE STUDY

To this end an examination was first made of certain printed documents [1] in order to ascertain the principles of athletic organization and administration in our universities, schools, and colleges. This preliminary study made evident that the administration and organization of athletics proceed in accordance with certain rather clearly defined types. Secondly, a number of colleges and universities, several public high schools, and a few private preparatory schools [2] were visited, the institutions being chosen with a

---

[1] Current handbooks and bulletins of various secondary schools, universities, and colleges, the current constitutions and by-laws of various state high school athletic associations, and, in particular, Dr. Thomas A. Storey's *Status of Hygiene Programs in Institutions of Higher Education in the United States*, Stanford University Press, 1927.

[2] Amherst, Hamilton, Pennsylvania State, Brown, Bucknell, Chicago, Colgate, Cornell, Harvard, Lafayette, Lehigh, Michigan, Minnesota, Pennsylvania, Princeton, Susquehanna, Syracuse, Wesleyan, Wisconsin, Yale. The following selected high schools were also visited: in New York City, the DeWitt Clinton and the Morris; in Brooklyn, New York, the Manual Training High

view to including clearly differentiated types of athletic administration. To a few universities [3] situated at a distance that rendered impracticable a personal visit, questionnaires were dispatched in an attempt to secure pertinent information; the meagre and incomplete results confirmed the general principle on which the enquiry as a whole was conducted, — that of not relying upon questionnaires as a means of gathering material. It is important to note that all of these steps were taken quite independently of the field work of the general enquiry and, indeed, supplemented it. The result was, of course, a sampling of conditions rather than an intensive survey, but it is believed that the sampling has been done with a care sufficient to make it typical of conditions in educational institutions the country over.

II. Current Athletic Practices at Representative Colleges and Universities

From the point of view of both the general student of college athletics and the college physician, it will be pertinent to enquire, first, what proportion of the students in these representative colleges and universities are affected physically, for good or for ill, by athletics; secondly, what is the relative incidence of serious injury or accident; thirdly, to what are these injuries due; and, finally, what data are available as to the compensating benefits of athletics to their participants?

A. Participation in Major Athletic Activities

At the twenty-two universities and colleges selected to represent conditions over the United States, some 43,923 male students engaged actively in thirteen branches of athletics during the seasons covered by the study. Tables A and B of the Appendix indicate the number of participants in these forms of both intercollegiate and intramural athletics. It is perhaps to be expected that more than twice as many students should engage in intramural contests as in intercollegiate athletics, even allowing for the fact that the figures involve a certain amount of unavoidable duplication owing to participation by one man in more than one branch. On the other hand, the fact that many students take part in such games as soft ball, speed ball, touch football, tennis, and golf, whether on an intercollegiate or an intramural basis, serves in a measure to compensate for duplication in the count. Hence it is highly probable that a participation of 25.7 per cent of these male student bodies in intercollegiate athletics and of 53.2 per cent in intramural athletics, with a total of about 78.9 per cent engaged in all forms, is approximately correct.

When the totals of participation in each branch are arranged in the descending order

School and Erasmus Hall; public schools in Ann Arbor, Michigan, and Ithaca and Groton, New York. In addition, private preparatory schools were visited as follows: St. Mark's, Phillips Andover Academy, Middlesex School, Lawrenceville School, and Groton School.

[3] California, Cincinnati, Indiana, Iowa, and Stanford.

of numbers, as in Table I, below, it appears that basketball is the sport most indulged in, and that baseball and track athletics stand next at a considerable interval.

TABLE I

Thirteen Branches of Athletics Arranged According to the Numbers of all Participants therein
At Twenty-two Representative Colleges

	Participants	
Branch	Indoor Branch	Outdoor Branch
Basketball	9626	
Baseball		6955
Track and field		5871
Football		5400
Swimming	4623	
Wrestling	2380	
Cross-country running		1852
Hockey		1673
Rowing		1474
Boxing	1435	
Soccer		1385
Lacrosse		640
Fencing	609	
Totals	18673	25250 43923

It appears that 18,673 men, who constitute more than 40 per cent of all of the participants in athletics, — roughly one-third of the men students, — at these representative institutions, engage in basketball, swimming, wrestling, boxing, and fencing, sports that are conducted indoors. Indeed, the popularity of basketball, swimming, and wrestling is largely due to the fact that, taking place under cover, they are little interfered with by seasonal weather conditions, and are not dependent upon daylight. But no one of these branches takes men — or women, for that matter — into the outdoor air or sunlight. It is therefore encouraging from the point of view of student health, that well over one-half of all athletic participation appearsto take place in the open air.

B. ATHLETIC INJURIES AND ACCIDENTS: THEIR INCIDENCE AND CAUSES

The second phase of our concern with the hygiene of athletic training in its bearings upon the physical welfare of college students brings up the questions: First, what serious or potentially serious accidents are sustained by the participants in these thirteen major athletic activities? Secondly, what causes these accidents? The answers outlined in the paragraphs that follow are based partly upon figures supplied from records at the twenty-two institutions previously referred to, partly from estimates made by team physicians, partly from a questionnaire addressed to former athletes at five Eastern colleges. The incidence of injury and accident as shown is probably smaller than the actual incidence because many injuries commonly are unrecorded.

The figures themselves, therefore, represent an understatement rather than an exaggeration.

Most physicians will agree that of the injuries that befall athletes, or the conditions that result from them, the following may be regarded as serious or potentially serious : chronic sprains that disable for three weeks or more, dislocations, fractures, concussions, collapse, and internal injuries.[4] Accordingly, these were the injuries concerning which specific data were sought. The figures are presented below in Table II. The periods of participation coincide with the periods during which the injuries were sustained.

TABLE II

Numbers of Cases of Serious Injuries and Accidents

Among 43,923 Participants in Intercollegiate and Intramural Athletics at Twenty-two Representative Colleges

Type of Injury or Accident	Injuries or Accidents to Participants					
	Number Incurred in			Percentage Incurred in		
	Total	*Intercollegiate Athletics*	*Intramural Athletics*	*Total*	*Inter-collegiate*	*Intra-mural*
Chronic sprains disabling for more than three weeks	523	405	118	1.19	.92	.26
Dislocations	318	237	81	.72	.54	.18
Concussions	240	205	35	.55	.47	.08
Fractures	188	153	35	.43	.35	.08
Collapse	30	24	6	.07	.05	.01
Internal Injuries	21	21	0	.05	.05	.00
	1320	1045	275	3.0	2.3	.61

The proportional frequencies of these different types of injuries and accidents may not astonish some persons who are inured to such figures, but the number of such cases may well give serious pause. All told, about three per cent of the men who took part in intercollegiate and intramural athletics during the period of observation sustained serious or potentially serious injuries.

The common notion that football is the most hazardous branch of athletics is abundantly substantiated by Table III, below, in which the thirteen branches are listed in the order of the frequency with which serious or potentially serious injuries or accidents befall contestants, both intercollegiate and intramural.

Although caution is necessary in using these figures for comparisons involving the relative hazards of various branches of athletics, and although it would be both fruitless and absurd to assert that, for example, basketball is one-tenth of one per cent more dangerous than track and field athletics, nevertheless the table affords a valid basis for a rough estimate of the comparative hazardousness of various branches.

[4] Nine cases of *myositis ossificans*, inflammation of a muscle accompanied by bony deposits, were reported, but are not included in the figures of the study.

TABLE III

The Number and Proportion of Serious Injuries Sustained in One Year
By Participants in Thirteen Branches of Intercollegiate and Intramural Athletics at Twenty-two
Colleges (in order of frequency)

Branch of Athletics	Participants			Injuries and Accidents						
					Number			Percentage of Participants		
	Total	Intercol-legiate	Intra-mural	Total	Intercol-legiate	Intra-mural	Total	Intercol-legiate	Intra-mural
Football	5400	2978	2422	649	525	124	12.0	17.6	5.1
Boxing	1435	164	1271	74	47	27	5.1	2.8	2.1
Lacrosse	640	568	72	31	31	0	4.8	4.8	0.0
Soccer	1385	660	725	64	64	0	4.6	4.6	0.0
Wrestling	2380	885	1495	80	66	14	3.3	7.5	0.9
Baseball	6955	1611	5344	166	116	50	2.4	7.2	0.9
Cross-Country	1852	915	937	27	22	5	1.5	2.5	0.5
Ice Hockey	1673	542	1131	23	18	5	1.4	3.3	0.4
Basketball	9626	1436	8190	130	102	28	1.3	7.2	0.3
Track and Field	5871	2559	3312	73	51	22	1.2	2.0	0.7
Rowing	1474	654	820	3	3	0	0.2	0.2	0.0
Swimming	4623	1094	3529	0	0	0	0.0	0.0	0.0
Fencing	609	263	346	0	0	0	0.0	0.0	0.0
Totals	43923	14329	29594	1320	1045	275	3.0	7.3	0.9

C. THE PHYSICAL DANGERS OF FOOTBALL

From the point of view of physical injury, it appears that football is the most
hazardous of college sports. Current opinion is thus confirmed by statistical analysis.

TABLE IV

Serious Injuries Sustained in Football
At Twenty-two Representative Colleges

College	Intercollegiate						Intramural					
	No. of Participants	Fractures, Dislo-cations, Chronic Sprains	Con-cussions	Internal Injuries	Total	Per Cent	No. of Participants	Fractures, Dislo-cations, Chronic Sprains	Con-cussions	Internal Injuries	Total	Per Cent
A	45	21	2	1	24	53.3	–	–	–	–	–	–
B	140	22	3	0	25	17.8	–	–	–	–	–	–
C	100	13	30	6	49	49.0	35	2	0	0	2	5.7
D	70	17	10	0	27	38.5	300	73	13	0	86	28.6
E	146	13	3	0	16	10.9	–	–	–	–	–	–
F	110	10	1	0	11	10.0	–	–	–	–	–	–
G	65	5	4	0	9	13.8	–	–	–	–	–	–
H	115	71	6	2	79	68.6	–	–	–	–	–	–
I	100	12	12	0	24	24.0	–	–	–	–	–	–
J	60	13	3	0	16	26.6	60	1	0	0	1	1.6
K	110	16	17	0	33	30.0	175	0	0	0	0	0.0
L	45	6	3	0	9	20.0	38	0	0	0	0	0.0
M	44	10	3	0	13	29.3	30	0	0	0	0	0.0
N	150	32	10	1	43	28.6	350	6	0	0	6	1.7
O	135	27	4	0	31	22.9	61	0	0	0	0	0.0
P	50	35	1	1	37	74.0	150	1	0	0	1	0.6
Q	343	8	3	0	11	3.2	–	–	–	–	–	–
R	140	5	1	0	6	4.2	–	–	–	–	–	–
S	300	18	6	0	24	8.0	1113	21	7	0	28	2.5
T	265	14	3	0	17	6.4	–	–	–	–	–	–
X	196	8	4	0	12	6.1	110	0	0	0	0	0.0
Z	249	6	3	0	9	3.6	–	–	–	–	–	–
22	2978	382	132	11	525	17.6	2422	104	20	0	124	5.1

But aside from the intrinsic dangers that arise from football as a hard, rough, body-contact game, other considerations shed light upon its relative dangers at various individual colleges.

1. Serious Football Injuries

When the comparative frequencies of a year's football injuries and accidents, serious or potentially serious, are set forth in tabular form by colleges (Table IV, above), a wide range of incidence appears; ranging from three per cent of the players (11 injuries) to no less than 73 per cent (37 injuries).

The median is 13.8 per cent, sustained among the 65 'varsity players at College G, the average 17.6 per cent. Certainly a college at which over 17 per cent (the average percentage) or 13 per cent (the approximate median) of all football players are seriously injured during a football season, may well consider the extent to which the injured men may be the victims of methods of coaching.

Bases of comparison in this matter are further indicated in Table V, below, which summarizes statistics, first, for all of the twenty-two colleges of the study, next for those eleven institutions which have intercollegiate football and intramural football, and finally for the other eleven institutions which do not include football in their intramural athletics, if any.

TABLE V

Range of Proportions of Serious Football Injuries to Participants
Among Twenty-two Representative Institutions

	Highest Percentage	Lowest Percentage	Average Percentage	Median Percentages
All football participants	68.6	3.2	12.0	between 13.8—11.7
Intercollegiate football players	74.0	3.2	17.6	between 22.9—20.0
Intramural football players	28.6	0.6	5.1	0.6

Among Eleven Institutions that play Intercollegiate and Intramural Football

All football participants	37.7	3.6	11.3	14.1
Intercollegiate football players	74.0	6.1	23.3	28.6
Intramural football players	28.6	0.0	5.1	0.6

Among Eleven Institutions that play Intercollegiate Football only

All intercollegiate players	68.6	3.2	13.4	10.9

Table VI, which exhibits the ranges of proportions of serious injuries to participants in thirteen sports, including football, intercollegiate and intramural, provides confirmation of these convictions.

Finally, twenty-one of the twenty-two institutions studied have instituted programs of intramural athletics, although of these colleges only eleven include football in

TABLE VI

Range of Proportions of Serious Injuries to Participants
In Thirteen Sports among Twenty-two Institutions

	Highest Percentage	Lowest Percentage	Average Percentage	Median Percentages
All sports	24.0	0.3	2.9	between 2.9—2.5
Intercollegiate sports	24.0	0.3	2.3	between 2.6—2.5
Intramural sports	9.3	0.07	0.6	0.3

intramural programs. Table VII, below, sets forth the figures at these twenty-one institutions.

TABLE VII

Range of Proportions of Serious Injuries to Participants
In Thirteen Sports among Twenty-one Institutions having Intercollegiate and Intramural Athletic Programs

	Highest Percentage	Lowest Percentage	Average Percentage	Median Percentages
All sports	16.9	0.3	2.8	2.5
Intercollegiate sports	13.7	0.3	6.9	2.5
Intramural sports	9.3	0.07	0.9	0.3

Certain generalizations appear to be justifiable with respect to the figures that now have been presented. It is believed that they are at least approximately true for a much larger number of colleges and universities, of which these twenty-two institutions are typical. But they are applicable to conditions at any individual institution only in the extent to which that individual institution is typical of the group.

From these figures, then, it may be inferred that intercollegiate football is more than three times as hazardous as intramural football, and that twelve out of every hundred football players are injured. On the other hand, intramural football is not more dangerous than boxing and only slightly more dangerous than lacrosse. Fractures, dislocations, and chronic sprains that disabled men for more than three weeks caused almost three-fourths (72 per cent) of the serious injuries in intercollegiate football, and more than four-fifths (83 per cent) of those in intramural football, for such injuries a total of about 75 per cent for all injuries received.

Among total injuries concussions show an incidence of about 25 per cent at intercollegiate football and about 16 per cent at intramural, or more than 23 per cent of the 650 serious injuries sustained. So important is concussion, that further light has been sought concerning it.

2. Concussions

Of all the injuries listed, the most difficult for even the expert and specially trained field physician to diagnose and to treat is concussion. The possible seriousness of concussion is attested by the fact that nearly one-half of the team physicians at the colleges and universities visited in the course of the field work on the hygiene of train-ing have observed that concussion, once suffered severely, tends to recur the more easily.

This observation is borne out by certain data collected by Professor Edgar Fauver, M.D., Director of Physical Education at Wesleyan University, who in 1917 sent ques-tionnaires to 374 former football players of Amherst, Dartmouth, Harvard, Princeton, Wesleyan, and Yale. These materials Dr. Fauver turned over to the Foundation for study. The tendency of concussion, once suffered, to be repeated is attested by Table VIII, which is made up from Professor Fauver's data.

TABLE VIII

Frequency of Concussions Suffered among 376 Former Football Players

Subjects (166)	Number of Concussions Sustained in College Football
134	1 or 2
21	3
2	4
2	5
5	6
1	8
1	12

Of the 376 former football players who replied to Professor Fauver's enquiry, 44.1 per cent had suffered concussion. From Table IV, above, it appears that 132 of 2,978 'varsity players at twenty-two representative institutions, or 4.4 per cent of these 'varsity players, suffered concussion. The frequency of concussion among the 2,422 intramural players as represented in Table IV is much lower, being twenty times or .8 per cent. College C, whose 'varsity football squad of one hundred men suffered thirty concussions, a ratio of 30 per cent, represents the highest incidence, although none of the thirty-five men at College C who played intramural football was con-cussed. College C is somewhat above the average percentage as regards all serious injuries sustained at intercollegiate football, while its incidence of 5.7 per cent of injuries at intramural football is not abnormal.

3. Summary

The figures and percentages that have been adduced concerning athletic injuries and accidents are provisional, and they do not by any means represent hard-and-fast criteria by which the dangers of athletics may be judged. On the other hand, it may be safely said that at a college where three-quarters or even one-quarter of the 'varsity football players receive serious injuries, attention may well be directed to the methods and teaching of the coaches. At those institutions at which the largest numbers engage in intercollegiate and intramural football, it is to be expected that the proportions of serious injuries should be lowest, because, first, the majority of the participants engage in intramural contests, which are far less vigorously prepared for and played than intercollegiate matches, and, secondly, the 'varsity squads being larger, there is less temptation for coaches to overwork their men.

Football, boxing, wrestling, and lacrosse — to mention only a few instances — are hard, vigorous, rough games. Indeed, any game that brings men into physical contact may be so regarded. From such games a higher proportion of physical danger, and therefore of injury, is to be expected than from such sports as golf, tennis, and swimming. At the same time, it is unquestionable that one sport, football, shows an excessively high incidence of injuries, and much the same is true of boxing, lacrosse, soccer, and wrestling (Table III). Five possible causes of such excessive incidence of injuries have been suggested by various team physicians and coaches: first, methods of coaching that ignore hazards to life and limb and look only to the winning of contests; second, the playing of men who are not properly conditioned; third, continuing in a game or a contest players who are overtired; fourth, inadequate medical examination and supervision of athletes; and, last, too rigorous schedules. Some of these matters are of such wide import that they demand detailed treatment.

D. PROBLEMS OF COACHING AND TRAINING

In considering college athletics it is not always recognized that coaching, to be regarded as satisfactory, must safeguard the health of participants, and that, conversely, coaching which does not safeguard the health of participants may, and indeed usually does, result in serious injury to athletes. To organize an extensive program of intramural football matches and then to omit to provide adequate coaching is merely to invite an excessive number of accidents and injuries. This may account for an interesting conflict of current opinion among directors and coaches concerning American football: Although the risk of excessive accidents is generally given as the reason for not including American football in the intramural programs of certain institutions, yet at not a few of those colleges and universities where it does find a place, its dangers are minimized. Moreover, from one Eastern institution, where there is no intercollegiate football and where intramural football is played in gymnasium suits and "sneakers," only two serious accidents have been reported in four years. On the other hand, a university which had organized an extensive program of intramural football, found it necessary to give up its schedule in mid-season because of an excessively high incidence of fractures. Had it been possible to afford satisfactory supervision for the program, the results might have been different.

Professional coaches, many of whom are well-trained men of good judgment, are universally provided in comparatively large numbers for intercollegiate teams and squads. Yet for intramural athletics, which engage more than twice as many students as intercollegiate athletics, the well-trained coaches are at best few and, in a great number of colleges, lacking altogether. Apparently the usual procedure is to provide a director of intramural athletics, who organizes schedules, finds equipment, and incites interest, but who makes little or no attempt to coach or actively to safeguard the welfare and health of participants. Of the twenty-two colleges visited for this phase of the enquiry, at only a few was serious effort made to provide coaching and active supervision for intramural activities, and in those few institutions such matters were largely in the hands of undergraduates of schools for physical directors.

1. The Football Coach and the Physical Welfare of Players

The fact must not be overlooked that among the professional coaches of intercollegiate athletics are some who aim steadfastly to protect the physical health of their charges. Yet, even within the numerical limits of the present study, evidence is to the effect that physical health has often been sacrificed to victory.

One football coach in the season of 1926 administered caffein tablets to his team in the final game against one of the other colleges visited. Another coach stated that as a player he had been given strychnin tablets by his former coach at a third college. On the other hand, a coach at a fourth college averred that "bread pills" are sometimes administered for their psychological effect upon very nervous athletes. At a fifth college, in 1926, a football coach offered to inject with cocaine the painful leg of a player so that the pain should not deter him from entering an important game. In spite of the objection of the team physician at a sixth college, the football coach sent into a game a player whose ankle had been badly sprained and had not yet mended. At the behest of the football coach at a seventh college, over the objection of the team physician, a trainer removed a plaster cast from a player's ankle and sent him into the game. In each of these cases the coach, who in no instance was qualified to take the step, ran counter to medical advice or opinion. In each case he exceeded his authority. In each case the coach, presumably after due consideration, chose deliberately to sacrifice the actual or potential physical welfare of a player or players to the putative exigencies of victory.

2. Extra-Hazardous Elements in Football Tactics and Play

Aside from such deliberate contraventions of common sense, certain technical matters of play, especially at football, although they effectually accomplish their purpose, appear to be generally recognized among coaches as particularly hazardous. Yet in spite of this general recognition, such methods are taught and employed. The result is an unnecessarily large number of injuries. The football coach of one college stated that three severe injuries to players on an opposing eleven resulted directly from the eleven of the second college having been coached in tackling to throw the body across the body of the runner; thus the head of the tackler was placed in an unnecessarily dangerous position in front of the runner instead of behind him. Among football coaches there exists a sharp difference of opinion as to whether recent efforts to "open up the game" by the use of the forward pass, the lateral pass, and other such innovations tend to reduce or to increase the hazards of football. Upon the merits of these opposing views, no judgment is here pronounced; it is sufficient to note the existence of the difference in opinion among practical men.

3. "Tapering-Off"

The desirability of relaxing the rigors of a season's hard training gradually and easily is widely recognized, not alone upon medical grounds but for the sake of the comfort of the athlete. Yet in none of the universities or colleges visited for this phase of our enquiry was there manifest any serious effort to "taper off" or "detrain." After a hard season of rowing, cross-country running, wrestling, or basketball, a tapering-off period is almost unknown. Indeed, at the colleges visited, many team physicians and coaches in these branches felt that detraining was unnecessary, and had never noted serious results from breaking training abruptly after a season. The general neglect of tapering-off is in a measure offset by the fact that some football coaches urge their players, after the season has closed, to participate in basketball or hockey, and to continue into track and baseball. The possible results of such advice are indicated in subsequent discussion. Moreover, in smaller colleges it is not uncommon to find men engaging successively in two, three, or even four branches of athletics. On the other hand, certain football coaches insist that their men shall rest on the conclusion of a schedule; and absolute inactivity on the part of less skilled athletes is common after a season's play.

4. The Trainer

At most of the colleges visited, the position of the trainer lacks definition. At some, the value of his work is questionable. As regards football, it is rare indeed that his functions include the conditioning of the team or squad, the coach confining his own efforts to the specialized technical instruction of his players. The result is that, sometimes gradually, sometimes abruptly, the trainer's duties have developed into supervising the equipment and its care, rendering first aid when the team physician is not available, and, under the team physician's direction, applying massage, baking, and other forms of physiotherapy. Although among trainers an experience of twenty years is not uncommon, yet in few instances has this experience been preceded by any scientific training. As a not infrequent result, tradition, superstition, and prejudice have usurped the place that should be filled by scientific reason and knowledge; the trainer's locker has become a quack cabinet overflowing with proprietary ointments, liniments, and washes, and his quarters a museum of old and new appliances for applying heat, water, light, massage, and electricity. The trainer who, having acquired a foundation of anatomical knowledge, realizes the functions of his calling and knows its boundaries with reference to the work of the team physician, is rare indeed.

5. A Retrospect

Whatever may be said of coaching, American athletic training of to-day has lost a great part of its spectacular element. The days of crucifying the flesh are gone. Although the American college athlete, in contrast with the British, still subjects himself to Spartan discipline, sometimes with a lack of humor that is itself comic, self-inflicted tortures, whether for dehydration or for other purposes, such as are detailed by one college historian concerning the "good old days" of 1873, are unknown.

> "The principal training rule," he writes, "was to reduce every man at least twenty-five pounds in weight regardless of figure, temperament or previous condition. The corpulent man had a comparatively easy time of it, for a few days of vigorous work and sweating would give him a natural figure once more. But it was serious business for the lean fellow to part with twenty-five pounds of adipose. To accomplish it the candidate was bundled up in flannel, and obliged to walk at top speed for several miles in the hot sun, and then run home. He was then covered up in bed, clothes on, and forced to parboil for about a half an hour; after this came the walk and rub down. Of course, the loss of so much perspiration caused a considerable reduction in weight and a feverish thirst. It was natural to drink, but this in adequate quantities would restore the lost weight, and therefore water was prohibited as far as possible. A cup of hot tea for breakfast and supper and a pint of Bass's ale for dinner was the invariable rule, and the fear of dismissal from the training table was sufficient to keep most of the boys to the rack. Sometimes, when the orthodox twenty-five pounds could not be reduced by sweating, purgatives were resorted to, and the result to the victim can readily be imagined. Well remembered are those days of torment. . . . Reduced in adipose until the muscles stood out like those of a Roman gladiator, and the ribs suggested a forty days' fast, parched with thirst, afflicted with boils, which made standing or lying the only endurable position, the days dragged slowly on. But, in spite of all this, twice a day the crew sat down to row, for old —— would not listen to excuses. It seemed like the self-inflicted torture of the Sioux warriors when dancing the snake dance, but pure grit made it possible without a murmur. What determination it took to sit by that cool spring, and hear the waters gurgle by in mocking tones without even taking a swallow."

E. The Medical Supervision of College Athletes

Concerning the medical supervision accorded to the participants in athletics, several topics are pertinent: the duties that the team physician now discharges; the forms employed in medical examinations of athletes and the uses to which the results of examinations are put; the stringency and the laxity of certain current practices; and the physical benefits which can be justly regarded as flowing from college athletics.

1. Functions of the Physician.

Of the twenty-two universities and colleges that were visited, all but one have so far recognized the hazards of intercollegiate football as to provide the services of a team physician, whose presence is assured at each match. Aside from this single requisite, the duties and responsibilities of the team physician vary widely. In only thirteen of the twenty-two colleges was he required to make a medical examination and take a heart history of each participant, even in intercollegiate football, before each season's practice. Seven out of fourteen training tables were under his direction. As regards intramural football, his responsibilities were much lighter. Their extent respecting the other twelve branches of athletics at the twenty-two institutions are exhibited in Table IX, below. To say the least, there is much confusion over the responsibilities of college medical men toward athletics.

TABLE IX

Medical Supervision of College Athletics
At Twenty-two Representative Institutions

Branch of Athletics	Intercollegiate or Intramural	Number of Institutions Involved	Heart History Prerequisite to Practice	Annual Medical Certification Prerequisite to Practice	Doctor Present at Each Contest	Doctor in Charge of Training Table
Football	ic	22	13	13	21	7 out of 14
	im	14	2	3	3	–
Rowing	ic	7	5	3	4	4–6
	im	7	2	3	4	–
Basketball	ic	22	11	10	12	7–14
	im	20	5	3	3	–
Cross-Country	ic	21	10	9	7	6–12
	im	9	1	2	1	–
Track and Field	ic	22	11	10	9	7–14
	im	14	3	4	4	–
Baseball	ic	22	10	9	9	7–14
	im	18	3	3	4	–
Soccer	ic	13	7	5	6	6–11
	im	7	1	1	2	–
Lacrosse	ic	11	6	4	7	5–11
	im	1	0	0	1	–
Boxing	ic	7	4	3	5	3–5
	im	14	4	4	5	–
Wrestling	ic	16	7	7	8	5–10
	im	15	3	3	4	–
Swimming	ic	17	8	7	4	6–11
	im	14	2	2	2	–
Ice Hockey	ic	11	5	4	6	5–6
	im	8	1	1	2	–
Fencing	ic	10	6	2	0	4–7
	im	5	2	2	0	–

Inspection of this table reveals that medical supervision is unevenly distributed over the various branches of college athletics, and that, although it is rigorous as regards intercollegiate football and fairly rigorous as regards intercollegiate basketball and track athletics, it is only passable in other branches of intercollegiate athletics. In respect of intramural athletics, it can be characterized only as lax.

2. Measurements, Health Data, and Research

Apparently, very few of the team physicians interviewed have accomplished much in measuring the results of college athletics upon the physical health of participants. At the time of the study, data regarding the effects of concussion were available or were being compiled at only two of the twenty-two institutions. Accurate records of injuries sustained year by year by participants in the various branches of athletics were also available at only two of the institutions. The effects of collapse had been studied at only four colleges. The heart had received more serious attention. At nine institutions data concerning the effects of athletics upon the heart were available or were being compiled. It is notable that no team physician had observed in the athletes under his care an undue incidence of diseases of the heart, or of nephritis, tuberculosis, or diabetes. Only one stated that he had noted an undue frequency of arterial hypertension among athletes.

Doubtless these facts are partly due to inadequacies of the blank forms used as guides in physical examinations and as repositories of data collected, including medical histories. Many of these blanks are so abbreviated that they provide no place in which to record apparently important items. Conditions which, if discovered and recorded, would disqualify a young man for athletics are not infrequently missed in physical examinations, and the results have sometimes been serious. At one college a student with chronic endocarditis continued as a member of the crew until cardiac decompensation threatened. At a second college a man afflicted with chronic nephritis continued his athletics until death terminated his efforts. At a third institution there are recorded two instances in which men affected by hyperthyroidism took part in athletics until severe symptoms occurred. Doubtless such cases could readily be multiplied to any desired number.

3. Unhealthful Practices and Expedients

Youthful enthusiasm and natural reluctance to be considered a "quitter" complicate the task of medical supervision, but many team physicians countenance the continuation of practices that, in any field of endeavor less tinted with romance, would be considered widely out of accord with present-day tenets and practice.

A few specifications will establish the fact. In cases of concussion sustained at football, a trainer and not a physician often makes the field examination to determine whether the player should resume play. Secondly, freak diets, and diets that, according to principles enumerated in the past, are too heavily weighted with protein, are much in use. Although at this writing the effects of a heavily protein diet are under enquiry with special regard to men engaged in physical activity, nevertheless it should be recalled that the college athlete presumably lives a life of which athletics are only a part. An entire crew was made ill by following orders to drink copiously from pails of cold water in which tea steeped indefinitely. Thirdly, men who are convalescent from fractures or illness are permitted to play in important contests because their services are "needed," even though participation entails a very considerable hazard. One college athlete, severely handicapped by tonsilitis, still was permitted to play basket-ball. A second athlete, a football man with a fractured fibula, was padded and band-aged and allowed to complete a game. Fourthly, wrestlers and others are permitted to "train down" in weight by intensive dehydration rather than by the use of dietary methods. At one institution the captain of the wrestling team, a man of splendid phy-sique who had suffered no previous illness, recently suffered a "nervous breakdown." He had been subjected to a rather severe process of "drying out" on several occasions before he could "make" the weight required for his class of event. Fifthly, the use of the common drinking-cup or water bottle and the common towel is generally suffered to continue without more than formal, ineffectual protest.[5]

4. Athletic Administration and the Health of Athletes

In view of the fact, indicated on many other pages of the present study, that the principal motive in the administration of present-day intercollegiate athletics is financial, it is scarcely astonishing to find that athletic directors and managers have been chosen rather because of their ability to make athletics, especially football, yield profits, to devise schedules that please various contingents, and to procure funds for stadiums, intercollegiate coaching, and other seeming needs, than for their interest in the health of athletes. Although a few of the twenty-two institutions studied have been able to devote football surpluses to intramural athletics, adequate provisions for organizing, equipping, coaching, and supervising are still to be made at practically all of the colleges of the study. The truth is that the physical health of about a third, and probably more, of the student bodies is little affected by athletic programs, — and this in spite of the time-worn cry, "Athletics for all."

On the other hand, the man who is regarded as a promising athlete of intercollegiate fame is permitted and even encouraged to overdo. "Three-sport-men" are by no means rare. Moreover, the attention that such athletic prowess attracts is almost certain to result in the athlete's election to office in several college societies and clubs, which although principally honorary, nevertheless consumes much time and energy. The net

[5] The Harvard Athletic Association is believed to have been the first to introduce the individual drinking-cup for players in foot-ball games. The innovation gave rise to much ignorant chaffing on the part of the spectators. Professor Thomas A. Storey, M.D., in his *Status of Hygiene Programs in Institutions of Higher Education in the United States*, page 99, describes a not uncommon practice: "The author observed a football team this season (1926), the members of which refused a tray of individual drinking-cups offered them by their hosts and, by obvious preference, mopped their grimy, sweaty, and sometimes bloody faces one after another with a single towel soaked and resoaked in a single bucket of water and then sucked the wash-water from the same towel and drank from the rim of the same bucket." The water cart with air pressure invented by Professor Storey for use at Stanford University has proved itself to be one of the most valuable devices for delivering fresh water to athletes on field and track. Accounts of the results of the first experiences of visiting teams with the water cart are entertaining, especially as reflecting a change from an attitude of amused tolerance to enthusiastic enjoyment of drinking the water from the cart, and spraying heads and necks first of the individual players and then of their friends.

result is frequently exhaustion or illness. To sustain through more than two of the three possible athletic seasons of the college year the exhausting and violent activity involved in intercollegiate athletics, to participate in the social activities that so often accompany athletic success, and at the same time to maintain acceptable scholastic standing, constitute a severe test of physical and nervous endurance for any youth. Yet a "two-sport rule," that limits any man's participation to one branch of athletics in its season and to not more than two branches in one year, is enforced at only two of the colleges of the study.

Such facts can easily be overrated in estimating the values and defects of athletics. It is wholesome to consider one or two other aspects of the physical results of college athletics and their administration. At College B, the medical records of 111 men whose athletic success had been rewarded with the right to wear the college letter, were compared with those of an equal number of non-athletes. The results follow in Table X:

TABLE X

Physical Data Concerning "Letter Men" and Non-Athletes
Graduated in 1926 from One College

	Letter Men	Non-Athletes	Excess, Letter Men
Average Age at Entrance	18.88 yrs.	19.85 yrs.	−.97 yrs.
Average Height at Entrance	69.19 ins.	68.99 ins.	.20 ins.
Average Height Senior Year	69.72 ins.	69.43 ins.	.29 ins.
Average Gain in Height during Four Years	.53 ins.	.44 ins.	.09 ins.
Average Weight at Entrance	146.05 lbs.	137.27 lbs.	8.68 lbs.
Average Weight Senior Year	155.99 lbs.	145.07 lbs.	10.92 lbs.
Average Gain in Weight during Four Years	9.94 lbs.	7.80 lbs.	2.14 lbs.
Number of Excuses Issued for Absence from Class on Account of Illness in Four-Year College Period	12.63	12.84	−.21

The care of athletic clothing is a part of the administration of college athletics. At seven of the institutions of the study, cases of "boils" and of "ringworm" were reported by team physicians in abnormal numbers. Having due regard to the origins and nature of these infections, only one inference is possible; namely, that the care of athletic clothing, mats, and shower and locker rooms at these seven institutions is inadequate as regards cleanliness.

Finally, it is a praiseworthy fact that, at all but one of the colleges visited, athletic injuries incurred by athletes on 'varsity squads are considered to be a responsibility of the college athletic association, which provides remedial treatment. Indeed, the provision of such treatment is one of the important functions of the association.

III. CURRENT ATHLETIC PRACTICES IN REPRESENTATIVE HIGH SCHOOLS

Manifestly, a detailed study of the ways and the means by which the health of high school pupils in the United States is protected and fostered through athletics would exceed the bounds of the present phase of the enquiry. It has, however, been possible to examine the regulations that apply to high school athletics in a number of states, to visit several public high schools, and to subject the facts thus gleaned to criticism kindly afforded by a number of authorities whose acquaintance with the field is both wide and detailed.

A. TYPICAL REGULATIONS OF HIGH SCHOOL ATHLETIC ASSOCIATIONS

Owing partly to the influence and standing of the seventeen state departments of physical education, partly to the efforts of interested and public-spirited citizens, the organization of local high school athletic associations into city or state high school athletic associations and the amalgamation of state bodies have provided much opportunity for disseminating information concerning desirable athletic practices in high schools and for safeguarding the health of boys and girls who take part in athletics. Although the constitution and by-laws of the National Federation of State High School Athletic Associations, which consists of some twenty-nine member bodies, is silent upon such matters as the purposes to be served by competition, the selection of suitable athletic events, periods and length of contests, the medical certification of players, the restriction of participants to limited numbers of events or branches of athletics, and similar matters, nevertheless these topics are dealt with in the regulations of not a few city and state high school athletic associations.

For example, ideals concerning purposes and values in high school athletics are emphasized by the Connecticut Interscholastic Athletic Conference, which recommends that "emphasis be placed upon health and physical fitness of all students and that opportunity for play be provided for the mass before the team." The Michigan High School Athletic Association, in a discussion of standards and practices of athletic administration, suggests that the school superintendent "judge the success of those in charge of the athletic program by the conduct of contestants and spectators rather than on the number of games won and lost." Similarly, respecting the attitude of the school coach, the suggestion is made that he regard his work "as an integral part of the school system with a definite contribution to make to the cause of education," and that "all other ends shall be made subservient to the main purpose of [his] profession — education." The New York State Public High School Athletic Association lays down the all-important principle that "athletics are for the boy, not the boy for athletics." On the other hand, the state high school athletic associations of Texas, South Carolina, California, and Illinois practically ignore the necessity of safeguarding student health in athletic programs so far as their constitutions and by-laws are concerned. Moreover, even in those states whose athletic associations attempt to set up regulations or proffer suggestions for safeguarding the health of pupils through athletics a considerable number of the high schools, not being members of the association, conduct their athletics independently of their standards. It is manifestly difficult for any school principal, however high his intentions, to enforce, in interscholastic competition and practice, standards that have not received the sanction of a state high school athletic association or a state department of physical education. Indeed, it appears that only some such central administrative body which is in sympathetic contact with the problems and practices of its component schools provides effectual means of bringing to the attention of principals, coaches, and teachers the measures that should be taken to safeguard pupil health through athletics.

The desirability of imposing certain restrictions upon participation with respect to the physical fitness of boys and girls, and the training that may produce it, finds place in the regulations or recommendations of a number of these associations. For instance, the Public Schools Athletic League of New York City in its "Athletic Rules for High Schools" requires of all pupils who would play football the approval of parents and a medical examination to determine their fitness. Respecting the administration of football the League requires that its member schools shall limit their contests to games played under the League's own restrictions. Schedules of not more than nine games must be submitted to the High School Games Committee and all games must take place on Fridays, Saturdays, or holidays. The first game of any schedule must be played sufficiently late for boys to get into proper physical condition. During October the time of play is only forty minutes. An echo of these provisions is to be found in the regulations of the Alabama High School Athletic Association : "Those taking part in contests should be in fit condition physically. This can only become possible as a result of properly conducted, systematic training. They should be provided with suitable protective clothing when such is needed." The New York State Public High School Athletic Association urges "that coaches shall confine practice periods in basketball to reasonable length and number. Excessive practice is recognized to be harmful to the boy." The hands of school principals are strengthened by the suggestion of the Michigan Association to the effect that a medical examination and the consent of parents be required before a student is allowed to compete. Similarly, this Association suggests that the school business manager or athletic director "make schedules which in addition to being financially advantageous leave the athlete ample time to complete his studies and do not place too great a physical strain upon him." Coaches are to have due regard for the physical condition of their boys, none of whom is to be sent into a contest unless he is "physically fit for the particular activity concerned." In addition to limiting the time of play in football contests, the Public Schools Athletic League of New York City restricts the halves of all basketball games to fifteen minutes, cross-country courses to two and one-half miles, and competition in all swimming events to one event for each boy. The League restricts competition in other branches by similarly stringent rules. The New York State Association provides that contestants in 440-yd, 880-yd, mile, and hurdle races are not to enter another event. "A contestant may elect to compete in any two field events. A contestant may compete in the 100-yd and 220-yd, or the 100-yd or 220-yd and any one field event, or in the 100-yd or 220-yd and one of these distances in a relay."

Not many state high school athletic associations follow the lead of the Southern Section California Interscholastic Federation in requiring that "a physician shall be in attendance at all semi-final and final games."

Respecting contests between junior high schools, some states lay down specific regulations with the intent of safeguarding the health of participants. Of such regulations those of the Michigan High School Athletic Association are very detailed. Pupils are restricted in competition to not more than three major sports in each year, and to not more than one major sport in each season, including football, whether Rugby or soccer, basketball, track athletics, and baseball. Quarters of Rugby football games are limited in length to eight minutes. Inter-city junior high school Rugby football is discouraged. Basketball contests for boys are limited to six-minute quarters with schedules of not more than seven inter-city games and not more than a total of nine games. For girls, quarters in basketball games are six minutes in length and schedules do not exceed five games. Inter-city contests for girls are prohibited. Regulations governing baseball schedules, track and field meetings, swimming contests, and soccer games are equally strict. For instance, it is suggested that from each of the following classes of events three be chosen to make up a program : (1) runs — 50-yd, 100-yd, 120-yd low hurdles, 440-yd relay, each runner covering 110-yds ; (2) field events — putting the 8-pound shot, football forward pass for distance and accuracy, drop kick, punt, place kick ; (3) foul-line shooting from basketball ; (4) climbing ; (5) jumps — broad (running, standing), high, hop-step-jump ; (6) pole vault (outdoor only, with a bamboo pole in a loose pit). No competition in Rugby football is permitted between junior and senior high school teams. Before a student competes in any athletic contest he must have passed an adequate physical examination given by a physician, and it is recommended that such examinations be made at least every month during the time of competition. "Where junior high schools desire to compete in weight divisions for the sake of uniformity, it is desirable that the weights of students be taken during the first month of each semester and certified by the principal. Three divisions are recommended : boys under 105 pounds, boys under 130 pounds, and boys 130 pounds and over."

From the quotations that have just been made it is apparent that no state department of physical education or state high school athletic association need lack information concerning measures that have been adjudged appropriate to the restriction of the character and number of events for boys and girls of high school age. On the other hand, it is not to be supposed that in all states in which such restrictions are set up they are followed with the integrity and the care that they deserve. Since 1919, however, more scrutiny has been given to selecting for high school pupils athletic contests and events that are suitable to their age and development, and the regulations of some interscholastic associations have given adequate attention to such matters, whether upon their own initiative, upon the prompting of state departments of physical education, or in response to the work of the Women's Division of the National Amateur Athletic Federation. These forces have wrought beneficial changes in a situation which threatened at one time to become dangerous.

B. TYPICAL HIGH SCHOOL ATHLETIC PROGRAMS

Visits to several large and several smaller high schools in the Eastern and Middle Western states have served to confirm certain of the observations which have just been made and to suggest further comments upon current athletic practices in their relation to the health of high school boys and girls. These visits and the visits of other qualified observers disclose that some of the high schools of the country have outdistanced colleges and universities in their efforts to control the spirit of "anything to win" and to make athletics contributory to the education and the health of pupils. At the same time, certain evils persist and even threaten the good results thus far obtained.

1. The Work of Physicians in High School Athletics

The physical examinations that are prerequisite to participation in high school athletics are in many instances hurried and inadequate. At a number of schools an entire football squad is examined in about one hour by a physician. Under such conditions thorough examination is impossible. The results of inadequate examinations may seriously impair confidence in the general principle of examination before competition. The fact is that in most high schools the physician has small opportunity to contribute the share which is to be expected of him to the purpose of safeguarding the health of athletes. In only a few high schools is provision made for medical supervision even at football contests, while practically no high school provides medical treatment of athletic injuries at the expense of the school or of its athletic association. One case was noted in which the captain of a school track team "competed against doctors' orders and finished fourth." In such a general situation the excellence of the work of physicians in certain large city high schools is an exceedingly hopeful sign.

2. The "Burning-Out" of High School Athletes

It is a common observation among college coaches that high school athletes have frequently indulged so extensively in athletic competition before reaching college that their physical powers are seriously impaired from the point of view of sport.

Two or three illustrations may indicate the manner in which such overexertion comes about. At one high school during the year 1926–27 an athlete who had already completed a season of football and a season of basketball entered upon a season of track and field competition. On May 2d, in a dual track meeting he won the 100-yd dash, the 220-yd dash, and the broad jump, took second place in the javelin throw, and ran as anchor man in the relay race. One week later, in another meeting, this boy won the 100-yd dash, the 440-yd run, and the broad jump, and again ran as anchor man in the relay race. At a second high school an instructor in physical education made a significant statement to the effect that a "good quarter-mile-er can be used twice a week through the year." For a boy of high school age such performance is excessive. In 1926–27 this high school scheduled no fewer than thirty basketball games, thirty track meetings, and fifteen relay races. A third high school engaged in twenty-five basketball games and twenty-six swimming meets during the same year. Similar instances abound. In the circumstances there is small wonder that high school athletes are so often "burned-out" before entering serious college athletic competition.

3. The Influence of the College upon High School Athletics

It has long been recognized that the influence of the college upon many phases of high school athletics has been and still is far from salutary. High school events are still modeled too closely after college athletics. Not infrequently they are obviously unsuited to the physiological age and ability of high school pupils. The medical reasons that underlie these statements are seldom clearly comprehended. It is well known that in the development of the adolescent each organ has its own "growth inning." The growth inning of the heart, for example, comes late in the period of development. Hence, it follows that the heart of the average fifteen-year-old boy is smaller in proportion to the size of his body than will be the case when he has reached the age of twenty years. Now, it is also well recognized that cross-country runs are a severe test of a man's endurance even at college age. Yet such events still find place in the athletic programs of high schools, although not usually to the extent that they were found at one school where, according to the principal, several cross-country runs were held over a four-mile course. The report of the Joint Committee of the National Education Association and the American Medical Association on Health Problems in Education expresses the conviction that endurance runs and crew races are contra-indicated at high school age.

4. Summary

Enough has perhaps been set down to indicate that although conditions of high school athletics that affect the health of pupils have improved during recent years, they are, to say the least, scarcely ideal. The work of competent heads of state departments of physical education and of certain directors of statewide high school athletic associations is commendable. It is necessary, however, that school boards, by close attention and study, should learn of the conditions that surround athletic competition in the schools under their charge, that principals give more heed to the details of high school athletics, and that more parents should be brought to take an intelligent interest in the athletic activities of their children.

IV. A Few Current Athletic Practices at Representative Private Schools

At the private schools the administration of the athletic program is now generally motivated by a sense of very definite responsibility for the health of the individual boy. This responsibility takes precedence over the desire to defeat opponents. Whether in older schools this condition is the result of ideals *in loco parentis* or of a more independent attitude toward alumni, sports writers, and townsmen, or of a clear comprehension of problems involved on the part of school administrators, the fact nevertheless remains that, as one school physician said, private schools have accomplished "certain reforms in athletic administration while colleges and high schools have been talking about them." Many private schools have made a reality out of the ideal that "athletics are for the boy, not the boy for athletics." Indeed, certain schools have much to offer in the field of the hygiene of athletic training and competition that is novel, practical, and valuable.

This does not mean that all of the private schools of the country have attained to these results. Even in those private schools which are most fortunate in respect to the integrity and the value of their athletic administration, defects may be discovered. At one school visited no medical examination or heart history is made before commencing practice in even such sports as rowing and cross-country running. Five private schools in no way limit the number of events that a boy may enter at a single track meeting, or the number of branches of athletics in which he may compete during the school year. At one school no physician is in attendance at football or other athletic contests. Only a single school was found to practice detraining or tapering-off. At each of three private schools a physician devotes only a part of his time to safeguarding the health of the student body. As a consequence the medical supervision of athletes suffers materially. Despite defects, however, the sums of money available to be devoted to such matters, the control of schoolboys which conditions of private school life afford, and perhaps above all the enlightened attitude of most of the headmasters of such schools have brought about a comparatively wholesome condition.

Conclusion

Because the present discussion has dealt with a more technical aspect of college and school athletics than some of the other chapters of the enquiry, the conclusion is divided into two parts: first, a summary of conditions; secondly, a series of suggestions approved by competent physicians and directors which have grown out of Dr. Smiley's visits to schools and colleges, and many hours of consultation on the part of the advisory group.

I. Summary

There can be no doubt that athletics, if well conducted, may be made to contribute significantly to the physical health of students. Certain facts, however, set forth in the text and in the tables of the present discussion clearly demonstrate that under the present system of conducting athletics too few students receive benefit and too many incur positive harm. Moreover, certain widespread athletic practices mentioned in preceding pages actually jeopardize the physical health of the participants. From the point of view of physical health, present-day athletic practices in American schools, colleges, and universities are open to adverse criticism in several respects.

In the first place, the notion appears to be very widespread that exercise in general and athletics in particular constitute a sort of panacea for all forms of ill-health from flat foot to melancholia. As a matter of fact, athletics should be regarded as somewhat in the nature of a powerful medicament to be prescribed for one individual in one strength, and for another individual in another strength, and for a third individual to be absolutely proscribed. Neither facilities nor incentive for participation in active sports are provided for a large group of students, high school and college, who are physically fit but who do not possess distinguishing qualities or abilities that might make them serious competitors for places on intercollegiate teams.

Secondly, there exist serious deficiencies in the relations of the medical profession to college athletics. All athletic aspirants are not subjected to adequate physical examinations to determine their physical fitness for participation in athletics in general and for any one sport in particular. Moreover, there is a lack of adequate medical care and supervision of athletic participants while engaged actively in training or in competition. Specifically, in case of accident, the team physician and not the trainer should go on the field to determine the nature of the injury and the advisability of continuing play. Upon the basis of a careful medical examination quite irrespective of the supposed exigencies of the situation, a doctor should decide the availability of a player when physical fitness or the effect of training upon him is in doubt. Participation in an excessive number of sports is still permitted and is too frequently urged upon prominent athletes. With regret it must be noted that too commonly the desire for victory still actuates managers, coaches, trainers, and even team physicians themselves.

Thirdly, it cannot be too often repeated that certain unhygienic practices that are common athletic practices would not be tolerated elsewhere. For example, very often the same athletic clothing is worn without washing throughout a four-year period of track competition. It would be difficult to discover a more virulent example of the working of superstition in modern life. The use of the common drinking-cup, water bottle, and sponge in other aspects of daily life than those pertaining to college athletics is now prohibited by law in most states of the Union. General uncleanliness of athletic clothing, locker rooms, and wrestling mats gives rise to such diseases of filth as ringworm and impetigo.

Finally, in high schools schedules of track and field meetings, swimming meets, and basketball games are commonly excessive. In both high schools and private schools athletes are permitted to compete in an excessive number of track and swimming events in the same meet and such participation is frequently urged upon them. Insufficient regard is had to the capabilities and well-being of the individual schoolboy athlete. In all these respects the situation is improving, but much still remains to be done.

II. Suggestions

Upon consideration of the foregoing criticisms, there follow certain suggestions for increasing the benefits to health that might be derived from participation in athletics.

A. The athletic team physician should be considered the key man in the supervision of the hygiene of athletic training and competition and be given full authority, —

1. To decide whether or not the physical condition of a student is such as to make athletic practice or competition justifiable and safe;

2. To direct the medical and surgical care of ill or injured athletes;

3. To direct the diet and in most instances the regimen of athletes in training;

4. To act in advisory capacity in the making of athletic schedules;

5. To act in advisory capacity in the choice of coaches and trainers;

6. To determine what athletic events are within the physiological limits of the athletes under his care. (For instance, the desirability of the six and one-half mile cross-country run and the four-mile crew race for college men, and of four-mile cross-country runs for high school players, may be seriously questioned on medical grounds.)

B. In view of these large responsibilities, the athletic team physician should be given proper equipment and assistance and be very carefully chosen with the following qualifications in mind:

1. He should have a considerable knowledge and appreciation of athletic competition.

2. He should have a medical degree from a Grade A medical school and at least one year's post-graduate surgical training in a hospital or surgical clinic with a large traumatic surgery practice.

3. He should have taken at least a six-weeks' post-graduate course in the hygiene of athletic training and the care and prevention of athletic injuries.[6]

C. Adequate provision should be made in every school, college, or university for a thorough medical examination, health history, and health-habit inventory of every student at least once a year. Upon the basis of this examination each student should be advised as to the type of athletics that he can take up with safety and benefit. The usual six- to ten-minute physical examination, given annually in accordance with many state medical inspection laws without even stripping the child, is inadequate. It is an open question whether the very limited funds now

[6] A few pioneer courses of this type have already been given in certain university summer school sessions for coaches. It is to be hoped that these courses will rapidly and soundly develop both in scope and in number. The character of such a course as defined by one of the early organizers of this type of course is as follows: "An intensive training course under competent direction and involving both theory and practice, for men who are responsible for the medical supervision of competing athletes. This course ought to consist of work along three principal lines, — (1) the minimum medical examination, its objectives and discriminating conclusions, which may serve as a basis for decision and advice regarding permission to compete in various events. This should include also the type of follow-up examination for the purpose of determining fitness to return to practice or competition after an illness or injury and to serve as a basis for a decision in border-line cases, particularly of the adolescent type; (2) the diagnosis and treatment of the various injuries and infections to which competing athletes are subject; (3) the organization and administration of a proper dietary for training tables where they exist."

used for this purpose would not be better spent in providing for each child a thorough physical examination three times during his school life, until the day when funds for more frequent, complete examinations are made available.

D. Participation in some form of athletic sport should be assumed for the vast majority of students, but since the games must be suited to the individual, facilities should be provided for a wide variety of sports. The success attending the policy of "athletics for all" has been such in the few institutions where it has become a reality that its expansion to all educational institutions is unquestionably indicated. At no time, however, should those few be lost sight of who need rest rather than exercise, or medication or operation more than physical activity.

E. Opportunity should be provided for out-of-door games during daylight hours, and without interference with the regular meal hours.

F. The coach should not usually be requested to take care of athletic injuries.

G. A student should be permitted to participate in not more than two training seasons a year.

H. Every effort should be made to match teams with opponents of approximately equal weight and skill, not for the sake of contests without victory, but as a safeguard of health.

I. Although, in order to obtain from athletics thé best values that they afford, each athlete must desire to win, nevertheless the notion that victory is to be achieved, no matter what the cost, must be eliminated if the values of athletics in respect to health are to be conserved and realized.

CHAPTER VIII
THE COACH IN COLLEGE ATHLETICS

BECAUSE over the past thirty-five years no single person connected with athletics has undergone so many changes of function and status as the coach, it is essential to define his fundamental duties. In the present discussion a coach is regarded as a man, or a woman, whose work it is to instruct members of college or university teams and candidates for positions on such teams in the technique and play of one or more branches of athletics.

The definition omits mention of many of the coach's activities which have grown to be regarded in the light of duties, and even qualifications for employment. It disregards questions of his character and influence, his relation to the health and well-being of players, his concern with the finances of athletics, the questions whether he devotes the whole or a part of his time to his work, whether he ought to instruct in more than one branch of athletics, and whether or not he is or should be a member of the faculty. His title, — whether or not he is appointed a director of physical education, or athletics, or intercollegiate contests, — and his salary, are not matters of immediate concern. In short, the definition is stated in its lowest terms.

If it were desirable to classify the coaches from whom information has been sought in the course of the study, it would be possible to divide them into several categories:

The first group would include seasonal coaches whose point of view and, indeed, whose regular occupation are those of the professional athlete and whose employment exemplifies the notion that games must be won without regard to cost. Second come those whole-year appointees who do not enjoy faculty status and who, after the close of their respective seasons of coaching, find their time practically unoccupied. The third group of coaches includes instructors or directors of physical training or physical education who coach in season, and out of season deliver a few lectures on hygiene and many lectures on athletic coaching, and who, except in their season, have so little to do that they welcome the opportunity to break their ennui by speaking tours away from the college campus and by activities which result in the recruiting of athletes for their teams. A fourth category would be composed of those coaching directors whose first concern is their football squads, but who are expected to direct the activities of a department of physical education and to coach or to supervise the coaching of all branches of athletics. Such men, occupied throughout the college year, truly represent full-time employment.[1] Fifth stands the teacher of academic subjects who in season, whether or not for compensation, coaches and supervises athletic teams. Last come the alumni coaches who, with the apparent exception of a single institution (Dalhousie), are paid for their work with or without appointment to a faculty.

I. The Training and Selection of Coaches

Before the actual appointment of a coach is considered, attention must be briefly directed to the origins of some of the coaches.

A. Origins and Training

The day is long past in American college athletics when the character and education of a coach were either taken for granted or disregarded altogether. The facts that football is essentially a college game and that ten years ago it was even more essentially a college game than it is to-day account for football coaches being almost without exception college men. For example, of one hundred and four head football coaches considered in this study, only eighteen are not college graduates. Of the remaining eighty-six, twenty-five are bachelors of arts, twenty-one bachelors of science, five are masters of arts, and an equal number are bachelors of law. The degrees of doctor of medicine, bachelor of physical education, doctor of philosophy, and master of science are represented by two coaches each. There were also found one bachelor of philosophy, a bachelor of commercial science, a doctor of jurisprudence, and a doctor of dental surgery. Eighteen other coaches are graduates of colleges, although their degrees were not ascertained. Without exception these men received their most influential training in football during college days.

In other branches of athletics coaches acquire their technique sometimes as under-

---

[1] Some of these and many of the other matters dealt with in the present chapter are treated in Dr. Harry A. Scott's *Personnel Study of Directors of Physical Education for Men in Colleges and Universities*, Teachers College, Columbia University, Contributions to Education No. 339, 1929. Dr. Scott's approach to his subject differs essentially from that of the present discussion, in that he regards his subject from the point of view of the personnel statistician of physical education, and not from that of the student of college athletics.

graduates, sometimes as employees of amateur athletic clubs and other similar organizations. Indeed, in track and field athletics it is not at all unusual for an intelligent trainer or rubber to advance to the position of a successful coach, whose influence upon young men is decidedly as wholesome as that of his academically trained colleagues. Baseball, however, presents a somewhat different situation. In a great number of cases its coaches, employed on a seasonal basis, are professional players or former professionals whose only relations with colleges have come in the course of their coaching. Despite individual exceptions, this fact explains in part the source of offers to college undergraduates for summer positions as members of professional or semi-professional baseball teams, and likewise tenders from teams in professional leagues. Indeed, some college baseball coaches of teams noted for winning, whose regular faculty status arises from their appointment as members of the teaching staff of the university, play professional baseball during the summer months. The professional influence in the coaching of college and university baseball nines is a powerful factor in undergraduate participation for money in summer baseball.

Some of the more technical aspects of the training of coaches for college posts have not been included in the present study. The number of schools, colleges, and universities that announce courses for the training of coaches or directors of physical education has never been accurately counted, but need not detain us. The work of institutions that pretend to train men for such positions appears to vary widely in quality, nor is it by any means certain that attendance upon a few courses in physical education or coaching offered at a university or at a summer school is earnest of the knowledge and the qualities of character that one who comes into intimate relationships with college undergraduates should possess. On the other hand, the impression was gathered in the course of the enquiry that coaches trained in good schools of physical education have a broader interest in the various branches of athletics than men whose professional preparation has been strictly specialized. The broadly trained man who is put in charge of a department of physical education appears to develop more rapidly a rounded athletic program, whereas the specialist, trained principally as a player, tends to carry specialization into his coaching. None of the dozen outstanding football coaches in the United States to-day has been trained in a school of physical education. It is entirely possible, however, to secure sound graduate training in physical education at a number of universities and colleges (New York University, Oberlin, Rochester, Teachers College Columbia University, Wisconsin, and other institutions). The much-emphasized demand for teachers trained in physical education in high schools and preparatory schools has led to the inauguration of undergraduate courses in the subject at all of the state universities and many privately endowed institutions. Parenthetically, it may be noted that the wisdom of requiring a coach to be a college physician is open to question unless he is more physician than coach.

B. The Selection and Appointment of Coaches

Any vacancy in the coaching staff of an institution that is at all prominent in athletics brings a large number of applications for the position. It is not unusual for as many as forty or fifty applicants to request consideration for appointment as head football coach (Amherst, Beloit, Brown, New York University, Northwestern, Oregon Agricultural College, Wesleyan). No matter whether appointments are to be contractual or seasonal, it is customary for aspirants to point to their records of victory and in some instances to the number of strong athletes whom they can bring with them to their new positions in case they are selected. The instances of this nature that are substantiated by letters available for study have involved principally high school coaches who are endeavoring to enter college athletics, but coaches in college positions are not by any means absent from the general run of such applicants.

1. Authority in the Selection of the Head Football Coach

Of one hundred and one institutions included in this study, at thirty-five selection of the head football coach entails coöperation between various individuals and groups, while at sixty-six the selection is made independently by a single group of individuals. At those colleges where the choice rests upon coöperation, in thirteen cases the president holds the weight of choice, in ten the director of athletics or graduate manager, in nine the alumni, and in three the faculty. These coöperate variously with the president, trustees, faculty, undergraduates, director or graduate manager, alumni, and athletic committees. At the institutions where no coöperation exists in selecting a head football coach the choice rests with the alumni at twelve colleges, the director or graduate manager at the same number, and with the president and the faculty at eleven each. In ten institutions the board of athletic control chooses the head football coach, in six the athletic council, in two the athletic association, and in one each the trustees and the undergraduates. Under such conditions it is not astonishing that so many coaches proffer applications for positions (or "shop round," as the saying is) when vacancies in coaching staffs appear. One prominent coach during the course of the enquiry wrote: "In most colleges coaches owe their jobs to different groups of alumni who are interested primarily in winning athletic contests for their institution." It is to be doubted if so sweeping a generalization is justified. On the other hand, at six institutions (Brown, Dartmouth, Northwestern, Western Maryland, Penn State, Syracuse) there have been indications that it is reasonably accurate as respects some appointments. In at least two of these instances irregularities of procedure accompanied appointment, while at another institution (Columbia) an attempt to name a coach in an irregular way was thwarted by the protests of the institution the coach was expected to leave.

2. Appointment

Once the duly authorized agency has selected the coach at football, the next step is his formal appointment. Of one hundred institutions studied in this connection the coaches at thirty-six are appointed by the trustees, at twenty-eight by the president, and at sixteen by the athletic council or similar body, while at seven institutions a committee on athletics, usually composed principally of alumni, has the deciding voice. The matter is more directly handled at four colleges where the alumni alone make the appointment. Three coaches are appointed by athletic directors, two each by the faculty and the athletic association, and one each by the graduate manager and an executive committee. In forty-six cases the appointment of a coach must be approved by the trustees of the institutions. This action is usually formal; recommendation by a president is seldom contravened by his trustees, although examples to the contrary (Centre, Syracuse, Texas) may be found.

3. Summary

It might be supposed that the status to which a prospective coach is to be appointed would be determined by the agency of selection, — in other words, that if a coach is to be a member of the faculty, the person who actually selects him would likewise be a faculty member or a college administrator. The history of a number of appointments, however, demonstrates that such is not the case. Probably in no other aspect of American academic life is the choosing of a member of the faculty so often affected by the decisions of persons not intimately connected with the administration of the institution.

II. THE STATUS AND TENURE OF COACHES

In the present connection the word "status" connotes the terms upon which the football or other coach is appointed. Tenure involves the length of the period during which the appointment is held, the power of dismissal, and other related matters. More specifically, discussion of the tenure of the coach quickly focuses itself upon the question whether the length of the appointment is dependent upon the number of victories won by the teams coached by the incumbent, and whether, in the event of the team's losing games, pressure is applied for his dismissal or resignation.

A. THE STATUS OF COACHES

The single aspect of the status of coaches that has been most discussed in recent years is thus the employment of coaches as full-time members of the regularly appointed teaching staff of a college or university. Here the term "faculty status" is often used indiscriminately. When applied to an athletic coach it probably implies that he is appointed by the same authority as other members of the teaching staff, with or without term, that his rank is comparable with that of heads of academic departments, professors, or instructors, that his reappointment is to be approached on the same basis, that sabbatical leave of absence is accorded to him just as it is to his colleagues in other departments, and that his post carries with it the right of membership in the deliberative or legislative body of the university or college with vote. In short, the term "faculty status" as used in connection with an athletic coach should mean that no distinctions exist between his status and the status of any academic colleague.[2]

At sixty-three institutions of the present study the head football coach holds a full-time faculty appointment and in respect of the foregoing definitions is to be regarded as possessing faculty status. Of these coaches, fifty-five are members of the department of physical education, while eight are teachers of academic subjects. The difference between the professor of physical education, a part of whose regular duties is the coaching of football and other branches of athletics, and the teacher of an academic subject, like Latin, or economics, or history, who, in addition to his duties, undertakes the coaching of a team or a crew, although obvious, is too often neglected.

A correspondent has enquired, "Is it not true that the past tendency to make specialized coaches over into all-year-round athletic directors is camouflage?" A categorical reply is scarcely warranted by the facts of the enquiry. If the question had dealt with full-time employment in its relation to full-time status and compensation, it could have been in part answered by pointing, on the one hand, to fully occupied coaches at Bowdoin, Coe, University of Chicago, University of Michigan, Ohio State University, and the University of Utah, as contrasted with men at some of the institutions of the Intercollegiate Conference, at certain Southern universities, and at Cornell, University of Missouri, New York University, Oregon Agricultural College, University of Southern California, Stanford, and the Universities of Texas and Washington. It is difficult to understand how coaching in one or two branches of athletics can be regarded as full-time service, especially when a number of coaches employed on a non-academic basis (Carnegie Institute of Technology, Dartmouth, Princeton) carry on intensive activities in business and other fields besides their work as coaches. From many points of view, the substitution of the academic costume for the football suit represents rather a yielding on the part of university authorities to demands made by influential and skilful coaches, whose services they fear to lose, than a desire to recognize physical education, whether or not as embodied in the person of a particular coach, as an appropriate subject for academic instruction and research.

Not all coaches or directors of physical education who are so fortunate as to possess faculty status live up to it. The activities of some in spying out, recruiting, and subsidizing athletes, their attempts to evade or to best both the letter and the spirit of rules, in the past their indulgence in unworthy associations, and the apparent absence

---

[2] The *Biennial Survey of Higher Education* (1922–24), issued as a Bulletin of the Bureau of Education in 1926, contains the following passage: "Abolition of professional coaches and substitution of faculty coaches in their place has received great impetus from its approval by representatives of twelve New York and New England colleges in 1922. This plan has been adopted by Union, Wesleyan, Bates, Trinity, and Hamilton, and submitted for consideration to Amherst, Bowdoin, Tufts, Middlebury, and Colby." Apparently no distinction is here made between the coach who takes faculty rank as a professor of physical education (Amherst, Bowdoin) and the full-time teacher of academic subjects who, in addition to his regular duties, undertakes also the coaching of athletic teams (Bates, Tufts). The difference between these two types of appointee involves very great distinctions, some of which are pointed out in the course of the present discussion.

of any code of honor among some of them, all combine to qualify the success of the attempt to transform coaching specialists into academic teachers.

On the other hand, the bestowal of academic status upon coaches appears to be a practical result of the essentially sound conviction that a coach should be a man whom the college is ready to welcome as a member of its faculty. Thus the motive behind the formula of faculty status for coaches is good. The practical results of the formula, however, are not always happy, not alone on the grounds of morals and influence, but also with respect to the coach's own comfort and tenure. Faculty status, it will be shown on subsequent pages, seldom carries with it so great a return in money as the coach could secure "elsewhere." It has not assured long tenure, nor has it protected him against the demands of alumni for victory. Finally, it has not guaranteed the coach's impeccability in matters of inducements and subsidizing. The best test of the value of faculty status as a formula to be used in solving the problems of athletic administration is this : Does faculty status assure to an institution scholastic standards and aims in policy and in education in which the institution may take pride ? Doubtless at some colleges the answer is in the affirmative. They are to be congratulated. At many others, however, the elevation of the coach to membership in the academic family has resulted merely in covering insincerity and dishonesty with the trappings of scholarship to the detriment of both learning and sport. Not every director of physical education should coach the football team, nor should every football coach be a professor of physical education.

Of the forty-one institutions where the football coach does not enjoy faculty status, seven employ full-time men in this capacity and thirty-four seasonal or part-time men, while five contract with the coach to take charge of other branches of athletics.[3] Divided authority and responsibility in football coaching has not worked well where the experiment has been tried (Oregon Agricultural College, Rutgers). At two institutions (North Carolina, Ohio Wesleyan) it appears that the head football coach has assumed and maintained an authority which was vested theoretically in a director of physical education. Many of these difficulties might be resolved, so far as coaches are concerned, if a line were drawn distinctly between intramural athletics with their concern for health and hygiene on the one hand, and, on the other, intercollegiate athletics with their spectacular and public panoply.

Thus, appointment as a member of a faculty as contrasted with employment on a part-time or seasonal basis confers no mystical assurance that the work of any coach shall "succeed" in developing habits of honesty, uprightness, courage, or self-reliance among the young men entrusted to his care. Of all the field of higher education, physical education shows the largest number of members with the rank of professor who have

---

[3] The late Dr. Frank A. March of Lafayette expressed the opinion that it is impossible to secure a satisfactory all-year-round coach for a number of branches of athletics, because a man who can coach football seldom succeeds as coach in other branches.

only the bachelor's degree or no degree whatever. In short, faculty status of itself guarantees to the institution nothing whatsoever with respect to the ability and character of the coach.

B. The Tenure of Coaches

In the present connection the word "tenure" is used to refer to the length of time during which a coach holds his position at one institution. In the Midwest, Southwest, and South the tenure of the head coach at football is approaching the permanent. There are indications also that in track athletics and in other branches tenure of coaches the country over is becoming longer. Owing principally to the employment of professional league players as baseball coaches, the tenure in this branch of athletics was at one time the least permanent of all. The changes which recent years have wrought are illustrated at the University of Chicago, Columbia, Holy Cross College, Princeton, University of Texas, and Yale. Two elements of tenure are important for both coach and institution: its length, and the causes assigned for termination of service.

1. Length of Tenure

All told, the enquiry has dealt with 272 coaches whose service has totaled 948 years in separate institutions. On the average the stay amounted to 3.49 years, while the median tenure was two years. Of the 82 head football coaches who held their positions at institutions of the study, the total service years at these institutions were 387, with an average of 4.72 years and a median of three years. Such facts as these, and others to follow, indicate that the length of the tenure of the coach, and especially of the head coach at football, is increasing.

Among these 82 coaches one had a tenure of thirty years, two of twenty-five years, three of ten years, one of eight years, three of seven, thirteen of three, nineteen of two years, and twenty-two of one year.

From sixty-four colleges and universities data were gathered concerning the number of head football coaches who had served the individual institutions during the past ten years. Thirteen institutions had one coach during that period, while eight had two coaches, sixteen had three, twelve had four, and one each had employed eight and nine coaches respectively. The average number of coaches so employed during the ten years was 3.34.

a. *The Relation between Tenure and Salary*

No very clear relationship exists between length of tenure and the salary received by head football coaches, although in the higher salary groups a few tendencies become fairly well defined. Seven coaches of the study received $10,000 or more as annual salary. Of these, three, at the time of the field visit, had been in office two years or less, while the other four had enjoyed tenures respectively of three, three and one-half, ten, and fifteen years. Thus the coaches who at the time of the field visits were enjoying the highest salaries for their services at football had had an average tenure of 5.23

years. The two men with the longest service averaged 12.5 years, while the five with the shortest service averaged 2.45 years.

The average salary of the fourteen coaches who, at the time of the visits to their respective institutions, had had ten or more years of tenure was $5,928. In this group the highest salary was $10,000, the lowest $3,500. Of these fourteen men, five had served twenty years or more in the same position. Their average salary was $6,900. The average salary of the remainder of the group, who, having discharged their present duties during from ten to fifteen years, had an average service of 12.1 years (the median service being twelve years), was $6,389, with their median salary $6,000. All of the salaries of $10,000 or more were paid by institutions having more than one thousand students eligible for participation in intercollegiate contests.

These facts disclose no special relation between coaches' salaries and length of their tenure. The size of the university or college is a more important factor in determining the salary paid.

b. *Tenure, Salary, and Faculty Status*

Among the group of fourteen coaches having to their credit ten or more years of service in the same position, eight enjoyed faculty status. Of the remaining six who were not members of faculties, three were seasonal appointees without formal duties after the football season, although the services of one or two were utilized in checking the academic standing of football players. Two were full-time appointees and one was a part-time appointee who, however, coached another branch of athletics in season. Thus, even with respect to those fourteen coaches who have filled the same position for upwards of ten years, no significant relation exists between tenure, salary, and status as a member of a faculty. For men of shorter tenure, the fact that the notion of faculty status has been in widespread operation for a comparatively short period of years has rendered inconclusive any attempts to generalize.

2. Causes Assigned for Termination of Service

In twenty-two instances of recent years in which head coaches at football have terminated their service at one institution to go to another, each migration involved the receipt of a higher salary. A number of such transfers were studied in detail. The causes assigned varied widely; indeed, in not a few cases it was impossible to verify or coördinate the reasons given by the two parties to the change. An attempt to classify the causes of migration beyond the offer of a higher salary has resulted in discovering only two specific reasons: first, lack of coöperation, and secondly, the loss of games.

a. *Coöperation as a Factor in the Migration of Coaches*

In a number of instances the principal factors which combined to end the tenure of a coach may be grouped together in the single statement, "He did not fit." The verdict implies an element of injustice to all coaches, inasmuch as further enquiry revealed the fact that in a few instances it was employed to cloak specific breaches of manners or morals. At two institutions coaches who were plainly unsuited to their positions were dispensed with after long and devious negotiations and intrigue. It is not too much to say that tenure frequently depends upon coöperation between the coach and other authorities. One prominent coach even went so far as to express his coöperative attitude in respect of certain abuses with which he claimed to be out of sympathy by stating that he did not wish to "bat out his own brains" by leading a reform. A beneficent compromise of a policy with the facts of a situation in football coaching is well illustrated by the coöperation existing at McGill University. By and large, the reason most commonly alleged for the resignation or dismissal of football coaches has been stated somewhat vaguely to be "temperament," the fact that they have not fitted the requirements of their positions, or that they could not handle their men successfully.

b. *Tenure in Relation to Victory*

At eighty-three different institutions of the study various coaches, presidents, deans, faculty members, and others were asked the question: "Is the tenure of the coach dependent here upon his producing winning teams?" When recent football history at any institution clearly led to the conclusion that victory was or was not essential to tenure, the facts of the case were given more weight in the study than the replies of officers, students, and alumni.

Of the replies, those at thirty-three institutions were affirmative and forty-six were negative, while conflicting opinions were expressed at four institutions. Six coaches, four presidents, four directors of physical education, and one faculty member were among those who replied in the affirmative. In nine instances action promptly following losing seasons at football proved conclusively that the tenure of the coach depended upon victory.

As regards the forty-six negative replies, six came from faculty members, nine from presidents or deans, five from coaches, and eight from directors or graduate managers, while six others were corroborated or inferred unmistakably from the evidences of recent official action. In four cases reservations accompanied answers in the negative. There were conflicts of opinion: in two instances coaches believed that tenure depended upon producing a victorious eleven, while their presidents denied it. In one instance the situation was reversed. In another, the alumni regarded tenure as dependent upon victory, while the college president did not. The athletic authorities at Cornell, Harvard, and Iowa have proved through action that victory is not essential to tenure. In a number of other cases of coaches' dismissal after losing seasons at football it is difficult to be certain that in any one instance a coach is dismissed or not reappointed on these grounds. Certainly, losing teams have been factors in not a few cases. One coach went so far as to state frankly that the subsidizing of athletes is essential if a coach's tenure depends upon victory. In the South it is not uncommonly regarded as unfair to coaches to check up on the scholastic standing of football players in mid-season because of the possibility of interfering with combinations for play through the removal of ineligible players and thus impairing the chances of the team and hence the tenure of the coach.

Comparing the foregoing evidence with what could be learned of conditions in the past, we believe that the tenure of the football coach is coming less and less to depend upon victory. The standard desired at present appears to be a "fair winning average" over a period of from five to ten years. Such an aggregate is being achieved through the operation of forces working from two directions: coaches, on their side, are demanding longer contracts, and institutions, on the other, are becoming less and less subject to the pressure for victory from a few rabid enthusiasts. And yet one striking injustice to the coach remains: Even though victory be not so essential to tenure as it was in the past, nevertheless if a coach believes it to be thus essential, the result of defeat upon his peace of mind is equally detrimental.

In any case, from the point of view of the coach, academic status and appointment to membership in a faculty, — not to mention even a professorship of physical education, — do not protect a coach's tenure when teams cease to win and the college administrator charged with the shaping of the institution's athletic policy wavers in his support. Nor, from the point of view of the institution, is "a seat on the faculty" a guarantee of the good character of the coach, his contentment with his post and its duties, or satisfactory teaching. Some time ago it was suggested that an endowment from the income of which a football or other coach might be paid would offer the best solution of all questions touching tenure and salary of coaches.

III. The Coach's Salary

During the enquiry many requests were received for information concerning the salaries paid to coaches. Doubtless these questions reflected not alone a common curiosity and a desire on the part of college administrators to conform to general practice, but also the notion that no coach ought to receive a higher salary than a full professor at the same institution. Accordingly, data were collected from about one hundred universities and colleges concerning the salaries paid to deans, the maximum salaries paid to full professors, the compensation of the head football coach, and the pay of the next highest paid coach. A few inferences concerning the maximum salaries of professors have appeared in the Twenty-third Annual Report of this Foundation (1928). All of the figures represent maximum salaries being paid at the time of the field visits to the respective institutions.

A. The Salary of the Head Football Coach in Relation to Other Salaries

At over one hundred universities and colleges the highest salary paid to a dean was $15,000, the median $6,000, the average $6,409. The highest-paid full professor received a salary of $12,000, while the median salary among such professors was $5,000 and the average $5,158. Among eighty-three directors of physical education or graduate managers, the highest salary was $14,000, the lowest $1,000 for part-time work, the median $4,800, and the average $5,095. Of ninety-six head football coaches, the highest paid drew a salary of $14,000, and the lowest $1,800, while the median salary was $6,000 and the average $6,107.

At ten colleges the salary of the head coach in football was paid partly by the athletic association or department and partly by the institution. Under these circumstances the highest pay was $14,000, the lowest $3,500, the median $7,500, and the average $7,700. The highest amount paid by an athletic association as its share of the total compensation of the head football coach was $9,500, the lowest amount $700, the median $3,151, and the average $4,115. The highest amount contributed by a college to such a divided salary was $5,000, the lowest $2,500, the median $3,449, the average $3,544. It appears, therefore, to be the general rule that, on the average, when the salary of the head football coach is paid partly by the athletic department or the athletic association and partly by the college, the athletic association or department bears the brunt of the burden. Apparently, in some instances the college has found the divided salary a somewhat inexpensive means of securing a high-priced coach for a comparatively small expenditure of the institution's own funds.

A further division of head football coaches' salaries on the basis of full-time or seasonal appointment involves fifty-nine coaches employed on a full-time basis and twenty-six on a seasonal basis. Of the fifty-nine full-time coaches the athletic association, which is the employer in nineteen cases, paid to the highest-paid $12,000, to the lowest-paid $1,800, to the median man $6,000, and on the average $6,468. In forty cases the institution paid the full-time football coach, and almost universally he enjoyed faculty status; the highest salary was $12,000, the lowest $2,300, the median $4,778, the average $5,058. A comparison of these average salaries of full-time coaches, — $6,466 when paid by the athletic association and $5,058 when paid by the college, — affords to the statistically minded an opportunity to infer that to the full-time football coach academic status costs, on the average, about $1,400 a year, or about 27.6 per cent of the salary that he receives from his college.

With respect to twenty-six seasonal head coaches at football, twenty-one were paid by the athletic association or department and five out of institutional funds. Among the twenty-one individuals of the first group, the highest salary was $12,000, the lowest $2,500, the median $6,667, and the average $6,822. That college administrations drive closer bargains with seasonal coaches than athletic associations may be inferred from the five salaries of men paid from institutional funds; of which the highest is $8,000, the lowest $3,500, the median $6,000, and the average $5,500. Thus the seasonal coach at football appears to be appreciably better paid than the full-time man, although if employed by the athletic association his maximum salary is the same as that of his full-time colleague. His minimum salary is the larger by nearly 50 per cent, his median salary by about 40 per cent, and the average salary for his group by perhaps 15 per cent. The athletic department or association pays about 24 per cent more for a seasonal coach than the college administration pays, and about 28 per cent more for a full-time man. From the point of view of expenditure, the institution is apparently the more economical employer.

In a consideration of the salaries of head football coaches as compared with the maximum salaries paid to full professors, a division suggests itself on the basis of the "large" and the "small" college. The number of institutions to be considered is reduced to ninety, all told, by the omission of Catholic institutions not employing lay teachers in one or more of the posts under observation and institutions for which any one of the sets of figures were uncertain or incomplete. For this comparison, then, the "small" college was defined as a university or a college in which the students eligible to compete in intercollegiate athletics numbered fewer than one thousand; a "large" college, as a college or a university in which those eligible for intercollegiate competition were more than one thousand in number.

At the thirty-two small colleges, then, the highest-paid professor received a salary of $6,000, while the lowest-paid received a maximum of $1,800. The median maximum salary was $3,700 and the average maximum salary $3,840. Although the minimum salary paid to a head football coach at an institution of this group was the same as the lowest maximum compensation received by a full professor, namely, $1,800, the highest paid football coach received $8,000, or $2,000 more than the highest-paid full professor, which exceeds the maximum salary for a dean at a small college by about $500. On the average, the head coach for football received $4,163, or $383 more than the highest-paid full professor, while the coaches' median salary was $3,600, as contrasted with the median maximum salary of $3,700 paid to a full professor.

At fifty-eight large colleges, the head football coach was still more highly paid. His highest maximum salary was $14,000, or $2,000 more than the maximum paid to a full professor, but his lowest minimum salary, — at a Southern institution where the head football coach engages in business and regards coaching as an avocation, — was only $2,000, or $1,000 less than the minimum salary of the full professors in the highest-paid group. The median and average salaries presented even more significant contrasts. For the professors the median maximum salary was $6,000; for the coaches, $6,500. The average maximum salary of the highest-paid full professors at these large colleges was $6,315; of the head football coaches, $6,926, — a difference in favor of the coaches averaging $611.

It is possible that, in general, the smaller colleges have been more successful than the larger in limiting the salaries of their head football coaches. Certainly, on the whole, the head football coach at a small college appears to be paid on a scale more nearly comparable to that of a professor than he is at a large college. Again it should be emphasized that the salaries of professors here dealt with are maxima. Consequently the average salary for all full professors at all of the institutions from which data were obtained would be much lower than figures herein set forth. Possibly also college administrators at smaller institutions are able to keep a steadier hand upon athletic expenditures, while larger institutions have a greater income from which to pay larger salaries to the men who create it. Elsewhere in the study it is indicated that the larger the sums that are available for athletics, the more will be spent upon athletics. Thus extravagance has grown by what it fed on.

B. The Salaries of Other Coaches

The salary of the head football coach touches only one phase of the matter; the salaries of coaches in other branches received consideration. Attention was directed principally to the coach to whom the second highest salary was paid. Upon this subject data were available for eighty colleges. For convenience, the coach who drew the second highest salary for coaching another branch of intercollegiate athletics than football will be referred to as the "second" coach.

The highest salary paid to such a coach, in rowing, was $10,000, the lowest $225, the median $3,500, and the average $4,609. These salaries, as a group, are considerably below the corresponding figures for maximum compensation paid to professors. When the institutions are divided into two groups, "small" colleges and "large" colleges, the results obtained are as follows:

At twenty-five "small" colleges, the highest salary paid to a "second" coach was $5,000, which was paid to a coach in track and field athletics. The lowest was $275, which represents a part-time appointment. If it be supposed that the part-time basis on which this salary was paid invalidates the figures, it must be recalled that this compensation represents the whole sum paid at the institution for coaching all work in one branch of intercollegiate athletics; the fact that the post does not involve sufficient work to justify a higher salary or a full-time appointment is somewhat beside the point. Of these salaries, the median is $2,800 and the average is $2,563. One "second" coach received a higher salary than the head football coach at the same institution, and one the same salary.

At fifty-five "large" colleges, three "second" coaches received a larger salary than the head football coaches at their respective institutions, and four received the same compensation. The highest salary of a "second" coach was $10,000, paid to a rowing coach. The lowest was $225, paid to a part-time football coach. The median salary was $3,756, and the average of eighty such salaries is $5,539. Thus, the "second" coaches at "large" colleges are much the more highly paid, — indeed, they receive on the average much more than double the salaries of their colleagues in the "smaller" colleges. The relations of their salaries to those of full professors may be understood by comparing the foregoing figures with those set down in the preceding section.

C. Notes on the Salaries of Coaches

Although a degree of caution is necessary in making or accepting the statement, nevertheless the tendency to increase the salaries of head football coaches is well defined. Probably the notion, expressed by President Kinley of Illinois, President Von Klein Schmid of Southern California, and Professor Charles W. Kennedy of Princeton, that such salaries must be governed by laws of supply and demand is responsible for the tendency. Expressions of contrary opinion embodied in the Harvard-Yale-Princeton agreement, in the rules of the Rocky Mountain Conference, and convention in the Intercollegiate Conference, — not to place too much stress upon the practice at Dartmouth, — serve but to test the general rule. It is noteworthy that the salary of one head football coach (Utah) was increased partly because of a desire to retain his services and thus to hold the interest of a public with whom he was popular during a campaign for a new stadium. Moreover, in three instances business men who consider football coaching as their avocation are not above accepting or even demanding increases of salary as head football coach.

From detailed study of the incidents that have led to the migration of coaches and from many other trustworthy facts, the inference is inescapable that the responsibility for the size of the salaries paid to football coaches rests finally with the college president. He it is who has bid, or through his permissive attitude has allowed others to bid, for the services of expert coaches. On the other hand, a football coach who is at once a gentleman, an expert in his calling, and a wholesome influence among his players is worthy of his hire. The problem is not so much to diminish coaches' salaries as to diminish the need for paying high salaries to coaches.

A word must be said concerning the annual sums lavished upon coaching and training at numerous institutions. Selected figures for such expenditures at eight universities (Harvard, Iowa, Ohio State, New York University, Pennsylvania, University of Washington, Wisconsin, Yale) have run as high as $84,600 for all branches and $41,800 for 'varsity and freshman football. In the group the lowest figure for football coaching alone is $15,000; for all branches, $35,400. At an interest rate of 4.75 per cent, $84,600 represents the income from about $1,700,000, and $41,800 the return from $880,000. These capital sums are greater than the endowments of many American colleges. Certainly $84,600, or $41,800, or $35,400 is in excess of the annual amounts spent for instruction in a great number of university and college departments. Such expenditures for coaching and training clearly reflect a distorted scale of academic and athletic values.

IV. THE WORK OF THE COACH

The reader who desires a complete discussion of the duties and activities of the coach is referred to some of the excellent treatises on such matters respecting numerous branches of athletics. The present section is concerned with few of the technical aspects of coaching. A coach is in every sense of the term a specialist, and, moreover, a specialist upon whose shoulders, willing or reluctant as the case may be, the past thirty years have placed an increasingly complicated burden. His duties and responsibilities are first to be examined, and then a few notes will be set forth concerning methods of coaching.

A. OFFICIAL AND OTHER DUTIES

Upon whatever basis a coach may be retained, the variety of his duties, official and otherwise, is comparable in the field of university education only with that of the college president.

1. Responsibilities

Inasmuch as the functions of the coach are rarely defined with clarity in his own mind or in that of his employer, except in so far as they are indicated by numerous clichés that have grown threadbare from overuse, it will be fruitful to examine only a few of the responsibilities that cluster about him. Professor Coleman R. Griffith was not the first to note that in most branches of athletics coaches now control the games and contests. It is seldom the duty of the coach to arouse interest in athletics, inter-collegiate or intramural, unless he serves also as director of physical education. So far as the game itself is concerned, the principal work of the coach relates almost univer-sally to strategy. Indeed, college football, baseball, and, not infrequently, basketball teams are acknowledged to be highly trained groups of automata that execute the will of their coaches. For example, the captain of the football team at a large Eastern university stated that he regarded the captaincy merely as an honor and himself as a figurehead with respect to the leadership of the team. At another Eastern institution it was indicated that in baseball the captain is of even less importance than in football because of the intricacy of both strategy and tactics. At a third institution (Prince-ton), however, the captain of the football team has such part in the direction of play as the team desires. At colleges like Amherst and Oberlin, the purpose of the coaches has been to train undergraduates not alone in strategy but in the initiative of tactics and judgment. Although at one Canadian university (McGill) the football coach occupies a spectator's seat at contests, a telephone connects him with the players' bench on the side lines.

The fact of the matter seems to be that, the country over, a college football or base-ball player has opportunity to exhibit little more initiative than a chessman. The exi-gencies of the game forbid original thinking. Not many coaches understand what it means to let their men work out their own plays and conduct their own teams accord-ingly. It is a commonplace of adverse criticism of present-day coaching methods that many coaches tend to occupy too much of their men's time with fundamentals, too little with playing the game under conditions of contest. In general, college football players grumble at weekday games; they live through drill and "skull practice" and save their energies, both physical and nervous, for the Saturday contest. Yet, if ath-letics are to be "educational," the player must be taught to do his own thinking. In every branch of athletics the strategy of the game should not be beyond the capacity of the alertly-minded undergraduate. As matters now stand, no branch owes even a vestige of its strategy to the undergraduates engaged. Such matters are the affair of the coach.

Aside from the strategy and most of the tactics of the branches of athletics, the coach has other responsibilities. In the fields of student health and physical develop-ment he has few, unless his duties are combined with those of the director of physical education. He is usually concerned with the use of equipment and accommodations for his teams, seldom with their provision. A Southern coach, who undeniably pampers his athletes, has objected more than once to attempts of the director of athletics to check expenditure upon luxuries of travel; the possibility that any member of this particular football team should occupy an upper berth was to this coach both abhorrent and pathetic. In general, the notion seems to be that no device that may contribute to the protection and the comfort of players should be withheld. The tenet is often carried rather far in securing specially fitted and individually made braces, pads, and other pieces of equipment, especially for football players in the backfield. Indeed, a well-known seller of athletic equipment stated that he was shocked at the extravagance in the use of football supplies at one large Eastern university.

With schedules of games the coach usually is not directly or initially concerned, although that institution is rare at which he is not consulted during the period when schedules are in the making. Most coaches naturally desire that members of their teams or squad shall stand well scholastically, — because high standing implies eligible players. After an athlete has played his allotted number of years, his academic standing fails to interest the coach. At a number of universities (Cornell, Harvard, New York University, Princeton, Purdue) the coaches have been praised for their efforts during off seasons, sometimes at the behest of college administrators, to spur athletes to better scholastic performance. On the other hand, in at least one instance the duties of football coaches appear to include something very like recruiting. Men who are wisely employed upon a full-time basis for physical education have little opportunity for such activities as these.

With respect to the inculcation of moral principles and qualities, most coaches, when questioned concerning the matter, place upon it a very strong emphasis, although doubt has frequently been expressed if the coach in any sport thinks so seriously of this phase of his work as a dean, to whom rather than to the teacher of academic subjects his responsibility relates him. In this connection it may well be noted that at Harvard and Yale members of the coaching staffs meet periodically for luncheon at a club, to the mutual advantage not alone of themselves but apparently of all concerned in their work. The unostentatious nature of the qualities of sportsmanship at these two institutions is due in part to the relations thus established. Discussion of the coach's responsibility in securing candidates for athletic teams and in other extramural relationships is for the present postponed. The president of one college commended his football coach because of his ability to establish and maintain the friendly interest of the alumni in the institution. At three larger universities, the activities of single coaches or of whole staffs have earned the gratitude of administrators in this particular. At most of the institutions of the Intercollegiate Conference the duties of the head football coach, after the conclusion of his season, embrace speaking at luncheons, high school assemblies, clubs of many kinds, and other engagements of a similar nature.

In short, the responsibility of the coach is much divided. A third of a century ago it was far simpler than it is to-day. Then he was concerned only with the specifically technical aspects of his duties ; now academic administrators are requiring of him a far wider activity and interest.

2. The Occupation of the Coach

It has been noted that at baseball the coach not infrequently is a professional player hired for a season to coach a college team. Instruction in basketball and in track and field athletics is often secured from members of departments of physical education or from others employed upon a full-time basis. In football, however, where a contrary condition exists, it is due principally to the notion that status as a member of a faculty is desirable from the point of view of both coach and institution.

An examination of the occupations of one hundred and four head football coaches, aside from their regular coaching duties, showed that sixty-seven (64 per cent) had no vocation other than football coaching, although eight others (7 per cent) taught academic subjects. Not a few of the sixty-seven coaches enjoyed teaching assignments in courses or schools that deal with football coaching during the regular or summer sessions (Iowa, Michigan, Wisconsin), and many others instructed in other branches of athletics or served as directors of physical education.

Of the remaining thirty-seven coaches who had other occupations than football, fifteen engaged in business. Three of the business men were connected with manufacturing, two with retail merchandizing, two with selling insurance, and one each with real estate, the sale of coal, publishing, and the activities of a local chamber of commerce. In seven instances the branch of business was not ascertained. In addition, three coaches were occupied with the law, as practitioner or judge, one with medicine, one with school teaching, one with dentistry and dental teaching, and one as a clergyman and social worker. For all of these thirty-seven men presumably the coaching of football was an avocation. Yet partisans of victory (Ohio State) have objected to one head football coach's instructing in a medical school, on the ground that his duties as teacher left him insufficient time to devote to the game and to his men. A second head coach (New York University) is engaged on an all-year-round basis with no other assignments than football, so that he may not be distracted from the duties which his position involves.

B. Notes on Methods of Coaching

Although the following notes on a few of the most discussed aspects of coaching deal principally with football, it is probable that not dissimilar situations and problems arise with respect to other branches of athletics. It is possible to commend, as regards individual branches, coaching systems at certain universities and colleges where academic instructors coach teams : Amherst, Bates, Colorado, Hobart, Massachusetts Institute of Technology, Pittsburgh, Queen's, Tufts.

1. Discipline and Severity of Method

An enquiry into the severity of discipline and method of most of the one hundred and four football coaches of the study prompts to observations concerning the amount of time that is spent upon football and the way in which that time is used.

The Intercollegiate Conference limits the duration of daily football practice to two hours. At one member institution (Wisconsin) athletes expressed gratitude to the Conference for this limitation and stated that they spent from three to four hours upon practice, if dressing be included. Comparable conditions were found at a rather large number of universities and colleges. At the height of the football season Colgate players have been required to devote as much as eight hours a day, namely, from one o'clock in the afternoon until nine o'clock in the evening to practice and drill.[4] At Cornell, however, stringent program requirements in the past materially reduced the amount of time that could be devoted by undergraduates to athletic exercise, including football. Indeed, at a number of technical and scientific institutions the amount of time allowed for organized athletics was minimal.

The ways in which the coach may choose to allot the time of his men during practice hours has even more importance. Often coaches overwork their players in drills and games. There is ample testimony to the effect that many an undergraduate is unable to compose himself for mental work during the two or three days succeeding an especially hard practice or contest. At one Eastern university students openly protested against excessive overwork on the football field. At another an assistant coach resigned because his objections to the overworking of men proved vain. For such conditions and for their results in individual cases and in respect of victory and defeat, some coaches blame the athletes for not having brought themselves into better physical condition. Occasionally men are kept in games much longer than is necessary.

Concerning this matter, the published testimony of two deservedly successful coaches is significant. Professor Stagg writes of "the necessity for a military obedience on the football field. A player must obey orders like a soldier where orders have been given, and, like a good soldier, act swiftly and surely on his own in an unforeseen contingency." [5] The character and appropriateness of the analogy need not at the moment detain us. "But a team cannot be clocked at full speed," wrote Mr. T. A. D. Jones,[6] "at every afternoon's practice and expect to derive much pleasure from their play. On the other hand, if they are not driven at full speed for the entire hour of practice which is at their disposal, then it is impossible to attain precision in the execution of plays either offensively or defensively."

The preference for the "driving" coach is not by any means confined to alumni. Mr. H. L. Mencken has told in detail of the care exercised in the selection of a Mid-Western football coach and of the dissatisfaction of undergraduates with his gentle methods. At a number of institutions, the names of which are omitted out of justice to the coaches concerned, athletes have expressed preference for the "driver," whose teams win, over the gentler man whose efforts end in defeat or mediocrity. In this connection enquiry was made into the charges of brutality which had been made both openly and covertly concerning the use of certain equipment by a coach at an Eastern

---

[4] Mr. W. A. Reid, Graduate Manager, letter of April 23, 1929: "Daily football practice is not in excess of four hours on any given day."

[5] A. A. Stagg and W. W. Stout, *Touchdown*, 1927, page 213.

[6] "How a Head Coach Looks at Football," reprinted in the *Harvard Alumni Bulletin*, November 17, 1927, from the *Outlook*.

institution. Assuredly, at the time of the field visit there was no basis for the rumor, if indeed it had ever been grounded in fact. From one passage in a discussion of coaching [7] it would appear that only two courses are open to coaches : weeks of study of the rules in order to map out the strategy of contests, or "cursing their men into a state of raving madness." Conversation with undergraduate athletes in comparatively large numbers over the United States and Canada leads to the conclusion that younger players usually prefer the coach who, although cursing them into "raving madness," makes their victory inevitable. With older players such is not the case. Their attitude suggests boredom over the eruptions of their mentor ; having heard them many times, the sophisticated regard them as interesting phenomena that are not to be taken too seriously. Considering the tendency of youth to glory in Spartan self-sacrifice for Alma Mater, it is perhaps not unnatural to find these young players preferring as coach the hard-bitten, driving martinet to the softer-spoken teacher of football in proportions of about two to one, provided always that the methods employed result in the winning of contests. The soft-spoken coach whose teams win is always popular.

2. Side-Line Coaching

Coaching from the side lines or from the players' bench is commonly discussed from the point of view of football. The practice obtains, however, in baseball, basketball, and other branches of athletics as well.

In football, side-line coaching is so common that its existence needs no proof. Its universality and the distrust that it engenders are attested by the suspicion directed at the field physician when his duties call him out upon the football field. Indeed, a former captain (Virginia) stated that after his team had advanced to an opponent's twenty-five-yard line their signals always issued from the coach on the bench. One novel expedient in side-line coaching deserves special mention. It so happened that on the football team of an Eastern university there played two brothers, Hawaiians, who were used by the coach to transmit signals to the team in action. One brother would be on the field ; the other would sit beside the coach on the bench. At the instance of the coach, the player on the bench shouted, in Hawaiian, to his brother with the team indications of the tactics that the coach desired the team to employ at critical moments.

Many persons who are interested in college athletics admit freely that side-line coaching is an abuse that should be ended, but few have attempted to mitigate it. The best authenticated case of a coach's ending the practice concerns a Western university (Southern California) where the coach has refused repeatedly to send by ingoing substitutes information or directions to players during a game. It is not to be denied that side-line coaching has robbed the undergraduate of many of the benefits that the game of football might without it confer.

3. Scouting in Football

In recent years no single phase of college football has been more argued than scout-

7 Coleman R. Griffith, *Psychology of Coaching*, 1926, page 89.

ing, which may be defined as an organized attempt on the part of a coach or a coaching staff to ascertain in advance the principles, methods, and details of play to be employed by opponents. Not all of the tales concerning devious expedients bent to this use need be credited in forming an opinion concerning it. In favor of scouting the arguments run about as follows: It gives the better team a better opportunity of winning. With it fewer victories are the results of chance advantage. Scouting relieves the almost unbearable strain that a football season imposes upon the coach, and it makes the occupation of coaching more interesting to those engaged in it. The abolition of scouting would encourage in the mind of the coach at any institution suspicion and distrust of other coaches. Moreover, attempts by college presidents to enforce non-scouting agreements upon coaches have resulted in dissatisfaction to all concerned. Finally, it is argued, a head coach at football cannot avoid receiving information concerning opposing teams and plays. Agreements to abolish scouting are complicated by interested alumni who, after attending a game in which the team of a future opponent of their own institution participates, write to their coach concerning it. The effectiveness of newspaper reporting to-day makes it almost impossible for any coach to remain long in ignorance of his opponent's strategy and tactics.

Those who oppose scouting at football attack it upon several grounds: They cite the testimony of certain coaches who state that scouting by enthusiastic but inexpert alumni has proved to be one of the most harmful attempts to aid in the development of a team. Respecting the cost of scouting, they refer to expenditure at a Catholic university of $800 a season for each scout employed. An expenditure of $2,500 for scouting is not uncommon, and occasionally the figure may reach $3,500. They point to an occasion upon which a coach at a New England college scouted a game so effectually with a stenographer that a contest resulted in overwhelming defeat for the scouted team, and that later, some of this information falling into the hands of another coach, a second contest resulted in a score of 43–0. Finally, they indicate that the elaborateness of the records of scouts and of outlines of games and plays, the pictures, both still and moving, now being taken of the teams of future opponents (Columbia, Dartmouth), and the highly technical nature of scouting lead directly to open professionalism in this activity.

Mr. Glenn Warner writes,[8] "Nearly every football coach has a competent and trustworthy football man who makes it a point to see each of the strongest rival teams play in at least one game, in order to note the opponents' style of offense and defense, and general style of play." "It was the scout's special duty to see just how the strongest plays were run off. Individual defects were also noted. With all this information in the hands of the head football coach he knew just how to attack his opponents and how to circumvent their strongest plays." "In the inner circles of school and college athletics it is not considered unethical or unsportsmanlike to scout opposing teams to the extent

[8]Glenn Scobey Warner, *Football for Coaches and Players*, 1927, pages 124, 125.

of seeing them play their games. It is perfectly legitimate to do that, but in some cases the practice is carried too far."

After an experiment lasting one year it was decided by the Yale Board of Athletic Control that non-scouting should be adopted as a permanent policy of football at Yale. Four of the institutions that Yale meets at football agreed to this convention. Yale, however, will scout no opponent regardless of that opponent's attitude toward scouting. The experimental period of abstention from scouting at Yale included an agreement between Mr. T. A. D. Jones and Captain L. McC. Jones of the United States Military Academy, which produced some difficulties of conscientious application but was honorably kept on both sides. Yale athletic officials, coaches, and athletes appear to be unanimous in their conviction that the absence of scouting decreases the importance of victory at football and augments the attractiveness of the game as a diversion.

The most practical argument against football scouting is the large expenditure that it involves. Yet with one or two exceptions those who have to do with athletic expenditures regard the cost of scouting as almost negligible. At only a few institutions is the cost considered significant. Whether or not the Canadian attitude be due to the influence of English university tradition, at the Dominion universities (McGill, Queen's, Toronto) scouting is considered unsportsmanlike and the athletic authorities of these institutions have agreed not to make use of it.

C. ONE ECONOMIC ASPECT OF THE COACH'S CALLING

In any discussion of coaching the fact must never be ignored that the coach, and particularly the football coach, is a specialist whose income has been made to depend upon producing "results." Moreover, in many instances the producing of "results" is a direct consideration in employment and reappointment. The loss of a few games, the jealousy of prominent players, an unintentional affront on the part of a coach may lead to dire consequences, affecting not only his own tenure but the food and shelter of his wife and children.

The results which the coach is expected to "produce" depend upon the ideals of the university or college with which he is connected. At best he must acknowledge many masters, — far more, indeed, than his academic colleagues. It is this hope of freedom from divided responsibility which induces him to sacrifice a fourth of his possible earnings at his occupation in exchange for a tenure which, he trusts, will provide him with a salary sufficient for the needs of himself and those dependent upon him.

V. A FEW OF THE EXTRAMURAL RELATIONSHIPS OF THE COACH

It is manifestly impossible to discuss in detail all of the relationships which the college athletic coach enjoys. All that can be ventured, therefore, is to select some five or six phases of the extramural contacts that apparently are common to most of the coaches, and to proffer a few notes upon each.

A. With Coaches at Other Colleges

In spite of rumors, printed or oral, it does not appear that antipathies between college coaches at the same or at different institutions are greater or more numerous than those that inevitably affect human relationships in other walks of life. Hence, the "temperamental" characteristics of the coach, to whatever results they may lead when a change in the personnel of a coaching staff becomes desirable, are not worthy of more serious administrative consideration than those of college teachers of academic subjects. Strained athletic relationships between institutions in the past have grown in a few instances from personal differences between instructors of teams; three well-substantiated cases have come to the attention of the study. A critic has remarked that in one respect football coaches appear to resemble the Indians of fiction; they never forget the offenses of a rival. To at least one other unfriendly relationship the passage of years has wrought for the two coaches involved a mutual tolerance and respect that is worthy of note.

B. With the Recruiting and Subsidizing of Athletes

The part played by some coaches in the recruiting and subsidizing of college athletes is discussed in Chapter X. For the moment only brief general observations are attempted. In the South and Middle West the restriction that coaches shall not initiate correspondence with candidates for admission to colleges, who have displayed promise as athletes, is evaded by two well-established procedures: In the first place, frequently contacts are initiated through personal interviews between coach and candidate which, although they are not literally classifiable as correspondence, nevertheless lead in the course of time to situations which it was the intent of the rules to obviate. In the second place, certain coaches secure the names of promising schoolboy athletes from newspapers. They then dispatch letters to alumni requesting them urgently to interview the boys and to ask them to write to the coaches. This procedure assuredly is equivalent to the initiation of correspondence. The sanctimonious attitude of the coach who thus violates the spirit of regulations would be despicable if it were not comic.

Although many coaches maintain that they do not desire the athlete who is on the lookout for perquisites and although several coaches, when interviewed, have stated emphatically that they had no room on their squads for men who had been recruited or subsidized, nevertheless the letters of coaches to such athletes show no discernible disaffection from them, even when prominent players, from knowledge in the possession of the coach or from suspicion which even he cannot escape, inevitably are regarded as hirelings. The experience of this study leads emphatically to the conclusion that any coach can end the subsidizing of athletes if it exists at the institution with which he is connected. Moreover, a gesture or a tone of voice would be sufficient to discontinue or considerably to modify the practice of local merchants in offering rewards to players who accomplish noteworthy individual feats.[9]

Journeys undertaken by the coach for the purpose of addressing high school assemblies and the ready conversion of such jaunts into recruiting tours are discussed in other pages.

C. With Alumni

From information gained in the present study it is clear that when a coach depends for salary or tenure upon the will of alumni, conditions unsatisfactory to the coach are most difficult to remedy. In such instances the power exercised by former students in certain aspects of athletics, always on the intercollegiate side, is likely to be great. Seldom is such a situation ideally comfortable. Occasionally, also, a coach is led to form such connections by the private hope that a summer camp which he conducts may prosper through favorable graduate opinion and an access of boys influenced by it. Unfortunately for the calling of the coach, in not a few instances the alumni appear to be an Olympian group to be placated at almost any sacrifice.

D. With Townsmen

Many a coach has found to his discomfort that friendship with individual members or small groups of townsmen can lead to an undue controlling interest on the part of fundamentally well-disposed individuals in the affairs of a university or college. The coach who, at the end of a victorious season, is the idol of the town is likely after a less fortunate schedule to find himself regarded less highly and even with suspicion. Those instances in which college administrators have attempted to capitalize for purposes of soliciting funds the friendly regard in which a coach is held by a local community have been fraught with the possibility of injustice to both the coaches and the institutions.

E. With the Press

Since the connection of newspapers and periodicals with college athletics is examined at length in a subsequent chapter, for the moment our concern is with a very limited portion of this subject. During the early days of this enquiry the statement was frequently made to members of the staff that the newspaper publicity accorded to many coaches was bought and paid for in cash or in kind. In view of the seriousness of the charge, special steps were taken to study it and the events which gave it rise. No such accusation was clearly substantiated. Although a statement to the effect that a coach's

---

[9] Cf. the article by Myles Lane in the *Dartmouth Literary Magazine*, May, 1928.

publicity is never paid for might be too sweeping, several test cases upon scrutiny proved to be motivated partly by sincere and intense admiration on the part of a sports writer for a coach, partly by the newspaper man's need for copy. It is, of course, possible that in some sections of the country newspaper writers on college athletics have been bribed by cash payments or by free tickets to discuss favorably the work of certain coaches. At the same time, in connection with such a wide distribution of complimentary tickets as takes place at certain California universities and at the University of Wisconsin, it has not been established that passes to games exert tangible influence upon reporters or sports editors.

With regard to interviews with newspaper reporters a former Eastern football coach has this to say : [10] "If we talked less in the press and more among ourselves we should get along better." A similar attitude on the part of responsible coaches would do much to diminish the notoriety achieved through newspaper stories concerning college athletes, the use of the names of young men in connection with the advertising of portable typewriters, clothing, sweaters, and other merchandise, and the publicity which attends the purchasing of the names and photographs of coaches and players for advertising cigarettes.

VI. Attitude and Influence

Athletic coaches, in spite of the notoriety that newspaper writers have bestowed upon them, differ not a whit from the generality of mankind. As with other men, the deepest tragedy among coaches is found where exigencies of the calling or of a situation have given rise to an increasing series of compromises with ideals which, starting in a coöperative yielding to comparatively innocuous practical considerations, increases with repetition until the life and influence of the man have come to be an almost perpetual negation of the verities. Happy is the coach to whom years and experience bring knowledge of the true relation of sport to education. Thrice happy is the college with which such a man is connected.

A. Attitude toward Contests

One of the great difficulties that beset the paid coach in any branch of athletics arises from the fact that having received, whether by his own choice or through the will of others, certain responsibilities, he must justify them publicly through the matches in which his teams or crews engage. In considering the resemblances that coaching bears to academic instruction, the fact is seldom noted that the responsibility of the coach for the "success" of his men, — however "success" be defined, — is tested by outside agencies frequently and immediately after he has imparted his instruction ; whereas the college professor of Latin or economics or engineering, under the American

[10] T. A. D. Jones, "How a Head Coach Looks at Football," reprinted in the *Harvard Alumni Bulletin*, November 17, 1927, from the *Outlook*.

system of examination, himself sets his immediate tests for his own pupils, and any larger ultimate tests of them as scholars or engineers or men of affairs are long deferred, in many cases until years after graduation. From the immediacy and the publicity of the tests to which athletes are subjected arises, on the part of those interested in college athletics, a scrutiny of methods and results which no coach can escape.

Careful consideration of individual instances leads to the conclusion that nowadays the coach who openly teaches his men to win by unfair means is very exceptional. Mr. T. A. D. Jones has well summarized the situation when he writes: "I do not believe that many men in football encourage this kind of thing; but I am convinced that there are still a very few not above turning a trick when they can do it handily. But, generally speaking, I am thoroughly sold on the men who are handling football." The statements of many athletes leave an inescapable impression that certain players, at the behest of their coaches, keep the rules when the rules do not stand in the way of gaining a point. It must be acknowledged with reluctance that the primitive fear of penalty or of loss is still in college athletics a powerful preventive of unfair play. If one could feel assured that all coaches were in this regard as conscientious as some coaches, there would be little question concerning the moral values to be gained from games and contests. At a meeting of coaches and football officials held in the spring of 1928, indications were not lacking that not all coaches desire to see the rules strictly and accurately enforced at all times. Hence their representation upon the Football Rules Committee by men whose livelihood is gained from college football is to be justified only by its results. The best of Canadian football coaches express in word and in deed an attitude toward their calling far different from that of their American colleagues.

B. THE COACH AND SPORTSMANSHIP

Effort has been made to ascertain the extent to which magnanimity, good manners, and friendliness in contests can be ascribed directly to the precepts or the example of coaches. The conclusion of this enquiry is stated with some reluctance. There is a series of striking instances in which much good feeling among players on opposing teams is traceable to the influence of coaches. But very few American coaches are consistently, actively, and practically concerned with the sportsmanship of their athletes. Some, indeed, preach it loudly but practice it only in restricted fashion. Some insist upon it occasionally. A few exemplify it quietly, earnestly, and thoroughly. These men, whether their salaries be high or low, whether their teams win or lose, are without price.

In this connection three observations have importance: First, it seems to be a fact of coaching practice that in the West athletes, especially football players, are coached to be more aggressive than in the East. Moreover, certain teams which meet Western or Mid-Western opponents have been so coached for specific games. Secondly, one prominent coach expressed the opinion that football is essentially a training, a laboratory period, and that it is not in reality a sport at all. Numerous instances, among them cases where football squads are composed of men engaged in the study of physical education and where large proportions of 'varsity teams are made up of subsidized athletes, bear widespread testimony to the growth of this notion. Thirdly, few coaches in the midst of their manifold technical duties and responsibilities are able, even if they were disposed, to give attention to ways and means of turning football players into good sportsmen.

Manifestly, it is absurd to expect a coach who himself is without the instincts of a sportsman to develop teams or crews who have those instincts. It is equally absurd to suppose that good may come from methods of a coach who says, in effect, "You men must be sportsmen, or I'll cut you off the squad." Youth has too much of the comic spirit to suffer such priggishness. Yet in so far as the character of a man, its making and its modification, are within his own control and the control of others, just so far also is the development of a spirit of magnanimous rivalry, whether between individuals or between institutions, within the power of those who bear the heat and burden of that rivalry. It has been repeatedly demonstrated that here, at any rate, men may add cubits to the spiritual stature of themselves and their fellows merely by taking thought.

C. THE INFLUENCE OF THE COACH

More or less intimate contacts with many coaches prompt to the belief that even the most advertised among them are not the evil geniuses they are supposed to be. During the study a certain football coach was stigmatized as a teacher of rough and unfair football and in support of the accusation the coach's own words were cited. Yet this is a summary of what an administrative officer at the college in question told a member of our staff: "We admire this coach, the boys admire him, and he was a good influence here. From a careful examination of the boys and from being present on the field, we have been unable to find evidence of instructions to cheat, or foul, or slug, but his oratory gets the upper hand. He talks too much. What he said was colored by those who repeated it, and he thereby injured not ourselves but our reputation." No matter what their status, coaches, having elected to wrest a living from athletics, must, like all others of their group, please their public. Doubtless a very great compensation lies in the esteem in which practically all of the coaches of this study are held upon their respective campuses, especially by the undergraduates. Yet, upon occasion, this popularity may be purchased at high cost. The coach who boldly demands monetary concessions for football men and at the same time permits misrepresentation of amounts paid to them as set down in eligibility blanks sent to other institutions of a conference is playing a double game, which profits neither his university nor his men. Through pressure for victory coaches have been known to pamper athletes in two respects:

First, young men have been led to value highly their own powers and to attempt to assure themselves of scholarships or aids or even direct financial payments before competing for teams (Ohio Wesleyan, various Pennsylvania colleges) ; and secondly, the scholastic pampering of athletes appears to be the chief responsibility of many football coaches after the close of their season. At three institutions partisanship for and against coaches has divided the respective student bodies to the extent that undergraduates are losing much of their zest for athletics. These cases are as exceptional as that of a young coach who, although he suffered from an unenviable reputation beyond the campus on which he worked, was there regarded as an exemplar of piety. Of this matter the important facts are two : Many coaches have earned the high opinion of college administrators, alumni, and undergraduates as wholesome influences in campus life. Not a few coaches, whether of this or of other types, sincerely enjoy working with young men and influencing their ideals and their conduct for good.

Conclusion

"The paid coach," remarked an Oxford don much respected for his interest and influence in college and university sports, "is at the bottom of all difficulties in American college athletics." From the British point of view the statement is entirely just. In English Rugby there is no such thing as a professional coach. The professional oarsman passed from British amateur rowing nearly a century ago. Paid coaches for university track and field athletics and association football at Oxford and Cambridge are employees solely. At the older and at most of the newer English universities coaching in intramural or in 'varsity sports rests upon a universally sincere regard for the status of the amateur.

To infer that British practice in this particular furnishes a model to be followed indiscriminately in the United States would be absurd. But it would be even more absurd to ignore British practice altogether. Between the two extremes of English and American coaching custom stands the Canadian, which has preserved, by the operation of the British sports tradition, more than a little of the English ideal of amateur coaching. It must not be forgotten that Englishmen have had in this particular far more and sharper experience than we. We should be guilty of wasting our opportunities if we neglected or disregarded what this experience has taught English and Canadian university sportsmen.

In coaching, as in other phases of college athletics, the American demands "the best"; his innate idealism makes him discontented with halfway measures. He believes that in coaching, as in other matters, he can procure the best by purchase and that the higher the price, the better the quality. Here his idealism may be and sometimes is misapplied. He fails to reckon with the devotion which a task commands and which in his business and commercial relationships he well knows has no price.

Doubtless at an ideal university professional coaching would find no place. It would be indeed a courageous college that abolished the paid coach. Yet among a group of colleges and universities a sincere coöperative effort, shorn of special pleading and the consideration of exceptional cases as if they were typical of all, to arrive at a common understanding of the place and function of the coach, paid or unpaid, in American college life would benefit not alone the institutions concerned in it but the very coaches whose situation would thereby be clarified.

Obviously, the position of a coach whose tenure depends upon victory is both unfortunate and unfair. The situation is deleterious to sport but especially to education, however it be defined. A coach who trusts to faculty status and fair words for safety in the hour of disapproval leans upon a broken reed. When the new ideals now stirring public and private school athletics reach their inevitable fruition in college and university sport, a change will come over the attitude of the coach toward his own calling. It remains to be seen whether coaches, through conviction, sound business judgment, or mere prudential shrewdness, will anticipate and hasten that change through their own efforts.

CHAPTER IX

EXTRAMURAL RELATIONSHIPS

JUST as the ripples from a stone cast into a pool widen till they reach its shores, so the relationships of college athletics broaden as they spread beyond the institution. Of these relationships, the most intimate concern the graduates and former students of the college. Rooted in a sentiment sown and fostered during undergraduate days, persisting among the most cherished memories of later life, they are for many graduates of American universities the most sacred of ties and obligations. Rather more primitive are the relationships between institutions, which affect all members of the college families. The widening circle of athletic relationships encounters next the conferences and associations that bind together the common interests of neighboring institutions, then the representative national bodies, and finally the organizations that provide channels for the contacts of American college athletes with the athletes of other nations. With these relationships and with a few of their implications the present discussion is concerned.

I. EXTRAMURAL RELATIONSHIPS AND THE ALUMNI

Although the alumnus is a member of the college family, yet in the great majority of cases his life and interests lie beyond college walls. Graduates of the older English universities maintain their connection with those institutions through "keeping their names on the books," that is, by the payment of certain fees under certain conditions which entitle them to voting membership in the university organization. Something of the same procedure obtains in Canada. At some of the Scottish universities alumni are being organized into associations. The direct connection of the American alumnus with his university is formally through the alumni association.

For many years American universities and colleges have expended much effort to interest their alumni. It will be convenient to consider first the more general aspects of the alumnus's relation to his college and then his influence and relation in college athletics.

A. THE RELATION OF THE ALUMNUS TO ALMA MATER

The tender and peculiar place which the university or the college should occupy in the affections of its alumni is not to be denied or impugned. It is compounded of gratitude which prompts to service, a love that springs from impressionable years passed as an undergraduate under the protection of the Fostering Mother, and the tendency common to many men and women to look into the past for the Golden Age. These considerations form the ideal basis for the relation of the alumnus to his college.

This ideal is rarely fulfilled. The failure is as much the fault of those who direct the college as it is of the graduates. Whether from shortcomings of modern civilization or from specific weaknesses in our educational processes, the attitude of the college toward its alumni and of the alumni toward their college is at the root materialistic. Between the graduate and the university there has for years existed a tacit bargain: for money and for activity of interest the college in effect offers certain rewards. The alumnus of to-day is thought of principally as a source of funds for endowment drives, operating expenses, and the maintenance of undergraduate activities. Seldom does he evince interest, without being solicited in support of a financial campaign. In return he receives prominence, the promise of power, and the self-satisfaction that these and his activities bring. With repetition of these conditions the attitude of the alumnus may end by becoming proprietary. The power which he has received takes the form of governance and trusteeship, whether of the university or of athletics.[1]

Four considerations must be kept in mind. In the first place, only a small proportion of the alumni of any university or college are active in the administration of the institution, whether in affairs of the alumni association or in athletics. Secondly, the aspects of American college life that have contributed to make graduates "self-starting and self-propelling" — to borrow the phrase of President Lowell — have been principally extra-curricular as distinguished from academic. Thirdly, in soliciting alumni support, the college has emphasized and received it in tangible matters; the interest of the alumni in the intangibles of American college or university life has been recognized only recently and its growth thus far has been limited. Fourthly, whether or not participation in athletics as an undergraduate prompts to graduate interest in the institution as a whole, it can at least be said of the graduates who manifest interest on behalf of the university that former athletes are likely to be interested in athletics, and especially in the branch in which they as students took part.

[1] Eighteenth Annual Report of the Carnegie Foundation, 1923, pages 38–39.

B. His Relation to Athletics

Just as an ideal relation occasionally exists between the alumnus and the general affairs of the university, so a corresponding ideal relationship may sometimes be found with respect to athletics. It is manifested by that rare alumnus who sees individual boys as the educational units in college life, who expends his best effort in developing not alone their physical prowess but also their contacts with their fellow students and especially their relationship to the things of the mind and of the spirit. To such an alumnus intellectual endeavor, a knowledge of the past, honesty, right living, industry, and love of athletic games all have their appropriate places in the life of the undergraduate. Such an alumnus is of wholesome influence, even though he can afford to give little in time or money.

On the other hand, the usual current relationship of alumni to athletics manifests itself in two ways: the control of policies, and the recruiting and financing of athletes. Probably not a fifth of all alumni are active in either direction.

1. Alumni Influence upon Details of Coaching

At a number of institutions (Brown, Rutgers, and other universities) not the least of the coach's difficulties has been the interference of alumni with the practical details of instruction, chiefly in football. The members of alumni advisory committees are nearly always prominent former players or erstwhile coaches. Naturally they have favorite theories and notions which they wish to see used. A coach who is passive by nature or who for reasons of harmony fears that he must give ear to the suggestions of advisory committees discovers too late that some of the best features of his own teaching have been modified.

2. Alumni and Athletic Policies

The influence and activity of alumni in formulating the policies of universities and colleges as regards athletics have already been discussed at length in Chapter V. Only a few brief observations need be added.

In the modern American university, the graduate manager or treasurer and his functions bear witness to the importance of the alumni and the esteem in which they are held. Their influence is felt in the appointment of coaches, the shaping and administering of coaching policies, the erection and size of stadiums, building programs, the provision and distribution of tickets, the making of schedules, and, indeed, in practically all of the extramural relationships of college athletics. Seldom do alumni manifest strong interest in intramural programs or competition. Although many play golf, tennis, squash, and handball, relatively few appear to realize the importance of cultivating in all undergraduates the experience of games that are suitable to his enjoyment and recreation in later life. The present-day attitude of alumni toward athletics is essentially the product of our long-standing emphasis upon extramural competition. It is likely that the growth of intramural games will give future graduates a different point of view.

Football attracts most of the alumni attention. During undergraduate days it draws and keeps the interest of men and women students to an extraordinary degree. After graduation the interest persists but does not manifest itself in active participation. Very few players take part in football games for more than five or six years after graduation. In the United States, contests at football between alumni and undergraduates have little to commend them; the graduates, "fat and scant of breath," endure, with little credit to their zeal, the falls, knocks, and runs of American football, while the student players receive small benefit from meeting a team possessing only antiquated strategy and tactics. That this should be so is one of the principal limitations of American football. True, a few alumni who have formerly played on college teams join local or amateur organizations after graduation. In California, for football, and in New York City, for basketball, athletic clubs provide opportunity and training accommodations for graduate athletes; teams representing these clubs are almost invariably more skilful than undergraduate college organizations. Some college graduates, especially from the Middle West, enter professional football for a few years, and a larger number take up coaching or physical education. But by their thirtieth birthdays the great majority of graduates feel more at home in their seats at a football spectacle than they would in suits upon any field. In Great Britain this is not the case. English Rugby, soccer, and the special football games of certain public schools, once mastered, are not infrequently played almost until middle age. The interest of the American changes early from the active to the passive. Usually it expresses itself in attending games, listening to broadcasts play-by-play, participating in the shaping of college athletic policies, subscribing money for equipment and increased facilities, and in other similar works. Much the same is true of other forms of athletics in American colleges and universities.

3. The Procurement and Support of Athletes

Although methods and procedure in recruiting and subsidizing college athletes are discussed at length in Chapter X, a word may be said here concerning the motives which lead alumni to these practices. The number of cases in which the entire support of athletes is furnished by alumni are far fewer than those in which a part is given and the athletes are provided with actual or nominal jobs through alumni efforts. Doubtless some alumni have a philanthropic and worthy desire to enable a deserving youth to obtain a college education, but comparatively seldom is this the genuine motive for subsidizing and recruiting. In the course of this study we have never heard it advanced except in defense of dishonest practices, in extenuation of the course of an institution, a group, or an individual, or in a theoretical and academic discussion. The pretended fear of doing injustice to some deserving boy is a bogeyman kept close at hand to justify all such doings. In view of the kindly solicitude that is lavished upon the athlete, the only injustice that he is likely to experience is the injustice that falls to any youth who is overcoddled and whose money comes too easily.

The guidance of alumni interest and activity in athletics presents one of the crucial problems of college administration. What is needed is not more interest on the part of graduates, but the direction of this interest to ends that will truly benefit under-graduates. At present, too few alumni look upon athletics as a factor of higher educa-tion which prepares for afterlife, where games and outdoor contests ought to play their part. The most active of the alumni in a number of institutions, consciously or uncon-sciously, tend to make college athletics a preparation for professional athletics.

II. Inter-college Rivalry in Athletics

Rivalry between institutions springs spontaneously from college pride. It is not confined to athletics. Annual competitions in glee and chorus singing, in debates, and, indeed, in any form of activity in which two institutions desire to test their skill, bear witness to the fact that rivalry exists in many phases of college life. But in no other form of competition is public interest so keen as in athletics. This was not always the case either in England or in the United States. Intercollegiate athletic rivalry in its early days was informal and important principally to undergraduates. The influence of alumni and the acceptance of the principle that their desires must be served grew later out of the sentiment engendered and cumulated in succeeding generations of undergraduates.

A. Wholesome Aspects of Intercollegiate Rivalry

It is not to be doubted that a wholesome and magnanimous rivalry in athletic compe-tition between two or more institutions represents a salutary condition in undergradu-ate life, especially as between two or more institutions of approximately the same size, with comparable ideals and traditions. Among the best examples of such rivalry in the East stands the relation between Amherst College, Wesleyan University, and Williams College, which for a number of years have competed keenly in both athletics and in other fields of endeavor, and, more recently, the relation of St. John's College, Annapolis, to some of its opponents. Not the least good resulting from such pleasant relationships is to be traced in the mutual respect, magnanimity, and hospitality between institu-tions and the inter-college friendships which individual undergraduates cherish. So long as relations such as these remain normal, there is little trace of the institutional jealousy and distrust which quickly become the sources of many evils. Under guidance, athletics can be made to contribute to pleasant inter-college or inter-university relationships. It is not a question of checking such rivalry, but of tempering and directing it to salutary ends.

B. HARMFUL ASPECTS OF INTERCOLLEGIATE RIVALRY

The discussion which follows is based upon a study of the intercollegiate relations of some forty colleges and universities in the United States and Canada.[2] Some of these relations are cordial, others are bitter, many have been severed. It is matter of history that many colleges and universities have been engaged in disputes with other institutions with which their relations should have been friendly and tolerant. The fact that in a great number of such instances the causes in dispute have been forgotten gives ground for the hope that much of the bad feeling which to-day exists in inter-university dealings may in time be replaced by a sportsmanlike magnanimity.

Unpleasant intercollegiate relationships have in some cases given rise to distrust, without leading to the abandonment of athletic competition. In other cases they have progressed so far that athletic contests have been abandoned.

1. Unsatisfactory Relations without Abandonment of Competition

To the attention of this study have come at least three instances in which the relations existing between colleges or universities have been for a number of years far from satisfactory but not so acute as to lead to the severance of athletic competition. During the past few years, contests between two Eastern institutions and between three universities in the Far West have been held not for reasons of friendship — which have long since disappeared — but for the sake of the financial return from gate receipts and guarantees. At a dinner tendered to two football squads representing Mid-Western universities, much of the evening was passed in charges and countercharges of recruiting and subsidizing of players at the respective institutions. It is doubtful if under such circumstances a continuance of athletic competition is desirable or beneficial. The attitude of distrust and suspicion invalidates whatever good might flow from a continuation of relationships.

[2] In collecting information concerning intercollegiate rivalry the following groups of relationships were considered: University of Alabama with Auburn Polytechnic Institute, Amherst College with Massachusetts Agricultural College, Baylor University with Texas Agricultural and Mechanical College, Brown University with Dartmouth College, University of California with University of Southern California, University of California with Stanford University, University of Chicago with Northwestern University, Columbia University with New York University, University of Georgia with the Georgia School of Technology, Harvard University with Princeton University, Harvard University with Yale University, Haskell Institute with several institutions that competed in the Drake University Relay Races, Holy Cross College with Harvard University, University of Iowa with Iowa State, University of Michigan with University of Minnesota, University of Michigan with Notre Dame University, Notre Dame University with University of Southern California, University of Oklahoma with University of Nebraska, University of Oklahoma with Oklahoma Agricultural College, University of Oregon with Oregon Agricultural College, University of Pittsburgh with University of Pennsylvania, Princeton University with University of Pennsylvania, Princeton University with Rutgers University, Rensselaer Polytechnic Institute with Union University, University of Toronto with McGill University and other Canadian institutions, U. S. Military Academy with Syracuse University, U. S. Military Academy with U. S. Naval Academy, Washington State College with University of Washington. In each instance an unprejudiced attempt was made to ascertain the views of all parties regarding relations or their severance. It is not intended in the present study to pass judgment upon the merits of any claim or dispute that may be involved in the relationships which are discussed.

2. The Severance of Athletic Relationships

The reasons which lead to the severance of athletic relations between institutions, in so far as they are ascertainable, are usually of the utmost complexity. Sometimes breaks have been of such long standing that it is impossible to discover what conditions occasioned them or whether the existing ill feeling arose after the break or before it. Usually many acts or conditions were involved, no one of which upon examination was apparently of sufficient strength alone to have caused the break. Frequently the reason which has been alleged for a discontinuance of athletic competition was merely an excuse. In every instance, however, the immediate cause was bad feeling between the partisans of the institutions. In almost every instance, its origin appears to have been an overweening desire for victory and the reputation that victory is supposed to bring.

Of the matters involved in these breaks the most direct and acutely contributing factor was disorder at or during football games. Certain other cases of ill feeling are ascribable to close scores and possibly to the lost wagers which they involved. In three instances a financial loss on gate receipts which made contests not sufficiently profitable is the reason alleged for the failure of natural rivals to compete. Questionable alumni activities at one institution and the desire on the part of a director to give his fellow-director at the rival university a means of combating the recruitment and subsidizing of athletes led to the abandonment of football games between two universities in the Mid-West. Jealousy of the apportionment of state aid to sister institutions and personal animosities of directors, coaches, and other officers have contributed to similar results. Personal animosities on the part of directors, managers, and alumni have been handed down from generation to generation for no justifiable cause ; even when changes have supervened in the personnel at rival institutions (Brown, Dartmouth ; Princeton, Pennsylvania), ill feeling may persist. Finally, in at least eight cases, a variety of reasons are put forth for abandoning competition. In a few instances an ill-disguised feeling of superiority on the part of one or both of the universities involved made contests impossible. Undergraduate pranks not connected with athletics and disputes over eligibility have played their part. Upon three occasions low scholastic standards have been advanced as the cause of the abandonment of competition. This excuse is frequently put forward by many private institutions to justify their refusal to compete with Catholic colleges and universities. It was also invoked recently in the disputes resulting from success of the team representing the Haskell Institute at the Drake University Relay Races. The counter-statement has been made that, during those races, when the Haskell team gave evidence of superlative excellence, the treatment accorded to its members by representatives of other institutions became markedly discourteous. Incidentally, the excuse of low standards has more than once been used to cloak real reasons for severance of relationships.

A study of these cases prompts the following observations : First, the source of the ill feeling that has resulted in a majority of these breaks has been intercollegiate football. Moreover, in many instances in which football relations have been severed, competition in other branches of athletics, including soccer, has survived the breaking off of relations in football. Such facts reflect the overvaluation of football, and its attendant importance in rousing bad feeling among colleges and universities in the United States. Far from invariably leading to friendly rivalry, clean and manly contests, and pleasant regard, as its proponents never tire of insisting, American football, whether from its intrinsic nature as a body-contact game or from the abuses that have grown up to choke it, has bred distrust, suspicion, jealousy, and physical violence.

Theoretically, any college, however small, should be able to compete with any institution, however large. Practically, competition between small and large universities has given rise to dissatisfaction and dishonesty. As one well-informed critic has written, "I am firmly convinced that no institution of less than one thousand male students can compete on an equal basis with an institution of two thousand or more students honestly." Although these criteria appear to be somewhat crude, the principle that underlies them is valid. It is impaired in its operation by the financial returns to be gained by competition with much larger institutions in the same conference (in the Intercollegiate Conference, Chicago, Northwestern, and Purdue, with eligibles ranging in number from five hundred to a thousand, compete with Michigan, Minnesota, and Wisconsin, whose eligibles number from four to six thousand; Idaho and Washington State in the Pacific Coast Conference). In some conferences small colleges suffer many inconveniences and even indignities rather than withdraw. The ambition to compete outside of a class has given rise to many deleterious influences and temptations.

Secondly, the regrettable fact appears that very few colleges and universities of the country make any genuine effort to understand life and conditions at other institutions, whether those institutions be athletic rivals or not. Such a state of affairs is doubly unfortunate in view of the value of a sincere college loyalty that grows from the understanding of even a few other universities, the mutual respect prompted thereby, and, no matter what superficial appearance may seem to indicate, a disposition to forbearance. Generally, the cultivation of a beneficent college loyalty in extramural relationships is a task of years that demands the sympathetic guidance and work of older men and women, — presidents, alumni, frequently members of faculties, who, understanding the implications of even latent hostilities, labor unobtrusively to change conditions that do no credit to any university or college. The resumption of athletic relationships between Amherst College and the Massachusetts Agricultural College, the long traditional rivalry between Harvard and Yale, Amherst and Williams, Purdue and Indiana in spite of divided appropriations from the state, may be cited as proof. In the majority of these instances the attitude of certain individuals, translated into action, has done much to bring about and maintain cordiality. The change of the word "Opponents" to "Visitors" on the score board of the Harvard stadium is a case in point. The hospitality of the University of Toronto to visiting teams, of Cornell University on the occasion of the annual indoor intercollegiate tennis tournament for the Larned cup, and of many other universities during May regattas, contrasts sharply with the fact that usually, when accommodations for two teams at one institution differ, the guests are assigned to the inferior quarters. Managers and directors have more or less apologetically attempted to justify the condition by explaining that, first, it would be unfair to the home team if visitors were better accommodated, since better accommodations might contribute to better physical condition and an advantage in the contest, and secondly, that since the home team is regularly established in the best available quarters, it is far simpler if they occupy them rather than yield them to their guests. The difference implied between athletic hospitality and other forms need not be elaborated. Bad feeling between institutions is often roused deliberately by coaches and by newspaper writers who report practice or contests. The undergraduate rally preceding a football game which does not emphasize the hospitality that should be shown visiting teams and spectators had best be abolished. Furthermore, instances have been rehearsed in which a partisan spirit among an undergraduate body has led even to the rebuke of men who have cheered opponents or recognized their excellence or skill. Comparatively few universities or colleges attempt to instill into their undergraduate bodies the notion that, on the occasion of the annual football game or other contest with the natural rival on home grounds, undergraduates are really hosts. Much the same is true of preparations for students to accompany teams to games played away from home. Too often visiting partisans not only exhibit the worst of manners, but indulge in recalcitrant disorders which disgrace both the institutions and the games. A private individual whose guests smash furniture, drink to excess, and generally make themselves obnoxious, is amply justified in no longer offering them hospitality.

The attitude of mind which many intercollegiate athletic contests reflect presents a problem that is really social. Hospitality on the part of a group can be cultivated, and the reason it is not more evidenced is a lack of initiative, or even an adverse sentiment on the part of older persons. If it were necessary to fix the responsibility for mutual understanding between colleges and universities, it would be salutary if the initiative in courtesy were taken by the larger institution.

Thirdly, undergraduate opinion upon the merits of institutional rivalry has demonstrated itself to be illogical, emotional, easily provoked by rumors emanating from players, coaches, alumni, and other partisans, false or one-sided newspaper accounts of games, all of which readily flame into hostility and contribute after graduation to an inimical sentiment among alumni.

Finally, it is a commentary upon American sportsmanship that when athletic relations are severed, the initiative is generally taken by the institution that has been losing games over a series of years.

III. Athletic Conferences

A third phase of extramural relations is represented by athletic conferences. Although these bodies differ widely in composition, nevertheless their organization, purposes, and methods exhibit many resemblances one to another.

The athletic conference of to-day may be described as a voluntary regional association of colleges and universities through elected or appointed representatives for discussion of problems concerning intercollegiate athletics, formulation of regulations to govern athletic contests between member institutions, and usually the conduct of competitions in various branches of inter-college and inter-school athletics. Thus its functions are deliberative, regulatory, and executive. Although the powers of conferences vary, most of the forty-two associations that have come to the attention of this study possess police functions respecting violation of their rules. One or two, notably the Intercollegiate Conference, have gone further than others in engaging a commissioner and a paid executive staff. Other bodies appropriate sums of money for secretarial allowances, clerical assistance, and various services. In certain instances the conference is based upon special mutual interests or affiliations; witness, the Colored Intercollegiate Athletic Conference and the so-called Eastern Jesuit Conference, which is less a formal conference than a mutual informal agreement. The athletic conference, as the term is used in the present discussion, being essentially regional, is to be distinguished from a national association in size, membership, and geographical extent. Thus, although the National Collegiate Athletic Association possesses many of the characteristics of an athletic conference, it is a national representative body.

A. Origins and Development of Athletic Conferences

The predecessors of the athletic conference, as we know it to-day, are to be traced in three organizations of the 1870's.

Of these, the first in respect of time was the Rowing Association of American Colleges which, formed in 1870, included most of the New England colleges and universities and three or four in New Jersey and New York State.[3] For six years the Association conducted intercollegiate regattas with varying success. The Rowing Association was apparently dominated by Harvard and Yale, "the minor colleges taking sides with either one or the other. This rivalry, together with the difficulty of managing and judging so many crews on the same course, led to much doubtful diplomacy and frequent controversies." [4] In 1876, the intense rivalry between Harvard and Yale led to their withdrawal and the wreck of the Association. A second tributary to the stream of college conferences was the Intercollegiate Association of Amateur Athletes of America, founded in 1875, while a third is to be traced in the convention of American colleges that met in New York City in 1876 to establish rules for intercollegiate football competition, — a predecessor of the Football Rules Committee of the present day.

[3] Sheldon, *Student Life and Customs*, New York, 1901, pages 230–255.
[4] Ibid., page 231.

A fourth intercollegiate agreement, formulated in 1878, bound together twelve colleges for competition not in athletics but in public speaking, essay writing, and exercises in Greek, Latin, mathematics, and mental science.[5] Doubtless the convenience, utility, and practicability of intercollegiate associations such as these led to the formation of intercollegiate conferences dealing exclusively with athletic competition. The Southern Intercollegiate Conference was founded in 1894, followed by the (Mid-Western) Intercollegiate Conference one year later. The dates of the founding of other conferences were as follows: Maine Intercollegiate Track and Field Association 1896, Northwest Conference 1904, Canadian Intercollegiate Athletic Union 1906, Missouri Valley Conference 1907, Rocky Mountain Faculty Athletic Conference 1909, Southwest Athletic Conference 1914, the original Harvard-Yale-Princeton agreement 1916, Pacific Northwest Intercollegiate Conference 1923, California Coast Conference 1926, Eastern Intercollegiate Athletic Conference 1928.

The methods and procedure of the earlier athletic conferences justified the designation. Representatives of colleges and universities met, discussed the governance of athletic competition, and bound their institutions to abide by the rules passed by the assembly for the common good. With the increase of available funds, the associations established central offices to act as clearing houses of athletic information, centres of mutual interests, and executors of the policies of the group as expressed in votes and regulations. Gradually the central offices acquired powers to enforce regulations by the imposition of penalties and assumed certain of the functions of investigating agencies. Some of the studies carried out under such auspices have exerted the utmost influence upon the conduct of competition and the formulation of organization policies. It may be noted, however, that the days of disinterested discussion in conference meetings appear to be long past.

B. Representative Regulations

It will suffice to consider a few of the important provisions laid down by some of the more influential conferences touching faculty control, eligibility, the general subject of compensation of players, including recruiting, proselyting, subsidies, and scholarships; training seasons, tables, and quarters; summer baseball, coaches, and sportsmanship. The great majority of conference regulations are designed to apply especially to football. Indeed, the framers of conference rules apparently place other forms of athletic competition, like baseball, basketball, and track and field events, in a decidedly subordinate position.

1. Faculty Control

A number of conferences emphasize control of athletics by faculties as a qualification for membership.

---

[5] Harold DeWolf Fuller, *New York University Alumnus*, Vol. VII, No. 9, 1926, page 9. The institutions subscribing to the agreement were Colgate (then Madison College), College of the City of New York, Cornell, Lafayette, New York University, Northwestern, Princeton, Rutgers, St. Johns, Syracuse, Wesleyan, and Williams.

For example, the (Mid-Western) Intercollegiate Conference, which has no written constitution, restricts its membership to "institutions having full and complete faculty control of athletics." Representatives must not be those who receive "pay primarily for services connected with athletics or the Department of Physical Education." But in this Conference, academic teachers, although vouchsafed theoretical control, do not actually control the athletics of their institutions. With the organization of the Directors Conference in 1922, directors and coaches have taken upon themselves some of the duties and prerogatives of the academic members. Being aggressive, they have taken the lead in nearly all official actions of the Conference since that date. The Rocky Mountain Conference goes so far as to stipulate for institutional representation in the Conference only on a basis of professorial rank and to bar from such functions any person "whose duties include those of a coach or manager." Here, although faculty representatives have no very large authority, the matter rests with the presidents who, however, act with little semblance of unanimity. The Southern Conference "requires faculty responsibility and control in intercollegiate athletics" and insists that the "faculty members of the athletic committees in the different institutions of the Conference must constitute a majority and must assume the full responsibility for carrying out the eligibility rules of the Conference." Perhaps the Southern Conference more than any other exemplifies actual control by academic teachers.

In some conferences that stipulate for "faculty control," rules are so vigorously interpreted that they lose their value. For example, in the (Mid-Western) Intercollegiate Conference restriction upon compensation to players is regarded at some institutions as forbidding only payment for summer baseball. At least one faculty chairman in the Southwest Conference, differing with the action of the local scholarship committee in awarding semi-athletic scholarships, signs eligibility blanks almost as a matter of form. Here and there in the United States there is too much rationalizing and dictating of interpretations of rules by coaches, managers, and directors to undergraduates who should be led rather to follow the dictates of their own consciences as regards eligibility than to accept the interpretation of older persons who in one sense are certainly "wiser than they."

2. Eligibility

The endeavor to place intercollegiate competition upon a fair and equitable basis leads to regulations concerning the eligibility of players.

The (Mid-Western) Intercollegiate and Rocky Mountain Conferences make detailed provision for due attendance of players upon university exercises. Certification of eligibility is required by the (Mid-Western) Intercollegiate Conference, the Missouri Valley, the Pacific Coast, the Rocky Mountain, the Southern, and the Southwest. Most of the requirements concerning eligibility are very specific and detailed. Among the most stringent stands Rule 10 of the (Mid-Western) Intercollegiate Conference, which requires certification of athletes at the beginning of the season in each intercollegiate branch by each institution to every other, and a statement from each registrar concerning residence, attendance, and scholarship. "As to the remaining rules, the certification shall be by the chairman of the athletic board or committee." However excellent the intention of this regulation, it has led to a divided responsibility. The business of the registrar is not the business of the chairman, and *vice versa*. On the contrary, eligibility certification in the Southern Conference, although it includes the registrar's statement, places the full responsibility for a player's status upon faculty chairmen of athletic committees. The Southwest Conference requires the approval of the chairman of the faculty committee of athletics upon each eligibility card of each player, which is mailed to the president of the Conference within one week after the opening of the session at every institution. Moreover, at the beginning and end of each playing season, lists are interchanged by the colleges of the Conference. A pre-season eligibility list must be in the hands of managers of opposing teams in the Rocky Mountain Conference five days before any game.

The (Mid-Western) Intercollegiate and Rocky Mountain Conferences are not alone in requiring from each athlete a statement over his own signature that he is eligible to compete in intercollegiate contests under the "letter and spirit" of the rules. The version of the Harvard-Yale-Princeton agreement, as revised in May, 1926, appears not to demand from the individual athlete a signed statement concerning his eligibility, but all three of the universities do in fact require it. In these three pacts and a number of others, the intention is to place the ultimate responsibility for the eligibility of any athlete upon his own honesty.

The general decrease in the number and complexity of the problems arising from the migration of athletes is probably ascribable in great measure to the very stringent regulation of almost all conferences concerning transfers. There is, however, no uniformity of detail. For example, the Pacific Coast Intercollegiate Conference lays down the rule that "a student who has established a residence in one institution loses the same when, upon entering a second institution, his fees shall become due; and he shall not represent the second institution until he has passed one season of each sport thereafter. He shall also lose one season's participation in each sport. However, registration for the summer session or quarter in a second institution shall not be considered as nullifying residence already established in the first." The supplementary agreement adopted by Harvard, Yale, and Princeton, and made effective January 1, 1923, provides that "any student who has, while enrolled in another university or college, taken part in competitive athletics as a member of his university, or college, or class team or crew while playing against opponents not members of that institution, shall be ineligible to represent Harvard, Yale, or Princeton in any sport in which he so represented his former college or university." This regulation as regards transferred students is probably the most stringent of any athletic pact.

Most of the American colleges restrict intercollegiate competition to undergraduates; Canadian institutions do not. Furthermore, all appear to require one year's residence before membership upon any 'varsity team, and the Intercollegiate Conference, under certain conditions, prohibits its teams from engaging "in athletic competition with institutions that do not require one year of residence before participation." [6] The restriction of intercollegiate play to three years of undergraduate connection with

[6] The Minutes of the Eighteenth Annual Meeting of the Association of New England Colleges for Conference on Athletics, held in May, 1925, reveal that in reply to a questionnaire sent out during that year by the Association, 3 colleges of the 21 members stated that they permitted freshmen to compete on university teams throughout the entire first year; 9, however, had a one-year rule, and 8 a partial-year rule. There is discernible among Eastern institutions a tendency to increase rather than to diminish the number of games on freshman schedules, although general opinion seems to be to the effect that a reduction of such schedules, besides preventing freshmen from participating on university teams, benefits the first-year men scholastically.

an institution is almost unanimous. To some of these requirements the United States Military Academy at West Point has felt that because of its peculiar constitution and position it could not subscribe. Finally, late registration by athletes is discouraged.

The subject of eligibility is much involved with certain other topics that are treated separately in these pages, for example, summer baseball and compensation to players. The great bulk of all intercollegiate rules, as set down by athletic conferences, represents an attempt to particularize eligibility as that status upon which any undergraduate in good academic standing, who is a genuine amateur athlete, may compete in intercollegiate contests as a member of an athletic organization representing his university or college.

3. Compensation to Players

Just as in the case of eligibility, so in the case of compensation to players in its broadest sense, the intention of the colleges and universities of the country is clear. Except in the matter of summer baseball, conferences and individual institutions agree that intercollegiate athletics are for the amateur and the amateur alone. The intent of all rules concerning recruiting, proselyting, and subsidizing of athletes is unmistakable.

The complexity and detail of conference rules governing these matters is the result of an attempt to specify and define *in extenso* as many as practicable of the acts or conditions which result in the giving and receiving of assistance in kind or in money, which impairs the amateur status of athletes. The intention may be commendable, but the attempt to cover every individual case by a regulation is futile. Of necessity it must result in the omission of certain instances or conditions in which no rule has been devised or, indeed, can be devised. Such omissions make possible covert agreements between individuals which, because they controvert both the regulations and their intent, can be regarded only as equivocal, detrimental, and dishonest. In conference regulations concerning recruiting and subsidizing, as in all other laws involving ethical values, "the letter killeth, but the spirit giveth life."

Although it is idle to quote examples in detail, it may be noted that the Harvard-Yale-Princeton agreement, now in force between Harvard and Yale and Princeton and Yale, appears to be unique in requiring that when assistance is given to an athlete, "the motives of those who extend the aid and the motives of those who receive it" shall be considered. The requirement in the supplementary agreement is that "no man who has ever received any pecuniary reward or its equivalent by reason of his connection with athletics — whether for playing, coaching, or acting as teacher in any branch of sport or engaging therein in any capacity — shall represent his university in any athletic team or crew except that the . . . [Two] Chairmen may permit such participation in intercollegiate athletics by men who might technically be debarred under the letter of the rule, but who in the judgment of the Committee have not commercialized their athletic ability nor offended against the spirit of the foregoing provision." In spite of the fact that the listing of "playing, coaching, or acting as teacher in any branch of sport or engaging therein in any capacity" has led to some equivocation and evasion, nevertheless, no other agreement appears to rest so precisely upon the honor of the institutions involved.

4. Training Regulations

Conference rules concerning the training of athletes deal principally with the maintenance of training tables, camps, and quarters. As regards training tables, there are two attitudes, the one permissive, the other prohibitive. For example, the Pacific Coast Intercollegiate Conference and the Southwest Conference countenance training tables, the former limiting the table to the evening meal for football and basketball and imposing special restrictions upon crews, the latter providing that the entire cost of training tables is to be paid by the students who participate in their privileges. The (Mid-Western) Intercollegiate Conference, the Missouri Valley Conference, and the Southern Intercollegiate Conference permit no training tables whatsoever. Apparently the great majority of conferences have now taken legislative action in this matter in one way or the other.

Camps for the preparation of teams, especially in football, are prohibited by the (Mid-Western) Intercollegiate, Southern, and, except upon home grounds or campus, the Southwest Conferences. The Pacific Coast Intercollegiate Conference provides that "in crew the participants, because of the remoteness of practice waters and other considerations, shall be allowed to associate themselves together for the purpose of better preparing themselves for the contest, this at an expense to them not less than the expense at their regular eating places." This regulation appears to permit the use of training quarters by crews. Certainly it would be difficult for any university eight representing an inland institution to be deprived of the privilege of training quarters.

5. Summer Baseball

Conference regulations respecting summer baseball are more elastic than those bearing upon any other single topic.

They range from absolute prohibition (Intercollegiate Conference, Rules 6 and 7) through restricted participation (Harvard-Yale-Princeton agreement, Pacific Coast Intercollegiate Conference), to practically complete permission (Rocky Mountain Conference). In the middle group the favorite restriction embodies the requirement that permission to play summer baseball must be secured from the student's university athletic authorities. The Harvard-Yale-Princeton agreement appears to recognize, although somewhat timidly, the principle that a professional in one branch of athletics is a professional in all: "A student who takes part in summer baseball or in the work of a summer camp, without first securing the approval of the University Committee on Eligibility jeopardizes his right thereafter to represent his university in any team or crew, and may in the discretion of the University Committee on Eligibility forfeit temporarily, or permanently, his right to do so." Two conferences, the Rocky Mountain and the Southern, restrict players to teams recognized by the National Baseball Commission. Although the Missouri Valley Conference "believes in the necessity of the amateur rule" it permits students to play summer baseball, presumably for pay, on home teams and agrees "to reinstate men who are technically ineligible through ignorance or through the acts of others." At the Nineteenth Annual Meeting of the Association of New England Colleges for Conference on Athletics it was stated by representatives present that Brown University allows its men to play baseball for money during the summer, as well as after-season football, and that four Maine colleges, namely Bates, Bowdoin, Colby, and the University of Maine, permit summer baseball except on professional teams operating under the national agreement. More than one college representative expressed the opinion that at present summer baseball playing cannot be controlled. In the words of Mr. C. A. O'Donnell, of Holy Cross College, "The attempt to cut out summer baseball is idealism. Only colleges where they have wealthy men can do it. The Western Conference claims to control it but it does not. Any boy who has a talent for baseball should be allowed to use it."

Few conferences or individual colleges have set their faces determinedly against summer baseball. Of the conferences, the (Mid-Western) Intercollegiate Conference has dealt commendably with the problem in its obvious phases as well as those most obscure. As a result, it probably suffers less from this form of commercialism than any other group of institutions in the country. The principle that the college should determine the eligibility of its players respecting summer baseball is, of course, no more efficacious than the practices that the colleges themselves permit under it. A very few institutions have taken a decided stand against summer baseball; for example, Cornell has strict regulations against it and enforces them conscientiously. The number of colleges that have followed the principle that an athlete who receives money for playing baseball at any time under any condition shall not represent them in intercollegiate contests would be negligible were it not for the honesty and the courage that such a course displays.

6. Coaching

With respect to the employment and status of coaches, only one tendency is common to all athletic conferences. Such associations as have legislated concerning the appointment of coaches agree upon the principle that members of the coaching staff shall be regularly employed by their institutions. Apparently none of the larger conferences recognize any distinction, whether in fact or in desirability, between (1) entrusting the coaching of teams or crews to men appointed primarily for work in academic subjects, (2) employing specialists in physical education, which is an essentially non-academic subject, as faculty members to coach, and (3) engaging as a coach with faculty status a former player whose occupation since graduation has been far from academic. The Southern Conference prohibits employing as a coach any football player "who plays as a member of a professional football team." The (Mid-Western) Intercollegiate Conference stipulates that "no coach shall be appointed except by university governing bodies on the recommendation of the faculty or president in the regular way." Harvard, Yale, and Princeton once agreed that "it should be the aim of each university, as far as practicable, to have the coaching of all teams done by members of its regular staff." Both provisions amount in the end to the same thing. It is, however, true that the second of the two affords an honest latitude in the selection of football coaches and permits the employment of men with due qualifications of skill and of character without "a seat on the faculty" to disguise their status as professional athletes. Most of the conferences that have legislated in the matter prohibit the coach's receiving from other than duly regularized sources any bonuses or extra compensation for his work.

7. Sportsmanship

Among the conferences whose rules have been subject to detailed examination, a growing number emphasize the principles of sportsmanship.

The Harvard-Yale-Princeton agreement was prefaced with a statement of the desire to keep the "spirit and uses of professionalism out of college sports and unreasonable hampering of them by the mere letter of rules," and the expression of a desire to maintain mutual confidence concerning eligibility. The Southern Conference enjoins upon each institution the duty of avoiding controversy over athletics and of using "every available means to encourage right feeling and courteous relations between the teams and student bodies of the representative institutions." A resolution passed by the Pacific Northwest Intercollegiate Conference some years after the original agreement in 1910 urges "upon the student body and upon the student newspaper correspondents of each member the necessity of close observance of the ideals of good sportsmanship." Too often where such resolutions exist they yield to expediency when coaches and other athletic officials must choose between theory and practice. On the other hand, as a rule college conferences in the past have laid too little stress upon good sportsmanship as a fundamental instrument in athletic competition. The Illinois Intercollegiate Conference states as its object "to encourage sportsmanlike conduct and fair play in all collegiate contests in which any or all the colleges of this Conference may engage; to promote the spirit of purity in college athletics and keep athletics free from professionalism; to provide for annual intercollegiate contests within the Conference and to formulate and enforce general rules for the government of all athletic contests between colleges of the Conference."

8. Summary

In respect of the seven topics just examined there appears to be general agreement among the conferences concerning at least four: namely, eligibility, compensation to players, training regulations, and coaching. Matters of faculty control and of sportsmanship are, it would appear, taken for granted in a number of sets of rules. Of all of these topics, summer baseball has produced the widest divergence of opinion and the greatest variety of practice. It is difficult to understand the logic of a representative body that in one paragraph of its regulations goes on record as upholding the status of the amateur and in another countenances the payment of its athletes for playing baseball with professionals during the summer months. Perhaps it is too much to expect consistency in such matters.

Whatever reasons are urged for countenancing procedures which contravene and nullify the fine phrases in which conferences indulge concerning the amateur status, the real reason is this : universities and colleges have found that unless they relax their rules regarding professionalism and wink at flagrant abuses they cannot win enough games to satisfy their constituents and continue their large expenditures.

C. Notes on the Execution of Conference Rules

Between the minutely detailed provisions of the constitutions and rules governing the Rocky Mountain Faculty Athletic Conference of 1923 and the general and elastic principles laid down in the Harvard-Yale-Princeton agreement as revised in the same year, most of the sets of conference rules occupy a mid-ground. Sometimes, as in the case of the Southern Conference, all of the regulations are to be classified in this middle position as regards detail. Sometimes certain rules are general, while others are much particularized, like, for example, the requirements of the (Mid-Western) Intercollegiate Conference respecting eligibility. It does not appear that any relationship exists between minuteness of provisions and the degree of thoroughness with which they are carried out.

On the other hand, in not a few sets of rules general principles are so modified by exceptions, both to theory and to operation, that they become nugatory. The Missouri Valley pronouncements on the amateur status and on participation in summer baseball on home teams is a case in point.[7]

It would be idle to complain that conference rules are not enforced. Considering their complexity, the overweening desire for victory, and the reprehensible tendency to win games by means of "jokers," exceptions, and far-fetched interpretations of rules or resolutions, the regulations of conferences are generally well administered. But he who believes that clean and sportsmanlike games, chivalrous rivalry, and magnanimous competition are to be attained through mere administrative provisions and procedure is indeed naïve. The tendency to assume that any abuses inherent in intercollegiate athletics will automatically disappear if a conference is formed and passes rules of a nature sufficiently lofty and stringent is absurd, no matter how much administrative

[7] Of eligibility rules adopted by athletic associations at various institutions, those concerning summer baseball at Amherst and Cornell appear to stand among the most stringent. The attitude of most conferences is reflected in the eleventh and thirteenth eligibility rules of Lehigh University (1925).

machinery is provided or how many teeth may be placed in regulations. The funda-mental problem concerns, not the enforcement of rules by conference administrators, but conscientious adherence to them and their honorable observance on the part of all whom they affect, — alumni, graduate managers, coaches, faculty members, college presidents, and undergraduates. In the course of the present study it has been proved again and again that no rule, however well intended, can be made binding without the consent and the active coöperation of those to whom it applies. Too often multiplicity of detail in regulations tends only to drive dishonest practices out of sight and to make them secret, not to eliminate them.

In this matter the American athlete can profit from the words of the Canadian Rugby Union quoted in Chapter III. If athletics in Canadian institutions offer to us who live south of the international boundary any principle that is worthy of our most active and sincere admiration and imitation, it is that principle which the Canadian Football Code embodies.

IV. Certain National Relationships of American College Athletics

In the United States, universities and colleges, although influential, have not dom-inated athletic and sporting tradition as they have in England and Canada. This fact, as regards the United States, is accounted for by three considerations, which have operated to dilute the effect of university life upon the life of the people : democratic conditions, political, and social ; both the vast expanse of territory and the distance between institutions of higher education ; and, above all, the nature of the interest that the American people have evinced in college games and contests. This interest is largely ascribable to the emphasis laid by our newspapers upon athletics in college life. Under these conditions, the day has not yet arrived when the college or the university may be regarded as furnishing all of the essentials of an American athletic tradition. That day will be delayed until our college men and women over a period of years act as regards athletics with a "leadership," a sincerity, and a courage of principle that shall com-mand the respect and the active emulation of other Americans.

Our present concern is with only two phases in the national relationships of American college athletics : representative legislative and executive bodies and their functions, and national contests as they involve individual college students as participants.

A. National Bodies

As far as colleges and universities are directly concerned, their present countrywide affiliations are with the National Collegiate Athletic Association, which is essentially deliberative and legislative in its activities, and with such directive and executive organizations as the Intercollegiate Association of Amateur Athletes of America,

which holds track and field meets and sponsors other activities in which college undergraduates participate. It should be remembered also that the National Collegiate
Athletic Association has held some seven annual track and field meetings in which,
however, Eastern participation has been much restricted. To certain very influential
bodies that govern the various branches of athletics and safeguard the standing of
participants in them and include both college and non-college athletes, — such bodies
as, for example, the Amateur Fencers League of America, the National Association of
Amateur Oarsmen, and the United States Golf Association, — American colleges and
universities have a certain relation, but it is less close than their connection with the
various intercollegiate associations in boxing, fencing, lawn tennis, rifle shooting, rowing, Rugby and association football, swimming, and wrestling. Moreover, college students, among others, participate in the annual games, some national, some regional in
their entries, conducted by such organizations as the Knights of Columbus and the
Young Men's Christian Association. The mazes of all these associations are too complicated to be threaded by the present discussion, which is concerned less with the listing of intercollegiate athletic bodies than with the relation of college athletics to
education.

1. The National Collegiate Athletic Association

Membership in the National Collegiate Athletic Association, originally organized
as the Intercollegiate Athletic Association in 1905, is open to "all colleges, universities, and institutions of learning in the United States."

Three classes of membership are provided: active, which includes some one hundred
and fifty universities and colleges; allied, embracing six conferences with about sixty
institutional members; and associate, in two classes, the first consisting of schools, the
second of "groups of colleges and universities that are organized for the purpose of
conducting mutual competition in sports," of which only one, the United States Intercollegiate Lacrosse Association, holds membership. The constituency of the National
Collegiate Athletic Association is divided into eight geographical districts, each with
its vice-president, who acts as arbitrator of charges concerning amateurism, adviser of
the conduct of intercollegiate athletics, and custodian of records, and who reports to
the annual convention of the Association concerning the strictness with which the
rules have been "enforced" during the year, "modifications or additions to the
eligibility code made by institutions individually or concertedly," progress toward
uniformity in the activities of intercollegiate athletic associations, of local conferences,
of leagues, district competitions if any, and other facts or recommendations which may
be of interest to the Association. A council of fifteen members, eight of whom are
members of faculties, conducts the affairs of the Association between meetings, and
the council elects its own executive committee of five. The Association chooses annually committees to frame the rules in twelve branches of athletics — football, soccer,
basketball, swimming, volley ball, boxing, track, wrestling, hockey, fencing, gymnastics, and lacrosse; to preserve college athletic records; to arbitrate; and, under the

approval of the executive committee, to publish the rules of various sports. Many of the items of receipt and expenditure in the accounts of the Association concern the preparation and publication of these rules.

a. *Purposes of the National Collegiate Athletic Association*

The purposes of the Association, which are laid down in its constitution as amended December 30, 1924, are so important and generally so wholesome that they are quoted in their entirety:

The purposes of this Association are:

(1) The upholding of the principle of institutional control of, and responsibility for, all collegiate sports.

(2) The stimulation and improvement of intramural and intercollegiate athletic sports.

(3) The promotion of physical exercise among the students of the educational institutions of the United States.

(4) The establishment of a uniform law of amateurism and of the principles of amateur sports.

(5) The encouragement of the adoption by its constituent members of strict eligibility rules to comply with high standards of scholarship, amateur standing, and good sportsmanship.

(6) The formulation, copyrighting, and publication of rules of play for the government of collegiate sports.

(7) The supervision of the regulation and conduct, by its constituent members, of intercollegiate sports in regional and national collegiate athletic contests, and the preservation of collegiate athletic records.

(8) In general, the study of the various phases of competitive athletics, physical training, and allied problems, the establishment of standards for amateur sports, and the promotion of the adoption of recommended measures, to the end that the colleges and universities of the United States may maintain their athletic activities on a high plane and may make efficient use of sports for character building.

The precise meaning of "amateurism," as the term is used by the Association, is defined in the seventh article of this constitution. The third section specifies six acts on the part of the participants that are considered to violate amateurism.

b. *Meetings and Carnivals*

Mention has been made of the annual track and field meeting held by the Association, usually in Chicago, and of the committees chosen annually by this body to frame rules. In the case of track athletics these functions have a very wide extent. Although only a single meet is conducted by the Association, nevertheless a conception of the extent to which its rules are influential may be gained from an enumeration of track and field meetings in which member institutions compete. National and sectional conference meets of this character number about twenty during each year. Collegiate state meets are slightly fewer. Over one hundred and twenty-five dual college meets, several triangular meets, and, usually, a meeting between four institutions are held. The popularity of the relay carnivals is shown by the fact that more than ten are held annually in the United States. In addition, about thirty-five scholastic track meets, practically the same number of interscholastic meets sponsored by conferences, associations, or colleges as members of the Association, and four or five high school relay contests take place during each year. Over such competition the National Collegiate Athletic Association appears to exercise no direct control. These responsibilities are undertaken by constituent bodies and universities.

c. Merits and Defects of the Organization

Certainly to the general principles upon which the National Collegiate Athletic Association is based few objections are to be taken. The Association fixes responsibilities in college athletics, favors the extension of athletics to include a widening circle of undergraduates, encourages strictness of regulations touching eligibility, and upholds the status of the amateur. Few universities and colleges would have either the desire or the temerity to attack openly these principles, which, so far as they go, appear to be almost impeccable. A critic may regret that more responsibility for the conduct of college athletics is not given to undergraduates, that students have no part in the affairs of the Association, that in the deliberations of this body the voice of the men to whom athletics are a vocation rather than an avocation tends to be more frequently heard than that of the amateur by the Association's own definition, and that at times the organization has appeared to be more concerned with enforcement of its standards than with persuasion to the end of coöperation.

On the whole, the influence of the National Collegiate Athletic Association has been salutary. But the past twenty years have witnessed a change in the tone and temper of its annual meetings. At its inception the Association appears to have been rather an informal coming-together of individuals possessed of mutual interests and aspirations than what it now is — a legislative assembly before which invited speakers set forth their views, coupled with an agency for holding track meets. The resumption by the Association of membership in the American Olympic Association closes happily a brief but unfortunate chapter in the history of both bodies.

2. The Intercollegiate Association of Amateur Athletes of America

The Intercollegiate Association of Amateur Athletes of America, which is allied to the Amateur Athletic Union, was organized in 1875. Its present constitution, framed in 1891, has been amended in every year since its adoption except 1912 and 1918.

The object of the Association is "the protection of the mutual interests of the different universities and colleges which comprise the Association, and the advancement and improvement of amateur athletic sports among universities and colleges." Its membership (1928) numbers forty colleges and universities, of which by far the greater number are situated in the Eastern States. Beyond the Middle Atlantic States and New England the members are the University of California, University of Cincinnati, University of Michigan, Michigan State College, University of Southern California, Stanford University, and the University of West Virginia. The Association "declares its absolute jurisdiction among its members" over competition in the following events: running (all distances), walking, jumping, pole vaulting, putting the shot, and throwing the hammer, weights, javelin, and discus. It conducts annually an indoor meeting in February under sets of rules which it promulgates and a track and field championship meeting in May. Since 1908, it has sponsored in each November a series of cross-country runs.

Officers of the Association are not permitted to receive remuneration for their services. In cases of infraction of its own amateur rules, the organization possesses a pardoning power. Under these rules, in 1927 some eighty-eight 'varsity meetings and seventeen freshman meetings were held, and during the preceding year more than seventy cross-country runs. The I.C.A.A.A.A. is officered entirely by undergraduates; graduate members act as advisers without vote. In this respect the Association is believed to be unique among national bodies.

3. The National Amateur Athletic Federation

The National Amateur Athletic Federation, organized in 1920, comprises two divisions, one for men, the other for women.

In the men's division are included eighteen bodies, among which may be mentioned the United States Army, Navy, and Marine Corps, the American Legion, the National Collegiate Athletic Association, the Young Men's Christian Association, the American Physical Education Association, the Jewish Welfare Board, and the Catholic Boys' Brigade of the United States. The Federation states its "mission" to be "to create and maintain in the United States a permanent organization representative of amateur athletics and of organizations devoted thereto; to establish and maintain the highest ideals of amateur sport in the United States; to promote the development of physical education; to encourage the standardization of the rules of all amateur athletic games and competitions and the participation of this country in the International Olympic Games." Its definition of an amateur and its pronouncement upon the spirit of "Amateurism" are those of the National Collegiate Athletic Association. The constitution provides that "each organization in the Federation shall direct its own activities, conduct its own competitions, and control its own athletes in accordance with the principles set forth by the Federation. Governmental agencies are exempt from all dues. These provisions appear to leave the Military and Naval Academies, as well as the Services, responsible for the formulation and application of their own regulations.

B. Individual Relationships to National Bodies and Competitions

Concerning the relationship of institutions and of individual athletes to national bodies and competitions, it will be possible to set down only a few observations.

1. The Athlete and the National Deliberative Body

The American university undergraduate who possesses any specific information concerning the processes and work of the National Collegiate Athletic Association is very rare. The reason, which has been foreshadowed in preceding pages, is reflected even more sharply in the vote of the Association at its twenty-second annual session "that the president of the Association be requested to send a letter before the time of the next convention to the president of the member colleges suggesting the desirability of their sending two delegates to the convention, one from the physical education department, and the other from the academic teaching staff." In short, the Association is not intended for undergraduates; the delegates who attend its meetings should, it is held, be evenly divided between professional physical educators and teachers of academic subjects who are interested in athletics. Such a representation doubtless facilitates procedure, but it none the less certainly provides a powerful professional leaning in the assembly and absolutely eliminates the possibility of student interest in the more general aspects of the Association, together with all the good that might flow from personal contacts between undergraduates of widely differing and separated institutions. The mere presence of a few score students as spectators at the deliberations of the Association would be well worth the cost in money, and might in a decade lend an entirely different cast to certain aspects of college athletics.

2. The Athlete and National Games and Meets

Much more intimate is the undergraduate's relation to the national or even the regional bodies that hold intercollegiate track meets and similar competitions. At the annual games of the Intercollegiate Association of Amateur Athletes of America, his position is similar to that of a guest; similarly, when such bodies as the Knights of Columbus and the Young Men's Christian Association hold invitation or closed meets that college athletes enter. The merging of individual interest in the scoring of points with the interest and success of the college is mainly wholesome, and in most track meets points scored for an institution have more importance than individual triumphs. Exception, of course, is to be found in those cases of very expert athletes, whose concern is almost wholly with their own performance and whose reputations have been established through newspaper publicity, prompted sometimes by the press agents of their universities. Trophies awarded on the basis of institutional rather than individual success serve to diminish the undue renown of these "stars." For such reasons the abandonment of team competition in the annual meets of the National Collegiate Athletic Association is regrettable. No force or incident that operates to merge the esteem in which the individual athlete is held with the honor of his college should be neglected.

Of late years one of the reasons most frequently advanced against national or regional competitions has been the distances that teams and supporters must travel to matches. It is also urged that academic work is seriously impaired by a week's absence from a university, that college discipline is weakened, and that such trips breed "over-emphasis." On the other hand, it is asserted, usually by coaches, students, or others who have an immediate interest in such trips, that through travel, seeing distant parts of the country, and the amicable contacts that athletes make one with another, much "educational" benefit accrues to the contestants, not to mention the favorable publicity that such contests bring to the institutions involved. With due respect to the arguments advanced by both sides, it must be said that the weight of fact and of policy appears to rest with those who oppose long trips.

The clearest example of what occurs is to be found in the relay carnivals. Beginning with such annual events as those sponsored by the University of Pennsylvania, relay meetings have spread to include those of Drake University and the sections of New England, Illinois, Texas, and the Far West. It is undeniable that the increase of such carnivals has dimmed the lustre of the "Penn Relays." On the other hand, the results of the movement have been in some respects wholesome because of the dilution of interest it has brought about.

These comments concerning intersectional matches, of course, refer only to non-commercial, college competitions. The commercial exploiting of any form of college athletics through intersectional contests and championships is reprehensible, and should not be countenanced by any university. Such interests as are involved in the California Tournaments of Roses can work only injury to college athletics in their relation to the general public, institutions, their teams, and the individual participants. Furthermore, the holding by universities of football, basketball, and track competitions on home grounds for school teams appears to be deleterious to the best interests of all. Certainly the benefits to the contesting schoolboys are negligible; from the point of view of physical welfare, and, indeed, from all other points of view, these boys might far better be competing on their own fields or courts. The supposed advantages to universities that hold such meetings in selecting promising schoolboy athletes to whom inducements, however mild, may be proffered, certainly are unsavory enough. The dangers to individual athletes that national, intersectional, or regional competitions breed arise from the exploiting of teams to increase gate receipts and the undue publicity lavished upon them. The educational advantages, if any, that accrue to the contestants from long trips are more than counteracted by unwholesome notoriety, fatigue, the impairment of studies, and the increase of commercialism in college athletics. The reputation that comes to any university whose teams are permitted to indulge in long trips is largely of commercial rather than of academic importance. In such circumstances it is not astonishing that the name of the modest gentleman who occupies the president's chair should be less widely known than that of the coach whom he hires to develop a team, every member of which is exploited for the commercialized dishonor of the institution and the enhancement of the factitious reputation of its coach.

V. THE INTERNATIONAL BEARINGS OF AMERICAN COLLEGE ATHLETICS

The widest of the extramural relationships in American college athletics is that which extends into other lands. It involves both the competition of American universities and colleges with particular institutions in other countries and the participation of athletes, whether as individuals or as members of teams, in international games. In both of these two types of competition the colleges and universities of the United States have met Canadian, English, and, in baseball, Japanese universities. In the second type, relationships have involved as principals nations rather than particular institutions, because they have been formed mainly through the medium of the Olympic Games.

A. INTERNATIONAL COMPETITION AND INTERNATIONAL AMITY

The conviction is frequently expressed that the surest road to friendship between nations lies through sport. The prospect is alluring: hosts of the youth of all countries coming to exalt by practical example the principles of sportsmanship and fair play, gaining through games the understanding that prompts to national friendships; wholesome rivalries that make impossible the suspicions which breed war between nations; a diplomacy of sport founded and upheld by numberless ambassadors of international amity, to the end that there shall come a parliament of sportsmanship, an athletic federation of the world. The view which these conceptions presents is based upon hope rather than upon past fulfillment. The history of international competition between schools and universities, between sections of countries, and between nations indicates that the good will of peoples is most substantially furthered through games and contests when the units represented are comparatively small and when patriotism is not debased to mere partisan prejudice. In short, it would appear that the road to international peace through sport is long, that the beginnings of the journey have only just been made, and that the surest hope for the consummation so devoutly wished by many rests upon the changing and broadening of their own attitudes.

B. COLLEGE AND SCHOOL CONTESTS

It is not to be denied that friendship between undergraduates of universities in different countries at present rests more firmly upon cordiality in athletic competition than upon the academic amenities.

1. With Canadian Universities

Contests between teams representing American universities and colleges and Canadian institutions, covering a wide field of athletic competition, began to come into public notice with the first football game between Harvard and McGill, in 1874.[8]

[8] Weyand, *American Football*, 1927, pages 8 ff.

Between Harvard on the one hand, and McGill University and certain Canadian amateur football clubs on the other, contests were continued sporadically until 1884, when football at Harvard was abolished on account of roughness. Meanwhile, Michigan, in 1880, played one match with Toronto, and Dartmouth one match with McGill. Since the divergence of the American rules from the Canadian code, which developed rapidly after the withdrawal of Harvard from the game, relations in football between the two countries have languished. Michigan played Windsor in 1885, Haskell Institute played the University of Toronto in 1912, and in the following year St. Lawrence University played Ottawa. The days when teams from Canadian and American universities could adapt the number of men on either side and the entire style of play to whichever rules were agreed upon have long passed. Happily, however, the playing of Rugby at Stanford and the University of California has provided in more recent years a basis of competition with the universities of British Columbia and Nova Scotia.

Although in track athletics and in soccer relations have not been so intimate as might be expected, they have prospered in other branches of athletics. Thus, teams chosen from various Canadian universities meet American intercollegiate representatives, chiefly of the two Service Academies that have fostered the contact, in annual assaults-at-arms, including fencing, wrestling, and, principally, boxing at Annapolis. The annual carnival of winter sports sponsored by Dartmouth College has brought Canadian undergraduates to Hanover for ski-ing and snow-shoeing, and several New England colleges are combining with McGill University to extend competition in this field. Individual swimmers and tennis players have, of course, entered American matches as representatives of Canadian universities. Ice hockey has become more intimately North American than other branches of athletics through the visits of Canadian teams to colleges in Maine and annual series of contests in Boston, Chicago, and New York City with various neighboring universities. The commercialized management of some of these series, prompted probably by the comparatively high cost of travel, is to be regretted. Here again, the most satisfactory relationships have sprung from visits of teams representing one university or college to the campus of another. It is notable that the trips of Canadian university players to the south of the boundary appear to have been much more numerous than the excursions of American teams to the north. Doubtless considerations of university discipline, the keenness of the rivalries between American colleges, the lack of extensive common ground in football, and the comparatively large number of neighboring institutions with which competition in the United States can be fostered without recourse to extended trips have all contributed to limit international contests between American and Canadian universities.

2. With English Universities

Of the twenty-six fields of sport in which British undergraduates indulge, representatives of universities in Great Britain meet American college competitors in only three : rowing, track and field athletics, and lacrosse. As regards rowing, crews of Columbia, Cornell, Harvard, the University of Pennsylvania, Princeton, Syracuse, and Yale upon a number of occasions have rowed against Oxford or Cambridge crews. The recent visit of the Kent School four to English waters was followed by the trip of the Browne and Nichols School eight to the Henley and other regattas in 1929. The jaunts of American college track athletes to England and of Oxford and Cambridge athletes to the United States have given rise to not a few personal friendships. Indeed, because of good sportsmanship and the pains that have been bestowed upon the entertainment of such visitors in both countries, it is doubtful if any other athletic pilgrimages have left such pleasant memories to both hosts and guests. Sporadically, lacrosse teams of certain of our Eastern universities have played against Oxford and Cambridge teams. The fruitfulness of all these contests is ascribable to their freedom from commercial exploitation, the intimacies arising from the close associations that they bring to pass between the undergraduates of both countries, and the acceptable personal qualities of members of teams or crews.

Thus far, the only universities of Great Britain which have entered into athletic relationships with American institutions have been Oxford and Cambridge. It should be noted that the British universities that compose the Inter-'Varsity Athletic Board offer an opportunity to open wider the field of international relationships in college athletics.

C. Organizations Possessing International Affiliations

Before briefly considering certain aspects of the relation of American colleges and universities to the Olympic Games it will be well to glance at some of the complexities which surround international university competition, and which have arisen from the desire of sportsmen in most countries to preserve the amateur status. What that status is and how it came to be defined need not enter into the present discussion. For the moment, our concern is with the relation of universities and colleges of the United States, through the Amateur Athletic Union of the United States and the International Amateur Athletic Federation, to the universities of other countries. Because this complicated matter has given rise to much controversy, some heated, some even bitter, and because it is involved in an understanding of a host of problems that beset American college athletics, it cannot be omitted from this enquiry.

1. The International Amateur Athletic Federation

Several international amateur sports federations antedate the revival of the Olympic Games at Athens in 1896. Before that year, associations or unions in gymnastics, swimming, rifle shooting, revolver shooting, and other branches had been dealing individually with problems arising from competition between countries. About the time of the Olympic Games of 1908, Mr. J. S. Edstrom of Sweden led a movement for international solidarity, with the result that by 1912, when the games were held at Stockholm, the International Amateur Athletic Federation had advanced beyond an experimental stage. It was not, however, until the summer of the following year, when the Federation met in Berlin, Mr. Edstrom presiding, that American representatives began to take active part in its affairs. Probably the most important work of the year was the adoption of an amateur rule.

The constitution of the Federation provides that in each country a single organization shall exercise jurisdiction over both international and national aspects of competition. Thus, for example, the Amateur Athletic Association of Great Britain and the Amateur Athletic Union of Canada perform these functions for their respective countries. Naturally, the strength of the International Federation, like the strength of any other alliance of a similar nature, resides in the vigor and the strictness with which each country maintains as a member the letter and the spirit of the pact. In spite of not a few attempts to break the authority of the Federation over international competition, based upon certificates and permits granted by each component national body, its powers have never been seriously threatened. The necessity of the Federation's maintaining an unbroken front, although obvious, has apparently been strengthened by politico-social conditions in Russia. The American body upon which the control, through sanctions and certification of eligibility, devolves is the Amateur Athletic Union of the United States.

2. The Amateur Athletic Union of the United States

The only American body duly recognized by the representative amateur athletic organizations of other countries, through the International Amateur Athletic Federation, as controlling the eligibility of American competitors, always as regards only certain sports enumerated below, is the Amateur Athletic Union.

Although the Union was not organized until 1888, nearly twenty years after American colleges began to compete with English universities in various branches of athletics, nevertheless when active American participation in the International Amateur Athletic Federation began in 1913 the Union was, with the possible exception of the American Olympic Committee, whose functions were highly specialized, the only American organization of sufficiently cosmopolitan composition, long experience, and variety of contacts to be considered capable of performing the important duties of the American member in the Federation. It is not to be expected that a body whose organization is very inclusive and whose officers receive no salaries for their services should exhibit either absolute unity or solidarity. The Union is somewhat loosely composed of twenty-three district associations or "active" regional bodies covering the United States on a geographical basis, each with its own officers and presumably its own constituency. To these regional organizations various colleges and universities are affiliated, as Columbia is connected through membership in the Metropolitan Association, Harvard in the New England Association, Yale in the Connecticut Association, and all three through the Intercollegiate Association of Amateur Athletes of America. Colleges west of the Alleghenies have not affiliated with the Union to the same extent as their Eastern neighbors. Moreover, the Army and Navy and their Service schools have not entered the relation.[9]

Now, it is a fact that the International Amateur Athletic Federation has been consistent in its refusal to recognize in any country any organization that does not hold membership in the Federation. It has, therefore, followed that an American athlete who desires to take part, for example, in international track and field competition must obtain permission from the Amateur Athletic Union. Unless this permission is forthcoming, no other country will allow him to enter into competition with its athletes. The policy appears to be sound. Its soundness, however, has not prevented attempts at Paris in 1924, at Prague in 1925, and at the Hague in 1926, on the part of representative Americans, to secure exceptions to this rule as it affects international intercollegiate contests, to the end that, for example, members of Cornell, Harvard, Princeton, and Yale track and field teams might compete in England against athletes from Oxford and Cambridge without the necessity of a sanction from the Amateur Athletic Union of the United States. Upon none of these petitions was favorable action taken by the Federation. Mr. Gustavus T. Kirby explains the grounds for the refusal somewhat as follows : The American type of university, and especially its control of amateur athletics and of its athletes, is practically, if not altogether, unknown on the Continent and quite generally unappreciated in England. In view of these facts, it is not astonishing that Europeans should oppose the American request on the ground that no distinction in principle can be made between athletes representing colleges in the United States and the athletes of Russia, because of the complications that always result from payment for "broken time." To the pleas that the American college athlete is of a very different type from the member of the Russian Soviet, and that the American college maintains athletic control over its students even after the close of the academic year, the reply is, in effect, that under these circumstances American colleges and universities should work in harmony with the American Athletic Union, to which they can and should appeal for permission for their athletes to compete outside of the United States. The provision for direct certification adopted by the A.A.U. in 1928 is a fortunate step. It would therefore appear that the concern of the Federation is solely with international events.

The actual procedure needed to secure a sanction for a track meeting between American and British universities is relatively simple. The athletic authorities of the American institution merely apply to the Intercollegiate Association of Amateur Athletes of America, a constituent of the Amateur Athletic Union in which forty institutions hold membership (1927), for the necessary sanction, which is always granted as a matter of course. Moreover, it is significant that no case is ascertainable

[9] John L. Griffith, "Why It Is Necessary to Supervise Athletics," four articles, Chicago *Daily News*, February, 1928.

in which a university or a college that desired to compete against an institution in another country ever failed to apply for a sanction, nor does the Union appear ever to have withheld its permission when request for it has been proffered. Private communications from English university athletes to members of the staff of this study reflect the European reluctance to compete in international university events against Americans who are not duly sanctioned through the processes and channels that now exist. At the present writing there is small likelihood that the International Amateur Athletic Federation will alter this feature of its policy in the immediate future.

Neither the International Amateur Athletic Federation, in its world-wide relation, nor the Amateur Athletic Union in the United States seeks to control all competition in track and field athletics. These bodies confine their mutual efforts only to "open competitions"; their provisions "do not apply to events that are 'closed,' that is, open only to members of a club, organization or group that is a member of any Association of this Union." Furthermore, over matches and games in which American college athletes meet only American college athletes the Union disclaims jurisdiction. When, however, an American college athlete competes against a member of any local amateur athletic association or club, including the Young Men's Christian Association, appeal must be made to the Union under the terms of its constitution and by-laws. In opposition to this arrangement it is frequently urged that it involves government without the consent of the governed, and a usurpation of powers that now reside in the colleges of the United States. This objection is more theoretical than practical.

Outside the constituency of the Union remain such universities and colleges as are not members, whether through the regional associations or the Intercollegiate Association of Amateur Athletes of America, the United States Military and Naval Academies, the Young Men's Christian Association, the National Amateur Athletic Federation, and the National Collegiate Athletic Association. With the Young Men's Christian Association and the accusation that its officers desire to dominate American college athletics the present discussion is not concerned. From the point of view, not of theory, but of existing fact, it would appear that a policy of coöperation as regards sanctions and international contests might well be furthered by those colleges and universities of this country which desire to compete against similar institutions in other lands. Apparently, the Amateur Athletic Union has not been unduly severe in any ascertainable case in which a sanction was requested for an American athlete to enter such competition; indeed, it seems likely that, if anything, it has been generous in issuing permissions to certain American college athletes who have derived something more than "pleasure and physical, mental, or social benefits" from college athletics.

We have now discussed the body whose function it is to govern formal international competition (the International Amateur Athletic Federation) and the constituent organization that represents this body in the United States (the Amateur Athletic Union of the United States). We turn now to the principal avenue of international competition, the Olympic Games. Although in general each country has its own Olympic Committee, whose function it is to select the nation's competitors and to arrange the details of its representation at the Games, we shall treat mainly of the work of the American Olympic Association.

3. The American Olympic Association

The certification of contestants in the Olympic Games is a complicated matter. All entries from any country must be certified by two agencies : (1) that country's member body of the International Amateur Athletic Federation which "governs" the particular sport in which certification is to be made, and (2) the national Olympic Committee. The application of this principle of dual certification in the United States is as follows : For those of the seventeen sports over which the Amateur Athletic Union of the United States claims jurisdiction, including, for example, boxing, running, jumping, pole vaulting, swimming, etc., the Union acts as the first of the two certifying bodies. For those branches over which the Union does not "claim jurisdiction," such, for example, as rowing and tennis, the national sports body governing the particular sport certifies. In these two examples certification would be made by the National Association of Amateur Oarsmen of America and the United States Lawn Tennis Association. In every instance, however, the American Olympic Committee acts as the second of the two certifying bodies.

The combination of selection and certification is even more complicated. If, for example, an undergraduate amateur athlete desired to enter an international competition such as the Olympic Games, he might be certificated directly by his college ; or he might be entered in the selective competitions through a subordinate body of the Union ; or, thirdly, he might enter one of the seven sets of semi-final regional tryouts from which winners may be certificated through the Intercollegiate Association of Amateur Athletes of America, and accredited either as a college representative or as an unattached athlete. It is matter of common knowledge that the Union has been adversely criticized for its alleged favoritism toward college and army athletes in not subjecting them to the same rigid processes as it subjects other competitors. So far as can be ascertained, the Union has striven to keep the avenues of competition open to the most capable amateur athletes in those branches over which it claims jurisdiction. As respects all branches, before any American contestant can engage in the respective Olympic contests against competitors from the other thirty-nine countries holding membership in the International Amateur Athletic Federation, the appropriate American governing sports body and the American Olympic Committee must certify to his status as an amateur.

The American Olympic Association grew out of the need for a central organization charged with the selection and management of American competitors in the Olympic Games, the revival of which is due directly to the energy of Baron Pierre de Coubertin. Having previously become acquainted with Dr. William Milligan Sloane, professor of history at Princeton, M. de Coubertin, upon coming from France to he United States to arouse interest in the revival of the Games, naturally placed himself in Professor Sloane's hands. A meeting attended by a few prominent American sportsmen was held at the University Club in New York City, and, as a result, an American team was entered in the Games at Athens in 1896. This team, which was practically a track and field group, was selected by the late James E. Sullivan without tryouts. Although an American Olympic Committee appears to have been in existence, its functions and influence were somewhat intangible and Mr. Sullivan alone became the judge of the eligibility of competitors. The games were won for America by a team consisting principally of students or recent graduates of Harvard, Princeton, and Columbia.

A rigid selection of American contestants in the Olympic Games by a continuing American committee was not inaugurated until after the Games at London in 1904. During a number of years in this period, Mr. Sullivan continued to choose members of the American committee, who every four years gathered together the best athletes available in the United States. Realizing in 1911 the impermanency of this arrangement, Mr. Sullivan, after consultation with influential athletic authorities, took steps to reorganize the American Olympic Committee and to secure financial support that would be adequate to permit participation in the Stockholm Games of 1912. From these beginnings grew the American Olympic Association, of which Colonel Robert M. Thompson was the first president. The occasion of the Stockholm Games represented the initial attempt of an American Olympic Committee of this Association to pass upon the eligibility of competitors for the teams. The effort was more theoretical than real, since such governing bodies as the American rifle, pistol, and track athletics associations in effect chose representatives with little if any guidance or advice. For the Olympic Games at Antwerp in 1920 the American Olympic Committee made a genuine effort to pass upon the qualifications of all members of teams rather than upon their technical skill or excellence, and a special committee was appointed. A similar procedure was followed in choosing the American representatives to the meeting at Paris in 1924.

The situation has led to much controversy between the somewhat conservative adherents to the established order and the proponents of international university competition to be conducted without reference to the duly constituted agencies. It would be neither seemly nor desirable to rehearse the charges and counter-charges to which this situation has given rise. For the present, it is sufficient to note that the National Amateur Athletic Federation and the National Collegiate Athletic Association have returned to full membership and participation in the American Olympic Association for the sake of "international amity and international sport."

4. Summary

Officers or representatives of the Amateur Athletic Union, the National Collegiate Athletic Association, and the National Amateur Athletic Federation have gone on record to the effect that athletic competitions of an international character between college athletes, whether as individuals or as representatives, should be regarded as "closed" meetings and therefore should lie wholly beyond the jurisdiction of any other body than the colleges or universities concerned. However desirable this may seem from the American point of view, there appears to be little likelihood that England or other countries of the world will accede to it. The Oxford or Cambridge athlete who comes to the United States certified by the British Amateur Athletic Union is free to compete in any college meeting without recourse or reference to the Amateur Athletic Union of the United States. Should he, however, wish to enter an "open meet" in which college, club, and unattached athletes participate, he may encounter difficulties. Indeed, as a safeguard to his amateur standing the certificate of the British body permits him only to enter sanctioned meets in which he contends only with amateurs so adjudged by the one American body internationally competent to certify to the eligibility of the individual competitor. A reciprocal relationship exists in cases in which American college athletes contend with undergraduates of British universities.

Conclusion

Although it has seemed best to discuss the principal extramural relationships of college athletics in a single chapter, few common inferences can be drawn. On the negative side one or two considerations are noteworthy. The extramural relationships of American college athletics have not always been friendly. Indeed, rivalry, whether or not alumni-bred, has been aggravated to jealousy and wrangling, which surely have no place in the American conception of sportsmanship. Some of the individuals who have been involved in these disputes have apparently been more concerned with justifying the payment of their own salaries and augmenting their own power and that of the body with which they are identified than with the encouragement of friendly feeling among athletes and supporters and their institutions.

Yet, on the other hand, there are men — and for these all sportsmen should be thankful — who concern themselves with the extramural relationships of our college athletics because of their desire to see them well and courteously fostered. With such persons motives of self-gratification and the acquisition of power are secondary to an ideal, seldom formulated mentally and very rarely expressed, — the ideal of service both to public and to university. The esteem in which these men are held and the influence that they wield because of unselfish and disinterested endeavor are their reward. The pity is that American college athletics, with all their glamour and popularity, have not brought forth more men of these capabilities and this character.

CHAPTER X
THE RECRUITING AND SUBSIDIZING OF ATHLETES

IN the pages that follow, the term "recruiting" denotes the solicitation of school athletes with a view to inducing them to attend a college or university. "Subsidizing" refers to the provision of financial or other assistance to athletes in consideration of their services on school or college teams or squads, whether in the year during which these services are rendered or in some other year. It should be noted parenthetically that in the past the term "proselyting," which, strictly speaking, is the solicitation of athletes who have already established academic affiliations, has been extended to cover the combined process of recruiting and subsidizing. Difficult though it may be to disassociate recruiting from subsidizing in the mass of practices that confront the enquirer, the distinction is essential if either subsidizing or recruiting is to be understood.

Considered liberally, certain forms of the soliciting of students to attend a college or university, without reference to the assistance that they may expect after matriculation, may be regarded as a part of the duty of the college toward the public. Moreover, soliciting may include offers of financial or personal assistance that are entirely consonant with the intellectual aims of the institution, and are not restricted to classes or groups, other than those formed on the basis of scholastic achievement or promise. It may even be conducted, more or less innocently, for institutions where men students are declining in numbers, or are outnumbered by women, or are sought, along with women students, to increase the total enrollment. In all such soliciting, which is motivated by general considerations, recruiting in the technical sense of the present discussion is not involved. Our concern is with the procurement of matriculates with the purpose of increasing an institution's prestige in athletics. Invariably, no exceptional or mitigating circumstances having been discovered, recruiting on this basis acquires a sinister aspect, since it involves a subsidy — an advantage for an individual or a group which is not available to others and which presupposes the possession and use of skill in sport.

Before setting forth the details of the recruiting and subsidizing of American college athletes, a brief general estimate of certain current tendencies is in order.

I. The Basis of Recruiting and Subsidizing

With all due allowance for the tendency to magnify the past in comparison with the present, there can be little doubt that the evils of soliciting and subsidizing athletes have diminished over the last twenty-five, twenty, or even fifteen years. A study of facts and opinions set forth from time to time since 1896 in the publications of various bodies, like the National Collegiate Athletic Association and the National Education Association, by men possessing much knowledge of the conditions involved, makes clear that matters have improved. On the other hand, letters, accounts, and other records indicate that this improvement has been one of degree but not of kind; some of these letters, a sampling of which is printed in the Appendix, might easily, if their dates were altered, do duty under present conditions.

A. Changes in Procedure

Before, say, 1917, recruiting appears to have been conducted by enthusiastic under-graduates and by athletes themselves more generally than it is to-day, except at a few institutions where fraternities have not yet outgrown such practices. The subsidizing that accompanied recruiting under these auspices was comparatively ineffectual and certainly crude. Since those days, a more businesslike procedure has been developed by older persons on the basis of experience in previous years and in the field of commerce. About 1919, there began to spread through the East and South and along the Pacific Coast a contagion of ready assistance to promising athletes, which was initiated and coördinated mainly by older hands. The result is that to-day, notwithstanding many statements to the contrary, the colleges and universities of the United States are confronted with acute problems of recruiting and subsidizing, especially with respect to intercollegiate football.

Nor is the abuse by any means confined to any particular sections of the country. In the Mid-West, the Intercollegiate Conference, regarded by many as the most thoroughly controlled of all conference bodies, has repeatedly called recruiting and subsidizing its most serious problem, and events in the spring of 1929 clearly demonstrated this fact. On the Pacific Coast, the larger institutions, having expended much ineffectual effort to control the abuse, are even now attempting to arrive at an equitable solution through common understanding. From similar cares the Southern Conference is by no means free. In the words of one of its coaches, there is "cut-throat competition" for prospective athletes. The president of another Southern university, newly founded, complained of the competition for a prominent athlete whom he himself had tried to secure. In the Rocky Mountain Conference, sentiment in favor of recruiting recurrently strikes certain institutions with full force. Parts of Pennsylvania and the adjacent territory have long accepted and openly practiced it as indispensable to victory in football. Organizations varying in type from the loosely informal group in the East to the oldest and strongest of conferences, although they have succeeded in influencing the evil, redirecting it, curtailing it, partly controlling it, or changing its form, have not permanently affected its existence or its results.

B. Methods of Attacking Recruiting and Subsidizing

For the most part, the attack upon subsidizing and recruiting has been conducted through the medium of conferences and associations. Thus far, little serious effort has been expended upon the problem. The principal means adopted to meet the situation has been the formulation of rules designed to curtail or eliminate specific practices, but such sentiment as has been roused has mainly resulted in slow or temporary or indecisive action.

This fact finds illustration in two conferences: Members of the Eastern Intercollegiate Conference adopted a regulation limiting the number of athletic scholarships and reducing their amounts as a preliminary step toward their abolition. Naturally, the next step would have been a further curtailment of subsidies, which, however, the conference failed to enact. In the Southern Intercollegiate Conference, a rule which required that, for intercollegiate participation, the names of persons who had held for more than one year scholarships or other financial aids should be published officially by their institutions, was abrogated because of the objection of influential conference members.

Certain measures, although containing at least the promise of better success, have not been entirely successful in application. In the Mid-West, Major John L. Griffith, commissioner of athletics for the Intercollegiate Conference, has attempted to inform high school principals concerning the methods and results of recruiting. The Association of Colleges and Secondary Schools of the Southern States and the North Central Association of Colleges and Secondary Schools have adopted educational standards concerning athletic policy to be required of member institutions. In two instances where such rules have been enforced against applicants for admission to associations, the institutions, although conscious that they have not been innocent of offense in the practices alleged, have known themselves to be no guiltier than many who had not been called in question, and not so guilty as certain others. Organizations with wider membership, like, for instance, the National Collegiate Athletic Association, have adopted amateur definitions which have proved ineffectual to curtail or check serious abuses. If the individual colleges and universities that hold membership in the N.C.A.A. had sincerely accepted its definition of an amateur, as quoted on previous pages, and had conscientiously — or even to a reasonable extent — followed it, the abuses of recruiting, proselyting, and subsidizing would have disappeared overnight. That they have not abated more, casts less discredit upon the N.C.A.A. than upon the individual institutions that are its members. Changing public opinion is a tedious task when the process runs counter to the material interests of some preparatory school principals and coaches, and of college coaches, directors, and alumni. Rules in this case, prepared usually by academic men, are somewhat readily evaded and, if too much particularized, even invite evasion. The efforts of conferences and other organized groups have produced in this direction little lasting good.

When, however, an occasional individual college, a change of policy having been determined upon, has courageously as a unit endeavored to reform its practices, has not been concerned with excusing its own abuses, and has acted in accordance with wholesome institutional dignity and a reasonable amateur standard, good results have followed. The excuse most frequently heard for recruiting and subsidizing is that "all the others are doing it." The statement is often followed by the assurance that "we are doing very little compared with our competitors." Such temporizing weakness is almost fatal. Attempts to extenuate offenses lead readily to even more persistent efforts to justify them. Far more self-respecting has been the policy pursued by those institutions that, disregarding what their competitors and others were reputed to be doing, have concerned themselves honestly with their own practices.

C. THE IMPECUNIOUS ATHLETE

In the United States the saying is common that "every athlete is a needy athlete." That football players, and, to some extent, other athletes, come from families whose means do not permit them to pay all of the expenses of a college course is generally accepted as fact and, indeed, is broadly true. To the general rule that many college athletes are either wholly or partially self-supporting, there are, of course, exceptions. But when such instances are distributed among the 800-odd colleges and universities reporting to the United States Bureau of Education, almost all of which maintain football teams, the well-to-do athlete becomes something of a rarity. Assistance extended to athletes who otherwise would not have thought of going to college, although it increases the disproportion, only accentuates a condition that is grounded in much deeper causes.

In Canada a far larger proportion of university athletes come from the more prosperous classes and are maintained entirely by their families. The needy athlete is comparatively rare, and even where he exists, he does not expect special consideration.

The presence of the impecunious athlete in American schools, his desire to secure the advantages of a college education, and his inability or unwillingness to distinguish between proper and improper assistance have combined to produce a fertile field in which to sow the tares of commercialized exploitation and subsidies.

II. THE RECRUITING OF ATHLETES

The present analysis of recruiting, as well as the subsequent discussion of subsidizing, is based upon a first-hand personal examination of correspondence, accounts, and other documents made available, at practically all of the institutions visited, through the ready coöperation of college officers, athletic officials, alumni, and others involved. Although it will be useful to consider these practices separately, they usually go hand in hand. Whenever competition or the athlete's own financial circumstances inject into his choice of a college the question of expense, the recruiter must perforce decide whether to offer subsidies or not. In most instances this initial decision is the turning-point for the recruiter, his college, and the schoolboy.

The varieties of recruiting are almost infinite. They range from rare and casual contacts made or directed by an individual in the athletic organization of the institu-tion (Chicago, University of Colorado, Cornell, Washington State College), in which the motive may be the general welfare of the institution or personal favor, to an in-tensively organized, sometimes subtle, system that may utilize or coördinate numbers of agents on or off the campus (Michigan, Northwestern, Oglethorpe, Southern Cali-fornia, Wisconsin[1]). Casual or incidental solicitation involves the minimum of recruit-ing. The use of a prearranged and usually secret plan gives to recruiting its most in-sidious form.

A. KINDS OF RECRUITING

From a slightly different point of view, recruiting may be distinguished as either professional or non-professional. In any one institution both sorts of activity may exist. When athletes are solicited by one or more individuals in the employ of the institution or its athletic department, the practice is certainly professional in method and often in spirit. Professional recruiting usually involves head coaches, members of the athletic staff, the alumni secretary, or even academic appointees who devote any part of their regular time to forming contacts with prospective athletes as a separate group. Pro-fessional also is the similar work, performed whether on a full-time or a part-time basis, by alumni or local organizations. What we here term non-professional recruiting is undertaken by members of the college family, usually alumni or students, who may wish an especially promising athlete to attend their particular institution. Into non-professional recruiting, subsidies may not enter at all, but even the most innocuous solicitation is transformed immediately into the most insidiously dangerous recruiting when financial assistance enters the negotiations, or when it is conducted by one who receives a salary or compensation from alumni or some other non-professional group.

Frequently it is difficult to determine the exact moment at which innocent enquiries end and recruiting begins. The schoolboy notion that athletic ability can be turned to advantage is so widespread that the mercenary athlete seldom waits for solicitation.

[1] *Northwestern*, President Walter Dill Scott, April 25, 1929: "I am not aware of such solicitation being 'officially' done." *Wisconsin*, statement of Professor J. F. A. Pyre, forwarded by Miss Julia M. Wilkinson, Executive Secretary, at the behest of President Glenn Frank, July 30, 1929: A statement that subsidizing is "in full force" is "in my opinion not justified by the facts. I find no evidence of overt [sic] violations of the Conference agreements in regard to recruiting or subsidizing." The statement in the text is based upon careful examination of much correspondence and many other documents.

In common parlance, he starts "shopping." Thus many of the contacts that eventuate in subsidies are initiated by the athletes themselves quite aside from the recruiting activities of institutional and other representatives. Some colleges limit solicitation almost exclusively to athletes who themselves initiate enquiries. Others profess this policy, but do not practice it. The line between active and passive recruiting is therefore tenuous.

B. DISTRIBUTION OF RECRUITING

Although the extent and intensity of recruiting elude geographical classification, it may be observed that soliciting, apart from subsidies, appears to be less strenuous in the Southwest and, with one or two exceptions, in New England than it is in the other Eastern and the Middle Atlantic States. In the Rocky Mountain Conference, the practice, although not yet general, is spreading. In the Mid-West and South, and on the Pacific Coast, soliciting and bidding for athletes are keen. Membership in a particular conference or group does not assure the presence or absence of recruiting. In some conferences, universities that solicit most actively stand side by side with others which do least in this respect. Quite aside from the question whose is the responsibility for honest athletic competition at any institution, the presence or absence of recruiting and subsidizing appears to rest immediately upon the character of the athletic staff and the duties entrusted openly or tacitly to them, particularly the director and head coaches.

C. LACK OF EVIDENCE OF RECRUITING

At a number of institutions evidence was lacking that recruiting existed. Absence or the curtailment of intercollegiate athletics is certainly not the reason, for most of these colleges and universities are keen athletic competitors in the principal branches of athletics, including football. Although the financial need of athletes, the availability of loan funds and general scholarships, and the activity of alumni interest all vary among these institutions, nevertheless, in every instance the absence of recruiting can be ascribed wholly or partly to the attitude and efforts of athletic officials and college officers in the face of as great temptations to recruit as exist in many other American colleges and universities (Bowdoin, Lehigh,[2] Massachusetts Agricultural, Middlebury, Trinity, Tufts, Tulane, College of Wooster; Emory, Reed, Massachusetts Institute of Technology). In addition, Canadian university sportsmanship is sufficiently strong to prevent recruiting. Occasional acts of single individuals with athletic or administrative connections (Amherst, Chicago, University of Colorado, Cornell, Oberlin,

[2] Lehigh University has recently made a significant and courageous change of policy respecting recruiting and subsidizing. The process entailed the exercise of much tact and patience on the part of athletic officials and university officers, and an admirable coöperation on the part of alumni. Although officials at Lehigh are too experienced in such matters to be overconfident, nevertheless the results obtained encourage them.

When, a few years ago, it was discovered that a large proportion of the Tulane football team had been recruited and was subsidized, seventeen members of the squad were immediately dismissed from the University. Doubtless this decisive action explains the absence of recruiting now at Tulane.

Vanderbilt[3]) are not regarded as of sufficient significance to justify grouping these institutions with those discussed on subsequent pages,— especially since it is possible that at other colleges and universities casual or occasional recruiting has occurred without its evidences coming to the attention of this enquiry.

D. Recruiting by Correspondence

The first contacts with many promising athletes are made through correspondence. When correspondence is started by schoolboys, it may be merely an innocent part of the process of choosing a college, but often it represents one phase of "shopping-round." When it is begun on behalf of a college or university, it may be entered upon directly or procured indirectly through some intermediary, such as a high school coach who is friendly with the college coach, an alumnus, or a friend of the institution or the schoolboy. Conference rules prohibiting the initiation of correspondence by coaches and directors are sometimes ignored and often evaded, with a naïveté that is astonishing in mature men. By whomever the interchange of letters is begun, — schoolboy, coach, director, alumnus, or friend, — it is likely to end in putting the athlete and the dispenser of subsidies in direct communication.

1. Letters from Schoolboy Athletes

Again it must be pointed out that numbers of enquiries come to all institutions from athletes who are genuinely interested in a particular college or university, and who quite naturally write for information concerning matriculation. In other cases, enquiries are not so innocent. Very large numbers of high school athletes in the United States have the notion that universities and colleges are bidding for their services. How this conception has arisen will be easily understood from typical letters assembled in the Appendix. The boy whose parent does not understand the essential nature of subsidizing, or whose school coach or friend has held out to him alluring promises of what can be gained by a little "shopping-round," is readily led to auction his athletic services to the highest bidder.

Long ago, college publicity taught the venal school athlete the use of newspaper clippings, a collection of which in praise of the athlete's exploits often accompanies his tenders of athletic skill to one or more colleges. Or the letter may state that his clippings will be forwarded as soon as they have been returned by another institution. For purposes of "shopping-round" one schoolboy (Evanston, Illinois), with an enterprise worthy of a more honorable cause, had an especially favorable press notice

[3] As regards the University of Chicago, among hundreds of letters examined, only one, which recommended candidates for rushing by fraternities, remotely suggested recruiting. At Cornell, of scores examined, only one savored at all of the recruiting motive, and only the strictest interpretation of this single letter leads to the inclusion of the University in the list. Chicago and Cornell may therefore be regarded as reflecting the absolute minimum of such activity. At the University of Colorado, in granting a personal favor, an athletic official temporarily passed over his responsibility to his institution. As abuses of standards accepted and usually adhered to at these universities, the instances cited are utterly insignificant. A minor official in the Oberlin administrative office appeared to be carrying on a recruiting correspondence with or concerning high school athletes without the knowledge or sanction of the athletic staff or the college authorities.

mimeographed from a local paper with some of its comments underscored. Almost identical letters of another high school athlete (New York City), who was hawking his services, were encountered at no fewer than five institutions. A third football "prospect," much solicited, furnished our enquiry with fifty-eight answers to his own tenders, with the comment that he had "been shopping, and this is the result." Indeed, so common has "shopping-round" become that many colleges of small athletic prominence and even others that have no intercollegiate athletics at all sometimes receive letters asking openly or between their lines, "What can you do to attract a promising but needy athlete?" Action upon such a letter reflects the policy of the institution respecting solicitation and, generally, subsidies.

The usual clearing-house for letters of this sort is the athletic department, and the individual, whether present on the campus or remote from it, who looks after enquiries of this nature, is generally the person who initiates correspondence with prospective athletes, in case this practice is countenanced by the particular institution.

2. Under the Auspices of the Department of Athletics

Recruiting correspondence, varying from the most innocuous and casual to the most purposive and systematized, was examined at a comparatively large number of the colleges and universities visited (Alabama, California, Columbia, Denver, Drake, Michigan, Montana State College, New York University, Ohio Wesleyan, Oregon Agricultural, Pennsylvania, Rutgers, Southern California, Vermont, Washington, Washington and Jefferson, Washington State College, Wisconsin [4]). At some of these institutions the amount and nature of correspondence demand that a member of the athletic staff or a coach out of season shall attend to the letters of prospective athletes, and in some cases the files contain literally hundreds of letters to or about promising schoolboy athletes scattered over a very wide area (Brown,[5] Dartmouth, Montana State College, New York University, Pennsylvania, Wisconsin).

Usually in a case of recruiting the head football coach has the opportunity to set a policy respecting the treatment of correspondence. At small institutions where the football coach acts also as director of athletics, and at a few of the larger institutions (California, New York University, Pennsylvania), he is likely to care for such correspondence himself. On the other hand, the majority of head football coaches at larger universities do not regard such tasks as a part of their duties (Cornell, Harvard, Missouri, Princeton, Southern California, Washington, Wisconsin, Yale, for example). Where the responsibility for establishing recruiting contacts rests upon a designated

[4] Respecting the University of Alabama, although correspondence seemed to be unnecessarily voluminous, it was written with a care for standards and addressed only to high school boys within the state. At Washington State College, the enthusiasm of a member of the athletic staff for a particular athlete carried him beyond what the member regards as his normal and conservative policy. At the University of Washington, a subordinate appeared to have forgotten momentarily the instruction of conscientious superiors.

[5] Brown, letter forwarded by President Faunce, and dated April 29, 1929: "No influence has been brought to bear to violate college regulations."

member of the athletic staff, letters from prospective athletes may be passed to him (Brown, Columbia, Purdue, Wisconsin), or they may be transmitted to the alumni secretary, if they contain matter within his province. In some instances, a coöperative effort may develop; the football coach, the director of athletics, a designated member of the athletic staff, and an alumni officer or an alumnus may unite to form and extend connections (Michigan, Oregon Agricultural, Pennsylvania). Occasionally some member of the business or administrative staff of the institution (Drake, Gettysburg, Oberlin) conducts the correspondence.

It is gratifying to note that at a considerable number of the colleges and universities visited examination of the files showed that letters from prospective athletes receive polite but reserved acknowledgment, with an indication of willingness to be of such assistance as circumstances allow and the reputation of the institution permits. But in view of the strong, universal expressions of disapproval by both athletic and academic officers concerning the commercializing attitude of the "shopping" athlete, it is astonishing not to find in replies to enquiries a similarly universal effort to correct this attitude. No less astonishing is the tendency of many coaches, directors, and other persons, who in theory deplore professional-minded approaches, to reply to thinly-veiled hints with encouragements of a purely financial or commercial nature, such as references to the low cost of living, the availability of jobs or scholarships, and the advertisement that may accrue from being in a particular conference or section of the country. Whatever the resources at the disposal of the writer of such a reply, the great majority of athletes value these answers in dollars and cents. Even in cases where money is not mentioned, replies are sometimes so laudatory or solicitous that the schoolboy thinks not at all of his own offense against amateurism in offering his athletic skill at a price, and swells with the self-importance that calls forth such acknowledgments from (to him) mighty athletic organizations. It is only later, in college, that he learns the true worth of such flattery.

If all who receive and answer athletes' letters showed in their replies the high-minded disapproval of these tenders that they exhibit in conversation and in speeches, before long the tone of such "feelers" from high school athletes would change. Evidence to this effect is found at those institutions (Bates, Bowdoin, Brigham Young, Chicago, Cornell, Lehigh, Stanford, Tulane, Virginia) where such phrases as follow set the tone of replies:

> The only inducement we offer to any student is that of a good education. This is all the right kind of athlete expects of us.

Although, upon receiving such a reply, many an enquiring athlete will merely look to other pastures for his grazing, nevertheless he has at least learned that the practice of soliciting athletes by correspondence is not universal.

Up to this point consideration has been directed principally to correspondence that, presumably, has not been initiated on behalf of the college. Those institutions whose files evidence mere casual or incidental recruiting very seldom make overtures. For the college or university that, on the contrary, solicits athletes, or countenances recruiting on its behalf by members or friends, there are many sources of information from which lists of prospects may be compiled; newspaper clippings, graduation lists, personal recommendations, — even those written by school officers who stress athletic prominence, — lists of "all-state" players, and other compilations. A conference rule against soliciting does not stop it, for a trail, more or less devious, can be laid around it. Methods used in evading such prohibitory regulations are illustrated in the following quotations:

> As you know, it is contrary to Conference rules for us to initiate correspondence with any high school athletes. However, were these boys to write us first, we could, of course, reply and then do our best to get them to come to ——. Perhaps you might wish to suggest this to them. Once I have had a letter from a prospective student, I always follow up the case vigorously.

> It might be well for you to secure the name and address of the boy and have him write me a letter of inquiry covering such things as he wants to know about. The athletic directors cannot initiate correspondence with any prospective athlete, but they do have the right to answer any enquiries made of them by prospective students.

> I will appreciate it if you will suggest to these two kids that they write me a letter so that I can communicate with them. One of the rules of the Conference prohibits any member of the staff of the University from writing directly to prospective students, but the lid is off if any one makes an inquiry.

Sometimes alumni are judged to need instruction in the fine art of recruiting. The following letter was written by a coach to an enthusiastic alumnus:

> Dear ——, Just thought I would drop you a line to remind you that this is a good time to start our work on preps who look good in athletics and try to interest them in ——. Between now and the time school is out and then in August is a good time to start our activities and pepper them up.

Another director-coach has written of "fat jobs saved" for promising athletes. He has stated also that "we can do something fancy in the way of a job," and that "I am willing to go to some extremes in jobs to get them." The impecunious athlete who receives such golden assurances is naturally drawn strongly toward the institution from which they emanate, and away from one where, he is told, "many of the students succeed in working their way," and where his name will be given to the university official "who has charge of employing students," but nothing can be guaranteed.

Frequently correspondence may preface the more intimate recruiting for an institution from which an agent goes out to establish contacts in person (Brown, Columbia, Oglethorpe, Wisconsin), or to which athletes can be brought for the purpose of establishing pleasant personal relationships (Oregon Agricultural, Pennsylvania, Southern California). The wary athletic official may so phrase his letters to prospective athletes that his institution cannot be accused of making offers. More naïve is the letter-writer who warns the prospect that "there are some things that cannot be written about," but that So-and-So will call upon him in the near future, or — what appears to be more effective — it will be made possible for the athlete to visit the campus and then "everything" can be gone over in detail.

In short, it is just to say that when letters from prospective matriculates are received or answered by members of the athletic department or the coaching staff of any university or college, the tempting way is open to recruiting by correspondence with athletic officials or others or to the activities of personal solicitors, whose functions are discussed on subsequent pages.

3. By Alumni Secretaries or Officers

The alumni secretary who has connections of varying intensity with the alumni on the one hand and with the athletic organization on the other (Amherst, Arizona, Drake, Michigan, Northwestern, Oregon Agricultural, Purdue, Southern California) may readily become a useful intermediary in recruiting. Such a situation is the natural result of the many-sided functions, both specific and general, that have gradually accrued to the office of the alumni secretary. In keeping his fellow-alumni informed and interested, he finds it convenient to be prepared with accurate and, as far as possible, encouraging reports of teams and contests. When he visits widely separated alumni groups, information concerning prospective athletes in whom alumni are interested almost forces itself upon him. Even if he does not travel about, letters from fellow-alumni often mention schoolboys of athletic promise. These phases of activity are almost inescapable duties of the alumni secretary. But at some colleges either he is called upon to take, or else he voluntarily assumes, an advisory capacity respecting athletics; and he may even be a member of the board that controls them. In these circumstances it is not astonishing to find that alumni secretaries or their assistants (Drake, Georgia School of Technology, Michigan, Northwestern, Oregon Agricultural, Southern California, Vermont, Washington and Jefferson) have become involved in recruiting, whether by correspondence or in person.

4. In Administrative Offices of Colleges and Universities

Occasionally a college administrative officer is encountered whose interest in athletics leads him to correspond with promising athletes. He may be the assistant secretary of the institution (Oberlin), or the assistant to the president (Gettysburg), or the business manager (Drake). The athletic department may or may not be cognizant of his activities; in the first instance cited, these were certainly inconsistent with the ideals expressed by the department and the institution.

5. Beyond the Immediate Jurisdiction of the Institution

Whether the reply to the "shopping" letter comes from an officer of the college, from a member of its athletic staff, or from some person less immediately connected with the institution, its effect upon the athlete is the same: the institution is credited with the recruiting activities of its partisans. In this there is a certain crude justice; for in almost every instance an open connection or a secret channel of information exists or has existed between the athletic or administrative staff and the more remote and active individual or organization. Enquiries received at the athletic office may pass to an unpaid alumnus (Dartmouth), who because of loyalty and personal pleasure in such contacts devotes much energy to them, or the alumnus agent may receive from a local organization (Brown, Purdue) a salary that lends a professional shade to his proceedings. When a club of local citizens sets out to secure through correspondence "a good live football team," all considerations of amateurism vanish under the pressure of commercial or business methods. The farther removed is the correspondent from the academic interests of the university, the less amenable is he to control by officers of the institution, and the less likely he is to feel any responsibility for honesty in college sport.

E. CIRCULARS AND ADVERTISEMENTS IN RECRUITING

Of all the uses of the mails for recruiting college athletes, the distribution of printed matter tends to be the least prejudicial to the amateur status. Sometimes, however, such material goes only to athletes in the senior classes of high and preparatory schools. When it emphasizes the athletic activities of the college, its relation to recruiting becomes closer. When, finally, this type of advertising is so elaborate and so concentrated upon athletics and courses in coaching as it was for a time at the University of Illinois, it lays the institution open to well-founded charges of professionalism, even though subsidies, except in the form of scholarships, be not a consideration.

F. RECRUITING THROUGH SOLICITATION IN PERSON

The recruiting of college athletes reaches most intense development at those institutions where it is professional in nature, that is, where it engages the paid services of one or more persons whose responsibility includes the making of personal contacts with promising athletes in order to influence their choice of a college. When the agent devotes full time to this work and is allowed by the institution or its athletic association transportation and liberal incidental expenses, his activities can readily include, in addition to voluminous correspondence, the interviewing and entertaining of prospects (Brown, Northwestern, Purdue, Wisconsin[6]).

1. Athletic Coaches as Recruiting Agents

Only a little less concentrated than the foregoing activities is the similar work of a coach who is expected or permitted to devote all or a necessary amount of his time to recruiting (Bucknell, Colgate, Columbia, University of Georgia, Georgia Institute of Technology, New York University, Oglethorpe, Tennessee, Washington and Jefferson, Western Maryland). If engaged partly for such work, a freshman coach of two or more branches of athletics may have to "scout" his athletes in off seasons or in the summer. On the other hand, the head coach of a single sport, who recruits, is fairly free, aside from his regular and off-season coaching, to divide his time between bolstering up the academic standing of his squads and establishing contacts that ultimately draw recruits.

At most institutions that make the establishing of contacts a part of the program of the athletic department, the responsibility is usually assigned to a single individual, such as the head coach, the freshman coach, a special employee engaged for the work, or the alumni secretary, a part of whose salary may be paid from athletic funds. On the other hand, the charge has been made, and evidence adduced to support it, that at a few institutions in the Mid-West and on the Pacific Coast, coaches, managers, athletes, and even university officers combine in a broad but intensive and systematic approach to prominent schoolboy athletes (Michigan, Ohio State, Purdue, Southern California, Wisconsin[7]). In defense of the practice it has been urged that athletes are not more sought than other promising high school students, but the fact that members of the athletic staff are assigned to the work casts doubt upon the validity of the contention. Such soliciting, whether general or specialized, breeds suspicion and distrust among colleges. Certainly it offers tempting opportunities for recruiting if agents are so minded. Furthermore, although it is maintained that speaking engagements of coaches and others are not utilized for interviewing and entertaining athletes, nevertheless careful examination of resulting correspondence and conversation with athletes themselves lead to a contrary conclusion. A comparison of speaking itineraries with a list of the home towns of promising athletes strengthens the argument against such methods of "putting the university before the people."

---

[6] *Brown*, letter forwarded by President Faunce, and dated April 29, 1929: "The Brown Club representative has no official or *semi-official* connection." *Northwestern*, President Walter Dill Scott: "I am not aware of such solicitation being 'officially' done.... The Assistant Alumni Secretary is not authorized to subsidize athletes. He may inform prospective students that there are a certain number of scholarships."

[7] *Wisconsin*, statement of Professor J. F. A. Pyre, forwarded by Miss Julia M. Wilkinson, Executive Secretary, at the behest of President Glenn Frank, July 30, 1929: "I find no evidence of any financial promises beyond the promise to provide jobs." That the Assistant to the Director, Department of Physical Education, "goes 'as far as the law allows' is evident from his correspondence. I find no evidence that he has overstepped that boundary." The statement in the text, however, is based upon a thorough examination of the correspondence files of this officer at the time of the field visit.

2. Alumni Soliciting and Recruiting

A common misconception touching the personal recruiting of athletes for inter-collegiate competition is that most of the work is done by alumni. The facts of our enquiry prove conclusively that this is not the case. Of one hundred and twelve colleges and universities visited, at only a little over thirty per cent was recruiting conducted by alumni. In slightly over half of the cases it was an affair of the athletic departments, and in eight per cent it rested upon administrative, executive, or academic officers. This apportionment of the responsibility for recruiting takes into account all activities of organizations, groups, or individuals concerning whom information has been sufficient to justify conclusions. In this particular, then, alumni are scarcely so black as they have been painted.

In a majority of the cases in which alumni recruit, the consent of the athletic department or the institution may amount to coöperation. The part played by correspondents and alumni secretaries has been indicated. The usual form of coöperation is that in which the athletic department directs the alumni in establishing contacts with prospective athletes. Alumni may be urged to coöperate with recruiting agents in the field by facilitating personal introductions and interviews.

Their aid is often enlisted in offering hospitality of various sorts to high school athletes. Alumni dinners, whether held at the university or at a distance, annually or as special gatherings in honor of victorious teams, are a fruitful source of contacts (Brown, Dartmouth, Rutgers). The announcement of such a dinner, held in New York City, reminded loyal sons that the occasion would be convenient and timely for work with sub-freshmen. At dinners held for the special purpose of entertaining prospective members of college athletic squads, members of the coaching staff and prominent athletes are often present; excellent opportunity is afforded for them to "talk things over" with schoolboys who may be interested. Although contacts of this nature are not necessarily utilized for recruiting, nevertheless they obviously and readily provide excellent openings. When, for the purpose of fostering alumni loyalty, college presidents or prominent administrative officers likewise attend, their presence is a handy screen behind which to begin the most subtle forms of recruiting.

The distribution of complimentary tickets to home athletic contests, although much curtailed by conference rules and in some cases completely stamped out, may be another factor in alumni recruiting. At one university (Southern California) alumni supply fraternities with tickets to football or other contests on the understanding that the fraternities will entertain prospective athletes whom alumni have invited to visit the campus. Again, an individual alumnus himself may buy the ticket for the athlete or provide him with transportation, in order that the schoolboy may enjoy the hospitality of the campus and "meet the fellows," among them the coaches. An Indiana high school boy, distinguished in several branches of athletics, was thus entertained from one to three times on the campus of every university in a large conference. In several such cases it was clear that alumni had practically forced fraternities to entertain prospective athletes. If fraternities feel it necessary to limit this form of free entertainment, the schoolboy may be provided with meal tickets for use at a local restaurant at the expense of the athletic organization.

Although only an alumnus of means is able to entertain school athletes upon such visits at his own expense, the burden of cost may be lightened by coöperation. One alumni athletic committee invited from all alumni of the university (Purdue) contributions of twenty-five dollars for each local group, and ten dollars a year from individuals for the dispensing of this hospitality and the employment of a field secretary. Another athletic department (Oregon Agricultural [8]) arranged to reimburse the alumnus host who has sponsored an athlete on a trip to see the campus. The reimbursement is more direct when the athlete is invited by the department of athletics (Pennsylvania) and draws his expense money upon presentation of his traveling account. Special funds are sometimes maintained by alumni clubs for such reimbursements. Incidentally, it was once the custom of an individual alumnus to operate a kind of recruiting excursion — several special Pullman cars hired at his own expense to take athletes from the city of his residence to the campus of his university (Indiana). Nor is the hospitality of an alumnus withheld in his own home. Week-end invitations from wealthy alumni readily serve the purposes of ingratiation and friendly relationships. Apparently in some instances a genuine personal interest is taken in the athletes aside from their athletic ability (Princeton, Stanford).

Although alumni who thus trade in hospitality display at times an enthusiastic loyalty to Alma Mater and great generosity toward worthy boys, one fact should not be overlooked. Their hospitality is sometimes prompted by those who have a more professional interest than they in successful teams. Practically never are their activities discouraged by athletic officials. For example, even at a university of high ideals (Michigan) the alumni treasurer writes to a fellow-alumnus who was willing to pay a school athlete's expenses in traveling about four hundred miles to visit the campus, that he is "spoken of most highly down at the Athletic Association offices and they certainly appreciate what you have done."

Three instances were encountered in which recruiting activities were being conducted by alumni apparently in opposition to the wishes of the responsible athletic authorities (Amherst, Princeton, Tennessee), and even in these cases a connection existed between other officers of the institution and the alumni engaged in this work.

[8] Statement forwarded by President W. J. Kerr, signed by Dean A. B. Cordley, Chairman, Board of Control, drafted by P. J. Schissler, Director of Athletics, C. A. Lodell, Graduate Manager, and Dean Cordley, and dated July 22, 1929 : "Entertainment for prospective athletes has never been made by athletic association funds." The statement in the text is made after a careful examination of accounts.

Indeed, at no institution visited did organized or semi-organized alumni recruiting exist without the knowledge of some official of the institution or the athletic staff, who received a salary for duties performed in athletic or administrative connections.

3. By Fraternities

One manifestation of the desire for publicity that afflicts fraternity chapters is the competition for athletic stars whose lustre presumably will shed glory on "the house" and distinction upon its members, present or prospective. Unfortunately, the fraternity chapter has proved itself to be as convenient a unit in a program of recruiting as it is in other more praiseworthy activities. Coöperation between fraternities, on the one hand, and individuals, whether alumni or members of the athletic staff, who solicit athletes, on the other, has been developed at a number of universities (California, Columbia, New York University, Ohio Wesleyan, Oregon Agricultural, Purdue, Southern California, Wisconsin, and other institutions[9]). School athletes, invited at their own expense or that of the athletic association or alumni, have been brought to the campus for a week-end or a game and lodged and entertained at fraternity houses.

High school athletic tournaments held on university grounds afford a convenient occasion for aggressive "rushing," whether at the behest of the athletic staff or on the initiative of the fraternities themselves. At one Western university (Southern California) a fraternity had listed for "rushing" the outstanding athletes of the region, giving for each the sport and position that he played; later, opportunity offered to entertain these athletes at the fraternity house. Variations of such activities, motivated always by institutional and fraternity loyalty, are found at other institutions. At parties or dinners prospective athletes are fed, among other good things, much propaganda concerning the university, and they are also enabled to see, meet, or hear the leading members of the coaching staff.

Many reputable national fraternities maintain a policy under which athletes are not unduly sought or favored over candidates possessing an interest in other extra-curricular activities. Conservative fraternity chapters have refused to put facilities at the disposal of the recruiting agent, and others who have acceded to his importunities have done so with varying degrees of reluctance. An opinion is growing to the effect that an athlete who possesses scholastic ability and who does not expect special considerations or concessions because he is an athlete stands among the most desirable of fraternity members.

[9] *Oregon State Agricultural College*, statement forwarded by President W. J. Kerr, prepared as indicated in Note 8, above, and dated July 22, 1929: "Entertainment for prospective athletes has never been made by athletic association funds. Fraternity groups sometimes entertain visiting prospective athletes." *Wisconsin*, statement of Professor J. F. A. Pyre, forwarded by Miss Julia M. Wilkinson, Executive Secretary, at the behest of President Glenn Frank, July 30, 1929: "Athletic officials make trips only on invitation of out-of-town organizations and their expenses are defrayed by the hosts, usually on the occasion of athletic 'banquets' and the like." A statement made after careful examination of the accounts of the Inter-Class Fund at Wisconsin that free transportation to the campus is provided for prospective athletes is, in Professor Pyre's words, "categorically false, if it is meant that such provision is made by an athletic officer or from any fund over which the athletic department exercises any form of supervision. There may have been a few cases in which such visits have been subsidized unofficially by alumni or friends of the University." Apparently, then, the Athletic Department exercises no supervision over the Inter-Class Fund.

4. Recruiting at Athletic Tournaments

Whatever other purposes high school tournaments may serve, they enable coaches and others similarly interested to see schoolboy athletes at their sports and to establish personal contacts with the more promising. Some coaches contend that they do not attend high school tournaments for purposes of recruiting. Testimony from high school athletes, however, indicates that coaches who attend tournaments do not neglect their opportunities in this direction. Clearly, the cure for the situation is not more stringent rules, which might tend to lessen the activity temporarily, but could do little toward permanent improvement. As long as high school tournaments are held, the only remedy for the abuse is that coaches shall voluntarily refrain from practices that are hostile to the best interests of college sport.

G. SUMMARY

The recruiting of American college athletes, be it active or passive, professional or non-professional, has reached the proportions of nationwide commerce. In spite of the efforts of not a few teachers and principals who have comprehended its dangers, its effect upon the character of the schoolboy has been profoundly deleterious. Its influence upon the nature and quality of American higher education has been no less noxious. The element that demoralizes is the subsidy, the monetary or material advantage that is used to attract the schoolboy athlete. It is seldom lacking in the general process of gathering "a winning team."

III. SUBSIDIES IN AMERICAN COLLEGE ATHLETICS

In amplification of the definition of subsidies set forth at the opening of the present chapter, a subsidy denotes any assistance, favor, gift, award, scholarship, or concession, direct or indirect, which advantages an athlete because of his athletic ability or reputation, and which sets him apart from his fellows in the undergraduate body. For both schoolboys and undergraduates the subsidy entails, first, an offer or a promise sufficiently definite to attract and hold the "prospect." The making of an offer implies, secondly, the procuring of subsidy funds, the preëmpting and listing of jobs, arranging for concessions, and similar preliminaries. The third factor in the process of subsidizing is the actual receipt of the subsidy, usually in a series of transactions. Any effort to reach a conclusion respecting the control of subsidizing involves appraisal of the responsibility for each of these three factors. If the athletic association or department is in any measure responsible for one or all of them, official action can be taken by the college or university. If all of them fall under the administrative authority of the institution, all can be controlled. If, however, there are rare cases where any of the three elements in the process is not susceptible to university or college regulation, then some or all of them will be difficult to curb.

A. Responsibility for Subsidizing

Subsidizing in some form or degree was found to exist at eighty-one of the one hundred and twelve institutions studied. At only twenty of these eighty-one universities and colleges was a single agency responsible for the practice: the institution was the sole dispenser of subsidies in eight instances, the alumni alone in eleven, and the athletic association alone in one.

With respect to the remaining sixty-one instances of subsidizing, various agencies combined in the work. For example, at fifty institutions, or 62 per cent of the whole number at which subsidizing was in force, the athletic department, the athletic association, or some member of the athletic staff was a party to the arrangements, including those institutions where subsidies take the form of jobs. Thus, the athletic department or association or a member of the athletic staff shared in all but eleven cases of combined effort.

At twenty-eight institutions, besides the eleven previously mentioned, alumni participated in the practice. Thus, the alumni were concerned in subsidizing at a total of slightly less than half of all the institutions at which subsidizing was found.

The institution itself participated in the process in nineteen instances, in addition to those in which it was the sole dispenser of subsidies, and townspeople in eleven instances.

Various forms of coöperation in subsidizing were encountered. In ten cases the athletic department or association and the alumni worked together; in six the association or department and the college administration; in three the alumni and the administration; in two the alumni and the fraternities; in seven the alumni and townspeople; in four the athletic department or association, the alumni, and the townspeople; and in two the athletic association, the alumni, and the institution.

The relation between subsidizing and recruiting has been discussed in previous pages, where it was pointed out that one seldom if ever exists without the other. Because of the origins of a large proportion of the most skilful college athletes, the recruiter, even if he wished, could not ignore the financial problems that a college education forces upon the schoolboy and his family. From the recruiter's point of view, it would be absurd not to be ready with a solution; hence, the vast number and variety of subsidizing expedients that competition has brought forth, ranging from a helpful interest and an offer to be of service, through an endless diversity of ways and means, open or secret, large or small, official or unofficial, to the frank and businesslike payments of expenses and even of compensation.

B. Unsubsidized College Athletics

The notion that intercollegiate competition is impossible, or at least impracticable, without subsidies is disproved by the fact that at twenty-eight of the one hundred and twelve colleges and universities visited for the enquiry no evidence was found that athletes were subsidized by any group or individual:

Bates	Queen's
Bowdoin	Reed
Carleton	Rochester
Chicago	University of Saskatchewan
Cornell University	Toronto
Dalhousie	Trinity
Emory	Tufts
Illinois	Tulane
Laval	United States Military Academy
McGill	University of Virginia
Marquette	Wesleyan
Massachusetts Agricultural College	Williams
Massachusetts Institute of Technology	College of Wooster
Ottawa	Yale

In this list stand colleges and universities of all sizes, sections of the continent, conferences, and unions. At some, the temptations to subsidize are less strong than at others. At some, there has been subsidizing in the past. Of any one it is impossible to say that there will not be subsidizing in the future. Possibly, also, at the time of the field visit subsidizing existed without being discovered, but in our enquiry an apparent absence of subsidizing inevitably occasioned the closest scrutiny.[10] Whatever may be the rights and wrongs of athletic subsidies, the conditions encountered at this group of institutions, especially at those enjoying keen intercollegiate competition, should encourage anyone who feels that subsidies ought to be eliminated from American college athletics.

C. The Practice of Subsidizing

The subsidizing of college athletes involves only four main instrumentalities: jobs and work of various kinds; loans; scholarships; and miscellaneous assistance.

1. Jobs and Employment

Athletic authorities commonly interpret conference and institutional rules against providing "financial assistance" to college athletes as not including the help afforded by employment and jobs that stand at the disposal of the department of athletics. It is obvious, however, that if on the initiative of the athletic authorities an athlete is given term-time employment that nets him $125 or $150 a month, he is receiving financial assistance that quite overshadows that involved in a job at trench-digging or

---

[10] One exception to the statement concerning coöperation was due to lack of understanding of such enquiries as ours and a resulting oversensitiveness, together with disharmony in the directing of athletics at the particular university.

dishwashing at forty cents an hour. Between these two extremes it would be possible, from the cases included in our enquiry, to construct a scale of subsidizing that would start at one extreme with the least remunerative tasks, involving hard and honestly performed manual labor, and end at the other with the few sinecures that have enabled their recipients to attend college, play on teams, and contribute to family support or put aside a capital sum with which to embark upon a business venture after graduation. Many a candid athlete acknowledges that his athletic ability has proved a "meal ticket" throughout his college course because of the readiness with which jobs were provided.

a. *The Offer to Assist in Securing Part-time Employment*

"I would like to attend your institution in the fall and if you can help a poor but honest schoolboy, with little money but a lot of ambition, I'd like to hear from you." Such an appeal can scarcely fail to arouse in any American coach, director of athletics, or teacher the liveliest impulses to help its author. But the athletic official who himself attempts to provide the assistance involved fails to recognize three facts: First, his apparently harmless favor is likely to lead to subsidizing. Secondly, it may lead to evils that profoundly affect the athlete, the institution, and college sport itself. Thirdly, dealing with such requests is the affair not of the athletic office but of the college employment bureau, committee, or officer. The coach who assumes no responsibility in job-hunting not only saves himself much unnecessary trouble, but gains a respect that is not accorded to the coach who scours the campus and the community for jobs wherewith to subsidize his players.

Although many schoolboys who request the opportunity to "work their way through college" while participating in athletics, are, of course, innocent of any desire to capitalize their athletic ability, a great many others are bent upon it. The motive that prompted the boy to write as follows to a prominent Southern college coach is unmistakable: "What chance has a fellow to work his way through your school . . . who has played regularly on the line of the most outstanding high school teams in the state?" and who, if the answer is "right," will bring with him three other equally valuable players? The boy believes this to be an adroit way of asking, "How much is my athletic ability worth to you?" or "Is it worth subsidizing?" The fact that so often the most desirable jobs in the athletic department and sometimes even on the campus are held by skilled athletes testifies to the same attitude of barter on the side of the institution. In not a few instances, such requests as have just been quoted are honored in accordance with the probable athletic gains that the young men may bring to the college, sometimes in comparison with the disadvantages that may arise from their playing on rival teams. The fact that in most cases campus jobs performed by athletes justify the compensation paid must be weighed with the fact that scores of other undergraduates who also need employment would do the work as well if not better than the athletes selected.

Further evidence concerning the job as subsidy is available in the following documentary citations:

> An alumnus who has enquired concerning help for two promising athletes is answered thus by the university business manager: "If you say these two boys can make the team then we sure want to take care of them."

> And again: "If he is an honest-to-goodness athlete, that is, one who can make our teams, we will, of course, do our best to help him with a job."

> A director-coach, in writing to a recruiting agent that he can provide a fifty-dollar job for an athlete who is good enough, and referring to a particular young man asks, "Is he worth it?" Regarding other athletes, he asks in the same letter, "How much are they worth?"

> At an Eastern preparatory school a highly remunerative campus job is available. The school coach writes to a college coach concerning a high school athlete whom the college coach has been considering. After a trial of the boy the college coach writes to the school coach: "He don't amount to much and I would not recommend him."

> Instructions from the chairman of a recruiting committee read: "If they [the prospective athletes] need financial assistance, find out how much. Understand, however, that our primary interest is in the football or other athletic ability of the candidate . . . a merely good man is not good enough. He must be *superlatively* good or you can't afford to waste any time with him."

> A university officer writes: "Under the circumstances, it seems we had better tell the boy we will be unable to help him in any special way since you say he is only a fair athlete in any sport and since we have many calls from big stars."

The foregoing quotations from the correspondence of athletic officials in various parts of the country represent no isolated or sporadic manifestation of the mercenary attitude. Indeed, in almost every instance of assistance provided for athletes as a special class, the motive can be called in question. In every instance, the unwisdom of such a policy is clear. However natural or philanthropic the desires of members of the athletic staff to assist their charges, the course under present conditions is neither necessary nor desirable. When an athletic department or association undertakes to provide employment for prospective athletes, it, to all intents, employs its time and funds for the purpose of subsidizing.

b. *The Athlete and the College Appointments Office*

Apparently a well-conducted college appointments office may care for athletes and non-athletes with equally good results, whether it be in charge of a Y.M.C.A. secretary, an administrative officer of the institution, or a manager specially employed for the work. Yet very commonly such an office is relieved of the responsibility of finding employment for athletes, although its results respecting other undergraduates are apparently satisfactory. The reason given by both athletes and athletic officials is that athletes who apply for positions receive insufficient attention. This, being interpreted, means that they must take their chances along with other undergraduates, without special privileges, — naturally an irksome process after the favors that have been lavished upon them by way of inducements. Such "unfairness" is not at all consonant with the privileged treatment that the recruited athlete has been led to expect. If, in response to his complaints, the coach or director, independently of the duly consti- tuted agency, endeavors to provide a job in keeping with the young man's promise or reputation as an athlete, the beginnings of a separate and illegitimate employment service have been made.

That such special privilege is entirely unnecessary is demonstrated at those institu- tions where the athletic department or association maintains no separate employment agency for the athletes and refers applicants to the university appointments office (Beloit, Bowdoin, Cornell, Stanford, Tulane; Brigham Young, Columbia, Yale, and other institutions in great measure).

c. *Employment Agencies in the Athletic Department*

Midway between the more regular methods of providing employment for athletes through the college appointments office and the irregular practice involving special services rendered under the auspices of the athletic department, stands the scheme by which a member of the athletic staff, under the instructions of the director, lists all applicants for work in order of application regardless of athletic prominence, to be cared for in turn as long as positions remain (Illinois). At a large number of colleges and universities, however, the responsibility of finding employment for athletes de- volves upon those who correspond with athletic prospects (Alabama, Amherst, Arizona, Brown, Chicago, Colgate, Columbia, Dartmouth, Denver, Drake, Georgia School of Technology, Idaho, Michigan, Missouri in part, Montana State College, Northwestern in part, Oglethorpe, Oklahoma, Oregon Agricultural, Purdue, Queen's, Rutgers, South Dakota, Southern Methodist, Tennessee, Utah, Vermont, Washington State College, University of Washington, Wisconsin[11]). The degree of specialization in the placement task varies widely. Sometimes the director, coach, or other athletic assistant attempts merely to apportion the jobs available in the department among the candidates (Ari- zona, Chicago, Missouri, Utah), no great effort is made to list other openings on or off the campus, and all applicants for whom jobs cannot be thus provided are referred to the regular university appointment officer. Sometimes the athletic employment agent

[11] *Wisconsin*, statement by Professor J. F. A. Pyre, forwarded by Miss Julia M. Wilkinson, Executive Secretary, at the behest of President Glenn Frank, July 30, 1929: That the Assistant to the Director, Department of Physical Education, "goes 'as far as the law allows' is evident from his correspondence."

makes with university authorities arrangements whereby a certain number of campus jobs in addition to those in the immediate disposal of the athletic department are pre-empted for athletes (Idaho, Oklahoma, Oregon Agricultural, South Dakota), an arrangement that may result in a practically complete monopoly (Idaho) or in a more or less fair allotment between athletes and non-athletes. Or concessions for the sale of refreshments at athletic contests may be allotted exclusively to athletes (Harvard[12]). A resourceful athletic employment agent may employ athletes to work for the department without additional cost or even at a slight saving over other students (Montana State College, Washington State College). A more specialized development is found at institutions where a member of the athletic staff or some other individual has had little to do but recruit and subsidize athletes and find them employment (Brown, Denver, Northwestern, Purdue, Wisconsin[13]). These agents, tireless in their efforts, come to look upon their protégés with an almost paternal interest, so strong as to overlook mediocre playing and even failure as an athlete. They discover every available job on the campus or in the community, win over the campus employer of labor, and convert townsmen to the duty of thus loyally supporting the college teams. If an employer becomes dissatisfied, they do their best to adjust difficulties. Under a system that permits them to exist at all, they are extremely useful.

The foregoing observations apply with varying force to those freshmen coaches, assistant coaches, or alumni who undertake the same sort of work (Alabama, Colgate, Columbia in part, Dartmouth).

Thus far our discussion of the employment of athletes has dealt with the procurement and apportionment of positions. We turn now to some of the many kinds of work for which athletes are engaged; we may classify them according to three types of employer.

d. *The Athletic Department or Association as Employer*

The operation of an extended program of intercollegiate and intramural athletics necessitates, in addition to the regular athletic staff, the employment of assistants in a number closely proportional to the number of participants. Certain tasks of undergraduate managers, assistants, and others were formerly performed on a voluntary basis. These positions, however, are increasingly coming to be regarded as work for which wages should be paid. In this development of paid assistance, the desire to provide jobs for needy athletes has been a factor. The expansion of athletic facilities offers additional opportunity to employ numerous undergraduates as laborers. A natural consequence has been that members of the athletic staff tend to regard certain kinds

[12] William J. Bingham, Director of Athletics, August 21, 1929: "Plans are at present under way for placing [certain concessions referred to in the text] beyond the control or direct interest of athletes," but this action is deferred by certain conditions which, it is hoped, are temporary.

[13] Statement of Professor J. F. A. Pyre, forwarded by Miss Julia M. Wilkinson, Executive Secretary, at the behest of President Glenn Frank, July 30, 1929: "I find no evidence of any financial promises beyond the promise to provide jobs."

of employment that lie at their disposal as legitimate subsidies to be allotted to promising or outstanding athletes (Allegheny, Colgate, Harvard, Idaho, Lebanon Valley, Missouri, Montana State College, New York University, Northwestern, Ohio State, Oklahoma, Southern Methodist, Syracuse, Texas, Utah, Wisconsin). Needless to say, the athletes have not been slow to reach a similar point of view, especially with regard to such relatively regular tasks as those of clerical assistants, caretakers, attendants for locker and equipment rooms, towel-dispensers, gymnasium janitors, gymnasium assistants, concessionaires, and field laborers. Other regular employment frequently is available as swimming pool guards, advertising solicitors, towel launderers, rubbers and assistant trainers, and waiters at training tables.

For such jobs compensation ranges from as low as thirty cents an hour to as high as seventy-five cents an hour, seldom higher. Or a weekly or monthly wage or allowance may be provided (Oklahoma, Oregon Agricultural, New York University, Wisconsin). The compensation depends upon several considerations, such as the athlete's need, the amount of the budget, academic standing, and athletic performance. Where he is paid an hourly wage he may, in case of absence even on an athletic trip, lose his time unless permitted to make it up upon his return. Generally athletic officials exhibit toward athletes thus employed a patience that amounts to leniency. During absence with teams, substitutes are provided, usually by the athletic organization. From a weekly or monthly wage, as a rule, no deduction is made to pay a substitute; the athletic department or organization pays not only the incumbent but his substitute as well. The conscientious athlete, who is not pressed with other duties, appears to render fair service at these tasks.

Unfortunately, at some jobs the athlete does not render satisfactory service. A number of superintendents of grounds and buildings, by no means unsympathetic with athletes, none the less prefer non-athletes as student workers. As janitor or monitor, especially when responsible to a member of the athletic staff, the athlete is not a success. A director-coach may find it necessary to sweep the gymnasium himself (Beloit). Sometimes athlete janitors are credited with hours of work out of all proportion to the amount actually performed; for example, twenty athletes are regularly employed for the tasks that some of them estimate would engage half that number of non-athletes (Oklahoma[14]). One superintendent of buildings (Oregon Agricultural[15]) holds athletic workers strictly to the hours of employment, six to eight a.m., but employs a regular force of janitors in addition. The payroll for these athletes is labeled "football help."

[14] President W. B. Bizzell, April 24, 1929: "I do not believe it quite accurate to say that the jobs assigned to athletes are regarded somewhat as sinecures. There may be some perhaps who think this is true." At the time of the field visit, a coach concerned with these jobs, as well as two athletes who had held them, apparently regarded them not only as sinecures, but as inducements.

[15] Statement forwarded by President W. J. Kerr, prepared as indicated in Note 8, above, and dated July 22, 1929: "All janitor jobs on campus changed from former sliding scale of forty to sixty cents an hour to forty cents an hour throughout. Recording of men engaged in athletics as football help in office of superintendent of buildings was made to assure exact supervision of time these men worked, thus assuring that they received no wages for time not put in on the job."

The rate of pay for non-athletes at such tasks is thirty cents an hour, and for athletes sixty cents, while the coach reports forty cents an hour on eligibility blanks in order to conform to conference regulations. At the time of one field visit (New York University) the condition of the squad quarters cared for by athletes was certainly unsatisfactory. Where such employment is not a disguised subsidy, similar results are not tolerated; with janitors' jobs placed on a competitive basis, open to all, and assigned fairly without prejudice, the work is better done (Brigham Young, Cornell, Massachusetts Agricultural, Middlebury).

As clerical assistants, locker room attendants, and towel dispensers, athletes are more proficient, but substitutes are leniently permitted or furnished. Sometimes towels are left to dispense themselves, while the athlete paid for this work spends his time in study or otherwise.

Working as gymnasium assistants and swimming pool guards, 'varsity athletes give at least as much satisfaction as non-athletes. Working as tutors in physical education courses, as long as the question of amateur standing is not raised (Y.M.C.A. College), they may be more desirable because of greater skill. To use athletes as towel launderers requires constant vigilance and close supervision (Montana State College, Oregon Agricultural, Washington State College). When not responsible to the athletic staff, athletes appear to give satisfactory service as field laborers. If, however, a regular weekly or monthly wage is paid, the force may be unnecessarily large (New York University, Oklahoma). In an extreme case thirty-two athletes and prospective athletes were employed to maintain a small playing field and do odd jobs (New York University). These men, whose work is assigned by the head football coach and who are responsible to an assistant coach or an ex-athlete, keep their own time, amounting to ten hours a week, besides week-end extra service, paid for at the rate of fifty cents an hour.[16]

At institutions where concessions within the control of the athletic department or association are allotted to athletes (Harvard,[17] Lehigh, Michigan, Minnesota, Missouri, Northwestern, Oklahoma, Syracuse, and other universities) profits are usually so restricted that, while not excessive, they afford what is considered to be just compensation. Commonly a member of the athletic staff or an outside agent supervises the concessions and the athletes act as salesmen at the contests. Advertising in football and other athletic programs may involve considerable sums, and frequently athletes prove to be successful solicitors, although the services performed are rarely commensurate with the compensation. To a select list of "loyal supporters," an athlete can sell enough

[16] Inspection of these labor accounts for one week during the football season showed a total of 320 hours of work and tended to support the opinion of one of the coaches that "the athletes are not overworked."

[17] *Harvard*, William J. Bingham, Director of Athletics, states in a letter of August 21, 1929, that "Plans are at present under way for placing [certain concessions referred to in the text] beyond the control or direct interest of athletes," but this action is deferred by certain conditions, which, it is hoped, are temporary.

advertising to make his allotted commission in a very short time, particularly when the athletic department (Missouri) coöperates with a group of townsmen. Indeed, coöperation reduces to a minimum the efforts required of a solicitor. When members of the athletic council pave the way by telephone calls or personal conversation with business associates (Pennsylvania), or when advertising space in the alumni directory of a large city is sold by prominent athletes (Michigan), the task may be not only easy but pleasant. Indeed, whenever university athletes are employed in selling advertising space in athletic or other publications, the solicitor's athletic reputation and the loyalty of the solicited are exploited unduly.

Of all jobs, legitimate or illegitimate, that are filled by athletes, waiting on table has proved to be the most convenient and satisfactory to the athletes employed. At training tables (Colorado, Columbia, Dartmouth, Harvard, Haskell, Pennsylvania, Yale) numbers of waiterships are usually available for 'varsity athletes or promising freshmen. In some instances these are so administered as to provide legitimate employment for athletes; in others they are clearly subsidies. For example, when they are divided without prejudice between athletes and non-athletes, or awarded to any needy student regardless of his athletic prominence, they can scarcely be regarded as subsidies. The situation is far different when several athletes are provided with living quarters at a "Freshman House" and wait at training table for their meals (Pennsylvania).

At universities where rubbing forms an important part of football training, athletes may be employed as rubbers (Minnesota, Missouri, Southern California, Wisconsin[18]), and freshmen are more conveniently used for the work than members of university squads. Some seventeen athletes at the University of Wisconsin, where athletes are most extensively employed in this capacity, appeared on the regular payrolls of the athletic department as "trainers and rubbers," with an average monthly wage of $33.67. With all due allowance for large squads and an intensive rubbing system, the number is generous.

Those who maintain that all jobs at the disposal of the athletic department should be given to prominent athletes often cite the practice of such other departments as chemistry, languages, or mathematics, that employ their better students as assistants. The analogy is pressed to the point where superior athletic skill is regarded as entitling its possessor to the more lucrative or influential posts. The resulting impairment of amateur standing in college sport is sometimes recognized by the advocates of the system, but seldom to the point of producing a reversal of policy.

e. *The University or College as an Employer of Athletes*

As an employer of athletes in various capacities on the campus, the college administration is generally more stringent than the athletic department or association. Excep-

[18] *Wisconsin*, statement of Professor J. F. A. Pyre, forwarded by Miss Julia M. Wilkinson, Executive Secretary, at the behest of President Glenn Frank, July 30, 1929: "This kind of employment is all *rigidly audited*." The italic is Professor Pyre's.

tions to this general rule arise from an excess of local interest in intercollegiate competition. At the institutions visited, about one-third of the campus jobs administered outside the athletic department and held by athletes, are janitorships which, for football players, at least, are less desirable than lighter work, such as waiting at table in common dining halls. Exceptionally, at the University of Texas, a specified number of athletes had been provided with employment in the Package Loan Library, a bureau of the Extension Division, at compensation ranging from ten to thirty dollars a month.[19] From the point of view of the university as employer, the chief deficiencies of the athlete are his proneness to discontent and his absences on trips. At Saturday and other part-time employments, if he is free to devote his attention to them, he has been found to give entire satisfaction.

f. Off-Campus Employers

The extent to which employment away from the college campus should be regarded as a subsidy depends partly upon the way in which such positions are secured and partly upon the industry that employers require of the athletes whom they hire. If an athlete secures his job without making his athletic connections his means of approach, and if he is required, like any other employee, to give service commensurate with his wages, jobs seldom are subsidies. Moreover, athletes who exhibit in their work those qualities of persistence, resourcefulness, and conscientiousness which athletics are supposed to develop, generally adopt a quite independent procedure in securing and filling positions. But an organized attempt, directed perhaps by a paid official, to provide and assign work away from the campus, approaches more nearly the nature of subsidizing (Denver, Drake, Southern California). Moreover, when employers, because of sympathy with the hard-worked athlete, permit him to draw his pay for purely nominal services, the situation is aggravated (Denver, Oregon Agricultural College, Wisconsin[20]). Business men, when questioned concerning their employment of athletes, have maintained that their chief motive is institutional loyalty, sympathy for the athlete, or general interest in athletics; nevertheless, they have not ignored the value of athletic reputation in pursuits that call for personal contact. Hence, athletes at a number of universities have been subsidized under the guise of salesmen of insurance or bonds (Columbia, Wisconsin), clothing store clerks (California, Drake, Ohio State), agents for business firms (Chicago, Colgate, University of Iowa, Southern Methodist, Wyo-

---

[19] The time sheets were turned in by a university officer, but the athletes were paid from funds in the custody of the Director of Athletics.

[20] *Oregon State Agricultural College*, statement forwarded by President W. J. Kerr, prepared as indicated in Note 8, above, and dated July 22, 1929: "Investigation of help given athletes by local business men shows that no subsidizing has existed during the past two years. One man was employed by a group of business men as janitor in doctors' offices at fifty dollars per month. This is the only evidence that can be found to show subsidizing of athletes by local business men during the past five years." *Wisconsin*, statement of Professor J. F. A. Pyre, forwarded by Miss Julia M. Wilkinson, Executive Secretary, at the behest of President Glenn Frank, July 30, 1929: "I fail to find any cases at the present time answering to these descriptions. . . . There are some athletes who have fairly remunerative jobs away from the campus during the summer vacation."

ming[21]), sporting goods salesmen (Dartmouth, Drake, Texas, University of Washington, Wyoming[21]), advertising solicitors (Michigan, Missouri, Northwestern, Pennsylvania), motion picture employees (Southern California), companions to children (Denver, Harvard), writers (Michigan), and otherwise. In view of everyone's natural impulse to accept all that his employer feels inclined to pay, it is doubtful whether, in the majority of cases, the notion ever enters the athlete's mind that he is professionalizing himself by trading in his athletic skill or reputation. Only a college athlete who is conscientiously devoted to the amateur ideal can be expected to avoid exploitation of any sort. Yet it requires no unusual code of honor to refuse to be paid an amount out of all proportion to service rendered.

Other positions off the campus filled by athletes include those of playground supervisors, life guards at summer resorts, letter-carriers, newspaper deliverers, theatre ushers, firemen, night watchmen, milk deliverymen, waiters, and filling-station clerks. No such position can be accounted a subsidy when the employer requires of his employee the same services as he would demand of other undergraduates not engaged in athletics. The self-respecting American undergraduate does not solicit charity, and little good flows from accustoming any young man to slack at his work.

2. Loans as Subsidies

Although successful general student loan funds are available to great numbers of American college students, the practice of lending money to young men because of athletic prominence or ability persists. Usually, such loans to athletes reflect a conscientious attempt to compromise between athletic scholarships or cash payments on the one hand, and the withholding of all financial assistance to athletes on the other. A loan to an athlete, even when its repayment is dubious, tends to ease the conscience of both lender and recipient. The sponsors of loans may be either individuals or organizations.

a. *By Individuals*

Even if it were possible to estimate the extent of loans to athletes by individual alumni, coaches, and friends, the information would be nearly valueless without trustworthy knowledge of the motives behind each transaction. A fair proportion — perhaps a seventh — of the athletes interviewed during our study were borrowing funds from individual friends to assist them through college. Of these young men, fully half believed that the loans had been made out of friendship or courtesy without reference to athletics at a particular institution, and expressed an evidently sincere intention to repay them in full.

The greater number of these loans by individuals are made by alumni of the athlete's

---

[21] President A. C. Crane, written statement, May 13, 1929 : "From 1924 to 1927 local alumni and business men subsidized athletes with jobs and loans; . . . this activity was discontinued in 1927."

own college. Occasionally a local business man (Southern Methodist) or a member of a board of trustees (Texas) thus helps athletes. Few coaches or directors of athletics now lend money to their athletes or endorse their notes (Drake, Georgia School of Technology, Texas); in one instance, losses on such transactions have fallen upon the sponsor. To a prudent director or coach, financial self-protection, his own reputation, and the good name of the institution are far more important than the temporary relief of a needy athlete. Moreover, a disgruntled or disloyal player who has borrowed from his coach or director may easily create a most embarrassing situation for the considerate lender and the institution with which he is affiliated.

b. *By Organizations*

Although it is not nowadays customary for an institution or an athletic organization to loan money officially to athletes as such, vestiges of such practices in past years have been found (Southern California). Loan funds sponsored or provided by alumni are usually dispensed at the direction of the athletic organization (Drake, Georgia School of Technology, Ohio Wesleyan, Vermont; Baylor, in process of formation at time of field visit [22]). One such special athletic loan fund that grew out of the vote of an athletic council was distributed to some forty nominees of the director of athletics and the coaches in return for notes; another, provided by alumni and friends of the institution, was managed by the athletic organization; a third, maintained by alumni, was in charge of a member of the athletic council; a fourth loan fund has superseded the practice, which formerly had the sanction of the university trustees, of stamping the registration card of athletes "paid" without any payment of institutional obligations being in fact made. This fund, for which an alumni secretary is now responsible, assists about a hundred athletes. None of its notes, which appear to be scarcely legal in form, has as yet fallen due, but efforts are made to impress the borrowers with their obligations.

Unfortunately, it appears that the notes of athletes are collectible in comparatively few instances, even when the loan fund is administered through a local bank in order to create a sense of responsibility on the part of the athlete-borrowers. The fact is that loans from funds provided by groups of persons and controlled or administered by athletic organizations or departments are practically the equivalent of gifts, and borrowers tend to regard them as subsidies, feel little responsibility for repayment, and

---

[22] *Drake*, President D. W. Morehouse, letter of April 24, 1929: " We are enforcing these collections wherever it is possible. Within the year a number of collections have been made from those who had ignored our statements before. We can cite name and date." In response to a later request, President Morehouse furnished information concerning payments from five individual borrowers as follows: (1) on September 13, 1928, $51.75; (2) on September 17, 1928, $18.50; (3) on January 24, 1929, $26.90; (4) on February 15, 1929, $59.74; (5) on May 4, 1929, a pledge of $20 a year for five years to the Drake Endowment and Dormitory Campaign, with the statement that " The Alumni Association holds my tuition notes for eight hundred dollars which I hope to pay, and this will take all I can spare for the next five years."

Ohio Wesleyan, President E. D. Soper, April 20, 1929: " They [the athletes] are put on exactly the same basis with other students in their relationships to the scholarship loan fund. . . . [The local alumni loan fund] has been done away with entirely and there is no such fund maintained at the present time whatsoever."

appear not to fear prosecution for default. In contrast, when bona-fide loans from officially constituted funds are wisely made and regularly collected, both athletes and non-athletes being included among the beneficiaries on equal terms (Columbia), no disproportionate losses are incurred through loaning to athletes and the essential nature of subsidies is lacking.

A few alumni loan funds have been administered independently of the athletic organization (Arizona, Brown,[23] Georgia School of Technology, Detroit Club of the University of Michigan, University of Washington). Apparently in no instance have large sums been involved.

Often citizens luncheon clubs of benevolent intent provide general loan funds for students. Where, however, interest in local college athletics runs high or athletic enthusiasts influence awards, such funds may be loaned only to athletes (Arizona, University of Colorado, Ohio State, Wyoming [24]). In one instance the fund developed out of impatience on the part of business men with the meagre encouragement given to athletes at the local institution. Although funds such as these are generally inaugurated with much enthusiasm, they tend to peter out.

3. Scholarships as Subsidies

If, in the assignment of a scholarship, whatever its designation, source, or form, the element of athletic ability or reputation is a determining factor, the award is, to all intents and purposes, an athletic scholarship. The term, however, has suffered more official disfavor than the practice.

Under present conditions, the notion is general, especially among high school athletes, that athletic scholarships are plentiful at American universities. Even at certain institutions that upon close examination are apparently innocent of the practice (Brown, Coe, officially awarded scholarships in Columbia College, Ohio Wesleyan), undergraduates as well as prospective students believe that scholarships are awarded on a basis of athletic prominence. No doubt this state of affairs is partly ascribable to misrepresentations or misunderstandings on the part of schoolboy athletes, inducements set forth in the name of other institutions, and an occasional offer from a solicitor couched in language that leaves the athlete under the impression that the assistance he may receive is in reality a subsidizing scholarship.

a. *Athletic Ability as a Scholarship Qualification*

No single factor has contributed more directly to the use of athletic scholarships in American colleges and universities than the second qualification set by the will of Cecil

---

[23] Emery M. Porter, M.D., president of the Brown Club, Providence, to President W. H. P. Faunce, of Brown University, letter of April 29, 1929: Only one loan has been made from the club's funds to an athlete since January, 1927.

[24] *Wyoming*, President A. C. Crane, written statement of May 13, 1929: "From 1924 to 1927 local alumni and business men subsidized athletes with . . . loans; approximately 10 athletes assisted; they were required to sign a note covering loan bearing 8% interest after graduation; this activity was discontinued in 1927."

Rhodes for recipients of the Oxford scholarships that bear his name.[25] Certain American institutions (for example, Dartmouth, Rutgers, Swarthmore) award scholarships upon what is termed an "all-round" basis, including, besides scholastic excellence, qualities of "leadership," interest in undergraduate activities, usually physical vigor, and, perhaps, value to the student body. Obviously, all of these qualifications except the first point in the direction of athletic ability. When, in awards, intellectual achievement is underrated and qualities of character and "leadership" thereby are given undue emphasis, an "all-round" scholarship is in reality granted on the basis of athletic skill and attainment. Examination of academic records among such scholarship-holders usually bears out this view. It is true that some instances in which a disproportionate award of aid appears to have been made to athletes from general scholarship funds may arise more or less naturally from the fact that official effort is made to provide tuition or part-tuition scholarships for all deserving undergraduates (Dartmouth, University of Iowa, Ohio Wesleyan), and that many athletes need assistance. Alert recruiters may be trusted to bring to the attention of the committee awarding such aid every impecunious athlete. In such circumstances the right use or the abuse of awards depends entirely upon the wisdom and fairness of those who make them. When examination of a list of scholarship-holders reveals that practically every important athlete at the institution enjoys a scholarship, the fact points to the use of general scholarship aid as an athletic subsidy.

b. *Special Scholarships*

The result of awards from certain funds that are provided by special regulations and that go principally to athletes is the same as in bestowing athletic scholarships (Columbia University Club scholarships at Columbia, Hobart, Undergraduate Division of New York University School of Commerce,[26] Southern California, Southern Methodist, Stanford, Ursinus). Although formal application may be required of a candidate, the enquiries preliminary to award rarely include the usual questions con-

[25] Founded in 1902, these awards are authorized by the will of the late Cecil J. Rhodes, in which he stipulated that "in the election of a student to a scholarship, regard shall be had to (1) his literary and scholastic attainments; (2) his fondness for and success in manly outdoor sports, such as cricket, football, and the like; (3) his qualities of manhood, truth, courage, devotion to duty, sympathy for and protection of the weak, kindliness, unselfishness, and fellowship; and (4) his exhibition during school days of moral force of character and of instincts to lead and to take an interest in his schoolmates."

A Memorandum on the Rhodes scholarships for the United States of America, 1928 (Department of the Interior, Bureau of Education, Washington, Higher Education Circular No. 34, February, 1928), restates the basis of selection: "In that section of the will in which he defined the general type of scholar he desired, Mr. Rhodes mentioned four groups of qualities, the first two of which he considered most important: (1) Literary and scholastic ability and attainments. (2) Qualities of manhood, truth, courage, devotion to duty, sympathy, kindliness, unselfishness, and fellowship. (3) Exhibition of moral force of character and of instincts to lead and to take an interest in his schoolmates. (4) Physical vigor, as shown by interest in outdoor sports or in other ways. . . . Participation and interest in open-air and athletic pursuits form an essential qualification for a Rhodes scholar, but exceptional athletic distinction is not to be treated as of equal importance with the other requirements."

It should be noted, however, that it is the earlier and not the later version of these qualifications which has influenced materially American theory and practice respecting the relation of athletic skill to the award of scholarships, etc.

[26] *New York University*, Chancellor Elmer Ellsworth Brown, letter of May 16, 1929: "Such tuition scholarships as are available to worthy applicants are available not alone in the School of Commerce, Accounts, and Finance, but in all other departments of the University."

cerning his origins, references, evidences of promise, and other qualifications upon which candidates for regular scholarships available to all students are examined. Most of the personal recommendations appear to come from alumni, coaches, and recruiting agents, who are interested in the athletic success of the institution. Indeed, for the actual appointments, or the nominations that are their practical equivalents, made by alumni or coaches, the officers of a university may merely act as recording agents (New York University,[27] Southern California, Stanford, Catholic institutions). Even when the actual appointments are made by the duly constituted scholarship agencies, the recommendations of recruiters may be influential (Columbia).

Only one step removed from this practice is the procedure by which a regular committee on scholarships appoints incumbents after the receipt of recommendations from persons intimately acquainted with candidates (Southern Methodist; proposed method at Stanford; Ursinus). A dean may permit a coach to dispose of a number of scholarships upon official approval of the dean (New York University[28]), or the alumni who provide the necessary funds may merely inform university officers that certain candidates are to receive credit for specified sums of money (Stanford). Even though appointments be nominally annual, it is usually understood that, once made, they will continue while the holder remains in residence.

The sources and value and the numbers of such special scholarships vary greatly among the institutions that make use of them. The principal sources are two : university funds allocated by presidents or trustees to provide a certain number of scholarships or amount of assistance (Drake, neither specified — converted into loans; New York University, seventy-five scholarships; Southern Methodist, twenty scholarships; Southern California, $40,000; Ursinus, twenty scholarships; certain Catholic institutions) ; or alumni contributions (Stanford, approximately fifty scholarships). If funds or numbers of scholarships available are limited, most of the awards usually go to football players (New York University,[29] Southern Methodist, Ursinus), but keenness of interest in other sports may bring a wider distribution (Columbia, Stanford). In no instance are awards of special scholarships confined exclusively to athletes. The popularity of this method of assistance probably flows from the convictions, first, that it is fairer than other methods to both athletes and non-athletes ; secondly, that under it the athletic situation is more nearly controlled and the interests involved are better subserved, possibly on a basis of compromise ; and, thirdly, that, if athletes are to be subsidized at all, the institution itself should dispense the subsidies.

[27] *New York University*, Chancellor Elmer Ellsworth Brown, letter of May 16, 1929 : "The award of such scholarships is never delegated to a coach, nor are coaches permitted to make commitments as to such awards." The statement in the text is based upon a newspaper interview with the head coach in November, 1926, upon letters written by him, copies of which were kindly supplied to our enquiry, and upon his oral statement to the same effect.

[28] See Notes 26 and 27, above.

[29] See Notes 26 and 27, above.

c. *Honorary Scholarships and the Athlete*

Another type of scholarships is hardly distinguishable from that just described. It includes those honor awards which, named from the donor, source, or purpose of the fund that provides them, almost invariably are bestowed upon athletes and are currently regarded by many as athletic scholarships (Brown, one scholarship; Des Moines, fifteen scholarships; University of Georgia, forty scholarships; Lehigh, one scholarship; Montana, five scholarships; Princeton, eight scholarships;[30] Southern California, two scholarships). If a traditional practice of awarding such scholarships to athletes exists, it may be in part due to the influence of alumni in urging the appointment of athletes whom they have encouraged to attend the university (Princeton[30]). Again, the scholarship funds may have been specially earmarked by their donors for athletes (Brown, Lehigh, Montana, Southern California); or a university may remit all or part of the tuition for an unspecified number of athletes as a tapering-off of a more extensive system (Des Moines); or a special fund may have been created by alumni (Georgia School of Technology, University of Georgia) in the hope of ultimately eliminating subsidies (University of Georgia). Although such controlled and duly recorded awards may represent a step in advance of extensive and indiscriminate subsidizing by outside agencies, the policy is not to be compared for firmness and courage with the action of the University of California in advocating a conference rule to deprive itself of a gift that would have established what would have proved to be an athletic scholarship.

d. *Athletic Scholarships*

Thus far our discussion has dealt with scholarships and awards, which, although their purposes and results may be very similar to those of veritable athletic scholarships, are not officially designated as such. We turn now to those forms of aid which are frankly and unequivocally termed athletic scholarships. The amounts or numbers of such awards available and the bases of award at the time of each field visit varied considerably (Blue Ridge, twelve; Colgate, twenty-five; Geneva, thirty-five; Georgetown, unspecified; Gettysburg, thirty; Fordham, forty; Lebanon Valley, sixteen; Muhlenberg, unspecified; Pennsylvania State College, seventy-five; Syracuse, $14,000; West Virginia Wesleyan, twenty; Ursinus, sixteen[31]).

The benefit is rarely paid in cash. The partial or complete remission of tuition

---

[30] Since the time of the field visit to Princeton, December 10–13, 1926, the method of awarding scholarships has been completely and soundly revised.   For the method now in force see the Princeton University Catalogue for 1929–30.

[31] *Pennsylvania State College*, President R. D. Hetzel, written statement of May 15, 1929: "There is a general sentiment on the part of the faculty and the students against giving athletic scholarships as inducements. In 1926, there were 75 'Trustee Athletic Scholarships' covering fees and room rent, or fees or room rent or board. The number is reduced to 28 holding a full scholarship which covers room rent, incidental fees, and, in some cases, non-resident tuition; one holding a partial scholarship which covers room rent and non-resident tuition; one which covers room rent only; and three which cover non-resident tuition only — a total of twenty-eight holding full scholarships, and five holding partial scholarships. The Board of Athletic Control passed an action two years ago that no new athletic scholarships should be offered, and none have been offered."

West Virginia Wesleyan College, President Homer E. Wark, letter of June 27, 1929: In December, 1926, "all assistance to players was stopped; no scholarships have been provided by the Athletic Board; no use of the 'gym' as a rooming place, and the training table was discontinued . . . and this year [1929–30] we want to abandon the training camp."

through athletic scholarships generally involves and often takes place in the offices of the institution, which devise methods of award to suit local conditions and the needs of athletes. Values of athletic scholarships range from part or full tuition at the lower end of the scale (Colgate), to allotments graduated in amount according to the number of teams for which the recipient is selected (Blue Ridge). In the first instance, athletic scholarships represent a step away from even graver forms of subsidizing; in the second, a step toward them. Usually the source of the fund in a measure conditions the selection of its beneficiaries, but in some instances coaches (Lebanon Valley) or a graduate manager (Syracuse) have chosen the recipients; or, again, the regularly constituted scholarship committee of the institution may distribute the scholarships.

e. *Publication of Lists of Scholarship-Holders*

Although it is generally customary in English-speaking countries that a trust or endowment operated for charitable educational purposes should make public the extent and nature of its benefactions, a few universities have felt it unwise to publish full statements of scholarship awards (Southern California, Stanford, certain Catholic institutions), with the result that natural but harmful suspicions have been aroused among athletic opponents. Suspicions such as these apparently do not arise when accurate information concerning all awards may be gathered from official publications of the university (Columbia, New York University, Princeton). In this connection, the suggestion has been made that awarding scholarships to undergraduates of questionable scholastic achievement is embarrassing to an institution that prides itself upon its academic standing. When academic standards rise, the award of a scholarship or other aid is preceded by scrutiny of the candidate's intellectual ability and promise, but where athletes are almost without exception regarded as special cases in such awards, it is difficult to discern in the practical results any very sincere regard for the academic reputation of the institution.

4. Subsidies in Money or Other Tangible Consideration

Campus jobs and scholarships, when used as subsidies, generally entail no payment in cash; they result in bookkeeping transactions, whereby the money credits obtained are applied to college bills. We turn now to various other types of subsidy, which are sometimes conferred in conjunction with athletic scholarships and which, in certain cases, involve the receipt of money or some value that is accepted in its stead.

a. *In Conjunction with Athletic Scholarships*

The practice of "caring for" a more or less definite number of athletes, ranging from twenty-five to fifty (Bucknell, Gettysburg, Muhlenberg, Oglethorpe, Pennsylvania State, Pittsburgh, West Virginia Wesleyan), is a somewhat less formal matter than the award of athletic scholarships. Its excuse is the competitive bids of rivals, and its limit is usually "all college expenses." Sometimes (Boston College, Holy Cross, Notre Dame) no definite promises are made; the athlete is merely assured that he will be "cared for." Neither procedure necessarily entails cash payments, although these may be present. The sources of the necessary funds or credits may include, singly or in combination, subscriptions from alumni as individuals or as groups and from local merchants, appropriations from the athletic treasury, and the remitting of tuition by the institution. Although the probable success of a candidate at athletics is usually a prerequisite to such arrangements, a further obligation of some sort is occasionally imposed: the performing of odd tasks about the campus, or recruiting — indeed, an athlete successful at recruiting may even be valued at his full college expenses without any other requirement than attendance at the university (Oglethorpe[32]). As is to be expected under a system that links the institution, through the bestowal of athletic scholarships, with other agencies and sources of provision, recommendations and appointments to subsidies are made by persons intimately acquainted with the institution's athletic affairs: coaches, graduate managers, athletic directors, the president's assistant (Gettysburg), or the president himself (Oglethorpe[33]).

b. *Subsidies without Athletic Scholarships*

At the time of the field visits to a number of institutions, athletes were subsidized on the basis of their financial needs or demands; that is, although the process closely resembled the awarding of athletic scholarships, the element of barter entered more frequently into the recruiting and maintenance of athletes than it does in the transactions previously discussed. Of course, an athlete is seldom subsidized thus unless he needs assistance. Funds for subsidizing according to need or demand may come, singly or in combination, from alumni or friends of the college, from the athletic association or organization, or from the institution (Allegheny, Carnegie Institute of Technology, Centre, Dickinson, Grove City, Lafayette, Lebanon Valley, Northwestern, University of Pennsylvania, Western Maryland[34]). At some preparatory schools, these subsidy expenses have been charged to advertising (Bellefonte,[35] Kiskiminetas) with a frank

---

[32] President Thornwell Jacobs, letter of April 19, 1929: "There are no students playing on any of the teams of Oglethorpe University who do not pay their entire expenses at the institution, either in cash or services. These services consist of various forms of self help work for which the University would otherwise have to pay cash."

[33] President Thornwell Jacobs, letter of April 19, 1929: "The President does not favor subsidy of athletes. He has never in his life attempted to proselyte an athlete." In a subsequent conversation, President Jacobs stated that he did not like the use of the terms "recruiting" and "subsidizing" to describe the *securing* of students, athletes and non-athletes, at Oglethorpe.

[34] *Centre*, President Charles J. Turck, letter of April 22, 1929, states that the emphasis on football has greatly decreased; only five out of nineteen football games have been won in the last two years. *Grove City*, President Weir C. Ketler, letter of April 22, 1929: During 1928–29, "only twenty-six boys engaged in athletics" are "receiving any sort of scholarship aid, and fewer will receive it next year." *Northwestern*, President Walter Dill Scott, letter of April 25, 1929: "There was a sum provided by alumni for scholarships. . . . It is quite possible that the sum of the funds paid for these sixteen scholarships amounted to $2900. These scholarships were awarded by the regular committee of the faculties and were not more generous in amounts than the scholarships assigned to other students." The statement in the text does not refer to scholarships awarded by the "regular committee of the faculty."

[35] *Bellefonte*, Headmaster J. R. Hughes, letter of May 14, 1929: The Academy has "abolished the practice of giving full scholarships. Very few athletic officials are paying the expenses of needy athletes in schools like Bellefonte."

appreciation of the appropriateness of the procedure. In the case of one college, this type of subsidy was distributed, with the knowledge of the athletic authorities, in addition to unorganized activities by individuals. Alumni subsidies are dispensed, sometimes by a member of the athletic staff or someone intimately connected with athletics, from a "slush fund" or "black box fund," and thus a close supervision of beneficiaries can be maintained. Wherever the head coach is influential in selecting candidates for subsidies in which the element of bargaining is present, players are expected to "make good" or forfeit all or part of their subsidies. The amounts available in slush funds vary (Carnegie Institute of Technology, $13,000; Centre, $600; Grove City, $8,000; Lafayette, $3,000) with the interest of contributors; but the number of beneficiaries varies less with the size of each fund than with the cost of living at the institutions (Carnegie Institute of Technology, thirty-two; Centre, eleven; Dickinson, twelve; Grove City, thirty-five; Lafayette, twelve; Lebanon Valley, sixteen; Northwestern, sixteen; Western Maryland, six[36]). The intensity of the practice depends upon conditions in the section or conference in which the college is situated and which may license, retard, or even stop the practice. Ordinarily, an interview between the recruiter — be he coach or agent — and the prospect settles the prospect's approximate need, which in at least one instance was supplemented on instructions from the recruiter's "superiors" to "match anything up to tuition, board, and room." The bargaining that results sometimes taxes the wits of both parties; one subsidizer personally and closely examined every candidate for assistance to ascertain his precise needs. Coöperation from fraternities in providing food and lodging, and from the athletic organization in supplying jobs, is, of course, very helpful. At no institution are all of the athletes thus subsidized, and at none, also, is it customary to grant subsidies in excess of the cost of tuition, food, lodging, books, supplies, and incidental fees.

In an extreme case of subsidizing, alumni and business men made contributions ranging from $10 to nearly $1,000 annually to a fund aggregating from $25,000 to $50,000 a year. From this the college expenses of all football players were paid and additional sums, termed "pay checks," were disbursed to leading performers (Washington and Jefferson). Later, the practice was modified to provide only tuitions, board, room, and fees, without cash payments.[37] The essentials of the practice may be the same, even though the fund be small (Franklin and Marshall).

In at least three instances the practices at the time of the field visits were explained as a tapering-off of more extensive operations (Centre, Lafayette, Northwestern).

c. *On a Basis of Guarantees*

As a variation of this practice, on a basis of estimated monthly expenses at an insti-

[36] *Centre, Grove City, Northwestern:* see Note 34 above.

[37] President S. S. Baker, in a letter of April 22, 1929, states that, instead of a reduction of from 10 per cent to 15 per cent, estimated by this study, "the actual reduction averages almost 40%."

tution, an athlete may be guaranteed $25 or $50 a month, to be secured partly through work at off-campus jobs (Tennessee, ten to twenty athletes) or outright, without reference to other than athletic services (University of West Virginia, twenty-five or thirty football players[38]). Funds for the purpose are raised and allotted by alumni. Under the first of these systems, a man who engages in three branches of athletics and finds his time too much occupied to work at other employment is, nevertheless, assured of a fixed income for the college year; the work performed appears to be of less importance than the guaranteed amount of the subsidy. From the point of view of the custodian of the fund, who equalizes the amounts under each guarantee, the advantage is that a hard-working young man will not need much assistance of this sort. Under the second system, an athlete who lives at home, instead of at the squad house, may be compensated by a similar process of equalization under his guarantee. One distinguishing feature of this method of subsidizing on a basis of guarantees is payment in cash or by check. The monthly basis testifies to the insecurity of employment as an athlete.

5. Subsidies in Kind, Favor, or Service

The types of subsidy about to be considered resemble those already discussed in purpose and sometimes in operation, but, for reasons which will become apparent, they are treated separately.

a. *Alumni Assistance to Athletes*

Some of the many ways in which groups or individuals among alumni assist athletes, especially in conjunction with other agencies, have been set forth. A little apart from these practices stands the over-enthusiastic alumnus, who, aroused by competition for athletes on behalf of rival colleges, is led on his own initiative to match or to exceed these inducements by assisting promising schoolboys, from two or three to ten in number, to attend his own Alma Mater (Dartmouth, University of Iowa, Pennsylvania, Southern California, Stanford). In no case studied were qualities other than athletic prominence apparently so important a consideration in the minds of the men who gave the assistance. Challenged in this traffic, the alumnus usually replies that he has a perfect right thus to help young men if he chooses. The fallacies of this position are outlined in Chapter XII. For the present it should be noted that much has been done (Dartmouth), and much more can be done, by genuine efforts to eliminate this independent type of subsidizing.

This practice in some particulars associates itself with a rather more farsighted effort on the part of alumni. In the East, relations have been established between

---

[38] President John R. Turner, letter of April 23, 1929: "We . . . have altogether discontinued the practice of subsidizing athletes. . . . I do not say, as in my judgment no college president can say, that no alumnus is making any contribution to the support of a member or members of our athletic teams. I must say, however, that after careful inquiry I have learned of no case where a student is receiving support because he plays on one of our athletic teams."

certain private preparatory schools on the one hand and certain colleges and universities on the other, whereby athletes, varying in number from one to as many as twenty, have been wholly or partly maintained at the schools until they are ready for college (Brown, Carnegie Institute of Technology, Dartmouth, Dickinson, Lafayette, New York University, Pittsburgh, Princeton,[39] Syracuse, Washington and Jefferson). Those most frequently responsible for the arrangement, which, whether old or new, is predicated upon mutual good will and a supposed advantage to both college and school, are alumni, headmasters, and coaches. The actual basis of operations may be a number of free places or scholarships in a school to which alumni as individuals or as groups may appoint athletes of promise, or merely a working understanding under which boys are induced to enter the school on such especially favorable financial conditions as the school coach or headmaster is able to arrange. In a few instances, the athlete's school expenses have been paid from a college athletic slush fund. It is only fair to state that rumors of similar subsidizing on behalf of certain other institutions have not been substantiated by the present enquiry.

b. *Training Tables and Subsidizing*

Experience at a number of universities and colleges tends to demonstrate that training tables provide a ready means of subsidizing that may appear difficult to stop. Rarely are training table board bills settled promptly and regularly. The subsidized athlete, seeing his fellows lax in these payments, quickly concludes that he, too, is entitled to his meals at someone else's expense. An easy-going official in charge of collections readily slips into the way of allowing large indebtednesses for meals to accumulate, while a conscientious steward is torn between his duty as collector and his sympathy for the impecunious athlete. Of course, an athlete who is "taken care of" to the extent of "all college expenses," pays no board bill. Board that is given, or practically given, by the athletic organization (Colgate, Columbia, Pennsylvania) is obviously a subsidy.

The situation is less serious when the athlete himself meets all, or almost all, of the training table expense (Amherst; Colorado, up to January, 1927; McGill). The dangers are minimized when bills are collected through the business office (Brown, Washington State College), or when only the evening meal is served (California, Lafayette, Lehigh, Southern California, Tulane, Vanderbilt).

c. *Fraternity Subsistence*

Besides the ways already detailed in which fraternities are exploited for subsidizing athletes, local chapters, as their contribution to a subsidizing program, may provide

---

[39] The practices at Princeton to which reference is made in the text have been abolished through the efforts of President John Grier Hibben, Dean L. P. Eisenhart, Professor Charles W. Kennedy, and Dr. Joseph A. Raycroft. This fact again indicates what can be accomplished when administrators, sincerely concerned for institutional honor and college sport, act with the same sincerity upon information, however distasteful, offered to them in a disinterested fashion.

certain athlete members with rooms or board or with both at so low a figure that
the arrangement can be regarded only as an athletic subsidy (Franklin and Marshall,
New York University, Ohio Wesleyan,[40] Oregon Agricultural, Pennsylvania State).
Usually not all of the fraternities at any one institution are given to this practice.
Sometimes a fraternity chapter is used as a kind of agency or clearing house for other
subsidizing transactions between an athlete and an alumnus or some other person
(University of Iowa, Ohio State, Stanford). Although these are usually termed
"loans," it is almost needless to say that, as in the case of other unofficial borrowings,
the record of collections is not good.

d. *Maintenance of Academic Standing*

It would be difficult to discover an institution in which the athlete, if hard pressed
to maintain his academic standing, is not afforded some gratuitous assistance in study
by his fellow undergraduates. If the help is intelligently given and utilized, it may
even become an important and valuable element in the intellectual development of all
concerned. From this natural condition, it is only a step to the notion that a degree of
responsibility devolves upon administrative or athletic officers for the academic standing of undergraduates who assumedly benefit the college through participation in
extra-curricular activities, especially intercollegiate athletics. Moreover, with increasing strictness of requirements of eligibility has come an increased concern, sometimes
prudential, on the part of coaches over the academic standing of their players. The
result has been that a number of institutions or athletic organizations have provided
professional tutoring or similar special instruction for athletes (Brown, California,
Carnegie Institute of Technology, Colgate, Columbia, Georgia School of Technology,
Oklahoma, Pennsylvania, Pennsylvania State, Southern California[41]). For practical
purposes, there appears to be little difference between this practice and relieving a
regular salaried member of the athletic staff from some of his other duties in order that
he may supervise the academic standing of athletes.

A further consideration respecting academic standing as a factor in the support of
athletes touches upon the average of grades required as a qualification for financial
assistance. Of seven institutions (Baylor, Columbia, Des Moines, Rutgers, Southern
California, Southern Methodist, Stanford), at which a minimum academic require-

---

[40] *Ohio Wesleyan*, President E. D. Soper, letter of April 20, 1929: "If this means that athletes receive board and room free of
charge, it is not true. . . . There are athletes, however, who work for their rooms and board in their fraternities in the same
way that other students work their way through college." The statement in the text does not refer to athletes "who work for
their rooms and board in their fraternities in the same way that other students work their way through college."

[41] *Brown*, President W. H. P. Faunce, forwards a statement, May 9, 1929: "Very rarely has the Brown Club paid for any tutoring
and then only in exceptional cases. The last time this was done was over two years ago. When possible [the Club tries] to get
some of the upper classmen in the fraternities to keep the men up to scholastic standards, but this work is entirely voluntary
and without pay." *Colgate*, Mr. W. A. Reid, Graduate Manager, in a letter of April 23, 1929, states that daily tutoring is conducted as follows: "Various boys on athletic teams who are exceptionally good students in the several given subjects tutor the
other boys for a half hour during the afternoon and in the season prior to going on the field for practice in the sport," and that
no compensation whatsoever is paid. The statement in the text refers to tutoring, for which canceled vouchers for payments to
a woman tutor were examined, with Mr. Reid's coöperation, in his accounts.

ment, usually an average of "C," is prescribed for the award of certain scholarships, it was approached at only two. In a third case, if the holder of a scholarship falls below the required average, the scholarship is withdrawn; but the athlete is provided with a loan on the understanding that it will become a gift if he regains his academic standing.

e. *Complimentary Tickets as Subsidies*

In the course of our study, conversations with a considerable number of athletes have indicated that it is common practice, particularly among certain football players, to sell the complimentary tickets allotted to them as members of squads, in some instances contrary to the exhortations of their coaches. Of course, the market price of such tickets increases with public demand. The value of complimentary tickets as subsidies in kind is illustrated by the fact that a football player at a university on the Pacific Coast sold his allotment at a profit of about $100 each for various major games of a single season. If an athlete sells his tickets to personal friends, one or more of whom may be financially interested in him as an athlete, the practice is difficult to check. Extensive abuse of the privilege has been reduced by cutting down the number of tickets allotted to each player, and the measures usually taken against "scalpers" have been found as fruitful here as in other similar violations of good faith respecting football tickets.

6. Athletic Subsidies at Catholic Colleges and Universities

In respect of other matters than subsidizing, athletics at Catholic universities and colleges are discussed in these pages jointly with athletics at the other institutions visited. As regards athletic subsidies, however, it has seemed best to treat of the Catholic institutions as a group because of certain considerations which, being common, if in varying degree, to these particular colleges, will enable the reader the better to understand their problems.

Without exception, the Catholic institutions visited coöperated fully and frankly in our enquiry through interviews and immediate and unrestricted access to files and other data. As a rule, their presiding officers are not so closely in touch with the views and actions of athletic conferences as the heads of many other institutions. The explanation is their more secluded lives and training. Hence, also, their general inclination to rely much upon advice from alumni touching athletic practices and policies. During the past two years a very important change in this respect is discernible. Catholic college presidents have begun to examine at first hand into athletic conditions and to act upon their own belief in the wisdom of certain limitations. Consequently, during this period the Jesuit colleges have adopted the usual rules limiting freshman competition and also a very severe regulation regarding transfers. More important still, most of the Jesuit presidents are now disposed to weigh the advice of alumni, instead of accepting it forthwith, and to discard it when it runs counter to what, to them, appears to be sound athletic practice.

It is, therefore, perhaps not astonishing that the subsidizing of athletes at certain Catholic universities and colleges appears to have rested less upon the expediency that generally motivates the practice than upon rationalized principles. These principles begin with a conviction that every young man who desires an education should be assisted in its pursuit. To this end all available resources are utilized. But the recipient of assistance is expected to prove himself worthy by honoring in some way his college or university: if gifted in music, he finds his place; if gifted as an athlete, he can participate in games; if industrious, a job of some sort will help him partly to compensate for the time and effort that are expended upon his education. Thus far the reasoning is simple and the conclusion natural. At this point, however, enter other factors which invalidate both. The resulting practices of Catholic institutions have been in general at least as objectionable as those of other colleges and universities.

The athletic teams of Catholic colleges compete with other teams upon supposedly equal terms of sportsmanship. Victory is dear to both sides. Where large profits from athletics are available to provide financial assistance to needy athletes, little is lacking except the athletes themselves. As regards the Catholic colleges, alumni and coaches, students, and sometimes parish priests have been given officially to understand that it is their duty to direct to the institutions young men of desirable character and athletic ability. To the loyal alumnus, the devoted priest, the enthusiastic undergraduate, the professional coach, athletic ability readily becomes the most important of these qualifications, and other qualities of character, if outstanding, tend to be taken for granted. Were this not the case, it is inconceivable that the officers of Catholic universities and the parish priests whom they themselves have trained would countenance what in the past has often occurred: the resulting perversion of a worthy and magnanimous principle.

Assistance to needy athletes at Catholic institutions takes several forms. It may be distributed as scholarships from athletic funds, covering wholly or partly tuition, board, and room, in addition to assistance from individual alumni (Fordham); or jobs that provide tuition, board, and room in return for very nominal services (Notre Dame); or an outright allocation of funds without return except in athletic participation (Georgetown). Occasionally, the attempt is made to balance awards to athletes with those to non-athletes (Holy Cross), so that no young man will "feel that his muscles alone are sufficient to get him through." Or priests may effect arrangements among their own parishioners, members of the faculty, or friends of their college by which athletes may be maintained (Boston College). From such practices as these, in the light of intercollegiate competition, an offer to assist young men to secure part-time work at the usual student rate of compensation (Marquette) is poles asunder.

7. Summary

The bearing of subsidizing upon the amateur status comes down at last to a question of motive. No matter what the source of the subsidy, if the reason behind it can be accurately determined, the status of the athlete becomes at once clear. Given a skilled full-back who is receiving from a head football coach $100 a month, if it can be proved that the motive for this provision concerns not at all the ability or prominence of the athlete, then the athlete is not thereby professionalized, whatever be the presumptions to the contrary. But in such a case, the mere assertion of innocence is not to be taken as proof. On the other hand, any favor, however small, that tends to assist an athlete financially, if it is done because he is an athlete, marks the beginning of professionalism. There is no valid reason why even the most worthy athlete should receive any consideration, favor, assistance, or attention that is not available, upon the same terms and with the same readiness, to the general body of undergraduates. Nor is it easy to see how the sincere amateur could expect such special consideration or advantage.

Conclusion

The foregoing exposition attempts to penetrate the deepest shadow that darkens American college and school athletics. Probably portions of the picture are even blacker than they have been painted. Yet in the murk there are many brighter patches. The absence of recruiting and of subsidizing at many institutions, the integrity of the men who have struggled against these evils with varying degrees of success, the unassailable fact that neither subsidizing nor recruiting is essential to college sport, and the improvement that has been manifest in these particulars during the last quarter-century, should hearten anyone who is battling against the corruptions here shown or deplores these perversions of common honesty. This much is certain : The university or college that, under capable leadership, makes up its collective mind to cast out these practices, can do so. What is needed is constancy of purpose and patience in the face of opposition from those whose self-interest, false pride, and mistaken loyalties make their recession difficult.

Experience has shown that, of all who are involved in these evils — administrative officers, teachers, directors of athletics, coaches, alumni, undergraduates, and townsmen — the man who is the most likely to succeed in uprooting the evils of recruiting and subsidizing is the college president. It is his duty to coördinate opinion and direct the progress of an institution. If neighboring presidents are like-minded, his task is a little lightened, but under no circumstances which we have been able to discover is it impossible even if he stands alone. It cannot be easy. But such are the position and the powers of the American college president that, once having informed himself of the facts, and being possessed of the requisite ability and courage, he will succeed.

CHAPTER XI
THE PRESS AND COLLEGE ATHLETICS

MANY college administrators hold that during the past twenty years the relations of the college to the public have been seriously impaired by the way in which American newspapers treat college athletics, but not all of those who hold this opinion have taken the trouble to enquire into the matter from other than their own point of view. The difficulties are not all on the side of the college administrator. Newspaper men themselves have noted that the growth of public interest in athletics is in large part the result of an attempt of the newspaper publisher and editor to satisfy a stimulated appetite of their readers. Professor James Melvin Lee has pointed out [1] that "the newspapers in the United States tend with the passing years to become more and more economic products." By the very nature of the present situation, the publisher or editor must regard college athletics as a single phase of sport, which in turn is only one phase of news, and news shares with editorials and "other interesting reading matter" that portion of the pages which is not offered to advertisers "at so much an inch."

Admitting, then, for the sake of argument, that the view of the college presented in the newspapers is distorted through overstressing of athletics, nevertheless college athletics are news, and news that appeals to many readers as the most consistently

[1] *Encyclopædia Britannica*, Thirteenth Edition, 1926, new Vol. II, page 1054c.

interesting and important aspect of college life. The present chapter points out some of the problems involved in the relationship of the press to college athletics.

I. THE GROWTH OF THE SPORTS PAGE IN AMERICAN NEWSPAPERS

The increased attention given by newspapers in the United States to athletic sports — the extension of the sports page, in a word, has coincided with a proportional growth in the space assigned to other departments of the newspaper. In this connection the contents of six representative newspapers published in various parts of the country were studied over corresponding weeks in the autumn of 1913, 1920, and 1927. This sampling may not adequately represent the 400-odd morning, the 1,200 and more evening, and the 500 Sunday newspapers of the United States, but the changes that it reflects are illuminating.

A. IN CERTAIN NEWSPAPERS OF NEW YORK CITY

The New York newspapers selected for study were the *Sun*, an evening paper, and the *New York Times* and the *World*, published in the morning.

1. The *Sun* (evening)

In six days of the week of November 17, 1913, the *Sun* published, not including for comparisons a Sunday edition which did not appear in 1920 or 1927, a total of ninety pages, of which nine pages, or 10 per cent, were devoted to sports. Those nine pages contained in all 865.5 inches of reading-matter concerning sports, divided as follows: professional, 436.5 inches, school and college, 378.5, other amateur sports, 50.5. Of matter with which we are especially concerned, fifteen and a half inches gave accounts of school and college games, while 119 inches dealt with practices. Only 3.5 inches of sporting news appeared on the *Sun's* first page during these six days, while editorial comment ran to 9.25 inches. No sporting news was signed; there were no columns and no "comics" on the sports pages. Advertisements on the sports pages dealt with clothing, theatres, and, especially, automobiles, with some classified advertising.

For the week of November 15, 1920, the *Sun* published in six days a total of 144 pages, of which twelve, or 8.3 per cent, were assigned to sports. The actual amount of sports reading-matter dropped to 842 inches, of which 306 inches dealt with professional athletics, forty-nine with miscellaneous sports, and 487 with school and college athletics. These 487 inches included 245 inches devoted to games, and 133.5 inches given to practices. The *Sun* had now become an evening newspaper. The increase in the news value of sports for evening papers is indicated by the fact that the *Sun's* first page held seventy-four inches of sports news during this week, of which seventy-three inches appeared on Saturday with a head that streamed across eight columns of one edition. Editorial comment on sport, however, totaled only a single inch. All told, 557 inches of sports reading-matter were signed, and 160.5 inches may be classified as "column." Comic strips ran about twenty-two inches a day, or 133 inches for the week. Racing results began to take on an added importance. Advertisements (492 inches) were of clothing, cars, and amusements, with some classified. The space emphasis has clearly shifted to amateur sports, especially school and college games.

This tendency is continued in the week of November 14, 1927, during which, out of a total of 262 pages, twenty-nine, or 11 per cent, were sporting pages. The total of sports reading-matter increased to no less than 1,956.5 inches, or 232 per cent of what it had been in 1920; professional 643.5 inches, or a little more than double that measured for 1920; school and college 1,217.5 inches, or two and a half times as much; and other amateur sports 95.5 inches, or about twice as much as for 1920. With respect to selected phases of sports news, only nine inches of the week's first pages dealt with sports, and all of this on Saturday, while editorial comment amounted to only four inches. Signed stories had become the rule; they totaled 1,186.5 inches for the week. Columns occupied 309.5 inches. The comic strip had disappeared from the week's sports pages, but advertising, 2,096 inches, had quadrupled since 1920 and now exceeded the reading-matter. Advertisements increased not only in amount but in variety; cars, clothing, travel, sporting goods, and beverages, together with classified.

The *Sun's* changes in emphasis respecting professional athletics and school and college sports from 1913 to 1927 may be gathered from the fact that, for the respective weeks, in 1913 professional sports bore to school and college sports a ratio of four to three; in 1920, a ratio of three to four; and in 1927, a ratio of one to two. In actual space professional sports claimed 436.5 inches in 1913, 306 inches in 1920, and 643.5 in 1927, a gain in fourteen years of about 50 per cent; while school and college sports had 378.5 inches in 1913, 487 inches in 1920, and 1,217.5 inches in 1927, a gain of more than 220 per cent between 1913 and 1927.

2. The *New York Times* (morning, daily, and Sunday)

For six days of the week of November 17, 1913, the *New York Times* published 114 pages, of which eleven, or 9.6 per cent, dealt with sports. On Sunday, Part V of the paper contained thirty pages, of which sixteen formed a Special Football Section and three pages were occupied by the regular sports news. During the entire week sports reading-matter totaled 1,159.5 inches — 418.5 inches of professional, 584 of college and school, and 157 of other amateur sports. All told, the Sunday *Times* ran 254 inches of school and college athletics, of which 128.5 inches dealt with games; only 2.5 inches pertained to games during the other six days of the week. Eight inches of the entire week's first page dealt with sports. There were no signed articles, no columns, and no editorial references. Advertisements offered cars and accessories, clothing, cigarettes, and whiskey, a total of 747 inches for weekdays and 778 inches for the entire week.

Seven years later, the *Times* printed 188 pages for six days of the corresponding week. Of these fifteen, or only about 8 per cent, were sporting pages. On Sunday, November 21, 1920, however, the *Times* devoted five pages to sports. For the seven days, sports reading-matter totaled 1,692.5 inches. Of this total, 477 inches were given to college or school athletics on Sunday — nearly as much as they received for the rest of the week (558 inches) and an increase of about 44 per cent over the same total seven years before. Other amateur athletics in 1920 occupied a total of 277.5 inches, —thirty-three inches only on Sunday, — and professional athletics about 366 inches. The signed article or the column had not yet appeared. A fourteen-inch Sunday editorial dealt with "The New Football." Advertisements to a length of 1,069 inches on weekdays and

1,311 inches including Sunday were used on the sports pages, principally for automobiles, clothes, racing, and cigars. The amount of space devoted to college and school athletics was still increasing.

In 1927, for the week of November 14, out of a six-day total of 292 pages the *Times* carried twenty-two pages, or only 7.5 per cent, of sports. On Sunday, November 20, 1927, it carried ten more sports pages. The six-day total of sports space was 2,110.5 inches — professional 772.5 inches, college and school 1,148 inches, other amateur 190 inches — while with Sunday's edition the total ran to 3,379 inches, of which 2,139 inches, or about 63 per cent, dealt with schools and colleges. For the seven-day week, professional athletics totaled 956 inches, and amateur athletics other than school and college, 284 inches. Games for the week had only 143 inches, but practice and prospects occupied 811.5 inches, or 231.5 for the first six days only. Signatures were attached to 297 inches for the first six days, a total of 539 inches including Sunday. The column appears with 191 inches for seven days, — about twenty-seven inches a day, double measure leaded. Advertisements totaling 1,102.5 inches for six days and 1,372.5 inches for seven have become rather more miscellaneous, but cars, tobacco, and clothing still predominate. Only 4.25 inches of the first news page are used for the Harvard-Yale and New York University-Allegheny games. Sports in this week far outran advertising on the sporting pages, with a strong leaning toward college and school games and practice.

The *Times* as well as the *Sun* has increased its emphasis upon school and college sports. In 1913, the ratio of space given to professional and to school and college athletics was about four to five; in 1920, about three to ten; in 1927, about three to seven. In 1913, the amount of space for professional sports was 418.5 inches; in 1920, 366 inches; and in 1927, 956 inches. School and college sports occupied in 1913, 584 inches; in 1920, 1,035 inches, and in 1927, 2,139 inches. Thus, while between 1913 and 1927 professional sports only a little more than doubled their space, school and college sports almost quadrupled their space.

3. The *World* (morning, daily, and Sunday)

The morning *World* for the six weekdays following November 16, 1913, ran six sporting pages totaling 642 inches out of 102 pages. On Sunday it printed two sporting pages instead of one, a total of eight for seven days. College and school sports claimed 484 inches out of a week's total of 866 inches, or well over half, while professional sports took 260.5 inches. Whereas during six days college and school games were given only twelve inches, as compared with 116.5 inches for practice, they received 108.5 inches on Sunday. The *World* had begun the use of signatures, as 106.5 inches for seven days testify. There were no columns and no editorial references, although the Harvard-Yale game took eighteen inches of the first news page of the Sunday edition. Advertisements totaled 190 inches for six days, or about 224.5 inches for the week's sports pages.

At the end of the following seven years the *World* had increased its weekday pages until they totaled 138, of which twelve, or about eight and a half per cent, were sporting pages. For six days sporting news ran to 747 inches, an increase of 105 inches; with the two Sunday sports pages the total was 1,064 inches, an increase of nearly 200 inches or about 23 per cent. Of these 1,064 inches, school and college athletics had 710.5 inches, professional 307, and other amateur sports 46.5. College and school games ran to 289 inches on Sunday, and only nine inches for the rest of the week. Four days' practice stories received 89.5 inches. The Harvard-Yale football game occupied the first two columns of the first Sunday page. Advertising on the sporting pages had increased greatly, to 722.5 inches for the week, with none on Sunday. Signed articles have for the week 235 inches, with 143 inches for six days. Advertising emphasizes principally clothing.

The week of November 14, 1927, indicates some striking changes in the *World's* sporting pages. In the first place, they had increased in number to three on weekdays and six on Sundays. For the whole week they carried 2,419.5 inches of sports reading-matter, of which 1,439 inches dealt with college and school sport. Of these 1,439 inches, 444 were given to school and college games. The total increase in seven years was about 127 per cent. Signed sport articles now aggregated 335 inches for the week, columns 234.5 inches, and first-page stories nine inches under a double-column head with pictures of the captains of opposing elevens. The lack of editorial reference continued. Sports page advertisements appear to have been crowded into only 301.5 inches for the whole week by the greatly increased reading-matter.[2]

From figures for the three weeks under discussion, it appears that the *World* has maintained between professional athletics and school and college athletics a space ratio of about one to two. The actual amounts of space, however, for professional sports were, for 1913, 260.5 inches; for 1920, 307 inches; and for 1927, 750.5 inches. The space devoted to professional athletics has therefore not quite trebled over the fourteen years. In 1913, school and college sports had 484 inches; in 1920, 710.5 inches; and in 1927, 1,439 inches. Here, too, the space has about trebled.

---

[2] Other data bearing on sports space in New York City morning papers, kindly furnished by Arthur S. Draper, Esq., of the *Herald Tribune*, may be condensed and adapted as follows:

DAILY AVERAGE OF COLUMNS OF SPACE IN FOUR NEW YORK CITY MORNING PAPERS WEEK OF FEBRUARY 4, 1928

	Total News	Sports	Total Reading Matter
American	33.75	16.5	144.5
Herald Tribune	48.5	20.5	157.0
New York Times	64.75	23.5	181.75
World	39.25	17.5	120.0

DAILY AVERAGE COLUMNS OF SPACE IN FOUR NEW YORK CITY NEWSPAPERS DURING AUGUST OF FOUR YEARS

	Total News	Sports	Total Reading Matter
American			
1924	23.0	16.5	105.25
1925	30.75	22.0	122.5
1926	32.25	22.0	135.5
1927	28.5	22.5	129.75
Herald Tribune			
1924	33.5	18.25	114.25
1925	34.0	21.0	121.75
1926	40.25	22.0	142.25
1927	40.75	24.0	147.0
New York Times			
1924	40.75	16.75	113.0
1925	51.5	17.75	133.75
1926	54.5	21.75	148.5
1927	62.0	29.5	172.5
World			
1924	37.5	16.0	93.75
1925	36.75	17.75	112.75
1926	38.0	20.5	123.5
1927	37.5	19.5	112.75

B. In Certain Newspapers in Other Cities

Many of the tendencies reflected in the three New York City newspapers just ex-
amined are visible also in three newspapers from other sections of the country: the
Boston *Transcript*, the Salt Lake City *Deseret News*, and the San Francisco *Chronicle*.
Of these, only the *Chronicle* issues a Sunday edition.

1. The Boston *Transcript* (evening)

During the selected weeks of November, the *Transcript* in 1913 devoted eleven of
its 148 total weekly pages to sport, a total of slightly more than seven per cent; in
1920, seven out of 176 pages, or about four per cent; in 1927, seventeen out of 228
pages, or about 7.5 per cent. The number of inches ran from 989 in 1913, of which 850
dealt with school and college athletics, to 9,405 in 1920, of which 871.5 dealt with
college and school, and to 1,779.5 in 1927, of which about 1,500 inches were devoted to
school and college sports. Signed sporting articles, absent in 1913, ran in 1920 to 302
inches, and in 1927 to 727.5 inches, while a column reached sixty-two inches in 1927.
Professional sport dropped from 81.5 inches in 1913 to thirty-six inches in 1920, but
increased to 244 inches in 1927. Advertisements, with space of 263.5, 121.5, and 596.5
inches for the three respective weeks, show a curiously similar tendency.

2. The *Deseret News* (evening)

Over the three selected weeks, the *Deseret News* increased its sporting pages from one
daily in 1913, one on each of five days and two on Saturday in 1920, to two in 1927.
The total numbers of pages were 108, 134, and 128 respectively. Total sports reading-
matter ran from 640 inches, of which 430 inches dealt with school and college in 1913,
to 877.5 with a slight increase in school and college to 475.5 inches in 1920, and to 1,614
inches in 1927, of which no less than 1,052 inches dealt with school and college athletics.
Professional sport increased from 140 inches in 1913 to 387 inches in 1920 and to 451
inches in 1927. Sports page advertising for the three years respectively totaled 188,
117, and 99.5 inches. In 1913 no sporting stories were signed, but in 1920, 69.5 inches,
and in 1927, 462 inches bore signatures. The only editorial reference to sports appears
on November 19, 1927, "To an Athlete's Memory," in appreciation of the late Chris-
topher Mathewson.

3. The San Francisco *Chronicle* (morning)

In the week of November 17, 1913, the emphasis of the two daily sports pages of
the *Chronicle* fell heavily upon professional sports, with 517 out of 890 inches for six
days and 692.5 inches out of 1,235.5 for seven days. School and college sports occupied
only 197.5 inches on weekdays and 305.5 inches, Sunday included. Seven years later
a distinct change is noted; out of 964 weekday inches, college and school athletics
claim 457.5, and out of 1,383.5 inches for seven days, no less than 827 inches. The figures
for the corresponding week of 1927 are: Total space on an average of four sports pages
for six days, 2,250 inches, of which 1,308 inches are given to school and college athletics
and only 580.5 inches to professional sports; for seven days, 2,800 inches, including
1,801 inches for college and school and 611.5 inches for professional sports. Signed

articles in 1913 occupied 376.5 inches for the whole week, in 1920, 380 inches, and in 1927, 745 inches. Columns had twelve inches in 1913, 46 inches in 1920, and 88 inches in 1927.

Sports page advertising increased from 370.5 inches devoted to theatres, clothing, cigars, and cures in 1913, to 604.5 inches in 1920, with fewer patent medicines offered, and declined to 446 inches in 1927, which, however, appeared to be of a distinctly better grade. In the Sunday edition of November 20, 1927, one page displayed 160 inches of football rotogravures.

C. The Space Emphasis upon College and School Athletics in Newspapers

To the extent that the six newspapers selected for analysis typify tendencies in American newspaper editing and publishing, the following generalizations are justified : First, sports have grown to an unprecedented importance as news. Secondly, amateur sports, especially college and school athletics, have been increasingly emphasized over the past fourteen years. Thirdly, on the whole, this emphasis has proved profitable to newspapers as regards both the influence and the respect in which they are held, and also the advertising carried on the sporting pages. As regards quantity, the growth of space emphasis is apparent. The only test of quality which these figures contain is to be found in the amount of signed sporting material published.

II. The Complaint Against the Present Treatment of School and College Athletics in American Newspapers

The extraordinary growth of the sporting page shown by the preceding figures has led to the charge that newspapers are exploiting college and school athletics for financial gain. Nor is this accusation directed against the daily press alone; it extends to monthly magazines and weekly publications. An attempt will be made to summarize these and other charges : sensationalism, petty graft, and the exploitation of school and college athletes.

A. The Sensational in Sports Writing

If it is the function of the newspaper to report the affairs of life according to recognized standards of sound journalistic taste and of that very intangible but much blamed criterion, "human interest," then some sort of sporting page is justified, whether the intelligent reader likes it or not. He who dislikes the sports columns of a newspaper need not purchase it. This, however, is not what we mean when we speak of sensationalism. In sports writing, as in other phases of newspaper work, sensationalism almost always originates in a deliberate policy of magnifying the supposed interest or emotional connotations of facts beyond the proportions that their intrinsic values justify. The less intelligent reader is the more likely to be attracted by the sensational in sports writing and much of the material on certain sporting pages represents an attempt to provide such persons with the kind of reading-matter which, because of years of carefully incited indulgence, they increasingly crave.

1. Sensationalism in Usage

Different though the standards of English usage on the sports page must be from those of the study or of scholarship, examination of the work of the better sports writers reveals an astonishingly accurate, serviceable, and cultivated style. Such men stand at the head of their profession. When, however, the inspection of sporting pages is extended beyond the metropolitan dailies, it reveals an ignorance of the canons of respectability in writing. Apparently, in many instances deliberate attempts are made to pervert the technical language of sports reporting to a sensationalism that violates not alone taste but fact.

It has long been customary in certain newspaper offices to write accounts of professional baseball games in a kind of jargon that contains an element of humor. From this cant use of language there grew the notion that the technical vocabulary of any game or contest was not properly used unless it was accompanied by exaggerations of phrase. The result has been not alone a certain humorous picturesqueness, but also a great preponderance of the sensational in the reports of most sporting events. Another phase of the development accompanied the transfer of terms from the prize ring to other sports. For example, it is still the mode in some newspaper offices, in writing a baseball story, to employ such phrases as "So-and-So clouted the ball on the nose." A football player suffering from concussion is referred to as having "taken the count." A third stage of the linguistic process is represented by the introduction of terms from war and the battlefield. Accounts of college football contests have suffered most from this use of metaphors. The corruption of the vocabulary of many sports reporters and in some instances their apparent inability to report a contest in workmanlike, technical English is one of the most astonishing results of sensational journalism, even though it be one of the least important. Alumni publications naturally exhibit on the whole far better discrimination in such matters than the daily press; they are written for a public of greater intelligence and their writers are relatively free from the pressure of time.

2. Fact and Fancy

It must be reluctantly noted that evidence occasionally points to a deliberate policy of sensationalism in athletic news or comment. It was a newspaper man who stated that always to agree with the decisions of football officials does not make for news. In the past two seasons more than one metropolitan daily has printed articles signed by members of their staff that imputed incompetency and even implied calculated prejudice among officials at football matches.

The serious charge has been made that newspapers publish false information concerning college athletics, especially preparation for contests. This has sometimes occurred, but the fault has been less the reporter's or the correspondent's than that of partisans, including alumni, coaches, players, and university publicity agents who have given out misleading information in order that it might deceive newspaper readers and especially future opponents concerning the strength of teams or crews. Before a college contest of moment, the athletic or physical condition of many athletes interests the public. The advance stories concerning Oxford and Cambridge crews testify to the fact that this interest is not an exclusively American phenomenon. On the other hand, a deliberate magnifying of rumor and reports concerning any isolated group of young men may, through an unhealthy and partisan insistence upon victory, take on a wholly unreasonable importance. It is sufficiently unfortunate that newspapers should reflect this distortion. When the chicanery of laymen forces it beyond the bounds of truth, the result is intolerable. Happily, once deceived thus, a sports editor is unlikely to be caught a second time.

With the best of intentions an inexpert correspondent, especially if he is an undergraduate immaturely loyal to his college, may send to his newspaper material founded in rumor which might far better be omitted from any sports page. Resort to such clichés as "it is said," "it is understood," and others of a similarly cautious nature is learned early by the budding journalist. These phrases may be all very well, provided they represent actual current opinion. Perverted from their legitimate uses they readily become mechanical devices that encourage space filling "at so much an inch." A man, be he novice or thoroughly seasoned reporter, who is pressed by editorial order or by his own hope of financial gain, to turn out a story, quickly perceives the uses to which such padding may be put.

The chief temptations to the adulteration of fact in sporting news are the "assignment," whether imposed by superior order or by the need of maintaining an average of pay; the "advance story," which is rapidly dropping into disfavor with the best sports media unless it is written by experts; and the necessity of employing less skilful personnel than the responsibility of any newspaper warrants. Even "experting" has been made to appear a somewhat ridiculous business.

3. The Exploitation of Persons and Personalities

Protests against the exploitation of school and college athletes are not new. Thirty years ago Professor Henry D. Sheldon read a "three-page newspaper account of a great football game in the West," consisting of a technical and a general story, "biographies of all the players, the opinions of the captains, coaches, and the presidents of the two universities. In a personal note, the emotions of the gray-haired father of one of the players are described in detail." The whole ran to "twenty columns of printed matter and seven columns of illustrations, including cartoons." Professor Sheldon comments: "Such a cheap notoriety tends to place the football player on a level with the prize-fighting and bicycle-riding profession." [3] It is entirely natural that a generation of such sensationalism should obscure the distinction between amateur and professional athletes. Nowadays, athletes are exploited in news stories, columns of comment, and illustrations, and even in advertisements.

a. *In News Stories*

The exploitation of the college athlete in news stories is so common that examples would be supererogatory. The matter has been given an even more sinister turn by the exploitation of football and other coaches. As Mr. E. K. Hall has pointed out, nowadays undergraduates appear to have no teams; all teams are commonly referred to by the names of their coaches. It is noteworthy, however, that many of the more seasoned writers on college athletics are departing from this practice; younger men might well follow their example.

b. *In "Columns"*

To any column of sporting comment personalities are as the breath of life. The best of the sports columnists write usually in good journalistic taste. Their interest in college athletics, in most instances acquired or strengthened by their own participation during undergraduate days, has kept them young, while the passing years have brought them a mature judgment and in many cases, whether or not they are college men, a lively appreciation of the problem of sport in relation to education. The best of these men write, as the saying is, with no axes to grind. Their versatility and the quality of their work, produced without intermission for every day of the year, commands the respect of numberless sportsmen. They constitute a decidedly wholesome force in college athletics in so far as they endeavor to maintain standards of honest and clean sportsmanship, whether amateur or professional. Their defects arise from the necessity of doing a daily stint, lack of time for reflection, and, occasionally, the necessity of conforming to a policy of publication with which they themselves lack sympathy.

One of their outstanding weaknesses is their propensity to name all-American football teams. If the late Caspar Whitney could have foreseen the abuses to which his device for honoring the most expert among American college football players has led, he would certainly not have inaugurated it. The absurd growth in the number of all-American teams has been prompted partly by the notion that if one sports writer was qualified to select such a group, other sports writers were equally capable. To this rivalry has been added the sentimental feeling that a selection of an all-American team by one man omits the names of many deserving players and thus works an "injustice" to them. Finally, the conception of news as an aggregation of names doubtless has played its part in the rapid growth, not only of a number of all-American teams but of all-sectional and all-state selections. The result is a collection of publicity that dilutes an intended honor to the level of the ridiculous, and, the country over, includes an astonishing number of mediocre players.

[3] Henry D. Sheldon, *Student Life and Customs*, 1901, page 236.

Among sports writers a feeling is growing that all-American teams are better left unnamed. One columnist whose work is widely read received from a managing editor instructions to nominate such a team. Although he was reluctant to comply, his protests availed nothing; the newspaper had always named an all-American team and therefore an all-American team must be selected. This writer finally solved his problem by selecting a burlesque eleven, which assuredly entertained many more readers and provided far more diversion than a serious selection could have produced.[4] One reason for the vogue of all-American teams is, of course, the profit that accrues to the newspaper owner who through this device exploits the name of his sports writer. Among the qualifications for membership in any such team sportsmanship and cleanness of play rarely receive the high rating that they should have.

c. *In Illustrations*

The growth and the changes of fashion in newspaper illustration during the past quarter-century would provide an interesting subject for study. As regards college athletics alone there is no reason to suppose that the increased use of half-tones, line drawings, and cartoons on sporting pages is other than what is to be expected in consideration of the changes that have been wrought in sports stories. Photographs of coaches, however, have much increased in numbers and frequency. Even superficial enquiry has shown that the number of pictures of single individuals has grown materially, while the use of group pictures or large cuts of games has not perceptibly diminished. The quest of the sensational leads to the publication in Sunday supplements of half-tones or rotogravure pictures of football captains and players who may be entirely respectable young men, but who in these sheets resemble cannibals or criminals. Finally, the captions placed on sporting illustrations of all kinds are open to adverse criticism from the point of view of both taste and accuracy.

d. *In Advertisements*

The advertiser has been among the most persistent exploiters of college athletes. He has discovered that the bestowal of a sweater, a typewriter, or some other article readily procures from many a college athlete a testimonial (written by the advertiser or his agent) which may contain statements or implications deliberately perverting fact. In the course of the enquiry a case was studied in which as part of an advertising campaign an already unduly exploited athlete was requested in exchange for a sweater to sign a statement that he had used this particular brand for years. As a matter of fact, the young man had never possessed a sweater of this make. In spite of repeated good counsel from the athletic authorities of his college, the young man signed the

---

[4] To an Englishman the all-American team is incomprehensible. The man who plays for Scotland or for England is a member of an all-Scottish or all-English eleven or fifteen which actually plays together. Hence, the Englishman is accustomed to seeing his all-national teams in action. He is not slow to ridicule the all-American team which, selected by a sports writer, is never assembled for a game, although at times it has been assembled for purposes of entertainment, and to point out that the team as an expert unit is never tested by the exigencies of a single contest.

statement and accepted the sweater, and in due course his name and likeness were published far and wide in recommendation of an article of which from long inexperience he knew nothing whatever. This is not an isolated instance. Testimonials from college athletes have been repeatedly purchased by payments in kind, if not in cash — by gifts to fraternities of which they were members, and by the bestowal of such valuable considerations as automobiles, clothes, typewriters, and haberdashery. It is a matter of record that at least one professional heavyweight champion has shown a much keener sense of the proprieties.

Fifteen years ago most sporting pages contained a liberal sprinkling of advertisements of patent medicines, liquors, and tobacco. Newspaper publishers have themselves barred columns of advertising that extol "cures" and quack medicines. In accordance with postal regulations and numerous laws they have dropped advertisements of whiskey. But so desirable is the space on certain sports pages that in 1928 advertisers of cigarettes offered for it premiums over the regular "position charges." There is no valid reason to exclude tobacco advertising from the sporting page through the censorship that every newspaper publisher reserves the right to exercise, but there is very good reason to refuse advertisements that violate good taste, misrepresent fact, and exploit college athletes and college sport.

4. The Effect of Sensationalism upon the College Athlete

The effect of newspaper notoriety upon secondary school athletes was well set forth by a writer in the *Harvard Graduate Magazine*, 1895 (Volume III, page 318): "A schoolboy finds his photograph and a sketch of his life put before the public, and he is described as a future star. The consequence is that the first few weeks, which ought to be spent developing him into a player, are spent in reducing, what is the natural result of his publicity, a 'swelled head.'" In 1901, Professor Sheldon concluded that "the results of the notoriety and fever of expectation are seen in (1) the recruiting of men, (2) the extravagant outlays of money, (3) the overtraining of teams, and (4) the fierceness and intensity of the contests." At the annual meeting of the National Collegiate Athletic Association, 1925, Professor J. F. A. Pyre, of the University of Wisconsin, noted that the publicity accorded college athletes in newspapers results in (1) the excessive pursuit of high school and migrant athletes by colleges and the offering of inducements, and (2) the development of a "pre-professional" type of college athlete. These are only a few of the critics who have pointed out the harm that sensationalism in newspapers has wrought, not only to college athletics but to the individual participant.

An indeterminate number of athletes deliberately set about capitalizing newspaper reports and stories of prowess. The usual means is the clipping or scrapbook, in which is pasted every available printed reference. Doubtless many such collections start as college memorabilia, but many more appear soon to reach the position of a stock in trade, to be treasured and used as a means of commercializing athletic ability. A football captain at a Mid-Western university, on the other hand, being determined to avoid some of the ill effects of publicity, scrupulously refrained from reading any newspaper stories in which his name appeared during the season.

B. The Accusation of "Graft"

The committee of the American Society of Newspaper Editors, reporting in 1927, whose function was to investigate "every improper attempt to influence sports publicity," reached three important conclusions. First, most of the things that it "had heard and suspected were true." Its chairman, the late Will Owen Jones, of the *Nebraska State Journal*, stated that the committee "could make a sickening list of bribery, improper influence, stupid betrayal of the public, venial participation in profits, and overplaying of mediocre events." But, second, the committee's task had hardly begun before the discovery was made that "cleansing processes of great potency are already at work." Third, these processes apparently are induced in part by the influx of high school and college graduates into the sporting departments of newspapers, and "such abuses as still persist will soon be reduced to a minimum by good sense, plain honesty, and competent management."

Although in Texas the number of free passes to college contests distributed to newspapers seems excessive, nevertheless, whatever temptations may assail the underpaid sports writer, college athletics the country over have not descended to the level of professional sports-promotion in offering of gifts, tickets, and even cash to sporting writers. The charge that college coaches, especially at football, always pay in some form or other for the publicity lavished upon them has not been substantiated in a single instance. Study of one case in which a man stated that he had seen money passed from a coach to a newspaper correspondent yielded no corroborative results beyond a more circumstantial reiteration of the allegations.

The motive that leads to the excessive distribution of passes to college games is plainly fear lest more open-handed rivals may receive more favorable press notices. The motive in accepting tickets that can be sold is more complex, but probably in many cases includes the inclination "to make a little on the side." Both motives are unworthy. Members of sporting departments of metropolitan newspapers are, as a rule, far less prone to accept perquisites from college athletics than reporters employed by smaller papers. Moreover, whether perquisites are involved or not, one veteran newspaper man has stated that "a small college town paper would not be able to exist if it gave impartial accounts of home-team games." The distribution of free passes to college games and the giving of perquisites have much decreased in recent years.

C. Summary

An analysis of the charges of sensationalism and of bribery that have been made against the sporting departments of newspapers suggests two inferences: First, that the ethics of the rapidly developed sports department have rarely been formulated with the same precision as has obtained in the case of the long-established editorial, news, advertising, and circulation departments; and, secondly, that in formulating accepted policies of treatment and display, too little attention has been paid to the essential distinctions between college and amateur athletics on the one hand and professional, openly commercial, sports on the other.

D. Other Periodical Publications

The recent revival of interest in college athletics on the part of magazine editors has been in the main wholesome. In so far as writers have been actuated by worthy motives, have eschewed mere rumor and scandal not substantiated by facts, and have guided their readers to sound views and a realization of the value of honesty in college sport, they have served well both their publishers and the colleges. On the other hand, one editor rejected a manuscript because it was not sufficiently scandalous, and another, in an athletic controversy between two great universities, solicited contributions that should have "punch" in them — in other words, that should be abusive or rankly partisan or accusatory. Such policies as these acts reflect debase both American sport and American education.

III. A Few of the Conditions Contributing to these Complaints

Such are some of the complaints against the way American college and school athletics are currently dealt with in newspapers and periodicals. We turn now to a few of the conditions in the newspaper office, on the campus, and in the community that explain much of the criticism that has come to be directed against the present mode of treating college athletics in American newspapers.

A. The Exigencies of Newspaper Work

The lay critic of the sporting page of an American newspaper is seldom aware of the number of persons involved in the publication of a single story dealing with college athletics.

Much of the local athletic news is gathered by a reporter or correspondent, who writes or telegraphs the story himself or telephones it to the editorial rooms of his paper to be put into form by a "re-write" man. For morning papers or late evening editions, accounts of important matches may consist of two or even three divisions: a general story, a story detailing the match play by play, and the "crowd story." Accounts received by telegraph are treated somewhat differently. In case one set of facts is to serve a number of metropolitan newspapers, the material is collected and bulletined to different offices by a news association, to be later revised in accordance with the needs and policies of particular papers. The copy-desk men and editors review the drafts of articles prepared as indicated, and on the larger papers they or others especially assigned to the task provide the headlines. First a sports editor and then perhaps other editors see the copy for the sporting page, revise it as seems best, and assign it provisionally to a position in the edition. The managing editor also sees it, if the story is to start on the first page. The story is then set in type. Proofs are pulled, to be scanned and corrected by proof-readers. After the necessary changes have been made in the proofs, the types are put into forms for pages by a "make-up" man. The forms are locked, matrices, or molds of paper pulp or other material, are fashioned for each form, cylinders of type metal are cast to fit the rolls of the press, and the paper is printed. Material distributed by national news-gathering agencies is received by telegraph or on thin sheets of duplicating paper and is passed, cut, or rejected, as occasion warrants. Meanwhile, illustrations for the story or the sports page have been secured from special or staff photographers or from distributors, captioned, and edited. The advertisements have been contracted for and prepared, and the distribution and sale of the papers has been arranged on the basis of orders received.

Of the men engaged in getting out a newspaper varying in number on different papers from as few as three [5] to as many as a hundred, only a few are known to readers by name. This is especially true of the sports department. Thirty years ago the number of signed sporting articles or columns was small. The practice had become common in French journalism and in our own Far West before it was adopted to any great extent by Eastern and Mid-Western papers. Nowadays, the country over, not only are columns of sporting comment, whether specially prepared or acquired through syndicates, signed with the names of their authors, but in not a few newspapers a great number of sporting stories, accounts of preparation for matches, and special articles on all phases of sports gain an added authority from the names attached to them. Apparently, a signature is accepted by the run of newspaper readers as a guarantee that the story to which it is attached is of a certain type and character; doubtless in many instances the signature actually does operate to increase the accuracy and trustworthiness of the individual writers. The value of the author's name is not less in sports writing than it is in other fields of journalism.

Many signatures are *bona fide*. But the names of certain widely known baseball players, boxers, golfers, and other athletes are signed to newspaper or magazine articles to which they have perhaps at the most contributed a few very scanty notions which have been put into intelligible language by "ghost writers." The practice is now so common that few except the most trusting of newspaper readers are hoaxed by the amiable and profitable deception.

---

[5] A small daily may charge an already burdened reporter or editor with the preparation, editing, and proof-reading of sports material, but at least two employees in the mechanical processes are necessary to place the sports page on the street.

These notes upon the preparation of a sporting page or of a single article appearing on it perhaps suffice to indicate the large number of persons involved in the process, its complexity, and the chances for error which it affords. They make no mention of three other factors which are of the utmost importance: first, the extreme rapidity with which much of our sporting news must be collected, written, edited, and printed; second, the difficulty of maintaining a personnel of sufficient expertness at the salaries that can be paid; and third, certain technical considerations. The adverse critics of the modern sporting page are too often unfamiliar with problems which, upon acquaintance, lead the layman to wonder at the accuracy, comprehensiveness, and interest that contemporary journalism attains.

1. The Element of Time

In newspaper work, as in college administration, it is extremely difficult to find the time for adequate reflection. The collection of athletic news, its writing, editing, and other preparation for printing are processes performed at a speed that makes errors, including misquotations, unavoidable. Moreover, a newspaper is an affair of each day and every day; twenty-four hours at the most after its appearance it is antiquated. The ephemeral character of newspaper writing is at once a safeguard against lasting harm to college athletics from a single article, and a hindrance to effectual improvement through insistence upon sound principles. Only by repeatedly emphasizing those aspects of college athletics which the policy of the newspaper is intended to perpetuate can any writer hope to impress his views upon his readers. The assertion so frequently made that a newspaper reporter exercises no discrimination in preparing his material is false. Because of the nature of his calling and the very process of writing, every newspaper man is a censor, whose work, good or bad, is highly selective. The difficulty is that his mistakes, most of which are due to haste, are made, so to speak, in public, and that correction of an error of fact or of interpretation necessarily draws attention anew to the error. No one relishes reminding himself of his own mistakes.

2. The Element of Personnel

The problem of securing an adequate personnel for a sporting department is no less serious than it is in other aspects of newspaper work. A comparatively large number of young reporters have the ambition to become sports writers, probably less from motives of financial return than because of the intrinsic interest of the calling.

In a number of cases situations similar to the following have arisen: On a Saturday in the height of the football season a sporting editor finds his staff of writers taxed to the utmost to cover even a few of the important contests. He must have more men for the day. It is impracticable to engage temporarily any new writers. He therefore enlists the services of young street men or others who may have had experience only in the covering of an entirely different type of news. To such relatively inexpert men are assigned some of the less important school and college games. These they report with a fair degree of satisfaction to their chiefs. The experience has given them a taste of a fascinating branch of newspaper work and renewed their ambition to proceed in it, but it has furnished them with very few of the technical qualifications that are needed in covering school and college sport. Again, the sports editor presses into emergency service writers who, although they can turn out satisfactory copy concerning a prize fight, a professional baseball game, or a wrestling match, have no notion of the significance of a college or school football game. From the point of view of the college, the use of either of these types of man may prove disastrous. It has been suggested that, as a general rule, only college graduates should be engaged to write of college athletics. This brings up such questions as these: How, in our present economic situation, could the smaller newspaper offer a career that would satisfy the ambitious alumnus? How reduce the dangers of rabid partisanship, so often displayed by younger alumni? Even if the course were practicable, it is no guarantee of the quality of the result. Among the most influential and wholesome sports writers stand men who have never attended college or university. They have achieved their standing because they combine a quick perception and an ability to seize upon the essential quality of a situation. These are attributes of any good newspaper man.

Nor is it wholly clear that increases in salary will purchase an adequate staff for the treatment of college athletics. On the large majority of newspapers in the United States sporting writers seem to be paid on a scale about equal to that in force for other departments. On the whole, competition between newspapers being what it is to-day, a man is very likely to be paid what he is worth. The rewards in salary, power, and influence to which the more industrious and talented writers attain are commensurate with their value to their newspapers.

Probably in no other calling is experience so essential. The most respected of the sports writers are men who know news writing and usually editing from many points of view; they have specialized only after they have learned the technique of other branches of the work, often having begun as general utility men on smaller papers and risen through their own talents and exertions. Only the very exceptional young man becomes a successful or even a readable sports writer without serving a tedious but highly useful apprenticeship in other branches of newspaper work. The requirements of sports writing are succinctly expressed by one editor as follows: "Our sports writers . . . are expected to write plain English and stick to the facts. Newspaper writing requires practical experience."

3. Technical Considerations

The problems of haste and of personnel are common to many forms of business enterprise. In newspaper work certain technical considerations also operate, of which only one can be stated in this place. Exigencies of space may compel the make-up man or the copy desk to delete from an account of a contest the paragraphs in which the reporter has endeavored to make clear the sportsmanlike qualities of players. When such paragraphs are discarded by the man who arranges the typographical contents of a page of a newspaper according to the space at his disposal, the deletion, always performed at top speed, against time, is a purely mechanical matter. When, however, the deletion is the result of editing by the copy desk, it may reflect a deliberately adopted editorial or financial policy.

B. The Contact of the College with the Press

Thirty years ago, and perhaps even more recently, at most of the smaller institutions and, indeed, at many universities, the reporting of college events for newspapers and news agencies was in the hands of undergraduates who were working their way wholly or partially. Exceptions to this rule were those athletic contests which were considered to be of sufficient importance to be written by professional newspaper men. This situation proved to be undesirable to both the college and the press, largely because of the lack of a feeling of responsibility on the part of the student reporters. Attempts to guide them failed in the face of payment "at so much an inch." The system, if such it may be called, is still in use at some universities and colleges, but at probably a large majority of institutions it has been either superseded or greatly modified by the college publicity agent or bureau, whose duty it is to gather items of news, to distribute "tips," and to prepare typewritten or mimeographed "releases." The function of the publicity agent is to "keep the college in the news."

Sometimes he is a duly appointed officer of the institution, who adds publicity to other duties. More frequently, in the Middle West, he is an employee of the athletic department. In cases in which his salary is paid from the athletic budget, his releases are usually of athletic news. Such a man often receives a high salary because of the naïve appetite of many an institution and its partisans, including especially some of its alumni, for publicity at any price.

This semi-official currying of journalistic favor by men whose salaries are paid out of athletic funds is yet to be justified either in theory or in practice. Few universities are so poverty-stricken in scholarship or in good works as to need a "press agent"— a paid employee operating on a strictly commercial basis, whose success is measured by the inches of reading-matter that he succeeds in placing in newspapers. On the other hand, the advantages of a central, responsible, and official source for university information or the verification of news items are obvious to both newspaper men and the college family. A well-operated athletic association or department should have little need of gratuitous advertising, except as a means of promoting the sales of tickets through which a stadium may be financed. The danger in respect of a college publicity officer is lest he forget that he is not a press agent but an educational official.

C. Community, College, and Press

On the whole, however, it is not so much the college as the community in which it is situated that to-day influences a newspaper's policy in the treatment of college athletics, for the community provides the circulation for the newspaper, and circulation is the standard by which the success or failure of a sports-page policy is measured. In the community must be reckoned those alumni whose blind partisanship leads them to protest against friendly references to the teams or the sportsmanship of other universities. The college graduate who becomes a sports editor or the owner of a newspaper affords to such alumni a clear target if his sports page offends them by omitting the complimentary references to the teams of Alma Mater which they expect. The day of writing to the editor and canceling subscriptions over these fancied slights is not yet past. Sometimes it is to such men as much as to local pride, and the subservience of the local newspapers to both of these forces, that the commercial setting of post-season contests is ascribable.

D. The Sources of these Conditions

To the desire of the colleges and their partisans for the good-will of the public is due much of the publicity hunting that now obtains in athletics. The natural wish of the alumnus for news of his college is one thing. The notion that a university's teams or crews must be referred to only in the most laudatory terms is quite another. In many instances the state of mind commonly referred to as an inferiority complex is the root of the desire for athletic notoriety, whether in the individual or in the group.

As for the newspapers themselves, this should be said: Although it is entirely natural that the alumnus who becomes the owner or editor of a newspaper should be led by affection for his college never to resist an opportunity to bring that college into favorable notice, as regards athletics or otherwise, nevertheless the editors or owners who push this tendency to the limits of good taste are after all very few. It may be a confession of sin, but it is also a symptom of regeneration, that the following observation should have been made by a publisher before a gathering of newspaper editors: "It strikes me, gentlemen, the time has come for the American newspaper to establish its own integrity and with courage support the things that are to be supported without regard to the box-office receipts. Too many of our policies are established in the business office."

IV. Recent Improvements in the Newspaper's Handling of College Athletics

It is certain that without the help of the American newspaper, little if any improvement is possible in college athletics. It is equally certain that this help will be lacking without the deliberate adoption for the American sporting page of a policy intelligently calculated to assist, without priggishness or display, in changing our college athletics for the better. Fortunately, a number of sporting writers have long pointed the way, and certain individual newspapers have already begun the process.

The ideal of newspaper reports of college games preserves the point of view of the college, recognizes sportsmanship, clean play, and expertness, indulges in no grotesqueries of language, bears a head in consonance with the story, and is placed in the edition in strict accordance with its importance in the news of the day. The same is true of all college athletic news. The great news-gathering agencies, like the Associated Press and the United Press, generally produce for distant newspapers accounts of games that are open to little adverse criticism. Whether these accounts appear with appropriate heads depends upon the policy of individual newspapers and the competence of editors, head-writers, and copy-desk men. For purposes of reporting, editing, and display, certain newspapers have regard to, first, a distinction between amateur and professional athletics, and, secondly, the question who profits, if at all, by admissions to contests. When an editor or a writer insists too ostentatiously that through his accounts of games he is providing his readers with a vicarious participation in sports and is thus performing a public service second only to affording active physical participation, he is laying himself open to the suspicion of distorting results to justify a commercialized sports policy. Factors in the shaping of a valid policy for the handling of college athletic news include the size of the newspaper, the size and character of the community that it serves, the rate of pay of its sports writers as compared with that of other employees, and, finally, the immediate return which the newspaper yields to its owner.

Doubtless many American newspapers have adopted for the guidance of their sports writers and editors a definite policy. The Chicago *Tribune* is said at one time to have made an effort to reduce its reports of certain professional games to "a bare news basis." The efforts of two other newspapers, which doubtless are representative of many more, will be considered in more detail.

A. THE DES MOINES *Register*

The Des Moines *Register* distinguishes, in the first place, between amateur and semi-professional sports on the one hand, and professional sports on the other. Special letters of instruction are issued to correspondents, and from some of these the following paragraphs, addressed especially to college correspondents, are taken:

> We want every correspondent to understand that we do not expect him to give away secrets or betray his team or coach. However, neither do we want false stories nor reports. We do not want a story that Jim Blood will not be able to play next Saturday because of an injured ankle when the correspondent, the coach and the entire campus know he will play. Nor do we want a story that the attack is being rebuilt around Blood, when everyone on the

campus knows he has a broken collar-bone and will not play. We are not concerned in winning or losing games for any team through the news columns. What we want is the news, while it is fresh and is still news. Remember The Register and Tribune-News, and not your college or coach pay your monthly correspondence checks.

Help us make our sports pages during the week something more than mere propaganda sheets for the college.

Concerning one special feature of the sports page of the *Register*, the following letter was dispatched over the signature of the sporting editor:

We believe a daily feature in our papers dealing with outstanding examples of good sportsmanship will make good reading. It is impossible to interview everyone personally so we are appealing to you to send us an account of the greatest piece of good sportsmanship you have ever witnessed.

Occasional stories about a college "team, its prospects, schedules, players, coaches, etc.," are used, but they must be short.

B. The New York *Herald Tribune*

In the autumn of 1927, the sports editor of the New York *Herald Tribune* sent out the following notice:

To Herald Tribune Correspondents:

In reports of football games and practice for the *Herald Tribune* emphasize as much as possible the names of the players, rather than the coach.
The tendency to play up the coach has grown to a point where the college, the captain and the players are in many instances submerged in the news reports, while the work of the coach has dominated the stories.
It is not our intention to overlook the coach or his methods. It is simply to make the coach secondary to the college and the football players.
The captain, the 'Varsity players, substitutes and scrubs should be the main subjects in the reports of the development of the eleven. The part played by the coach must not be disregarded, but it should not be the subject of the lead of the story.

These instructions form a part of a carefully considered policy concerning the handling of sporting news, including the emphasis to be placed, through character of news, way of writing, position, and display, upon amateur, including school and college, sports and professional games and contests.

C. The Effect of a Considered Sporting-Page Policy

The best test of the success or failure of an editorial policy is to be found in circulation. The net paid circulation, however, is not conclusive evidence, because other factors than editorial policy enter into it and in part modify the results. On the other hand, an unsuccessful sport policy is reflected in circulation figures, to an extent which it is impossible to gauge with accuracy. Figures, partly from the Audit Bureau of Circulation, published in *Standard Rate and Data Service* for June, 1927 and 1928, show the following facts: As of March 31, 1927, the average net paid circulation of the Des Moines *Register* for which the figures were computed was, daily, 106,392;[7] Sunday,[6] 161,871.[7] Similar figures for the *Herald Tribune* as of March 31, 1927, were, daily, 289,674; Sunday, 366,220. In June, 1928, as of March 31, 1928, the same sources assigned to the Des Moines *Register* average net paid circulation daily of 109,499, Sunday of 169,248,[6] and to the *Herald Tribune* daily, 302,365, Sunday, 398,766.[6] The increases tend to show that an enlightened sports policy has not been fatal to circulation. It is probable that the same inference could be drawn concerning other newspapers which have adopted similarly commendable policies.

V. The Interest of the Newspaper Publisher in the Sporting Page

To those concerned with the publishing of a newspaper, athletic games and contests are important in at least three aspects, all closely interrelated: the general reputation and influence of the newspaper among its readers, its circulation, and its advertising. None of the very special and technical problems raised by these matters can be more than suggested here.

A. Sports and the Newspaper's Reputation

The highly intangible force known as good-will, which in newspaper publishing depends upon the attitude of the newspaper reading public toward a particular journal, stands among the most valuable assets of all newspapers. An indefinite but none the less certainly recognizable portion of the reputation of any newspaper among a portion of its readers depends upon the length, detail, accuracy, and tone of its sporting news. In identifiable cases, a newspaper's reputation and, as a result, its influence have been enhanced by an improvement of its sporting pages. On the other hand, when sports pages are neglected or are permitted to decline, the effect upon the good-will of the public toward the newspaper is as quickly reflected. The aphorism that "a newspaper is no better than its sporting page," although it indicates the close relation that exists between a single department and the whole newspaper, is, of course, an exaggeration. With equal truth it might be said that a newspaper is no better than its editorial page, or its financial page, or its first page, or its advertising. The general policy of a newspaper, however, is reflected at least as sharply in the sports pages as in any others, and

---

[6] Not an A. B. C. Figure.

[7] The Des Moines *Register* figures for 1927 run from February 14 to March 31. The increases between figures for 1926 and 1928 for this newspaper were even more marked.

it is also true that the good-will of a considerable proportion of the readers of a metropolitan daily depends upon the repute of its sporting pages.

B. SPORTS AND NEWSPAPER ADVERTISING

A generalization often heard is that "the American newspaper field is divided into New York City and the rest of the country." Its basis may be seen by a comparison of the advertising rates and practices of some thirty-five newspapers, of which twelve are published in New York City and the rest in other parts of the United States.

The twelve New York City newspapers have a combined net paid daily circulation of 4,485,000 copies,[8] six having a Sunday circulation of 4,253,000, in a population area of 5,970,000 (estimated) and a trade area of 9,500,000. All of these twelve papers maintain a "position charge" for certain advertising; that is, for specified preferred portions of the paper, like designated pages, the columns next to reading-matter, or the tops of columns, a premium must be paid over and above the rate for general advertising or special classes. Moreover, four, with a daily circulation of 1,596,000 copies specify a premium for advertising on their sporting pages, while four others, selling 1,252,000 copies daily, include the sporting pages in the class of "other designated pages," for which a premium is charged. Sunday newspapers that make an extra charge for advertising on the sporting pages number three, with a circulation of 1,573,000. The New York *Evening Post* announces "specified position not sold on . . . sports . . . page," and the New York *Graphic* makes a position charge for pages two or three, neither of which is a sports page. It should be noted that in a number of cases the society pages, financial sections, and the columns opposite editorial pages are also rated as preferred positions. In three instances the premium charged for position on the sporting pages are the highest of all position charges imposed by the respective newspapers.

In a word, publishers of New York newspapers have been fully alert to the interest of their public in athletics.

Outside of New York City, apparently, conditions are different. Three influential New England papers, with a combined daily circulation of 326,000 copies in different cities, charge a premium for "selected pages." One Boston paper makes "no charge for position. A desired position will be given when possible." Certain newspapers in California and Missouri, however, with a combined daily circulation of 330,000 copies, maintain a position charge. None of these twenty-three newspapers published outside of New York City specifies a position charge for the sporting page by name. Their combined daily circulation is 4,506,000 copies, or only slightly more than all of the twelve dailies studied for New York City taken together. It therefore appears that the sports page is not capitalized outside of New York City to anything like the extent to which it is capitalized in Manhattan.

C. CIRCULATION AND SPORTS

The regard in which a newspaper is held by the general public is reflected in its

[8] The statistical material concerning newspaper advertising is drawn from *Standard Rate and Data Service*, June, 1928, which for each daily newspaper gives circulation figures vouched for in many instances by the Audit Bureau of Circulation or by the United States Government. In the present discussion, circulation figures are given in round numbers.

circulation. The relation between circulation and sports is indicated by two statements by the late Will Owen Jones, of the *Nebraska State Journal*, chairman of the Committee on Sports Publicity, before the annual meeting of the American Society of Newspaper Editors in 1927. After noting that about one-half of the one hundred and twenty-five newspapers studied by the Committee devoted more than fifteen per cent of their "reader allowance of space" to sport, the total average being a little more than ten columns of sport a day and from two to three times as much on Sundays, Mr. Jones stated that seven give more than twenty per cent and five more than twenty-five per cent, while "some have 'no limit' on the space devoted to sports." "The circulation department," said Mr. Jones, "demands more and more sport; city editors and managing editors, overburdened with their regular duties and uncertain as to how this young giant is to be handled, permit it to do things that could not be tolerated on any of the other pages."

It seems clear that a great many circulation departments — and these departments are the thermometers of public interest and financial success — are more concerned with the quantity of sporting news than with its quality. On the other hand, newspapers of a certain standing, which number among their readers a greater proportion of college men and women, do give much attention to the quality of their sporting pages. In short, sporting news, in quantity proportionate to other news and of quality equal to that of the rest of the newspaper, appears to pay its own way. Examination of certain Canadian and British papers confirms this view.

D. SUMMARY

From various indications, it might be inferred that the interest of the newspaper publisher in the treatment of games and contests is almost wholly financial, — a question of profit or loss. It is not to be denied that in newspaper publishing, as elsewhere, financial prosperity has come to assume much importance in our scale of values. On the other hand, the traditions of the great names of American journalism — Benjamin Franklin, Greeley, Bolles, Dana, and Pulitzer — have not by any means been submerged in the rising tide of commercialism. These eminent exponents of individual journalism have been succeeded by other men with a power to direct the general sentiment of which their predecessors never dreamed. The great news-gathering agencies, the chains of newspapers, and the syndicates afford almost unlimited opportunity for a single publisher or for small groups of newspaper owners to give the public not alone what it wants but what, by every standard of taste and merit, it deserves. Nor do these men as a group possess a less lively sense of public welfare than their predecessors. Outside or on the fringes of the reputable group of publishers who endeavor to meet the responsibilities that power brings, there stand and will probably always stand the commercially minded owners of newspapers, devoted to the making of money through a debauched sensationalism without regard to the intangible values involved. The problems which the sports page presents to the publisher differ in essence not at all from the problems of other departments. A worthy policy of publication will reflect itself as quickly in the treatment of college athletics as in any other phase of newspaper proprietorship, and it need not be displayed in sixty-point type across seven or eight columns to become effectual.

Conclusion

The person upon whom rests the final responsibility for a newspaper's sports policy is not the reporter, or the desk man, or the sports editor, or the editorial writer, or, indeed, the managing editor; it is the owner or publisher, who initiates or approves the policies which his employees effectuate. In several instances publishers have adopted, usually without announcement in their newspapers, enlightened policies that have improved both emphasis and quality in their sporting pages. Without detracting from the interest of the sports pages, such policies have significantly affected the standards of sports reporting, writing, and editing. In leading public opinion to esteem the true value of the amateur status for American higher education, to cease to view, with a kind of cynical admiration, evasion or open defiance of the amateur convention, and to appreciate both amateurism and honest professionalism as tests of the sportsman's personal integrity, the publisher serves not alone education and sport, but the best ideals of our national life.

CHAPTER XII

VALUES IN AMERICAN COLLEGE ATHLETICS

IN considering the values that reside in American college athletics, the authors of the present study make no claim to originality. They desire only that their conclusions be grounded in the facts of the enquiry and a devotion to the truth as they see it. Inasmuch as their concern has been less with school than with college athletics, they may be pardoned if they turn from school athletics with the summary observation that, except for commercialism in some of its local aspects, certain phases of school hygiene, and the blight that college recruiting and subsidizing have cast upon the school and its pupils, those in charge of school athletics are giving daily increased evidence of disposition and ability to deal with their problems effectually. Indeed, if the salutary changes already begun in school athletics are permitted full, sincere, and consistent development, they will in the course of, say, ten or fifteen years materially modify college athletics for the better. But it must be clearly understood that the problems of school athletics, although related intimately to those of college athletics, are not identical with them, and that many of the principles which operate successfully in the one cannot justifiably be taken over bodily into the other.

As for American college athletics, their improvement during the past thirty years has been marked. Let that improvement continue — let their physical, moral, and spiritual potentialities in the education of youth be clearly understood and sincerely acted upon, and their value in our national life will be immeasurably enhanced. If the reader ask, What is delaying this consummation? the answer, as we conceive it, is set forth toward the end of the present chapter.

In the meantime, certain features of college and university athletics must be weighed: their educational bearings, the amateur status, and the interest of the public.

I. The Educational Bearings of College Athletics

That college athletics bear upon the educational process few will deny. The notion that they possess inherent "educational values" and the question whether they are to-day so administered as to exert such values may be discussed quite independently of whatever conception of education may be favored. In general, modern American theory respecting the purposes of education exhibits two fairly well distinguished trends : On the one hand, there are those who believe the university, the college, and the school, to be essentially intellectual institutions that should train the habits and powers of the mind. On the other hand, the school and the college, and, indeed, parts of the university are regarded by many as socializing agencies that prepare for various aspects of life.[1] The question whether the tendency to regard the college as a socializing agency has grown from an attempt to justify uncontrolled conditions in our higher education on the basis of existing phenomena need not detain us. Either of these fundamental conceptions recognizes the importance of athletics. If training the habits and powers of the mind is to be the function of education, athletics may provide recreation and contrast and may tend to develop moral qualities of perseverance, honesty, courage, and the desirable ethical characteristics that comprise sportsmanship. If, again, education is regarded as the greatest of the socializing forces, then athletics may directly prepare for life through their physical and their moral and ethical aspects. Thus, in whatever philosophical background education be viewed, both intercollegiate and intramural athletics may contribute, either indirectly in the case of the first view or directly in the case of the second, their share to the process. The channel through which athletics make their contribution is habits, physical and psychological, moral, or social. Any commendation or condemnation of college athletics may therefore be tested by the habits that they mold in youth.

A. The Tangible Aspects

For the present, only two of the tangible bearings of athletics upon the American college need consideration : physical health and the effects of athletic success upon college enrollment. Other tangibles, the material and financial, are reserved for later discussion.

1. Physical Health

Chapter VII shows that the effects of athletics and athletic exercise upon the bodily condition and growth of undergraduates, in spite of some conditions that call for

---

[1] This second view is well particularized in Meriam and associates' *Problems of Indian Administration*, Washington, 1928, page 373. "The real goals of education are not 'reading, writing and arithmetic' . . . but sound health both mental and physical, good citizenship in the sense of an understanding participation in community life, ability to earn one's living honestly and efficiently, in a socially worthwhile vocation, comfortable and desirable home and family life, and good character. These are the real aims of education ; reading, writing, numbers, geography, history, and other 'subjects' or skills are only useful to the extent that they contribute directly or indirectly to these fundamental objectives." It should be noted that athletics also may be regarded as a skill.

obvious improvement, are in the main beneficial. Both young men and young women who participate in intramural and intercollegiate athletics improve their health in a way that can be measured in anthropometric terms. College athletics have upon the nation a direct physical effect that justifies not alone their continuance but also their encouragement and further development, especially in their intramural phases.

2. Athletic Success and College Enrollment

The usual approach to discussion of the relation between athletic success and college enrollment has been somewhat like this: On the assumption that the one promotes the other, enthusiastic alumni have argued that athletic success must be secured at all costs for the sake of the college, while their critics have maintained that such a course implies a prostitution of educational ideals. This controversy is all more or less beside the point. As a matter of fact, the athletic reputation of a college or university, and especially its success at football, have little if anything to do with college registration. A successful college football or other athletic season comes too late in the school course to influence materially the choice of college by the great majority of boys, because that choice will have been made perhaps as long as four years previously. Even a succession of three or four victorious football teams appears not to be sufficient, of itself, to affect registration appreciably. The factor of material prosperity among parents exerts a far more important effect upon college enrollment, and a conviction that college or university training makes for success in life, however the term be defined, also contributes its share. There may be a trivial increase in attendance when these matters are used as "talking points" by recruiters or "boosters" in "selling" the college to expert athletes. An influx of such matriculates, eager for concessions at every turn, exerts upon the quality of intellectual work in any college a markedly deleterious effect.

3. The Educational Bearings of Physical Training

An institution that sets for its purpose the training of habits and powers of the mind does not entirely serve those ideals if it admits to its curriculum courses in football playing, coaching, and other phases of college athletics, or if it grants toward the degree credits in physical training awarded for participation in intercollegiate contests. On the other hand, the institution that regards itself as primarily a socializing agency will welcome the thorough training of the body as one of its essential functions. Numbers of American colleges and universities have taken up a position somewhere between these two views, and included intercollegiate athletics, occasional lectures in "hygiene," some intramural athletics (often all too perfunctory), a minimum of corrective exercises, and sometimes medical attention in a "Department of Physical Education." As in the spread of the term "university" in the United States, the adoption of the term "physical education" has been largely a process of imitation in terminology. Only at a minority of institutions where "physical education" has been widely advertised have the meaning of the term and the component factors that justify it been sincerely weighed and thoroughly effectuated. Very few institutions have recalled that in American college life athletic sports and pastimes long antedate physical training or physical education as represented in an organized body of knowledge.

B. The Intangibles

President Eliot, who was once erroneously regarded as opponent of our college athletics but who in reality stood among their friendliest critics, gave testimony in his Annual Report for 1892–93 to their intangible values:

> Athletic sports [he wrote] have infused into boys and young men a greater respect for bodily excellence and a desire to attain it; they have supplied a new and effective motive for resisting all sins which weaken or corrupt the body; they have quickened admiration for such manly qualities as courage, fortitude, and presence of mind in emergencies and under difficulties; they have cultivated in a few the habit of command, and in many the habit of quick obedience and intelligent subordination; and finally they have set before young men prizes and distinctions which are uncontaminated by any commercial value, and which no one can win who does not possess much patience, perseverance, and self-control in addition to rare bodily endowments.

In the thirty-five years that have passed since these words were written the intangible values which President Eliot so well appreciated have in some aspects become more scientifically understood, but by no one have they been more justly set forth. In the past, popular reasoning concerning them has run somewhat in this way: College athletics, especially football, and other body-contact games, *inculcate* in participants such desirable qualities as courage, perseverance, initiative, uprightness, coöperation, and honesty. Thereby they contribute very essentially to the popular welfare, because these estimable qualities, once established in youth, persist into manhood as habits and thus benefit society and its members. Upon these notions modern psychology and moral science have cast much doubt. For the moment it will repay us to summarize very briefly a few of the sounder tenets concerning these matters.

Such moral qualities as courage, initiative, and the group of characteristics included in the term "sportsmanship" are probably not *inculcated* by athletics at all. If through inheritance a young man or woman possesses them in whatever degree, athletic contests and games may effectually exercise them and through use strengthen them. The most that can be justifiably claimed is that athletics tend to develop in participants certain moral qualities that are already present. The medium through which this development may be accomplished is habits. No amount of athletic participation will create qualities that are inherently lacking. But the earlier in the school life of the pupil the attempt is made, not too ostentatiously, to emphasize the active qualities of sportsmanship and to make them habitual in his experience, the better for school and college athletics, and indeed for all forms of sport.

The question whether the moral qualities developed by athletics persist in the affairs of daily life is somewhat more complicated, principally because it involves what is technically known as "carry-over" or "spread of training." Summarily, the hypothesis may be stated as probable, that the moral qualities developed by athletics are carried over into the affairs of daily life when the conditions underlying both athletics and daily life are similar, and furthermore, that the extent of the "carry-over" is in large measure determined by the degree of that similarity. Further than this in claiming advantages for college athletics it is at present unwise to go.[2]

1. Socializing Values

For our purposes the term "socializing values" designates those influences or forces which enable men and women to take their places worthily among their fellows. Obviously, such values will affect life in college more immediately than life after graduation.

a. *In School and College*

Assuredly, "coming out for the team" has assisted in overcoming shyness, developing self-confidence, and widening the acquaintanceship of numbers of undergraduates. In the well-administered college or university athletics beneficially fill many leisure hours. At institutions where undue attention is devoted to games and contests, emphasis upon some of these forces may narrow rather than widen social contacts. Unfortunately, the relative emphasis placed by college opinion upon the various branches of athletics does not in any way correspond with their comparative use in student leisure.[3] Moreover, athletics contribute little to an appreciation of the past, whether in history, art, or literature, with the possible exception of Greek civilization.

And yet so important a part of college life have athletics become that it is not unfair to regard student activities as composed of athletics on the one hand, and all other non-academic activities, musical, dramatic, intellectual, on the other. A reflection of this situation is discernible in college discipline. In the "emotional intemperance of the football season" certain psychologists discern serious dangers that point toward

---

[2] Cf. The extreme view in opposition is represented by the following sentences: "Those who claim moral training for sports make the mistake of assuming that character traits are acquired by going through the motions." "The conclusion that there is a transfer of moral qualities from athletics to life situations is entirely hypothetical, and especially if the life situations are different from those of the game." Edwards, Artman, and Fisher, *Undergraduates*, 1928, pages 147, 148, quoting a psychologist in a men's college.

[3] "Of the activities which had been learned in physical education and used in leisure time by more than 50 students, swimming had the highest percentage of use in present leisure. Hiking, tennis, dancing, baseball, and volleyball follow in the order named with basketball having the smallest percentage of use in students' leisure." Ethel Julia Sexman, *Students' Use in Leisure-Time of Activities Learned in Physical Education in State Teachers' Colleges*, New York, Teachers College, Columbia University, 1926 (Contributions to education, No. 217).

crowd hysteria. Again, the body to which the disciplinary powers of the college are usually delegated is charged also with instruction and with the guidance of non-athletic activities such as dramatic and musical interests, and social events; yet only in rare instances does a glee club, a dramatic club, a college magazine or newspaper, or even a fraternity chapter test the disciplinary powers of a faculty or a dean as an athletic organization tests them.

Were there no signs of a changing perspective among American undergraduates regarding the place of athletics in college life the prospect would be gloomy. Fortunately, many indications point to a growing feeling at perhaps a dozen Eastern institutions that athletics are far from the most important feature of college days. If, as is most probable, this feeling spreads to other universities and colleges, and if it betokens a genuine reappreciation of the place of sport in undergraduate affairs, and not a shrinking from physical or moral competition, the effect upon American education will be most salutary.[4]

b. *After Graduation*

It is to be regretted that the good results of college sport in life after graduation are not more numerous and widespread. One explanation is that intercollegiate competition has been so hotly encouraged as to rob general athletics of much of their interest.

Nevertheless, some of the advantageous effects of college sport in later life are worthy of note. First, if there is good reason to believe that schoolboy athletics tend to decrease such crimes as larceny, burglary, embezzlement, assault, manslaughter, and murder, there is no less reason to believe in similar powers for college sports.

Secondly, habits of athletic participation may guide the wise use of leisure. On the one hand, the knowledge of games acquired in undergraduate days can be applied to later life for the benefit of psychological health. On the other, the enjoyment of the spectators at any athletic contest is increased if their appreciation is founded in experience. The college that encourages extravagance or a discernibly wrong emphasis in its athletics is not fulfilling its functions as an institution of higher education, regardless of the point of view adopted in educational theory.

Thirdly, the loyalty that motivates participation in college athletics is a source at once of strength and of weakness. Among undergraduates its strength lies in its driving power, which, when exerted by a group, forms a body of campus opinion which is practically irresistible. Among alumni its principal weakness lies in the fact that loyalty — albeit perhaps mistaken loyalty — may stand in the way of essential changes or improvements in the college. This conservative and conserving power among graduates, which is a matter not of reason but of emotion coupled with memory, has in the

---

[4] It is highly significant that the list of "objectives" for intercollegiate athletics adopted by athletic directors of the (Mid-Western) Intercollegiate Conference on May 27, 1927, places fun among the secondary "objectives" of intercollegiate competition. The brief code derived therefrom does not mention fun at all.

past upon occasion stood in the way of bettering certain practices that are harming both sport and education. The college loyalty that the best ideals of sportsmanship enhance looks constantly to the service of the college in all things that work together for good.

2. Anti-Social Influences

We turn now to those influences in college athletics, which, if the theory of the spread of training is accepted, work to impair the relationship of men and women to their fellows.

Both in management and conduct and in the technique of play college athletics of the present day exhibit phases of dishonesty, deceit, chicanery, and other undesirable qualities. Perhaps this is to be expected in view of long-standing abuses in which some present-day alumni participated as undergraduates. But a contention that most of these qualities are the results of the machinations of older persons and that they are not now initiated by undergraduates fails to take into account numerous representative cases cited in Chapter X. The fact is that the subsidized college athlete of to-day connives at disreputable and shameful practices for the sake of material returns and for honors falsely achieved. Arguments in support of such practices are specious, calculated to mislead, and fundamentally insincere. Viewed in the light of common honesty, this fabric of organized deceit constitutes the darkest single blot upon American college sport.

If it be argued that the desirable social effects of participation in college athletics persist into afterlife, it is just as probable that their evil effects also persist. The matter does not lend itself to statistical proof, but on the basis of moral analogy, a knowledge of the charms of material comforts easily won, and even a rudimentary appreciation of human fallibility under temptation, it is more than probable. Under just what conditions of life a business man will be dishonest who in undergraduate days was subsidized to play football and yet passed himself off as an amateur, it is impossible to state ; but the fact that his earlier deceit was successful over a period of years is to be reckoned with in accounting for his adult character and acts. Such a man, of course, may not go to prison. But we are concerned with those undiscovered acts which may not reach the stage of criminality, yet nevertheless bulk large in the welfare of society and the relations of a man to his fellows.

If, then, we deplore the actions of those young men who under the guise of sportsmen profit by the dishonesty that recruiting and subsidizing involve, we must condemn utterly the activities of those older persons, be they alumni, townsmen, or college officers, who recruit and subsidize athletes, corrupt young habits under the guise of charity, and imperil private morals to the detriment of society. They stand among the secret enemies of the social order.

3. Preparation for Success in Life

The notion that athletics "prepare for life" is, of course, based upon the theory of the spread of training and the persistence of habits. As we have noted, this theory depends for its validity upon an assumed similarity between athletic competition and modern life. Even when this notion is accepted, together with the concomitant notion that life is very like a team game, present-day college athletics may exert both advantageous and deleterious effects upon individuals, and through them upon the groups of individuals that we call society.

We lack objective evidence to show that success in athletics is an index to success in life after graduation. On the other hand, recent studies tend to demonstrate that a high quality of intellectual accomplishment in college has relationship to later success, however that term be defined. Accordingly, it is probable that the qualities of character that give rise to what we understand as success in life have developed less from the pursuit of college athletics than from the best academic achievement.[5] From such a working hypothesis it follows directly that college athletics should be so conducted as to exercise as many as possible of the desirable social qualities, — honesty, sincerity, persistence, thoughtfulness of others, coöperation, initiative, modesty, self-control, and the rest — that may contribute to the welfare of society; that they should assist and by no means interfere with intellectual pursuits, success in which gives earnest of later achievement; and that they should be shorn of anti-socializing tendencies. Although this ideal may never be completely fulfilled, it can be served far more sincerely than it has been up to the present time by the American college.

4. Morals and a Few Ethical Considerations

The line between the social and the moral values of college athletics is not sharply drawn. We set forth at this point a series of ethical and moral considerations, some of which have been touched upon but not emphasized in preceding pages.

From observations made during the enquiry it appears that the most vigorous attempts at direct inculcation of precepts — what we are accustomed to regard as "moral education" — exist at denominational colleges and universities. Notably, exacting instruction in such matters is given at the Catholic colleges. But, so far as could be ascertained, in no institution, Protestant or Catholic, are the moral precepts, instructions, and exercises of the lecture room carried into the open air of the playing field, or the moral practices of the playing field related by conscious effort to other phases of college life. As a result, the theoretical and the practical aspects of direct moral education in many American colleges lie far asunder. It is not unlikely that the

---

[5] It is likely that the reason for the War Department's preference of athletes as promising officer-material rests upon two facts: First, athletes are athletes because of personal qualities which conduce both to athletic and to military success and are developed, but not inculcated, by athletics. The similarities between "combative" athletics and war were emphasized many years ago by the late Walter Camp. Secondly, athletes possess physical strength and endurance above those of non-athletes.

details of scholastic, or, indeed, any other systematic philosophy, might be brought the more nearly home to the affairs of everyday life by reference to that portion of undergraduate life which is associated with the playing field and the stadium.

Testimony from a number of deans and other administrative officers is to the effect that problems of college discipline tend to be less acute when larger proportions of undergraduates participate in athletics. The same opinion has been expressed by many masters in English public schools. In the course of the enquiry there were studied several instances in which non-participating partisans, who accompany teams on comparatively long trips, indulged in misconduct that varied from tipsiness to downright immorality. It seems reasonable to believe that such misconduct, being fairly common in college towns, passes without much comment unless its uproariousness reaches the ears of disciplinary officers, but that, publicly indulged and paraded in less accustomed communities and in railroad trains, it becomes rightly a subject of sharp condemnation. In respect of university discipline, it is entirely possible that the present generation of college men and women possess, on the whole, more self-control and better manners than their predecessors. In any event, it is impossible, in considering breaches that attend upon athletic contests, to know whether they are chargeable more to athletics than to standards of daily life in the American community.

Previously in the study the statement was made that betting and gambling upon athletics touched the American undergraduate only occasionally. Possibly for this reason the more egregious examples appear to be especially reprehensible. Intersectional contests of all kinds, however, provide a fruitful field for the professional gambler and his familiars. Furthermore, it is likely that the number of college men who bet is materially increased through the mistaken loyalty that intersectional contests call forth. The efforts of the (Mid-Western) Intercollegiate Conference to eliminate betting among undergraduates have been fruitful, and the report of the Committee of the Southern Association of Colleges and Secondary Schools upon Athletics, in 1922, has also done much good in this particular.

Among the most distasteful aspects of that violent partisanship which overrides all ethical decency stands the tendency, too often abetted by newspaper writers, to protest, sometimes forcibly, the decisions of referees and umpires. The punishment of a Canadian football player who struck an official, life suspension from the game, is severe but justified. The efforts of those football officials who have discussed with alumni the problems of their duties on the field have tended to reduce, through an appeal to sportsmanship, the dissatisfaction with the earnest efforts of almost any referee or umpire that had grown astoundingly during the past fifteen years. Over a like period, says a much respected football official, the quality of sportsmanship displayed in intercollegiate contests has much improved. Players foul less and behave better. Coaches, too, are becoming better sportsmen. It is perhaps too much to hope that the manners of a crowd of spectators, numbers of whom possess little appreciation of the seemly, should be reformed completely forthwith. Perhaps, however, when members of the college family preponderate as spectators at intercollegiate contests the situation will be less offensive.

In short, respecting the ethical and moral considerations involved in certain phases of college athletics, the dilution of partisanship and intensity of rivalry that a more widespread participation in athletics at American colleges can bring, will in time work its changes in both active participants and spectators. Here, as elsewhere, the problem is to perpetuate the advantages that flow from college athletics and to eliminate as many as possible of the disadvantages.

C. SUMMARY: ATHLETICS IN EDUCATION

The boasted "educational values" of athletics as they exist to-day in the American college leave much to be desired. The educational advantages that flow from inter-college contests are principally by-products. Those which result from intramural athletics are neither so strong nor so widespread as they could and should be made. It is true that, in spite of comparatively high incidence of fatalities and injuries, athletics tend to confer much physical benefit upon participants. On the other hand, however strong may be the conviction that they inculcate or increase in young men courage, initiative, and other moral qualities, this remains to be scientifically established. More than a decade ago it was pointed out that excessive desire for victory has deprived us of one of the most important educational advantages of athletics, since coaching from the side-lines removes from the players the essential quality of initiative. The precision of play engendered by modern American coaching methods in practically all branches of athletics becomes a habit which exerts itself to shape conduct when conditions arise in games or in life similar to those that have been experienced in preparation. The amount of independent or individual thinking on the part of a college athlete which modern methods of athletic coaching, and in many instances supervision in management, induce is minimal. If the theory be adopted that education consists in the pupil's experiencing a series of situations as similar as possible to those he will encounter in after-school life, the notion that our college athletics are "educational" falls miserably to pieces. Tested by this standard, physical education, to the extent that it includes many branches of intercollegiate athletics, has little value. Much the same is true with reference to those intramural sports in which interest and participation are grounded in compulsion to obtain credits for the degree.

The educational problem of the future for the improvement of American college athletics is, therefore, upon the improving groundwork of school athletics to set up methods of coaching, management, and participation in which young men and young women may be accustomed to the making of decisions and in which a mental appreciation of problems replaces the present almost automatic reactions to stimuli applied under a comparatively hard and fast series of conditions. The problems of moral education implied are of still wider extent, but they come down at last to an exemplification of sportsmanlike qualities, especially those which begin and end in sincerity and honesty. These ends can be secured through a series of carefully graduated steps, which, although they must be appreciated and guided by older persons, need not and should not be vaunted. Beginning with the college freshman, the entire athletic activity of the college should be so reframed as progressively to increase the amount of responsibility for athletics and their conduct that the group of undergraduates sustain, this burden being lightened for individuals by spreading it over increased numbers, until at the end of the senior year the undergraduate shall have derived every possible benefit, in body, mind, and character, that college sport can yield. In devising such a program, the service of undergraduates of good judgment should be enlisted; in its execution their good-will and interest are obviously a *sine qua non*.

II. The Amateur Status in College Athletics

At no other point in the whole field of college athletics is honesty so severely tested as it is in connection with the convention of amateurism. The reason can be readily comprehended. Those who have sought to uphold the status of the amateur in the United States have proceeded, consciously or unconsciously, upon the notion that the man who plays a game for fun, or for the love of it, or for sport's sake, is in some way advantaged over the man who makes a living at it. Certainly the advantage cannot pertain to skill, for the general run of professional athletes tend to be far more expert at their sports than the general run of amateurs. Nor has either group a proprietary claim upon the exemplification of sportsmanship. The root of all difficulties with the amateur status touches the desires of certain athletes to retain the prestige that amateurism confers and at the same time to reap the monetary or material rewards of professionalism. The results in college athletics and probably in other forms of competition have included equivocation, false statements concerning eligibility, and other forms of dishonesty, which are to be numbered among the fruits of commercialism.

The values that argue for the preservation of the amateur status in American college athletics bear, first, upon the educational process, whatever its fundamental purpose, and secondly, upon the individual undergraduate. It must be kept in mind that amateurism is a convention. Furthermore, it is a social convention, in that it affects not alone the individual but also his relationships to his fellows, both participants and non-participants.

A. AMATEURISM AND THE EDUCATIONAL PROCESS

It is important that the doctrine of amateurism in college athletics be preserved, whether the college is regarded as an intellectual agency or as a socializing agency.

1. In an Intellectual Agency

The direct bearing of amateurism and of its antithesis, professionalism, upon American higher education was set forth a few years ago by a committee of the faculty of Purdue University:

> The average individual does not appreciate the real evil of professionalism in college athletics. He sees nothing inherently wrong in the acceptance of money for playing, any more than in accepting compensation for any other kind of legitimate performance. Why, then, should faculties make so much noise about it? The fact is, that mere playing for compensation is not, in itself, wrong, but the admission to the university of students who are financed because of their athletic prowess and because of their ability to round out winning athletic teams, cannot do otherwise than result in disaster to our educational program and to its standards of scholarship.

Particular instances in which athletes have been subsidized or otherwise professionalized to the detriment of the intellectual aims of a college or university will recur to many readers. The presence of a man whose prime interest in college is dependent upon payment for his athletic services delays and reduces academic instruction to his intellectual level and speed, both in the classroom and in every other phase of college work. It invokes concessions at entrance and at every point at which an academic requirement is set. It leads in the direction of special privilege in tests and examinations, the relaxation of standards of grading in class and in written work, the granting of special opportunities to repair academic standing when it is injured by the close attention to athletic practice that subsidies entail, and much excusing from the obligation to meet academic appointments promptly and sincerely. It disunifies the student body and soon brings other undergraduates to feel that efforts to fulfil the intellectual purposes of the institution avail nothing if men are to be supported merely for the sake of winning games. No other force so completely vitiates the intellectual aims of an institution and each of its members.

All this would be true if professionalism were practiced frankly and openly. Where, however, its practice is concealed, an even deadlier blow is struck at spiritual values.

2. In a Socializing Agency

If the American college be regarded as a socializing agency, the effects of professionalism, open or covert, in its sports are even more deleterious. Contravention of the amateur status in college sport strikes at the root of educational democracy.

The term "educational democracy" stands in need of definition. For present purposes, it denotes that characteristic of our educational process which vouchsafes to each and sundry equal opportunity to develop his habits and powers, of the mind, the body, or the spirit, in accordance with his capacities. The effect of importing subsidized or professionalized athletes into any institution seriously impairs not alone the incentive but also the privilege of every other student to develop to the full his interests and powers, intellectual, spiritual, or physical. If college athletics have the socializing values that are attributed to them, then the infraction of the amateur convention usually gives to the man who possesses athletic talent that he develops with a view to financial return, an advantage over his less skilful fellows which, because of the desirability of victory, destroys at one blow that democracy of the playing field and the river which is rightly numbered among the most precious merits of college sport.

From the point of view of American ideals in physical education, professionalism is an even more serious evil. Now, amateurism, as Professor Hetherington pointed out twenty years ago, "aims to conserve the natural rights of the many as against the privileges of the few." Thus, the convention of amateurism represents a guarantee on the part of the American college that every undergraduate shall have his fair and equal chance to develop his physical powers for the honor of his fellows, his own self-satisfaction, and the good of the nation. This guarantee any form of professionalism in a college or a school tends to destroy.

The stock arguments of those who would countenance defiance of the amateur convention in college athletics are as follows: A man with musical talent is permitted without comment to represent his college on a glee club and at the same time to sing for pay in a church; or another person may edit a college periodical and sell as many stories as he can to magazines. Why, then, should not an athlete represent his college and simultaneously be compensated for this or any other athletic success if his skill be sufficient? Is he not suffering from unfavorable discrimination if he is not permitted thus to capitalize his talent?

The answer, for present purposes, is soon made. In college life such pursuits as singing, acting, public speaking, debating, and writing make up a general group of undergraduate activities that are directly related to the arts. The "skills" upon which expertness in them depends are primarily mental or emotional; physical skill enters only as a part of the mechanics of expression. These pursuits, in their more competitive development, afford tests of even temper and self-control, but such tests are in general not sudden or violent; in other words, they offer opportunity for a degree of reflection which may considerably delay and modify the reaction to any stimulus.

On the other hand, such pursuits as football, baseball, tennis, golf, and rifle-shooting belong to a special group of undergraduate activities that collectively are termed sport. Sport involves the larger muscles of the human body and their coördination, almost always in violent exertion. Its "skills" are primarily physical; mental and emotional "skills" are present, but they vary between sports. Sport in general implies the over-coming of opposition or an obstacle — physical, mental, moral — which is immediate. The resulting contest is carried on under certain conventions. Through the relation of these conventions to the desire to excel, sport tests the good temper and chivalry of its participants. These tests, which involve the control of reactions, and our primal in-heritance of admiration for physical prowess, give rise to much of the aura with which sport is surrounded.

The conventions of sport are of two kinds: One sort — rules, written or otherwise established — pertains to the conditions under which contests take place. Appropriate rules are as essential to a general activity as to a sport, if competition is present. The second set of conventions, some of which are expressed in rules, penetrate deeper into the essential nature of sport; they are extended to the general activities only by a process of analogy. These conventions reflect the conflict between certain primal, inherited characteristics on the one hand, and certain traditions of social behavior on the other, — the moral struggle between force and the uses to which, with the sanction of our civilization, it may and should be put.

The difference between representing a college in athletic competition and represent-ing it on a glee club is the difference between sport and some other form of diversion.

The amateur convention is thus a social convention, — that is, a convention that the present order of society maintains for its own good. Against the maintenance of the amateur convention in college sport, the most powerful argument is that it does not work. But no human convention operates to perfection. The reason amateurism does not work perfectly inheres, not in its essential qualities or disadvantages, but in the very human weakness of those who would justify through victory the means whereby victory is sometimes achieved. An athlete has every personal right to professionalize himself so long as he deceives no one concerning his status.

The proposal that the amateur convention in college sport be abolished, is a counsel of defeat. Such a step is far from justified by present conditions. The abolition of the amateur code, — assuming for the moment that it could be abolished, — not only would destroy the best that is now gained from college sport, but would bring with it a new set of evils that would be infinitely worse than any that now obtain.

The solution of the problem is a wider and more conscientious adherence to the con-vention. It has already been noted that if all who iniquitously recruit, subsidize, and otherwise debauch college athletes would expend a fraction of such efforts upon honestly and conscientiously upholding the amateur status, the ethical aspects of our college athletics that are summarized in the term "sportsmanship" would largely care for themselves. So long as there is personal honor among undergraduates, alumni, and all others who are interested in college sport, the honest preservation of the amateur status will be respected and its impairment will be deprecated.

B. The Amateur Status and the Individual Undergraduate

The difficulty with the prevalent attitude toward violators of the amateur rule in college sport, through subsidies given or accepted, by summer baseball, or otherwise, is that to many alumni, faculty members, and undergraduates violations have apparently little consequence.[6] Yet evasion of the amateur rule is comparable in dishonesty with any other infraction of the moral code that does not involve the property right. For example, it presents many parallels with cribbing; the type of man who looks lightly upon cribbing tends to look lightly also upon violation of the amateur status. The greatest disservice that can be done a youth is teaching him that dishonesty is desirable. The effect upon his own morals is likely to prove irreparable. The effect upon his fellow-undergraduates will spread the corruption, especially by engendering a desire to profit by similar deceptions. Those who tempt young men to barter their honesty for the supposed advantages of a college course, dishonestly achieved, are the Fagins of American sport and of American higher education.

III. The Public and College Athletics

That portion of the American public which is without college interests or affiliations naturally regards college athletics solely from the point of view of popular amusement. The diverting and spectacular elements are paramount.

Surely an interest in clean, hard-played games conducted in the open air is to be preferred above addiction to any of the thousand and one forms of indoor entertainment that compete for popular favor. On the other hand, there is much to be regretted in the proprietary influence over college athletics that the general public of to-day is permitted to exert. In sacrificing many phases of the guidance of college athletics to popular whim, those charged with their conduct are subserving two forces that are unjustifiable from any point of view in education: commercialism, and the special privileges of small groups of alumni. Much of the distortion of the popular attitude toward the college has flowed from the fact that intercollegiate contests appear to be almost the only phase of college life that is regarded as news.

Very few of the beneficial results of the public's interest in college athletics could have been achieved under a policy that restricted attendance at college contests to the college family. It is true that a physical benefit to children and young men is traceable to their emulation of athletic heroes. Nearly thirty years ago Professor Sheldon pointed out that college "games have diffused a greater desire for bodily excellence, and a greater admiration for such manly qualities as courage and fortitude among the

---

[6] Note, for example, the words of a writer, a college graduate, in the New York *Sun*, on June 26, 1928. "Many condemn [a certain athlete] because of these things, but such condemnation seems unfounded. He has hurdled the shibboleths of amateurism and capitalized on his track ability about as successfully as any professional. But he has stayed within the literal interpretation of the rules, and that's all that the solons of amateur athletics demand." The metaphor needs no commentary.

schoolboys of the country." Granting all of this, there still remains the fact that the physical and other benefits that accrue to the spectators at intercollegiate contests are inferior in number and in force to those that are gained from the active participation in outdoor pastimes to which well-conducted intramural school and college athletics contribute, both quantitatively and qualitatively, through the formation of habits of physical activity. In view of such considerations a university must experience considerable difficulty in justifying in the name of education or valid public service the commercialization of intercollegiate athletics that exploits undergraduate loyalty and athletic skill, however much amusement it may afford the general public.

In the course of time, habits of athletic participation sufficiently diffused among our population may well restore to the nation some of the beneficial forces that lapsed with our loss of pioneer conditions. As for the individual, except for a sustainment of interest in sports, it is doubtful if occupying a stadium seat for three hours of the most delectable of autumn afternoons affords anyone physical or moral benefits that compare to those which accrue even from eighteen holes of very bad golf on a public course or from a two-hour walk through city streets. The advantages of vicarious participation in intercollegiate athletics have been greatly overemphasized.

IV. The Causes of the Present Defects in American College Athletics

The fundamental causes of the defects of American college athletics are two : commercialism, and a negligent attitude toward the educational opportunity for which the college exists. To one, and generally to both, of these inter-acting causes, every shortcoming of college sport can be traced. Both may be abated, even if neither, in view of the imperfectibility of human nature, can ever be absolutely eliminated.

A. Commercialism

We have defined commercialism as that condition which exists when the monetary and material returns from sport are more highly valued than the returns in play, recreation, and bodily and moral well-being. Through the medium of self-interest it affects every person whom it touches : college officers, teachers, undergraduates, and alumni, the press, and the public. Because some of its results are desirable, as many other material things are desirable, it is frequently argued that commercialism can be beneficent as well as harmful. This argument neglects the influence of time, which in its passage withers the beneficent aspects of commercialism into evils that are the more difficult to eradicate because of the depth of their roots.

Commercialism has made possible the erection of fine academic buildings and the increase of equipment from the profits of college athletics, but those profits have been gained because colleges have permitted the youths entrusted to their care to be openly exploited. At such colleges and universities the primary emphasis has been transferred from the things of the spirit or the mind to the material.

In general, university trustees are relatively innocent of commercialism by formal or tacit delegation of their responsibilities. Yet they have profited by it; the task of finding money for new equipment and buildings has been lightened. As for members of faculties, commercialism has added to their numbers through providing from athletic profits a part of the salaries of certain teachers. Rising gate receipts have brought them enlarged facilities. But the college teacher finds also that commercialism has complicated the instructional task through the admission of the unfit, the lowering of academic standards for the sake of gain, and the pressure exerted from various sources at a great number of points not to be "unfair" to athletes. Through commercialism the coach or director of physical education has received very great increases in salary, luxurious trappings, and sometimes the means and the opportunity to attract and subsidize athletes of unusual skill.

Commercialism has added to the amusement of alumni, but it has corrupted the moral fibre of not a few of them through its temptations to recruit and subsidize. It has deprived the college of the loyalties of some of her sons, whose encouragement and devotion she most needs. Although it has given to graduates stadiums of which to be proud and to boast, these gains would appear less gratifying in a less distorted scheme of values. It has given the general public more seats at football games, but it has impaired their attitude toward sports at some points, even while improving it at others. For newspaper men its results have provided inexhaustible "copy" and augmented profits and salaries.

It is the undergraduates who have suffered most and will continue most to suffer from commercialism and its results. True, the commercial policy has provided medical attention and hospitalization for injured athletes, but far fewer injuries would have resulted from uncommercialized games. It has rendered attendance at contests held on alien fields for the sake of profits, expensive and sometimes impossible. It has provided increased seating space for home games, and in some instances has added to the playing space available to all undergraduates, although usually increases of playing space are used for the benefit of participants in intercollegiate athletics. At some colleges, it has alienated the sympathies of considerable numbers of undergraduates, not alone from intercollegiate athletics but — what is more important — from intramural athletics; and it has impaired loyalties that would have been most precious to any institution. Commercialism motivates the recruiting and subsidizing of players, and the commercial attitude has enabled many young men to acquire college educations at the cost of honesty and sincerity. More than any other force, it has tended to distort the values of college life and to increase its emphasis upon the material and the monetary. Indeed, at no point in the educational process has commercialism in college athletics wrought more mischief than in its effect upon the American undergraduate. And the distressing fact is that the college, the Fostering Mother, has permitted and even encouraged it to do these things in the name of education.

The argument that commercialism in college athletics is merely a reflection of the commercialism of modern life is specious. It is not the affair of the college or the university to reflect modern life. If the university is to be a socializing agency worthy of the name, it must endeavor to ameliorate the conditions of existence, spiritual as well as physical, and to train the men and women who shall lead the nations out of the bondage of those conditions. To neither of these missions does commercialism in college athletics soundly contribute.

B. NEGLIGENCE RESPECTING EDUCATIONAL OPPORTUNITY

At a time when higher education in the United States is being much scrutinized, it is fitting that enquiry should be directed as well at its informal as at its formal aspects. In an agency primarily intellectual, athletics may take their place among the devices of informal education and recreation. In a socializing agency, the functions of athletics become more formal and more closely associated with the activities of the curriculum. But if at their best they are to be made to contribute indirectly or directly to the education of youth, their essential nature as sport must be preserved.

Occasionally a college president has attempted to improve athletics at his own institution. In certain cases failure has resulted because fellow presidents, for various reasons, have refused coöperation or have coöperated only in limited measure, or because pressure from alumni, townsmen, or friends of the college has grown too great to be resisted. Such presidents have been beaten at the game largely because they have tried, or have had, to play it single-handed.

The country over, college athletics present few isolated conditions or temptations. They are grounded in fundamental characteristics of young men and women, which, once recognized with clear vision, afford a basis for determining the place of athletics in the educational procedure. What that place may be depends upon the educational aims that the college sets for itself under the guidance of its officers.

We turn now to three respects in which the college has been negligent in its relating of athletics to college education. To characterize them thus implies no lack of discussion or theory; it does imply a certain poverty of lasting good results from action, ascribable principally to the workings of commercialism.

1. The Lack of Intellectual Challenge

It has been recently pointed out that a fundamental defect in the American college is its lack of intellectual challenge to the young and alert mind. If this is true respecting its academic aspects, it is doubly true of college athletics as they are at present conducted. Their governance has been delivered utterly into the hands of older persons, whose decisions are made with little reference to the benefits that the reasoning processes involved might confer upon younger minds. Most intercollegiate contests entail little independence of judgment on the part of players, whether in preparation or in actual participation. At every turn, our college athletics are mechanized into automatism, and our athletes and managers are puppets pulled by older hands. What intellectual challenge intercollegiate sport might afford has given way before the forces of commercialism. Fortunately for the future, intramural athletics have not succumbed to the deadening touch; but they are even now dependent for their existence upon the profits from intercollegiate football. If the spiritual and intellectual challenge of intramural sport can in time rejuvenate intercollegiate athletics, no man should withhold his hand from the task.

2. Control through Formula; Imitation

The problems of college athletics, like other problems in human relationships, are not to be completely solved by formula, however much they may be temporarily changed. As in the case of single branches of competitive athletics, standards and rules form the conventions of sport, and so long as sport exists, it will have its conventions. But conventions are not formulas. It is often assumed that if college athletics, as distinct from school athletics, are to contribute to education, they must be controlled (that is, restricted and curbed) through the direct action of faculties. This formula has failed at two points: If, on the one hand, it means delivering college athletics into the hands of men whose chief professional interest and means of livelihood they are, the result is not to check but to propagate commercialism. If, on the other hand, academic teachers on college faculties are placed in control, such men, being specialists, only in comparatively rare instances can and do give to the governance of college athletics that concentrated attention and devotion which they bestow upon their chosen fields of teaching and scholarship. Probably more than any other single factor, the operation of faculty control, even at its best, has tended to deprive the undergraduate of that opportunity of maturing under progressively increasing responsibility which an enlightened policy of guidance affords.

Imitation in the control of college athletics has wrought an equal havoc. To assume that the athletic policies and regulations that appear to work well at one university or in one section of the land can without modification be taken over successfully into another is fallacious. A clear understanding of the functions of athletics in their relation to the educational process, however that process be conceived, a sincere and uniform recognition of the principles of human conduct that athletics involve, and an honorable adherence to the spirit as well as the letter of the conventions of sport, have wrought vastly beneficial changes in college athletics wherever they have been effectuated with due reference to specific phases of local sentiment. The solution of the problem of control is not imitation but adaption, not repression but guidance by college presidents, deans, teachers, directors of physical education, or alumni who understand the implications of the term "sport," whose generosity prompts the gift of many hours without compensation, and whose honesty is beyond self-interest or commercialism.

3. Morals and Conduct

In the field of conduct and morals, vociferous proponents of college athletics have claimed for participants far greater benefits than athletics can probably ever yield, and, in attempting to evaluate these supposed benefits, have hailed the shadow as the substance. The workings of commercialism have almost obliterated the non-material aspects of athletics. And yet such qualities as loyalty, self-reliance, modesty, co-operation, self-sacrifice, courage, and, above all, honesty, can be more readily and directly cultivated through the activities and habits of the playing field than in almost any other phase of college life. What, therefore, is needed is not one set of moral and ethical standards for sports and games, and another for all other phases of college life, but a single set of standards so sincerely valued that by taking thought they can be made operative in life's every aspect. The transfer or spread of training implied is as much the affair of the academic teacher as of the coach or the director of physical education. It must begin with a diminished emphasis upon the material benefits of college athletics and a sincere resolution to substitute other and more lasting values for those that now are prized.

Conclusion

The prime needs of our college athletics are two, — one particular and one general. The first is a change of values in a field that is sodden with the commercial and the material and the vested interests that these forces have created. Commercialism in college athletics must be diminished and college sport must rise to a point where it is esteemed primarily and sincerely for the opportunities it affords to mature youth under responsibility, to exercise at once the body and the mind, and to foster habits both of bodily health and of those high qualities of character which, until they are revealed in action, we accept on faith.

The second need is more fundamental. The American college must renew within itself the force that will challenge the best intellectual capabilities of the undergraduate. Happily, this task is now engaging the attention of numerous college officers and teachers. Better still, the fact is becoming recognized that the granting of opportunity for the fulfillment of intellectual promise need not impair the socializing qualities of college sport. It is not necessary to "include athletics in the curriculum" of the undergraduate or to legislate out of them their life and spirit in order to extract what educational values they promise in terms of courage, independent thinking, coöperation, initiative, habits of bodily activity, and, above all, honesty in dealings between man and man. Whichever conception of the function of the American college, intellectual or socializing agency, be adopted, let only the chosen ideal be followed with sincerity and clear vision, and in the course of years our college sport will largely take care of itself.

APPENDIX

APPENDIX

I

UNIVERSITIES, COLLEGES, AND SCHOOLS VISITED FOR THE ENQUIRY

NOTE: The institutions marked by an asterisk in the first of the two lists were visited in connection with the study of the Hygiene of Athletic Training. The second list sets forth the names of other institutions visited in this same connection.

New England States

*Amherst College	Amherst, Massachusetts
Bates College	Lewiston, Maine
Boston College	Chestnut Hill, Massachusetts
Bowdoin College	Brunswick, Maine
*Brown University	Providence, Rhode Island
Dartmouth College	Hanover, New Hampshire
Deerfield Academy	Deerfield, Massachusetts
*Harvard University	Cambridge, Massachusetts
Holy Cross College	Worcester, Massachusetts
Massachusetts Agricultural College	Amherst, Massachusetts
Massachusetts Institute of Technology	Cambridge, Massachusetts
Middlebury College	Middlebury, Vermont
Trinity College	Hartford, Connecticut
Tufts College	Tufts College, Massachusetts
University of Vermont	Burlington, Vermont
*Wesleyan University	Middletown, Connecticut
Williams College	Williamstown, Massachusetts
Yale University	New Haven, Connecticut
Young Men's Christian Association College	Springfield, Massachusetts

Mid-Atlantic States

Allegheny College	Meadville, Pennsylvania
Bellefonte Academy	Bellefonte, Pennsylvania
*Bucknell University	Lewisburg, Pennsylvania
Carnegie Institute of Technology	Pittsburgh, Pennsylvania
*Colgate University	Hamilton, New York
Columbia University	New York, New York
*Cornell University	Ithaca, New York
*DeWitt Clinton High School	New York, New York
Dickinson College	Carlisle, Pennsylvania
Fordham University	New York, New York
Franklin and Marshall College	Lancaster, Pennsylvania
Geneva College	Beaver Falls, Pennsylvania
Gettysburg College	Gettysburg, Pennsylvania
Grove City College	Grove City, Pennsylvania
Hobart College	Geneva, New York

Kiskiminetas Springs School	Saltsburg, Pennsylvania
*Lafayette College	Easton, Pennsylvania
Lebanon Valley College	Annville, Pennsylvania
*Lehigh University	Bethlehem, Pennsylvania
*Manual Training High School	Brooklyn, New York
Muhlenberg College	Allentown, Pennsylvania
New Utrecht High School	Brooklyn, New York
New York University	New York, New York
*University of Pennsylvania	Philadelphia, Pennsylvania
*Pennsylvania State College	State College, Pennsylvania
University of Pittsburgh	Pittsburgh, Pennsylvania
*Princeton University	Princeton, New Jersey
University of Rochester	Rochester, New York
Rutgers University	New Brunswick, New Jersey
*Syracuse University	Syracuse, New York
United States Military Academy	West Point, New York
Ursinus College	Collegeville, Pennsylvania
Washington and Jefferson College	Washington, Pennsylvania

South Atlantic States

Blue Ridge College	New Windsor, Maryland
Emory University	Atlanta, Georgia
University of Georgia	Athens, Georgia
Georgia School of Technology	Atlanta, Georgia
Georgetown University	Washington, D. C.
University of North Carolina	Chapel Hill, North Carolina
Oglethorpe University	Oglethorpe University, Georgia
University of Virginia	Charlottesville, Virginia
West Virginia University	Morgantown, West Virginia
West Virginia Wesleyan College	Buckhannon, West Virginia
Western Maryland College	Westminster, Maryland

East North Central States

Beloit College	Beloit, Wisconsin
*University of Chicago	Chicago, Illinois
University of Illinois	Urbana, Illinois
Marquette University	Milwaukee, Wisconsin
*University of Michigan	Ann Arbor, Michigan
Northwestern University	Evanston, Illinois
University of Notre Dame	Notre Dame, Indiana
Oberlin College	Oberlin, Ohio
Ohio State University	Columbus, Ohio
Ohio Wesleyan University	Delaware, Ohio
Purdue University	Lafayette, Indiana
*University of Wisconsin	Madison, Wisconsin
College of Wooster	Wooster, Ohio

West North Central States

Carleton College	Northfield, Minnesota
Coe College	Cedar Rapids, Iowa
Des Moines University	Des Moines, Iowa
Drake University	Des Moines, Iowa
Haskell Institute	Lawrence, Kansas
University of Iowa	Iowa City, Iowa
*University of Minnesota	Minneapolis, Minnesota
University of Missouri	Columbia, Missouri
University of South Dakota	Vermillion, South Dakota

East South Central States

University of Alabama	University, Alabama
Centre College	Danville, Kentucky
University of Tennessee	Knoxville, Tennessee
Vanderbilt University	Nashville, Tennessee

West South Central States

Baylor University	Waco, Texas
University of Oklahoma	Norman, Oklahoma
Southern Methodist University	Dallas, Texas
University of Texas	Austin, Texas
Tulane University of Louisiana	New Orleans, Louisiana

Rocky Mountain States

University of Arizona	Tucson, Arizona
Brigham Young University	Provo, Utah
University of Colorado	Boulder, Colorado
University of Denver	Denver, Colorado
University of Idaho	Moscow, Idaho
Montana State College	Bozeman, Montana
University of Utah	Salt Lake City, Utah
University of Wyoming	Laramie, Wyoming

Pacific States

University of California	Berkeley, California
Oregon State Agricultural College	Corvallis, Oregon
Reed College	Portland, Oregon
University of Southern California	Los Angeles, California
Stanford University	Palo Alto, California
University of Washington	Seattle, Washington
Washington State College	Pullman, Washington
High School	Los Angeles, California
High School	San Bernardino, California

Dominion of Canada

Dalhousie University	Halifax, Nova Scotia
Laval University	Quebec, Quebec
McGill University	Montreal, Quebec
University of Ottawa	Ottawa, Ottawa
Queen's University	Kingston, Ontario
University of Saskatchewan	Saskatoon, Saskatchewan
University of Toronto	Toronto, Ontario

Other Universities, Colleges, and Schools visited for the study concerning

THE HYGIENE OF ATHLETIC TRAINING

New England States

Groton School	Groton, Massachusetts
Middlesex School	Concord, Massachusetts
Phillips Academy	Andover, Massachusetts
Saint Mark's School	Southboro, Massachusetts

Mid-Atlantic States

Erasmus Hall High School	Brooklyn, New York
Hamilton College	Clinton, New York
Lawrenceville School	Lawrenceville, New Jersey
Morris High School	New York, New York
Susquehanna University	Selinsgrove, Pennsylvania
Public High School	Groton, New York
Public High School	Ithaca, New York

East North Central States

Public High School	Ann Arbor, Michigan

II

EXCERPTS FROM MATERIALS ON RECRUITING

The purpose of printing excerpts from the mass of letters and other materials concerning the recruiting of athletes which has found its way to our enquiry is to demonstrate that the first step toward discovering the truth of the matter at any college or university is an examination of correspondence and other files. The items here presented make up a representative and, with two exceptions, a recent sampling. The substitution of symbols for names and the omissions that have been made for various reasons in no way invalidate the general purpose.

A. The Initiation of Correspondence

1. by a schoolboy athlete "shopping round"

The Initial Letter

Coach of Football,
    Makt University,
My dear Sir,
    Wonder if you can help me in going to Makt this fall,
    I have played football for fours [*sic*] at [a New England high school], making all Scholastic end for the years 192– and 192–, All Suburban 192– & 192– all [State] 192– & 192–, In basketball I play left forward for three years. In baseball I played 1st base for three years Track I run in 20 & 44s. Captain 192– & 192–
    Hoping you can help me I am,

Yours sincerely
Mnd Okdp

Write to
Mnd Okdp
  [Address omitted]
(over)

[Reverse of page]

I have had offers from Northern Colleges but prefer the South as I have spent some time there.
I am 5 ft 11 in 160 lbs 20 yrs old

M Kdp

The Coach's Reply

My dear Mr. Kdp:
    Makt University would be proud to have you register as one of our students, but the only inducement we can offer is a good education, providing you are desirous of same.

Yours very truly,

2. by the father of a schoolboy athlete writing to a coach

Dear Sir:
    What have you to offer in an Athletic Scholarship, to Xyd "Bugs" Cldst 3 years Backfield Star at Aeos High School, and who last season Was Captain of the Team that won 10 games and lost 1 and that game was lost by 1 point. Cldst also plays Basket Ball, Base Ball and Track for Recommendations write to Nes Fdai Head Coach or Rht Nag Faculty Mgr. of Athletics. . . .
    Hoping to hear from you soon

I remain yours Very Truly
Mtg Cldst
Father of "Bugs" . . .

3. by a college athlete to a coach

The Initial Letter

Coach P. D. Ldax
Sept. 11, 1899
    Trmd, Egim.
Dear Sir:
    You will doubtless be surprised to receive a letter from me. . . . I have been training here about a week for football, but am not entirely satisfied with the way affairs are conducted here, and am willing to

leave if sufficient inducements are offered. I am 5 ft. 9 in. tall, weigh 212 lbs. stripped and am in good physical condition. Am either a guard or a center. Good amateur standing. If you will guarantee to get me some kind of a job outside of school hours that will pay my way through school, I will consider your proposition. Hoping that this matter will be held strictly confidential between you and me, and awaiting a reply, I am,

Yours respectfully,
Ykxl W. Imxx

The Coach's Reply

Sept. 14, 1899

Mr. Ykxl W. Imxx, . . .
Dear Sir : —

In reply to your letter of September 11 I will say that we are not permitted by our rules or by our consciences to secure jobs for athletes who desire to enter our University. There are quite a number of athletic men here who are working their way but they have come here without any inducement on our part and have secured their employment without any assistance from us whatever. We cannot offer you any assistance, much as we should be pleased to have the services of a heavy line man.

Sincerely,
P. D. Ldax

4. BY A DIRECTOR

My dear Svtg : —

Your letter of April 8th in reference to [a certain school athlete] has just been received. I am turning this letter over to those in charge of looking after such matters as you make enquiry.

It might be well for you to secure the name and address of the boy and have him write me a letter of inquiry covering such things as he wants to know. The Athletic Directors cannot initiate correspondence with any prospective athlete but they do have the right to answer any inquiries made of them by prospective students. . . .

Sincerely
Director

5. BY TWO SCHOOLBOY ATHLETES "SHOPPING ROUND"

4590 13th St.
Piyr, Ljgv.

Dear Mr. Hlxg

I thought I 'd write you and see how the chance is to come to Jkdy next year to play football. We are two boys who have had three years' of high school experience. Ukj got his leg broke this year at the first of the season and did n't get to make the team here. We 're going to Ljcv. Oqid was not quite good enough to make the first string . . . but he is a fair little halfback. I play end. Of course, we realize that football down here is not played as it is up there, but we think that in a couple of years we could do something under your coaching. Xgzh weighs 150 and plays end and quarter. He is pretty fast, too. He made the [All-state] team at end, as did Oqid. We played with Qjdf and Jdul high schools. Oqid weight 155 and is 5'11" tall, and can pass and carry the ball, but is not extra good on kicking. Xgzh kicks both punts and drop-kicks. What we want to find out is how the chance is for a job up there, and what it would cost us, etc. Could you send us a catalog? We have offers from . . . here, and from Sᴅxɢ Lᴊɢᴠ State College, Wᴋᴊᴜ and the Dᴄsᴢ University. I guess that's about all. Be sure and write us and tell us what you think.

Respectfully,

Cʟʜǫ Oǫɪᴅ

Uᴋᴊ Xɢᴢʜ

B. Refusals to Recruit Athletes

1. a coach replies to an alumnus

Dear Sir:

Your letters of September 4, in reference to Mr. Kʟsᴡᴛ and Mr. Pʟᴀᴅ, have been received. I am returning the clippings which you kindly sent. I have never felt it was right to do trading for athletes, and therefore, while most people regard it as perfectly legitimate to get jobs for incoming athletes, I have never done so at the University. . . . Undoubtedly, these young men are entirely worthy and I hope they will be able to get a college education. Unfortunately, the tuition at the University . . . is $270.00 per year, which makes it difficult for a boy to work his way unless he has some help from home.

Thanking you for your courtesy in writing, I am

Sincerely,

X. L. Mᴅᴀɴ

2. a graduate manager replies to a "shopper's" letter

Dear Sir:

Mr. Gᴀᴇɪ Kᴘᴛɢ has referred to me for answer your letter to him of January 6th.

I am much interested to learn of the possibility of your coming to Gᴋʏᴏ.

There are no scholarships here whatever except those awarded on the basis of competitive examinations and there is no way in which tuition fees may be waived or reduced for anyone. I may say, however, that a substantial number of students earn their way through in part and some of them support themselves entirely.

While there are no jobs in the gift or under the control of the Athletic Association it is generally possible to secure one's board in return for waiting on table. It is more difficult but nevertheless frequently possible to secure one's room in return for such services as taking care of furnaces, shoveling sidewalks, mowing the grass and that sort of thing. A good many students earn substantial sums through acting as agents for the sale of commodities, representing newspapers, etc. Jobs of this latter character, however, are highly competitive and it is seldom that the better ones are secured prior to the junior year.

It's a pretty difficult job for a man to maintain himself financially, keep a satisfactory grade in his studies and at the same time take part in athletics. Nevertheless it has been and is done by a good many and everyone here is anxious to serve and help men who are tempted to do that sort of thing. There is, however, at Gᴋʏᴏ nothing whatever in the way·of an athletic scholarship or a cinch job for athletes.

What I have said may sound cold and discouraging but it is, I believe, unfair to encourage anyone to come to Gᴋʏᴏ under a misapprehension of the facts. We'd like you to come and we'll do everything legitimate and proper to help you help yourself.

If there is anything I can do further with respect to this matter or in connection with the getting of your credentials for admission here please command me.

Very truly yours,

Graduate Manager.

C. Enlisting the Fraternity Chapter

A UNIVERSITY FIELD AGENT WRITES TO THE PRESIDENT OF A FRATERNITY CHAPTER

My dear Sybm,

It is to your interest as well as mine that your chapter considers at this time whether or no they will be able to assist some freshman athlete in earning his room and board next year. We have a number of fine prospects in line and plan on having most of them visit Xmnp sometime before school is out in June. These men will all be good athletes who should make good men for your fraternity as well as for the school.

I will, sometime in the near future, talk to you personally about the situation and give you a slant at our side of the question. It is needless to say, perhaps, but you know the only means we have of helping men is through our fraternities. The alumni is not large enough and rich enough to compete with the larger schools . . . so all we have to offer our prospects is "room and board". If we can not get it from the fraternities we have no other way of getting men to come to Xmnp. Your fraternity and all of the individuals concerned want to see a "Greater Xmnp" in athletics but this will be impossible without the coöperation of every fraternity.

Can you call a special meeting of your chapter and find out definitely, if possible, whether you will be able to help one or more men? If you can write me about the results you obtain at such a meeting it will save much time. We are anxious to get an idea of just how many men we can hope to place. If you are too busy to write, I shall be glad if you will stop me on the street to give me the data but please let us come to some definite understanding as soon as possible.

I will be glad to meet your chapter anytime at your convenience and answer any questions that you may have. I am in hope that I will hear from you soon, either by pen or word, and I wish to remind you again that this is all for a "Greater Xmnp" in athletics.

Yours very truly,

R. S. Mtdx

D. Alumni and Recruiting

1. Arousing Groups of Alumni

A University Field Agent writes to an Alumnus

Dear Sir:

For the past five or six years there has been a gradual improvement in the varsity athletic situation at Jhro University. A survey shows about as follows:

Football has improved materially. This year we had the best team that Jhro has had in years. It was not, however, good enough to be considered by the authorities as a serious contender for conference championship honors or rating as one of the class A teams of the country. . . .

We have held our own in basketball, a sport that is increasing in popularity with a corresponding increase in the caliber of the teams whom we meet.

Last year's baseball team was better than Jhro has had for several years, although not a world beater.

Our track team is, as it always has been, that is, except for an occasional star we have had no track team to speak of.

This gradual improvement has been due in part to the activity of the "General Alumni Committee on athletics." Unfortunately, this committee became disorganized because of lack of sufficient financial support. A new committee has been formed but cannot hope to function unless it gets the required financial support. Several Alumni associations have guaranteed to send the committee a definite amount each month for a period of three years to defray expenses. . . .

J<small>HRO</small> men have the reputation of being more loyal to their Alma Mater than most other schools. The only trouble with them is that they are human and inclined to devote all their energies to their business activities and personal affairs, hoping that someone else will do the hard work connected with J<small>HRO</small> matters and let them come in on the cheering end when the team wins a ball game. Won't you and your association change this situation? Get together now and support us financially. Help us build teams that we can all cheer for.

We want your support in the form of a guarantee that your association will send the Field Secretary's office $25.00 per month between the first and tenth of each month for a period of three years. . . .

As stated above, we are going to have to have money quickly or this committee will be defunct and non-operating. Do not misinterpret our request. We are not going to buy athletes. A bought athlete is no good anyhow. A boy that goes into the game for the love of the sport and love of his school gives all that is in him. A bought athlete never does.

Won't you please advise the committee what you are doing and when we may expect your guarantee.

Yours very truly,

D. I. K<small>ROV</small>

An Alumni Secretary writes to an Alumnus

Dear D<small>QFO</small>:

I am very much put out that this office has not had your correct address for the last few years — hope that we do better in the future. . . .

There is one very important thing that we must depend upon you fellows to put over for L<small>FDB</small> College and that is to send B<small>DLF</small> O<small>DGD</small>, who, I understand, is your outstanding athlete, down here next fall. If you are not already in touch with him I hope you can make contact as soon as possible and let me know if you need any help from this end.

My information says the boy is interested in L<small>FDB</small>. I also know that your high school coach is a good friend of Coach C<small>ODT</small> so that should make a good start. You, of course, understand that the coach cannot make direct contact with players but he can answer any letters he receives and I am always ready to take matters up with him if you write me. If any of our folks are driving down this way it would be fine if O<small>DGD</small> could be brought along to look over the campus. . . .

Will you write me as soon as possible about O<small>DGD</small>?

Sincerely,

Alumni Secretary

2. A RECRUITER REPORTS TO ONE OF A GROUP OF ALUMNI

Dear Sir:

As a contributor to the fund raised by C<small>DGF</small> alumni of the University . . . for the purpose of sending a group of High School seniors to look over the Campus in J<small>QEK</small>, I know you will be interested in a brief report on the trip.

I recently received a letter from [1] Coach O<small>KGB</small> asking me to get in touch with two boys at the F<small>QJI</small> High School. It is interesting to note in passing that their former coach, R<small>DSC</small> U<small>QDI</small>, is a graduate of K<small>UHD</small> — but because of his regard for Q<small>OHX</small> O<small>KGB</small>, he wanted to see his players go to J<small>QEK</small>. I got hold of O<small>DS</small> I<small>FSK</small>, a U. man, and we went out to meet the boys, and through them met two others from the same school, all having

---

[1]This sentence acquires a special interest in view of certain definitions of illegitimate recruiting contained in an agreement entered into by directors of athletics of the conference, September 1, 1926, which runs as follows:
"It is not considered legitimate for Directors and coaches to initiate correspondence or interviews with high school athletes; to request letter men, other students or alumni to initiate correspondence with prospective athletes; or to give names of prospective athletes to the fraternities with the understanding that the fraternity men will rush these athletes."

played on the splendid football team turned out during the past three years. Four great big strapping Polish boys, excelling in baseball, track, basketball, etc. all eager to enter the same university.

We then decided to telephone about 15 men in our club, asking contributions to finance the trip to Jqek. Two hundred and ten dollars was raised, not enough to finance a trip by train, so it fell upon me to offer my car.

Ods Ifsk, the four boys, and I left Cdgf Friday morning — spending the night in Dykd and arriving in Jqek Saturday noon. Ukh Qech, Mr. Okgb's assistant, met us royally and had arranged meals and beds for us at the Dnk Lwk House. Two Dykd Alumni were also in town for the weekend with four boys. . . . .

Then followed a very good baseball game with Hlgf Ezjd, our team winning 5–3 against the pitching of De Szow's son. While we were winning that day in baseball, our track team was trimming Khyd at Jfsx, our golf team beating Lihf, and our tennis team on top in their game — so it was a big Skwd day. . . .

That evening while our four boys were being entertained at the Dnk Lwk House, Ods and I were invited to dine with Mr. and Mrs. Okgb. He certainly is a bundle of energy — working about 12–15 hours a day, just bubbling over with enthusiasm for Skwd and his program every minute. Every one on the Campus is for him — the townspeople, the people all through the state have all felt the influence of his wonderful personality and are all awake and up and at 'em, which is certainly a new atmosphere in Jqek. He introduced us to a big, strapping, nice looking boy named Kdoc, who was working in the house and yard that day. Just a year ago one of our Alumni in Docg, drove with Kdoc to Jqek. Result : he enters school last Fall, was a bear cat on the Freshman team — is working his way through school — and if ever I saw a boy with real Skwd spirit he is the one. He tells me he is bringing three others from Docg with him next fall. That Docg Alumnus has done something for the school, and also for that boy.

The next morning we drove our boys around Clgz — and then went to the Sjin Bimq House for dinner, Mr. and Mrs. Okgb being there also. I was interested to see how the boys in both fraternities did their part in selling Skwd to our boys — also to see the coöperative spirit in the athletic department in making their visitors comfortable and at home; talking with our boys about suitable work they might do to help pay their way through school, etc., etc.

I can't help but feel that the old pendulum has started to swing our way — bound to result in a better athletic situation, and a bigger and better university. Our alumni Association in Dykd has raised a fund of $2500 for the purpose of taking Dykd boys to Jqek with an idea of interesting them in the school.

We left Jqek that afternoon, spending the night in Tzfh, and arriving home Monday evening. Just a word of appreciation to each one of you for your contribution — I will return to our treasurer a small balance which I hope will be conserved for a future trip of similar nature. I only wish each of you could have made the trip for I know you would have got just as much kick out of it as I did.

Yours very truly,

Bejo J. Tigk

3. AN ALUMNUS IS INSTRUCTED IN THE FINE ART OF PROSELYTING

Dear Mr. Jhbc:

When I talked with Lh Dsog recently for suggestions as to whom I should write in the Kndu district on a matter of Ljgd interest, he informed me that you were the generally recognized and highly efficient representative in that part of the country. Since Lh has been appointed chairman of the Alumni Fund it has been necessary for him to give up the work he has been doing for the past three years. I have been delegated to attempt to fill the vacancy.

The matter before us at the present time concerns the case of Fdak Adgj, formerly of Piyr, who was a freshman at the Zcbm School, University of Mbcz, last year. Without doubt you are more or less familiar with this man's athletic ability. Some three years ago while in a Qetu preparatory school he was headed for

LJGD, but since he did not have the necessary credits went to PIYR for a year. While in the latter place JGDV, the MBCZ coach, influenced hi[m] to enter MBCZ in the fall of 1923. He completed the year in June and expected to return this fall. At the present time he is working for his father in QETU and does not wish to return to MBCZ, although JGDV expects him to go back at the beginning of the February term. He desires, very much, to transfer to LJGD, and along this line wrote to JGDA a week before the KHFS game. JGDA turned the letter over to me when I was in MBCZ some 10 days ago and asked me to investigate the circumstances.

ADGJ reports to me that he passed nine out of his ten courses in the two terms last year, and he believes that he ranks in the upper third of his class. You probably know that this latter requirement is necessary for consideration as a transfer to LJGD. Owing to the fact, however, that we know that considerable pressure will be brought to bear on ADGJ as soon as certain of the MBCZ alumni learned of what he has in mind, we believe it best to try to obtain the necessary information through unofficial channels before putting the case up to the Dean at MBCZ. For example, we thought it possible that you could see the Dean at the ZCBM School, and mentioning the fact that FDAK ADGJ had applied for a position in such and such a company you could learn from the Dean just how ADGJ was considered last year, and where he stood relatively in his class. Since you are more familiar with local conditions at MBCZ you, perhaps, will know of a better way of approaching the subject to obtain the desired information. ADGJ's expenses were being paid by a MBCZ alumnus in KNDU, and naturally ADGJ is very anxious that his desire to transfer should not be known until the case is well in hand. While we do not wish to underestimate the ethics of the authorities at ZCBM School, we have been tipped off that it is possible that they would make an unfavorable report of ADGJ's standing if the athletic authorities took a hand in the matter.

Up to the present time this matter has not been brought to the attention of the Dean in MBCZ, and I will await a report from you before taking any further steps. If you could find out that ADGJ stood in the upper third of the class I believe that it would be very easy for us to swing the matter. Your report, of course, would not be mentioned to MBCZ authorities, but we would simply have ADGJ make application for transfer through the regular channels, and the Dean of MBCZ would then write to ZCBM School for the data, which we hope to obtain before hand from you.

Needless to say, we would like very much to see ADGJ at MBCZ, and hope that this roundabout method of attack will enable us to obtain the correct facts from ZCBM School.

Cordially
BJLU CGJO

4. ANOTHER ALUMNUS RECEIVES INSTRUCTION FROM A GENERAL MANAGER

Dear XGZH:

Referring to your letter to Coach LJGDZ relative to MBCET OUTEQ, we certainly are interested in seeing him at KUHTF College. I believe that there is only one way to get OUTEQ interested to the extent that he will want to be in school here and that is to have him on the campus some time this spring, the sooner the better. It does not look any too well to send someone from here to get him and bring him back.

I believe that the best way to bring OUTEQ to the campus is for you to bring him here and then take him back with you. In this way he is merely making a trip with you and we are protecting ourselves at the same time. I will, of course, take care of any expenses which you may incur for the trip. I will appreciate very much an early answer and trust that you can arrange to bring him down at an early date. Bring him any time you can get away, a week end would be better of course. . . .

Hoping to see you soon, I am

Sincerely yours,
[General Manager].

5. A UNIVERSITY PUBLICITY AGENT PROMISES TO HELP AN ALUMNUS IN HIS RECRUITING

Dear Sir:

[The Director of Athletics] has referred yours of July 2nd, regarding AXTDN PLDMJ to me.

As for getting Mr. PLDMJ a job at the [undergraduates clubhouse], I am not at all sure of this but I can promise you that we will be able to get him a job at one of the fraternities or at a restaurant thru which he can easily earn his board.

I wish you would take this up with Mr. PLDMJ and let me know what he decides.

With best wishes I am,

Very truly yours,

[Signature]

E. OFFICE RECORD CARDS FOR RECRUITING

1. RECORD FROM A "PROSPECT" FILE (3 X 5 CARD)

JMFF, KOE L.   FQOO high school
358 PIYR Street
FQOO, ZCBM.

19 years old; 5'10½; varsity football. All-State tackle 1925; fullback; basketball; track; and baseball. Wants a job. XKE FKEI referred him to Coach QETU. Wrote to QETU himself.

2. FORM OF CARD FROM "PROSPECT" FILE (5 X 8 CARD) [2]

	Football	Baseball	Basketball		Swimming	Tennis	Track

Name in full_____ Home address_____

Preparatory School_____ Class_____

Name of parent or guardian_____ Address_____

Father's occupation_____ Can he afford to send son to college_____

Does boy anticipate going to college_____ Where_____

Will he be obliged to work to pay his college expenses_____ Entirely_____ Part_____

What course is he now taking in school:

Classical_____ English_____ Scientific_____

What is his school record as a student_____

What course will he take in college:_____

A.B._____ Ph.B._____ S.B._____ Engineering:

Mechanical_____

Civil_____

Electrical_____

Alumni or undergraduate acquaintances: Give names and addresses

Written	By Whom	Reply	Written	By Whom	Reply

Remarks

[2] This card bears the following notation: "O-Library Bureau 11-36027."

[Reverse of card]

Please fill this side out very carefully

Athletic Record

Age	Weight		Height	

Football	Baseball	Basketball	Swimming	Tennis
Centre	Pitcher	Centre	Short Dist.	
Guard	Catcher	Guard	Long Dist.	
Tackle	1st Base	Forward	Plunger	
End	2d Base		Diving	
Q. Back	3rd Base		Polo	
H. Back	Short Stop			
F. Back	Outfield			

Track Events

Event	Record	Event	Record	Event	Record	Event	Record
100 yd Dash		880 yd Run		120 yd Hurdles		Broad Jump	
220 yd Dash		1 Mile Run		220 yd Hurdles		Pole Vault	
440 yd Run		2 Mile Run		High Jump		Shot Put	

Event	Record
Hammer Throw	
Discus Throw	
Cross Country	

Remarks

3. A FORM OF CARD FROM A "PROSPECT" FILE (5 x 8 CARD)

ATHLETIC PROSPECT CARD   **NUMBER**

Name_____ Address_____

    (Last)   (First)

Prep School_____ Date Graduation_____ Character_____

Recommended by_____ Address_____ Date_____

Alumni in vicinity_____

_____

_____

College Preference_____ Course Desired_____

Branches of Sport	Football	Basketball	Baseball	Track	Minor
Position Played					

Age_____ Height_____ Weight_____

Characteristics of Playing_____

_____

_____

Wrote_____ Reply_____ Answered_____

Catalogue Sent_____ College Life Number Sent _____ Application Blanks_____

F. Dealing with Academic Obstacles

1. A recruiter approaches a college teacher

Dear Mr. Gfls: —

. . .

I am writing to you concerning a Freshman now at Sfhk by the name of Loku whom you had in Freshman English this year. As you know, Loku is one of three men in the Freshman class to receive numerals in three major sports and wherein [sic] I do not maintain that an athlete should be favored as far as marks are concerned, I do feel that a man who can arrive at four B's in four other subjects, and possibly two A's and two B's in these same subjects, should be checked up a little more closely than a man who is low in all of his subjects. Neither do I believe in making an individual case out of any low grade.

I wonder, Mr. Gfls, if you are thoroughly acquainted with Loku's position in regard to finances. Loku is at Sfhk on a scholarship which this last year amounted to, I believe, $200 and through working for his meals and doing various other work in the town, put himself through entirely on this money and no more which, I believe, is a very good record since he found time to participate in three major sports. He cannot look to home for any financial aid due to the fact that his father is dead and his mother is working for a big lawyer in Boston who is a Sfhk man. He, therefore, has to depend solely, as I understand it, upon his scholarship in putting him through Sfhk, and, of course, a low grade or a grade that fails to pass him will very materially cut down this scholarship, and I understand if it is cut down and no other financial aid can be secured, he will have to give up his course and go to work.

For that reason, Mr. Gfls, I am taking the liberty of cashing in on a personal connection which I believe to have with you, and writing to you to see if it will be at all possible for you to re-examine Loku's paper and if at all possible pass him in this course.

It is not because of any fraternal or personal reason that I am writing you but simply because I believe Loku' [sic] to be a good man for Sfhk and we should all give him a helping hand where possible.

I have recently done quite a little business in Hlfs, both at the . . . National Bank with Mr. Lurf Mbde, and at the . . . Savings Bank with Mr. Eqsh, and in the event that you should see them please extend to them my very best regards.

With kind personal regards to you, I am

Very truly yours,
K. D. Kqeo

2. The college teacher replies

Dear Mr. Kqeo —

I was glad to receive your letter of June 23.

Regarding Loku — I shall be willing to re-examine his examination book, although it will not be possible for me to do it until September. Frankly, I doubt if any re-reading will result in changing his grade. He had a low term average, and his examination paper was decidedly poor. It was gone over — as is the custom in the Department — by two other instructors, who O.K.'d the mark I gave him. His book, if I mistake not, is in the possession of Prof. Lhdf Mngo, chairman of the course and of the Department, and I suggest that if you think it necessary to obtain prompt action you write to him, informing him of your correspondence with me, and of the situation in general. I am inclined to think the greatest liberality should be shown in Loku's case and that even with a condition in English . . . he should be allowed to retain his scholarship and go on with his work. I believe that might well be the attitude of the Administration if it were put up to them in the right light. But I don't think that the standards of the English Department can rightly be lowered to compromise the case of one man.

I hope the matter may be adjusted satisfactorily.

Sincerely yours,

LINF Q. GFLS

G. A RECRUITING ENTERPRISE

DOKH High School,

DOKH, KEBU.

February, ____.

Mr. SFHK OUTE

Director of Athletics

MNBF College

ODAF, KEBU

Dear Mr. OUTE: —

It would be more convenient for me, as I busy with my school work, to have your representative come to DOKH and see me. He can see me in the high school any time from Monday until Friday inclusive. If a representative should come and see me he can see my scholastic record on file in the Principal's office.

I have completed, I think, all of the required subjects for admission to MNBF College if I should desire to go there.

If you would rather that I come to MNBF College for an interview, it would be preferable that the time be arranged for some Saturday or Sunday.

Very truly yours,

ADGJ ZCBM

Dear Mr. ZCBM: —

Your letter has been turned over to me since I am the representative for the purpose of looking up football material for the coming year. I am very glad that you are interested in MNBF College and I feel sure you will never regret it if you make up your mind to come to MNBF.

MNBF entrance requirements are as follows: Two years of foreign language, two and a half years of mathematics which means a year and a half of algebra and a year of plane geometry. The total number of high school credits required for entrance is sixteen.

It is impossible at the present time for me to inform you when I could come to DOKH to see you, probably it will be not before March 1st. So if it is possible for you to come to MNBF College for an interview between now and then, it would be entirely satisfactory to me. If you decide to come to ODAF, you can find me at the MNBF Training House. If you decide to come, be sure to write and let me know when you are coming and I will be on the lookout for you.

With best wishes, I beg to remain,

Sincerely yours,

[Freshman Coach]

May, ____.

Dear ADGJ:

Yesterday I received a letter from Mr. GDNP informing me that you had requested him to secure for you the necessary entrance papers for MNBF. I am enclosing herewith the papers.

You will observe that on the application blank there is a request that you send five dollars with your application. This is just a guarantee of good faith to assure the Registrar at MNBF that you are sincere in sending in your entrance credits. We will appreciate your sending this fee to the Registrar. This amount will be refunded to you as soon as school opens.

I am very much pleased that you have definitely decided to enter MNBF. As I have told you before we have a wonderful school here and I am sure that you will never regret your choice. If I can be of service to you at any time or in any way, please advise me.

With kind personal regards and with best wishes, I am,

Sincerely yours,
[Athletic Director]

June, ____.

Mr. K. K. GDNP,
DOKH, KEBU.

Dear Mr. GDNP : —

I am herewith enclosing a letter from ADGJ ZCBM and also my reply to same. It seems as if the young man was wavering somewhat and it may be necessary for all of us to give him a lot of attention. As I have stated in my letter to him, through the general alumni scholarship fund, we can guarantee him his tuition, room and board. As a general rule, this offer is made upon condition that an athlete comes here and makes good. I feel, however, that in the case of ZCBM that he is such a splendid fellow, good student and fine athlete that we can make this proposition unconditionally. I wish you would impress upon him the fact that our proposition to him is not a conditional one. If he comes to MNBF we will take care of him. I will appreciate your keeping after this case and doing all you can to see that he finally comes to MNBF. From his letter you will notice that OJFS is now also in the competition. This means that we will have to continue to work hard on this boy to land him. I will appreciate your keeping me informed upon the status of this case. If you deem it advisable, we will be glad to have another conference with the young man.

With kind personal regards, I am,

Sincerely yours,
[Athletic Director]

P.S.

In his letter, ZCBM says that it will be necessary for him to work, if he entered MNBF and that this might pull down his scholastic and athletic standing. Tell him that it will not be necessary for him to do any outside work during football season. Furthermore, I feel sure that any work he does during the rest of the year will not in any way affect his scholastic or athletic standing. Please impress this upon the young man. I will appreciate your returning his letter to me.

DOKH, KEBU.
July, ____.

Dear Sir : —

Parents did n't come home till 11 o'clock that night and I thought it was too late, and did n't bother to call. Anyhow as soon as they came into the house, I fired questions on them. Their answers were almost the ones I desired which means they are turning my way to a great extent. In the meanwhile I 'll take a little time and discuss it further with them and know I 'll get the decision. I mentioned that fact about the fraternities and they were stunned. That stunt of getting Father LIJY to write home will put over the deciding blow and my victory. Please excuse my writing as I am writing with a anxious heart and a nervous hand. I am doing it right after I came home from work.

Sincerely yours,
ADGJ ZCBM

July, ____.

Dear ADGJ: —

I am very glad to know that your family are giving in to the arguments that you have presented. You have no doubt received the letter from Father LIJY telling you exactly the conditions that exist at MNBF. I am very anxious to learn exactly what your parents think about your coming to MNBF and I hope it is all very favorable to everybody concerned.

We would be glad to have your mother and father come to ODAF and visit the school and know exactly what we have to present to our freshman prospects. I feel sure that this little visit will settle your difficulty once and for all. Be sure to let me know when you plan this visit and I will be on hand.

Just as soon as you have decided on coming to MNBF, you should send your high school credits to our Registrar so that everything will be all set for your entering school this September.

If there is any further information I can give you, do not hesitate in writing to me. With kind personal regards, I am,

Sincerely yours,
[Freshman Coach.]

July, ____.

Dear Mr. [Freshman coach]: —

I received your letter and proceeded to follow its directions when I was detained by a business matter I had to put it aside for the present. I have discovered that the principal had left on his vacation last Tuesday and will not be back until August. Until that time, I will have to occupy my mind with something else. I assure you that I will send those credits to you, the day he hits town and I catch hold of him. I express my gratitude the fact that I can enter MNBF freely and without any further intervenance. My parents have consented and now do believe I did right by choosing your school. I wish to state further that you can take all my trouble off your minds. I am going confident, sincere and determined to make that team next year. I have started to watch my eating and sleeping am taking a few exercises daily. I am ready to take any orders you want me to carry out.

Sincerely yours,
ADGJ ZCBM

August, ____.

Dear ADGJ: —

I have just returned from my vacation and [Freshman coach] has just shown me your last letter to him. I am delighted to know that you have been able to adjust your differences with your parents and that you are coming to MNBF with their approval. As I have told you previously, all of us at MNBF will lend you our best efforts to help make your time at MNBF happy and satisfactory from the standpoint of securing a first class college education. I have no doubt that you will make good at MNBF in every way. I want you to feel that we are your friends and if at any time we can be of service to you, we will be glad to do so.

In due time you will receive definite notice as to the time for your reporting for football. I am glad to know that you are already thinking seriously of football and that you are making an effort to get yourself into the proper physical condition. I shall be glad to hear from you when you feel that you have time to write. . . .

Sincerely yours,
[Athletic Director]

H. An Unsuccessful Attempt to Recruit

LETTERS OF AN ASSISTANT GRADUATE MANAGER TO A HIGH SCHOOL GRADUATE

December, _____.

Dear Sir:

I have been following your record this year on the football team and I am anxious to know when you finish school. I would be pleased to have a list of your credits, together with a record of your age, height, weight and positions played on various teams.

No doubt you are aware of the standing of our school both athletically and scholastically. Our courses are nationally recognized and I feel sure you would make no mistake by looking them over.

I am anxious to have a talk with you and as soon as I can get the above information will make arrangements to see you.

Very truly yours,
[Asst. Graduate Manager]

December, _____.

Dear Sir: —

I was surely very glad to get your letter and the information that you sent.

Your credits look very good and I will make plans to see you sometime in January. I would like to have you come here for it will give you a better chance to look the school over. If it is not convenient for you to get down let me know and I will arrange to call and see you. I will ask you to suggest a date that is suitable to you.

Wishing you a very Merry Christmas and a Happy New Year, I remain,

Very truly yours,
[Asst. Graduate Manager]

January, _____.

Dear Sir:

Would like to meet you at the [hotel] Wednesday, about five thirty or six o'clock.

We will have dinner there and talk matters over in regard to college next fall.

Very truly yours,
[Asst. Graduate Manager]

If not suitable wire me Tuesday.

February, _____.

Dear Sir:

Since our conversation sometime ago, I have been wondering how you are coming along with your school work and if you have been able to get sufficient credits to enter here in the Fall.

Our Basketball Team has been going at a pretty good clip and last week defeated . . . our city rival. They are on an Eastern trip this week and we hope it will be a successful one. Next week we play Hlgf Eqjc, Szhe, and Sfqs, which means a big week for the boys.

I surely hope that you have been able to get your schedule arranged and that we will find your credits in good shape in the Spring.

Please let me hear from you as to how you are coming along.

Very truly yours,
[Asst. Graduate Manager]

March, ____.

Dear SKDI:

I am enclosing an application blank which I wish you would return immediately so that the Registrar can get your credits and we will know exactly how you are fixed for entrance in the Fall. Even though your credits this semester will not be sent, if our Registrar knows what subjects you are taking now he can act on your total credits accordingly.

Please return this application at your earliest possible convenience for it is necessary to have your credits acted upon as soon as possible.

Very truly yours,
[Asst. Graduate Manager]

March, ____.

Dear GLT:

It has been sometime since I have seen you, and I am quite anxious to have a talk with you in the near future. I am wondering if it will be possible for you to get down Saturday morning, . . . at our expense. Either of these dates suits me alright, but pick the one that suits you best.

I surely hope that you can find it possible to get down, and if not, please let me know and I will try to come up to see you.

Very truly yours,
[Asst. Graduate Manager]

April, ____.

Dear GLT:

Well how is work going by this time? You have picked a rather cold winter to work it seems to me, but one has no jurisdiction over such things.

Exams are all over and the boys came through in good shape. Every one of the varsity and freshman teams are still in school and doing well. The freshmen came through in fine order and we are going to keep a close tab on them the rest of the year so they will all be back in the fall. We sure expect to have one sweet line next year as we only lost IFKW on the varsity line and the Fresh coming on are going to make things interesting. There are not so many good backs, but more than usual and enough to get by in good shape. We have an extra hard schedule next year though in such teams as SZHE, LJFV, ECGF, HDSN, DGJT, HLGF EQJC. It makes six hard ones, but we should come thru in good order. The Fresh have about the same schedule as last year and we are going to have just as good a team as this year. It is hard to find good linemen though.

About your brace, if you could come down some time this summer I think GDFH JEMH could devise a good pad and then we could have Spauldings make it up special. I am sure we can get you fixed up though. Could you come down for a basketball game sometime this winter. We play some good games at home soon and if you could come let me know.

I was also wondering if you plan to take applied art or architecture next fall. I would like to know about this so I can look up your credits. Well lots of luck GLT and let me hear from you soon.

Sincerely,
[Asst. Graduate Manager]

April, ____.

Dear GLT:

I was pleased to get your letter and application last week and I hope that your credits are sent in very soon. I am anxious to have these acted on so if any difficulty arises in regard to same we will have plenty of time to get it fixed up.

I hope that you succeed in getting down to the Track Meet for I would like to have another talk with you sometime this Spring. If you do not get down, I would like to have you down for [Festivities] Week. . . . this is our big home coming affair and I am sure that you will enjoy same.

Hoping to hear from you as to whether you can get down on one of these dates or not, I remain

Very truly yours,
[Asst. Graduate Manager]

April, _____.

Dear Sir:

I understand from the Registrar's Office that the certificate which they sent for your credits has not been returned as yet. I am very anxious to have your credits acted on immediately and I hope that you will send this in as soon as possible.

If the delay is in your Principal's office, I wish you would speak to them and have them hurry it along as much as possible. If there is any reason that this cannot be sent in now, please let me know so that I can explain the trouble to the Registrar.

Very truly yours,
[Asst. Graduate Manager]

P.S. I would like to know soon as to whether you plan to get down with your Track Team on [date]

April, _____.

Dear GLT:

We have succeeded in arranging a personal interview for you with our Registrar. It is necessary though that your credits be acted upon before this time. I wish you would have your Principal send these to us immediately so that they will be acted upon, before you are down here for the Track Meet, at which time we can interview the Registrar and get all difficulties straightened out.

Trusting that you will send these immediately, I remain

Very truly yours,
[Asst. Graduate Manager]

April, _____.

Dear GLT:

Received your letter and am glad to know that you will be down.

In regard to your credits, would suggest that you speak to your principal and ask him to send in the credits, that you already have and state in a letter the subjects that you are taking this semester and then when the semester is over all they will have to send in is the remaining credits.

I[t] would also be a good idea to have him send a letter of recommend with these credits, stating how you stand scholastically. A letter of this kind will help a lot.

Hoping to see you. . . .

Sincerely,
[Asst. Graduate Manager]

May, _____.

Dear GLT:

As soon as you possibly can, I wish you would send in your credits, for I am very anxious to have these acted upon in the near future. No doubt your school is about finished now, and your Principal will be willing to send these in, I hope right away.

As I suggested, I wish you would have him send a letter of recommendation with it so that if possible it will help your credits along to some extent.

We are counting strong on having you with us in the fall, and as things look now, we are going to have a fine Freshman team.

I trust that you will get these in very soon and that we will find them in good shape.

Very truly yours,
[Asst. Graduate Manager]

May, ——.

Dear GLT:

I am sorry to have been delayed in answering your letter, . . .

In regard to the camp job. The boy here at school who had the job is going to take it as he does not have to go to summer school as he thought. I have called our employment bureau and if there is anything that way turned in now I will get it for you, but I doubt if there will be now.

Your credits have not arrived yet GLT and if you would have your principal hurry these along it would help a lot.

Things sure look fine for the Freshman team and I am getting anxious for Sept. to roll around. I am sorry about the job.

Sincerely yours,
[Asst. Graduate Manager]

June, ——.

Dear GLT:

I was very glad to learn in the Registrar's Office the other day that your credits had been accepted, and that you were admitted without examinations. You will have a technical test though, which you will have no trouble in passing. It does not come until September so you can take that when you are down here at Football Camp.

It has been sometime since I have heard from you, and I am wondering how you are getting along. I surely hope that you were able to locate some work so that you can keep going during the summer.

Things are surely lining up fine for fall, and I can assure you that you will feel good when you report and see the various Freshmen who will be playing with you.

Please let me hear from you, as I am eager to know how you are getting along.

Very truly yours,
[Asst. Graduate Manager]

July, ——.

Dear SKDI:

Not hearing from you for some time, I have been wondering what you are doing this summer and how you are getting along. We are counting strongly on having you with us when Camp opens. . . . I surely hope that you will plan to be here at the opening, for Camp does a great deal in the way of getting one in condition.

I am enclosing our Freshman football schedule for next fall, and I am sure that you will agree with me that our team will have to be in good condition to get away with it as successfully as we hope to.

I can assure you that I would appreciate hearing from you as to what you are doing and how you are getting along.

Very truly yours,
[Asst. Graduate Manager]

Special Delivery

July, ——.

Dear GLT:

I was surely very much disappointed when I received your letter stating that you were thinking of not entering here in the fall. I have been counting very strongly on having you with us and I know that you would be more than satisfied with our School, also. If I would call at your home Thursday of this week, in the afternoon, after you are home from work, would it be possible for me to see you and your father? I would like very much to have a talk with him and explain our courses here more thoroughly.

Unless I receive a wire from you, you may expect me sometime Thursday afternoon.

Very truly yours,

[Asst. Graduate Manager]

August, ——.

Dear GLT:

I am very sorry that you have decided not to enter here this Fall and I can assure you that you have my best wishes at VFZH. I feel sure that you will make good no matter where you go.

If, by any chance, your arrangements at VFZH should fall through between now and September 1, I can assure you that I would be glad to have you report here.

Wishing you all kinds of luck I remain

Very truly yours,

[Asst. Graduate Manager]

December, ——.

Dear GLT:

Where have you been keeping yourself all year. No doubt by this time you are a millionaire and very prosperous. I am sorry that you were n't with our freshmen this year, for we could have used a man of your type just fine. The freshies had a fine year though and are sure making good in their school work too. Things look fine for next fall.

How do you stand for next fall? We sure want you back here with us and I hope that you figure the same. If you want to get in (architecture, building const.,) or one of the other courses, let me know so if there is anything to be done about your credits we can start now to fix them up.

If you know of any good high school boys, particularly good big linemen, please send me their names.

Let me hear from you very soon GLT and wishing you a very Merry Christmas, I remain

Sincerely,

[Asst. Graduate Manager]

February, ——.

Dear GLT:

I was over to see the registrar the other day about your credits and I also asked him how your credits apply for architecture. As I remember you were short your geometry, but I think you can get a condition in that subject.

I am enclosing an application blank, which I wish you would return so that the registrar will have it on file.

The boys all came through fine in exams. We only lost one man from the freshman team.

Sincerely,

[Asst. Graduate Manager]

J. Relations between School and University Coaches

1. A school coach writes to his friend, a college coach

Dear Dykd,

Received yours and I was glad to hear from you. We play here Saturday evenings January 2nd and Saturday January 29th. we play at Zhel but play here February fifth and Saturday February 12th so that only Saturday date we play away from home during January or February is at Zhel on Saturday January 29th.

Idox, Jmfl, Clgb all set for you. Dzhe said Hdsn was too big but I will have him go over to see you when he is over at Jlmh Fdvh spring vacation last of March. K. Xjkg is at Hlgf Czjc this year and Dzhe thinks well of Hlgf Czjc as only objection to Hdsn is size of city too many attractions and too near Jlmh Fdvh.

Get Vlok to get you Xzfb, Sydo and Ydsk fine quarterbacks very shifty good drop kicker 165. Jmfl of Lgnj Khfs. lives in Hdou near me and he was out to house last summer to come to Cdzh but Nvdw Ouhf sent him to Lgnj. five feet 9½ weighs about 200 and I heard he went big for Lgnj this year. I have couple or three other fellows here that want to go to Zdvc as they have friends attending Zdvc and they have been boosting Zdvc but I can get them for you although they think Hdsn a little too large. Let me know if you want them. Get those three from Zdvc if you. Kvlh from Ouhk is at Vkje School with Gdac. Let me know when you are planning on coming to Ncge. I am at home every Sunday so come out to house and stay.

Yours truly,

Diljh

2. The college coach replies

Dear Diljh:

Your letter of . . . received. Hope you keep after Gdac. I will be in Ncge sometime in July and will see him also.

I am glad to know Idox, Clgb and Jmfl are all set and hope Jnbd will be to. I told Fklf to have his brother write you and you will hear from him shortly. Dlhy is O.K. and so is Vhme. I will get in touch with Lonr when I get to Zdvc, and we will know about him shortly.

Zect of Zdvc is going to be a high class tackle and will talk to him when I get to Zdvc.

Let me know if anything develops on Gdac.

Sincerely yours,

Ljih D. Jegc

3. A school coach places an athlete

Dear Fbjm:

This will introduce you to Jzfg who played end here last two years. Jzfg will be one of your regular varsity men with a year on freshman team weighs 178 stripped 19 years old. If you cannot fix him up same as other men why look after him with full tuition and a job for board and room waiting on table as he is willing to work for board and room.

Best of luck.

Yours truly

Ckoh

III

THE EMPLOYMENT OF ATHLETES

NOTE: The following schedule indicates the nature of the part-time employment pursued by a total of 1,292 athletes studied in the course of the enquiry.

Nature of Employment		Number of Athletes Employed	
Waiterships, etc.			
Waiters for board at boarding houses, etc.		270	
Waiters for board at fraternity houses		122	
Waiters faculty club		1	
Waiters sorority house		1	
Total waiters			394
Managers fraternity houses for board and room		20	
Commissary fraternity house		4	
Treasurer fraternity house		1	
Steward fraternity house		2	
Janitor fraternity house		1	
Total fraternity house employees			28
Dishwashers		20	
Kitchen assistants		17	
Furnace tenders		12	
Doormen, 'varsity club		4	
Houseman		1	
Total			54
Athletic Department			
Gatemen at games	60	Policemen at games	5
Gymnasium	36	Swimming guards	5
Athletic department	26	Clerks athletic office	4
Ticket sellers	21	University laundry	3
Wash towels in gymnasium	17	Training room	3
Check room	17	Publicity department	2
Labor athletic field	14	Clean gymnasium pool	1
Athletic equipment	14	Stadium office	1
Concessions	13	Store room	1
Life guard	12	Instructor boxing	1
Stadium labor	7	Instructor swimming	1
Selling advertising for programs	6	Stenographer athletic department	1
Athletic programs	6	Total	277
Employ of University			
Janitors university buildings	94	Alumni office	2
Labor	39	Agriculture dept.	2
Painting	26	Building dept.	2
School labor	24	Accounting dept.	2

Clerks	24	Wash windows	2
Student assistants	12	Dramatic art dept.	1
Dormitories, monitors	9	Extension dept.	1
Nightwatchmen	7	Custodian Student Union	1
Readers	6	Stenographer	1
Library assistants	5	Laboratory instructor	1
Checking privileges, dances	4	Delivery copy	1
University employ	3	Binding in library	1
Prefects	3	Secretary-Treasurer office	1
		Total	274

Other Work

Clerks	34	Unknown	102
Dance officials	20	Delicatessen	1
Salesmen	13	Agent	1
Theatres	7	Collector	1
Hotels	7	Telephone collector	1
Filling stations	7	Sports writer	1
Post office employees	7	Paper carrier	1
Refreshment stands	5	Ambulance driver	1
Taxi drivers	4	Office work	1
Waiters at cafés	4	Mail room	1
Musicians, singers	4	Cashier	1
Officials at games	3	Repairing typewriters	1
Oil company	3	Chores	1
Railroad	2	Work in private home	1
Trust company	2	Bellboy	1
Firemen	2	Canning factory	1
Singers	2	Office boy	1
Hospital assistants	2	Power and light co.	1
Laundry	2	Coaching	1
Salesmen insurance	2	Tutor	1
Cleaning	2	Gardener	1
Armory	1	Stenographer	1
Sporting goods	1	Baker	1
Drug store	1	Multigraph operator	1
Clothing store	1	Electrician	1
Chauffeur	1	Total	265
		GRAND TOTAL,	1,292

IV

MATERIALS ON THE HYGIENE OF ATHLETIC TRAINING

NOTE: For lists of the universities, colleges, and schools visited in connection with the enquiry into the Hygiene of Athletic Training, which forms the subject of Chapter VII of this study, see Appendix I, above. In the following tables, the colleges and universities are indicated by letters. T = total. IC = intercollegiate. IM = intramural.

TABLE A

Participation in Athletics at Twenty-two Universities and Colleges

College	Enrollment	Football Total	i.c.	i.m.	Crew Total	i.c.	i.m.	Basketball Total	i.c.	i.m.	Cross-Country Total	i.c.	i.m.
A	3925	45	45	0				40	40	0			
B	3590	140	140	0	104	40	64	740	40	700	180	20	160
C	1465	135	100	35				135	35	100	25	25	0
D	3799	370	70	300							100	100	0
E	1370	146	146	0				333	60	273	28	28	0
F	852	110	110	0				279	54	225	35	35	0
G	420	65	65	0				143	35	108	20	20	0
H	2800	115	115	0	66	34	32	214	30	184	29	29	0
I	697	100	100	0				40	40	0	15	15	0
J	500	120	60	60				160	30	130	25	25	0
K	3000	285	110	175				560	40	520	70	70	0
L	215	83	45	38				124	24	100	18	0	18
M	715	74	44	30				165	90	75			
N	5421	500	150	350	500	150	350	400	100	300	35	35	0
O	2157	196	135	61	333	132	201	451	57	394	60	20	40
P	1000	200	50	150				95	20	75	10	10	0
Q	5531	343	343	0				1910	175	1735	391	40	351
R	2370	140	140	0				572	37	535	66	25	41
S	4766	1413	300	1113	80	80	0	1350	100	1250	299	119	180
T	5334	265	265	0				1032	222	810	214	154	60
X	3048	306	196	110	391	218	173	199	84	115	95	95	0
Z	2649	249	249	0				684	123	561	137	50	87
Totals 22	55,624	5400	2978	2422	1474	654	820	9626	1434	8190	1852	915	937

College	Enrollment	Track Total	i.c.	i.m.	Baseball Total	i.c.	i.m.	Soccer Total	i.c.	i.m.	Lacrosse Total	i.c.	i.m.	Boxing Total	i.c.	i.m.
A	3925	80	80	0	65	65	0							15	15	0
B	3590	120	120	0	456	36	420	405	30	375	40	40	0	40	0	40
C	1465	80	30	50	85	50	35	25	25	0	40	40	0	20	0	20
D	3799	450	150	300	300	25	275	25	25	0	25	25	0			
E	1370	359	105	254	367	51	316	34	34	0	34	34	0			
F	852	72	72	0	130	130	0				38	38	0			
G	420	60	60	0	40	40	0	60	60	0						
H	2800	127	35	92	235	28	207	41	41	0	56	56	0	28	28	0
I	697	225	150	75	85	85	0	40	40	0				50	0	50
J	500	130	100	30	155	25	130	95	30	65						
K	3000	340	90	250	755	40	715	50	50	0	30	30	0	205	30	175
L	215	65	30	35	90	30	60	40	0	40				14	0	14
M	715	50	50	0	240	30	210							13	0	13
N	5421	375	125	250	325	75	250	200	75	125	65	65	0	440	40	400
O	2157	401	210	191	375	65	310	200	140	60	197	125	72	16	0	16
P	1000	50	50	0	145	25	120	30	30	0	30	30	0	20	0	20
Q	5531	665	185	480	481	241	240	60	0	60				230	0	230
R	2370	232	120	112	50	50	0							28	0	28
S	4766	652	162	490	965	85	880									
T	5334	480	125	355	580	120	460							175	0	175
X	3048	205	205	0	275	150	125	80	80	0	85	85	0	121	51	70
Z	2649	653	305	348	756	165	591							20	0	20
Totals 22	55,624	5871	2559	3312	6955	1611	5344	1385	660	725	640	568	72	1435	164	1271

College	Enrollment	Wrestling Total	i.c.	i.m.	Swimming Total	i.c.	i.m.	Hockey Total	i.c.	i.m.	Fencing Total	i.c.	i.m.	Total	i.c.	i.m.
A	3925	15	15	0	30	30	0							290	290	0
B	3590	40	20	20	70	15	55	170	20	150	20	20	0	2525	541	1984
C	1465	100	100	0	375	25	350				20	20	0	1040	450	590
D	3799							125	25	100				1395	420	975
E	1370	88	58	30	223	91	132	35	0	35				1647	607	1040
F	852				30	30	0							694	469	225
G	420							10	10	0	40	40	0	447	339	108
H	2800	31	31	0	17	17	0	19	19	0	9	9	0	987	472	515
I	697	25	0	25	125	50	75	105	45	60				810	525	285
J	500	40	0	40	150	35	115							875	305	570
K	3000	215	40	175							25	25	0	2535	525	2010
L	215	6	0	6										440	129	311
M	715													542	214	328
N	5421	425	125	300	475	75	400				150	25	125	3890	1040	2850
O	2157	105	75	30	232	100	132	189	45	144	47	12	35	2802	1116	1686
P	1000	45	15	30	50	25	25							675	255	420
Q	5531	451	81	370	1003	68	935	87	87	0	95	0	95	5716	1220	4496
R	2370	95	15	80	350	50	300							1533	437	1096
S	4766	195	65	130	425	85	340	346	46	300	36	0	36	5761	1042	4719
T	5334	176	86	90	535	85	450	382	120	262				3839	1177	2662
X	3048	85	85	0	446	226	220	196	116	80	167	112	55	2651	1703	948
Z	2649	243	74	169	87	87	0							2829	1053	1776
Totals 22	55,624	2380	885	1495	4623	1094	3629	1673	542	1131	609	263	346	43,923	14,329	29,594

TABLE B

Number of Participants in Thirteen Specified Sports—Intercollegiate and Intramural

College	Number of Male Students Enrolled	Football		Crew		Basketball		Cross-Country		Track		Baseball	
		i.c.	i.m.	i.c.	i.m.	i.c.	i.m.	i.c.	i.m.	i.c.	i.m.	i.c.	i.m.
I	500	100	†	†	†	40	†	15	†	150	75	85	†
E	1200	146	†	†	†	60	273	28	†	105	254	51	316
M	600	44	30	†	†	90	75	†	†	50	†	30	210
Y	6200	135	275	87	72	30	808	†	10	181	160	126	630
R	3000	140	†	†	†	37	535	25	41	120	112	50	†
A	2500	45	†	†	†	40	†	†	†	80	†	65	†
F	900	110	†	†	†	54	225	35	†	72	†	130	†
B	4200	140	†	40	64	40	700	20	160	120	†	36	420
G	450	65	†	†	†	35	108	20	†	60	†	40	†
D	6300	70	300	*	*	*	*	100	†	150	300	25	275
AB	2800	175	†	†	†	133	265	25	55	150	76	80	321
Z	3000	249	†	†	†	123	561	50	87	305	348	165	591
P	1000	50	150	†	†	20	75	10	†	50	†	25	120
C	1500	100	35	†	†	35	100	25	†	30	50	50	35
Q	7200	343	†	†	†	175	1735	40	351	185	480	241	240
T	6700	265	†	†	†	222	810	154	60	125	355	120	460
N	8000	150	350	150	350	100	300	35	†	125	250	75	250
K	3200	110	175	†	†	40	520	70	†	90	250	40	115
O	2400	135	61	132	201	57	394	20	40	210	191	65	310
L	215	45	38	†	†	24	100	†	18	30	35	30	60
H	2800	115	†	34	32	30	184	29	†	35	92	25	207
J	550	60	60	†	†	30	130	25	†	100	30	25	130
S	4837	300	1113	80	†	100	1250	119	180	162	490	85	880
X	3051	196	110	218	173	84	115	95	†	205	†	150	125
U	*	*	*	†	†	*	*	*	*	*	*	*	*
Totals 25	73,103	3288	2697	741	892	1599	9263	940	1002	2890	3498	1717	6295

College	Number of Male Students Enrolled	Soccer		Lacrosse		Boxing		Wrestling		Swimming		Hockey		Fencing	
		i.c.	i.m.	i.c.	i.m.	i.c.	i.m.	i.c.	i.m.	i.c.	i.m.	i.c.	i.m.	i.c.	i.m.
I	500	40	†	†	†	†	50	†	25	50	75	45	60	†	†
E	1200	34	†	34	†	†	†	58	30	91	132	†	35	†	†
M	600	†	†	†	†	13	†	†	†	†	†	†	†	†	†
Y	6200	65	75	†	†	26	33	20	26	51	95	†	†	18	21
R	3000	†	†	†	†	†	28	15	80	50	300	†	†	†	†
A	2500	†	†	†	†	15	†	15	†	30	†	†	†	†	†
F	900	†	†	38	†	†	†	†	†	30	†	†	†	†	†
B	4200	30	375	40	†	†	40	20	20	15	55	20	150	20	†
G	450	60	†	†	†	†	†	†	†	†	†	19	†	40	†
D	6300	25	†	25	†	*	*	*	*	†	*	25	100	*	*
AB	2800	†	†	†	†	20	35	45	42	30	66	†	†	†	†
Z	3000	†	†	†	†	†	20	74	169	87	†	†	†	†	†
P	1000	30	†	30	†	†	20	15	30	25	25	†	†	†	†
C	1500	25	†	40	†	†	20	20	100	25	350	†	†	20	†
Q	7200	†	60	†	†	†	230	81	370	68	935	87	†	†	95
T	6700	†	†	†	†	†	175	86	90	85	450	120	262	†	†
N	8000	75	125	65	†	40	400	125	300	75	400	†	†	25	125
K	3200	50	†	30	†	30	175	40	175	†	†	†	†	25	†
O	2400	140	60	125	72	†	16	75	30	100	132	45	144	12	35
L	215	†	40	†	†	†	14	†	6	†	†	†	†	†	†
H	2800	41	†	56	†	28	†	31	†	17	†	19	†	9	†
J	550	30	65	†	†	†	†	†	40	35	115	†	†	†	†
S	4837	†	†	†	†	†	†	65	130	85	340	46	300	36	†
X	3051	80	†	85	†	51	70	85	†	226	220	116	80	112	55
U	*	*	*	†	†	*	*	*	*	*	*	†	†	*	*
Totals 25	73,103	725	800	568	72	223	1326	950	1563	1175	3670	542	1131	317	331

(NOTE) * Data lacking.
† Sport not engaged in.

Table C

Number of Fractures, Dislocations, and Chronic Sprains Occurring Yearly in Thirteen Sports—Intercollegiate and Intramural

College	Football						Crew			Basketball						Cross-Country				Track						Baseball					
	Fractures i.c.	Fractures i.m.	Dislocations i.c.	Dislocations i.m.	Cr. Sprains i.c.	Cr. Sprains i.m.	Fractures	Dislocations	Cr. Sprains	Fractures i.c.	Fractures i.m.	Dislocations i.c.	Dislocations i.m.	Cr. Sprains i.c.	Cr. Sprains i.m.	Fractures	Dislocations	Cr. Sprains i.c.	Cr. Sprains i.m.	Fractures i.c.	Fractures i.m.	Dislocations i.c.	Dislocations i.m.	Cr. Sprains i.c.	Cr. Sprains i.m.	Fractures i.c.	Fractures i.m.	Dislocations i.c.	Dislocations i.m.	Cr. Sprains i.c.	Cr. Sprains i.m.
I	3	†	0	†	9	†	(None)	(None)	(None)	0	†	0	†	2	†	(None)	(None)	0	†	0	0	0	0	5	0	0	†	0	†	3	†
E	4	†	4	†	5	†				2	0	1	0	3	0			0	0	0	0	0	0	2½	0	1	0	0	0	1	†
M	3	0	1	0	6	†				2	0	1	1	4	0			†	†	0	†	0	†	0	†	0	0	0	0	0	0
Y	*	*	*	*	*	*				*	*	*	*	*	*			†	*	*	*	*	*	*	*	*	*	*	*	*	*
R	0	†	1	0	4	0				0	0	0	0	2	0			0	0	0	0	0	0	3	0	0	†	0	0	0	0
A	4	†	2	†	15	†				1	†	2	†	5	†			0	†	0	†	0	†	5	†	5	†	5	†	2	†
F	0	†	3½	†	5½	†				0	1	0	0	4	0			0	†	0	†	0	†	0	†	3	†	0	†	0	†
B	4	†	12	†	6	†				1	0	⅓	?	2	?			½	0	½	†	⅓	†	2	†	1	2	½	?	1	0
G	0	†	2	†	3	†				0	0	1	0	1	0			2	†	0	†	0	†	5	†	0	†	6½	†	2½	†
D	1	9	6	44	10	20				3	0	4	1	4	2			4	†	0	0	0	0	5	15	3	0	2	0	10	20
AB	*	†	*	†	*	†				*	*	*	*	*	*			*	*	*	*	*	*	*	*	*	†	*	*	*	*
Z	2	†	2	†	2	†				0	0	0	0	1	0			0	0	0	0	0	0	0	0	0	0	0	0	0	0
P	1	1	2	0	32	0				0	0	0	0	5½	0			0	†	0	†	0	†	0	†	1	0	0	0	4	1
C	8	2	2	0	3	0				0	0	0	0	1	0			0	†	0	†	0	†	0	†	3	0	5	0	1	0
Q	1	†	2	†	5	†				0	0	0	0	3	0			0	0	0	0	0	0	0	0	0	0	0	0	0	0
T	2	†	5	†	7	†				1	0	0	0	0	0			0	0	1	0	0	0	3	0	0	0	1	0	1	0
N	3	1	22	5	7	0				1	0	1	0	0	0			0	†	0	0	0	0	1	0	0	0	2	0	0	0
K	5	0	5	0	6	0				0	0	0	0	3	0			1	†	0	0	0	0	0	0	1	0	2	0	2	0
O	2	0	9	0	16	†				0	0	2	0	0	6			0	0	0	0	0	0	0	0	0	0	0	0	0	0
L	1	0	3	0	2	0				1	0	0	0	0	0			†	0	0	0	0	0	0	0	1	0	0	0	0	0
H	20	†	39	†	12	†				0	0	10	0	4½	6½			6½	†	0	0	0	0	3½	†	0	0	0	4	5	0
J	6	0	6	0	1	1				0	0	0	0	1	2			0	†	5	0	0	0	0	0	0	0	4½	0	2	1
S	3	3	5	6	10	12				0	0	3	4	4	5			1	2	0	0	0	0	4	5	2	4	6	6	10	12
X	3	0	2	0	3	0				0	0	0	0	0	0			0	†	0	†	0	†	0	†	3	0	0	0	0	0
U	*	*	*	*	*	*				*	*	*	*	*	*			*	*	*	*	*	*	*	*	*	*	*	*	*	*
Totals 25	76	16	135	55	169	33				12	1	25	6	50	21			15	2	6	0	⅓	0	39	20	24	6	34	10	44	34

College	Soccer						Lacrosse						Boxing						Wrestling						Swimming			Hockey					Fencing		
	Fractures i.c.	Fractures i.m.	Dislocations i.c.	Dislocations i.m.	Cr. Sprains i.c.	Cr. Sprains i.m.	Fractures i.c.	Fractures i.m.	Dislocations i.c.	Dislocations i.m.	Cr. Sprains i.c.	Cr. Sprains i.m.	Fractures i.c.	Fractures i.m.	Dislocations i.c.	Dislocations i.m.	Cr. Sprains i.c.	Cr. Sprains i.m.	Fractures i.c.	Fractures i.m.	Dislocations i.c.	Dislocations i.m.	Cr. Sprains i.c.	Cr. Sprains i.m.	Fractures	Dislocations	Cr. Sprains	Fractures i.c.	Fractures i.m.	Dislocations	Cr. Sprains i.c.	Cr. Sprains i.m.	Fractures	Dislocations	Cr. Sprains
I	0	†	0	†	0	†	†	†	†	†	†	†	†	0	†	0	†	0	†	0	†	2	†	1½	(None)	(None)	(None)	0	0	(None)	0	0	(None)	(None)	(None)
E	0	†	0	0	2	0	0	†	1	†	3	†	†	†	†	†	†	†	0	0	1	0	1	0				†	0		0	0			
M	†	†	†	†	†	†	†	†	†	†	†	†	0	†	0	†	0	†	†	†	†	†	†	†				†	†		†	†			
Y	*	*	*	*	*	*	†	†	†	†	†	†	*	*	*	*	*	*	*	*	*	*	*	*				*	*		†	†			
R	†	†	†	†	†	†	†	†	†	†	†	†	†	0	†	0	†	0	0	0	0	0	0	0				†	†		†	†			
A	†	†	†	†	†	†	†	†	†	†	†	†	1	†	1	†	3	†	0	†	0	†	3	†				†	†		†	†			
F	†	†	†	†	†	†	3	†	0	†	1	†	†	†	†	†	†	†	†	†	†	†	†	†				†	†		†	†			
B	⅓	0	1	0	1	0	0	†	0	†	1	†	†	2	†	½	†	3	½	0	⅓	0	1	0				0	0		0	0			
G	0	†	0	†	0	†	†	†	†	†	†	†	†	†	†	†	†	†	†	†	†	†	†	†				0	†		0	†			
D	0	†	0	†	10	†	2	†	0	†	5	†	2	†	0	0	2	0	1	0	8	2	8	2				1	0		3	1			
AB	†	†	†	†	†	†	†	†	†	†	†	†	*	*	*	*	*	*	*	*	*	*	*	*				†	†		†	†			
Z	†	†	†	†	†	†	†	†	†	†	†	†	†	0	†	0	†	0	1	0	0	0	2	0				†	†		†	†			
P	1	†	0	†	12	†	0	†	0	†	0	†	†	0	†	0	†	5	0	0	0	0	0	0				†	†		†	†			
C	3	†	0	†	3	†	4	†	0	†	3	†	†	0	†	0	†	0	0	†	0	†	1	†				†	†		†	†			
Q	†	0	†	0	†	0	†	†	†	†	†	†	†	0	†	0	†	0	1	0	2	0	0	0				0	†		0	†			
T	†	†	†	†	†	†	†	†	†	†	†	†	†	1	†	0	†	0	1	0	0	0	1	0				1	0		0	0			
N	1	0	2	0	2	0	0	†	0	†	0	†	4	0	0	0	0	0	3	0	3	3	0	0				†	†		†	†			
K	0	†	0	†	2	†	1	†	0	†	0	†	0	4	0	0	0	2	0	0	3	0	0	0				†	†		†	†			
O	1	0	½	0	5	0	0	0	1	0	0	0	†	1	†	2	†	0	1	0	1	0	0	0				0	0		3	0			
L	†	0	†	0	†	0	†	†	†	†	†	†	†	0	†	0	†	0	†	0	†	0	†	0				†	†		†	†			
H	0	†	11	†	3	†	0	†	3	†	0	†	0	†	0	†	2	†	0	†	4	†	5	†				0	†		0	†			
J	0	0	0	0	0	0	†	†	†	†	†	†	†	†	†	†	†	†	†	0	†	0	†	0				†	†		†	†			
S	†	†	†	†	†	†	†	†	†	†	†	†	†	†	†	†	†	†	1	2	1	1	0	0				1	2		0	0			
X	0	†	1	†	0	†	0	†	0	†	1	†	1	0	0	0	0	0	0	†	0	†	2	†				0	0		0	0			
U	*	*	*	*	*	*	†	†	†	†	†	†	*	*	*	*	*	*	*	*	*	*	*	*				†	†		†	†			
Totals 25	6	0	15	0	40	0	10	0	5	0	14	0	8	8	1	2	7	10	9	2	23	8	24	3				3	2		6	1			

(NOTE) * Data lacking.
† Sport not engaged in.

TABLE D

Number of Cases of Internal Injury, Collapse, and Concussion Occurring Yearly in Thirteen Sports—Intercollegiate and Intramural

Football columns are split into intercollegiate (i.c.) and intramural (i.m.) values. *Data lacking; † Sport not engaged in.

College	Football — Int. Injuries (i.c. i.m.)	Football — Collapse	Football — Concussion	Crew — Int. Injuries / Collapse	Crew — Concussion	Basketball — Int. Injuries	Basketball — Collapse	Basketball — Concussion	Cross-Country — Int. Inj. / Collapse	C.C. Concussion	Track — Collapse	Track Int.Inj/Conc.	Baseball — Collapse	Baseball — Concussion	Baseball Int.Inj
I	0 †	0 †	12 †	(None)	(None)	0 †	0 †	6 †	0 / 2 0	(None)	0 0	(None)	0 †	6 †	(None)
E	0 †	0 †	3 †	† †		0 0	0 0	0 0	† / †		0 0		0 0	1 0	
M	0 0	0 3	3 0	* *		0 0	1 0	0 0	† / *		0 †		0 0	0 0	
Y	* *	* *	* *	† †		* *	* *	* *	0 / 1		* *		* *	* *	
R	0 †	0 †	1 †	† †		0 0	0 0	0 0	0 / 0		0 0		0 0	0 0	
A	1 †	0 †	2 †	† †		1 †	0 0	0 0	0 / 0		0 †		1 †	1 †	
F	0 †	0 †	1 †	0 0		0 0	0 0	0 0	0 / 0		0 †		0 †	1 0	
B	0 †	0 †	3 †	† †		0 0	0 0	0 0	0 / 0		0 †		0 0	1 0	
G	0 †	0 †	4 †	† †		0 0	0 0	0 0	0 / †		3 †		0 †	0 †	
D	0 0	0 0	10 13	3 0		1 0	0 0	0 0	2 / †		0 0		0 0	2 0	
AB	* †	0 †	3 †	† †		* *	* *	* *	* / *		* *		* *	* *	
Z	0 †	0 †	3 †	† †		0 0	0 0	0 0	0 / 0		2 0		0 0	0 0	
P	0 0	1 0	1 0	† †		0 0	0 0	0 0	0 / †		0 †		0 0	1 0	
C	6 0	0 0	30 0	† †		0 0	0 0	3 2	2 / †		0 †		0 0	2 0	
Q	0 †	0 †	3 †	† †		0 0	0 0	0 0	0 / 0		0 0		0 0	0 0	
T	0 0	0 0	3 0	0 0		0 0	0 0	0 0	0 / 0		0 0		0 0	0 0	
N	1 0	0 0	10 0	† †		0 0	0 0	1 0	0 / 1		0 0		0 0	2 0	
K	0 0	0 0	17 0	0 0		0 0	0 0	1 0	0 / 1		0 0		0 0	0 0	
O	0 †	0 †	4 †	0 0		0 0	0 0	0 0	0 / 0		0 0		0 0	0 0	
L	0 0	0 0	3 0	0 0		0 0	0 0	0 0	† / 0		0 0		0 0	0 0	
H	2 †	0 †	6 †	0 0		0 0	0 0	0 0	0 / †		0 0		0 0	0 0	
J	0 0	0 0	3 0	† †		0 0	0 0	0 0	0 / †		1 0		0 0	0 0	
S	0 0	0 0	6 7	0 †		0 0	0 0	3 4	1 / 2		1 2		0 0	0 0	
X	0 0	0 0	4 0	† †		0 0	0 0	0 0	1 / †		0 †		0 0	0 0	
U	* *	* *	* *	† †		* *	* *	* *	* / *		* *		* *	* *	
Totals (25)	**10 0**	**1 0**	**132 20**	**3 0**		**2 0**	**1 0**	**14 6**	**8 / 3**		**7 2**		**1 0**	**16 0**	

College	Soccer — Int. Injuries	Soccer — Concussion	Lacrosse — Concussion	Boxing — Int. Injuries	Boxing — Collapse	Boxing — Concussion	Wrestling — Int. Injuries	Wrestling — Collapse	Wrestling — Concussion	Swimming	Hockey — Collapse / Concussion	Fencing
I	0 †	0 0	0 †	0 †	0 †	0 2	0 0	0 0	0 0	(None)	3 0 / 1 0	(None)
E	0 0	0 0	† †	0 †	0 †	0 †	† †	† †	† †		† †	
M	* *	* *	* *	* *	* *	* *	* *	* *	* *		* *	
Y	† †	† †	† †	† †	† †	† †	† †	† †	† †		† †	
R	† †	† †	† †	4 1	1 1	1 0	2 †	1 †	1 †		0 0	
A	† †	† †	0 †	0 †	0 †	0 2	0 0	½ †	† †		0 0	
F	0 0	0 0	† †	½ 0	0 0	0 0	0 0	0 0	0 0		0 0	
B	0 0	0 0	0 †	0 †	0 †	0 3	0 0	0 0	0 0		2 †	
G	0 †	0 †	0 †	0 0	0 0	3 0	0 0	0 0	0 0		1 1	
D	0 0	0 0	0 †	0 0	0 0	0 0	0 0	0 0	0 0		1 0	
AB	* *	* *	* *	* *	* *	* *	* *	* *	* *		† †	
Z	† †	† †	† †	0 †	0 †	0 0	0 0	1 0	2 0		† †	
P	† †	† †	0 †	0 †	0 †	0 0	0 0	0 0	0 0		0 0	
C	1 †	1 †	0 †	0 †	0 †	0 0	0 †	0 †	1 0		0 0	
Q	† 0	† 0	† †	0 †	0 †	2 0	2 0	0 0	0 0		0 0	
T	† †	† †	† †	0 0	0 5	0 0	0 †	0 0	0 0		† †	
N	0 0	0 0	1 †	0 0	0 17	0 1	0 0	0 0	0 0		1 1	
K	0 0	0 0	0 †	0 0	0 0	0 1	0 0	0 0	0 0		0 †	
O	0 0	1 0	† †	0 †	0 †	0 0	1 0	0 †	0 †		† †	
L	0 0	0 0	0 †	0 †	0 †	0 0	† 0	0 0	0 0		1 1	
H	0 0	0 †	† †	0 †	0 †	0 0	1 0	1 1	0 0		0 †	
J	0 0	0 0	0 †	0 0	0 0	0 0	0 0	0 0	0 0		† †	
S	† †	† †	† †	0 †	0 †	0 0	0 0	1 †	0 0		0 0	
X	0 †	0 †	0 †	0 †	0 0	0 0	0 0	1 0	0 0		1 0	
U	* *	* *	† †	* *	* *	* *	* *	* *	* *		† †	
Totals (25)	**1 0**	**2 0**	**2 0**	**4 ½**	**1 0**	**26 7**	**3 0**	**3 1**	**4 0**		**9 2**	

(NOTE) * Data lacking.
        † Sport not engaged in.

TABLE E

Medical Supervision of Athletes in Thirteen Specified Sports—Intercollegiate and Intramural

College	i.c.	i.m.	Football 1	2	3	Crew 1	2	3	Basketball 1	2	3	Cross-Country 1	2	3
I	x	o	x †	o †	o †	† †	† †	† †	o †	o †	o †	o †	o †	o †
E	x	o	x †	x †	o †	† †	† †	† †	o o	x o	o o	o o	x o	o o
M	x	o	o o	x o	x o	† †	† †	† †	o o	o o	o o	† †	† †	† †
Y	x	x	x x	x x	x x	x x	x x	x x	x x	x x	x x	† x	† x	† x
R	x	o	x o	x o	o o	† †	† †	† †	x o	o o	o o	o o	x x	o o
A	x	o	x †	x †	x †	† †	† †	† †	x o	x †	x †	o †	x †	x †
F	x	o	x †	o †	x †	† †	† †	† †	x o	o o	x x	o †	o †	x †
B	x	o	x †	o †	x †	o o	o o	x o	x o	o o	x o	x o	o o	x o
G	o	o	x †	o †	x †	† †	† †	† †	o o	o o	x x	x †	o †	x †
D	x	x	x x	x x	x x	x x	x x	x x	x o	x x	x x	x †	x †	x †
AB	x	o	x †	o †	o †	† †	† †	† †	x o	o o	o o	o o	o o	o o
Z	x	o	x o	x x	x †	† †	† †	† †	x o	x x	x x	x o	x x	x x
P	x	o	x o	o o	o o	† †	† †	† †	o o	o o	o o	o †	o †	o †
C	x	o	x o	o o	o o	† †	† †	† †	o o	o o	o o	o †	o †	o †
Q	x	x	x †	x †	o †	† †	† †	† †	o o	o o	o o	o o	o o	o o
T	x	x	x o	x o	o o	† †	† †	† †	o o	x o	o o	o o	x o	o o
N	x	o	x x	x x	x x	x x	x x	x x	x x	x x	x x	x †	x †	x †
K	x	o	x o	o †	o †	† †	† †	† †	x o	o o	o o	o †	o †	o †
O	x	o	x x	o o	x o	x x	o o	o o	x x	o o	o o	x x	o o	o o
L	x	x	x o	x o	o o	† †	† †	† †	o o	o o	o o	† o	† o	† o
H	x	o	x †	o †	x †	x x	o o	x o	x x	o o	x o	x †	o †	x †
J	x	o	x o	x o	x o	† †	† †	† †	o o	x o	x o	o †	x †	x †
S	x	x	x o	x o	x o	o †	o †	o †	x o	x o	x o	o †	x †	x †
X	x	x	x o	x o	x o	o o	x o	x o	x o	x o	x o	o †	x †	x †
U	x	o	x o	x o	x x	† †	† †	† †	o o	o o	x x	x o	x o	x x
Totals	**25**	**24 7**	**24 4**	**15 4**	**15 4**	**5 5**	**4 3**	**6 3**	**15 4**	**11 4**	**13 7**	**7 2**	**10 3**	**11 3**

College	i.c.	i.m.	Track 1	2	3	Baseball 1	2	3	Soccer 1	2	3	Lacrosse 1	2	3
I	x	o	o o	o o	o o	o †	o †	o †	o †	o †	o †	† †	† †	† †
E	x	o	o o	x o	o o	o o	x o	o o	o o	x o	o o	o †	x †	o †
M	x	o	o †	x †	x †	o o	o o	o o	† †	† †	† †	† †	† †	† †
Y	x	x	x x	x x	x x	x x	x x	x x	x x	x x	x x	† †	† †	† †
R	x	o	o o	x x	o o	o o	o o	o o	† †	† †	† †	† †	† †	† †
A	x	o	x †	x †	x †	x †	x †	x †	† †	† †	† †	† †	† †	† †
F	x	o	o †	o †	x †	x †	o †	x †	† †	† †	† †	x †	o †	x †
B	x	o	x †	o †	x †	x o	x o	x o	x o	o o	x o	x †	o †	x †
G	o	o	x †	o †	x †	o †	o †	x †	o †	o †	x †	† †	† †	† †
D	x	x	x x	x x	x x	x x	x x	x x	x †	x †	x †	x †	x †	x †
AB	x	o	o o	o o	o o	x o	o o	o o	† †	† †	† †	† †	† †	† †
Z	x	o	x o	x x	x x	x x	x x	x x	† †	† †	† †	† †	† †	† †
P	x	o	o †	o †	o †	o o	o o	o o	o †	o †	o †	o †	o †	o †
C	x	o	o †	o †	o †	o o	o o	o o	o †	o †	o †	o †	o †	o †
Q	x	x	o o	o o	o o	o o	o o	o o	† o	† o	† o	† †	† †	† †
T	x	x	o o	x o	o o	o o	o o	o o	† †	† †	† †	† †	† †	† †
N	x	o	x x	x x	x x	x x	x x	x x	x x	x x	x x	x †	x †	x †
K	x	o	o o	o o	o o	o o	o o	o o	o †	o †	o †	o †	o †	o †
O	x	o	x x	o o	o o	x x	o o	o o	x x	o o	o o	x x	o o	o o
L	x	x	o o	o o	o o	x x	o o	x o	† o	† o	† o	† †	† †	† †
H	x	o	x x	o o	x o	x x	o o	x o	x †	o †	x †	x †	o †	x. †
J	x	o	o o	x o	x o	o o	x o	x o	o o	x o	x o	† †	† †	† †
S	x	x	o o	o o	o o	o o	o o	o o	† †	† †	† †	† †	† †	† †
X	x	x	x †	x †	x †	x o	x o	x o	x †	x †	x †	x †	x †	x †
U	x	o	x o	o o	x x	o o	o o	x x	o o	o o	x x	† †	† †	† †
Totals	**25**	**24 7**	**11 5**	**11 5**	**13 5**	**11 5**	**10 4**	**12 5**	**7 3**	**6 2**	**9 3**	**7 1**	**4 1**	**6 0**

(NOTE) 1 Doctor at each contest.
     2 Medical O.K. prerequisite to practice each year.
     3 Heart-history prerequisite to practice each year.
     † Sport not engaged in.
     x Yes.
     o No.

TABLE E (*concluded*)

College	Authorities responsible for remedying injuries of athletes i.c.	i.m.	Boxing 1	2	3	Wrestling 1	2	3	Swimming 1	2	3	Hockey 1	2	3	Fencing 1	2	3
I	x	o	† x	† o	† o	† x	† o	† o	o o	o o	o o	o o	o o	o o	† †	† †	† †
E	x	o	† †	† †	† †	o o	x o	o o	o o	x o	o o	o o	x o	o o	† †	† †	† †
M	x	o	o †	o †	o †	† †	† †	† †	† †	† †	† †	† †	† †	† †	† †	† †	† †
Y	x	x	x x	x x	x x	x x	x x	x x	x x	x x	x x	† †	† †	† †	o o	x x	x x
R	x	o	† o	† o	† o	o o	o o	o o	o o	o o	o o	† †	† †	† †	† †	† †	† †
A	x	o	o †	o †	o †	o †	x †	x †	x †	x †	x †	† †	† †	† †	† †	† †	† †
F	x	o	† †	† †	† †	† †	† †	† †	o †	o †	x †	† †	† †	† †	† †	† †	† †
B	x	o	† x	† o	† x	x o	o o	x o	o o	o o	x o	x o	o o	x o	o †	o †	x †
G	o	o	† †	† †	† †	† †	† †	† †	† †	† †	† †	x †	o †	x †	† †	o †	x †
D	x	x	x x	x x	x x	x x	x x	x x	† o	† x	† x	x x	x x	x x	? ?	x x	x x
AB	x	o	o o	o o	o o	x o	o o	o o	o o	o o	o o	† †	† †	† †	† †	† †	† †
Z	x	o	† o	† x	† x	x o	x x	x x	o †	x †	x †	† †	† †	† †	† †	† †	† †
P	x	o	† o	† o	† o	o o	o o	o o	o o	o o	o o	† †	† †	† †	† †	† †	† †
C	x	o	† o	† o	† o	o †	o †	o †	o o	o o	o o	† †	† †	† †	o †	o †	o †
Q	x	x	† o	† o	† o	o o	o o	o o	o o	o o	o o	o †	o †	o †	† o	† o	† o
T	x	x	† o	† x	† o	o o	x o	o o	o o	x o	o o	o o	x o	o o	† †	† †	† †
N	x	o	x x	x x	x x	x x	x x	x x	x x	x x	x x	† †	† †	† †	o o	x x	x x
K	x	o	x o	o o	o o	x o	o o	o o	† †	† †	† †	† †	† †	† †	o †	o †	o †
O	x	o	† x	† o	† o	x x	o o	o o	x x	o o	o o	x x	o o	o o	o o	o o	o o
L	x	x	† o	† o	† o	† o	† o	† o	† †	† †	† †	† †	† †	† †	† †	† †	† †
H	x	o	x †	o †	x †	x †	o †	x †	† †	† †	† †	x †	o †	x †	o †	o †	x †
J	x	o	† †	† †	† †	† o	o †	† o	o o	x o	x o	† †	† †	† †	o †	o †	o †
S	x	x	† †	† †	† †	† †	† †	† †	o o	o o	o o	o o	o o	o o	o †	o †	o †
X	x	x	x o	x o	x o	x †	x †	x †	o o	x o	x o	x o	x o	x o	o o	x o	x o
U	x	o	o o	o o	x x	o o	o o	x x	o o	o o	x x	† †	† †	† †	? ?	o o	x x
Totals 25	**24**	**7**	**6 6**	**4 5**	**6 6**	**10 5**	**8 4**	**9 5**	**5 3**	**8 3**	**10 4**	**6 2**	**4 1**	**5 1**	**0 0**	**4 3**	**8 4**

TABLE F

Other Information

College	Team physician in charge of training table	Collecting data on cerebral concussion	Team physician states that concussion once incurred tends to recur more easily	Team physician states that concussion effects often felt for many months	Collecting data on effects of collapse	Collecting data on cardiac hypertrophy
I	x	o	o	o	o	o
E	o	o	x	o	o	o
M	no t.t.	o	o	o	o	o
Y	o	o	o	x	o	o
R	no t.t.	o	o	o	o	x
A	x	o	x	o	o	x
F	o	o	o	o	o	o
B	x	x	x	o	o	x
G	no t.t.	o	x	x	o	o
D	x	x	o	x	x	x
AB	no t.t.	o	x	o	o	o
Z	no t.t.	o	o	o	o	o
P	o	o	o	o	o	o
C	o	o	o	o	o	o
Q	no t.t.	o	o	o	o	o
T	no t.t.	o	o	o	o	o
N	o	o	x	o	o	x
K	o	o	o	o	o	o
O	x	o	x	o	x	x
L	o	o	o	o	o	o
H	x	o	o	o	x	x
J	no t.t.	o	x	o	o	o
S	no t.t.	o	o	o	x	x
X	x	o	x	x	o	x
U	no t.t.	o	x	o	o	o
Totals 25	7	2	10	6	4	9

College	Team physician states that he has observed the occurrence in students in his care with undue frequency					
	Heart Disease	Kidney Disease	Tuberculosis	Arterial Hypertension	Diabetes	Boils
I	o	o	o	o	o	o
E	o	o	o	o	o	o
M	o	o	o	o	o	x
Y	o	o	o	o	o	o
R	o	o	o	o	o	x
A	o	o	o	o	o	o
F	o	o	o	x	o	o
B	o	o	o	o	o	o
G	o	o	o	o	o	o
D	o	o	o	o	o	o
AB	o	o	o	o	o	o
Z	o	o	o	o	o	x
P	o	o	o	o	o	o
C	o	o	o	o	o	o
Q	o	o	o	o	o	x
T	o	o	o	o	o	o
N	o	o	o	o	o	x
K	o	o	o	o	o	o
O	o	o	o	o	o	o
L	o	o	o	o	o	o
H	o	o	o	o	o	x
J	o	o	o	o	o	o
S	o	o	o	o	o	x
X	o	o	o	o	o	o
U	o	o	o	o	o	o
Totals 25	0	0	0	1	0	7

(NOTE)   x   Yes.
         o   No.
     no t.t.   No training table.

V

PARTICIPATION IN THE BRANCHES OF INTERCOLLEGIATE AND INTRAMURAL ATHLETICS AT THE COLLEGES AND UNIVERSITIES OF THE STUDY

TABLE G

At Institutions Using the Same Branches for both Intercollegiate and Intramural Competition

Sport	Intercollegiate & Intramural				Intercollegiate				Intramural			
	No. of Institutions	Registration	No. of Participants	Per cent	No. of Institutions	Registration	No. of Participants	Per cent	No. of Institutions	Registration	No. of Participants	Per cent
Baseball	50	100757	10215	10.1	49	97519	3283	3.4	27	67473	6782	10.0
Basketball	23	63122	13200	20.9	55	114734	2892	2.5	27	74156	6315	8.5
Boxing & Wrestling*	14	49105	3290	6.7	31	83887	1631	1.9	16	45685	1527	3.3
Cross-Country	13	36599	2615	7.1	32	79210	1160	1.4	16	42403	2450	5.8
Fencing	5	20935	336	1.1	7	26617	184	0.7	7	31935	389	1.2
Football	12	34866	4319	12.4	67	129588	7286	5.6	13	33270	2822	8.5
Golf	10	37544	1287	3.4	17	48496	640	1.3	16	50196	1553	3.1
Gymnasium	3	14602	308	2.1	8	36653	207	0.5	6	17409	676	3.9
Hockey†					9	19724	432	2.2	7	17040	673	3.9
Lacrosse	1	1500	112	7.5	6	9803	402	4.1	5	17404	772	4.4
Polo†					2	4619	68	1.5	3	15087	539	3.5
Rifle or Pistol	1	5800	295	5.1	5	13497	164	1.2	2	12300	463	3.8
Rowing	2	5497	550	10.0	5	17412	614	3.5	4	7602	469	6.1
Soccer	2	9271	371	4.0	7	18876	556	2.9	13	38384	1622	4.2
Swimming	14	42959	3597	8.4	31	77897	1331	1.7	18	46107	3659	7.9
Tennis	19	59557	6147	10.3	37	95834	1285	1.2	22	62179	4375	7.0
Track & Field	3	10385	574	5.5	52	111334	5455	4.9	25	58762	5222	8.9
Water Basketball	1	2685	55	2.0	1	2685	25	0.87	1	2685	32	1.1
Wrestling									15	37336	1104	2.9

* Intramural figures for boxing only.

† In hockey and polo figures for intercollegiate and intramural participation at the same institutions were not reported separately.

TABLE H

At Institutions Using Branches for Intramural Competition Only

Sports	Number of institutions using the sport	Registration	Participation	Per cent
Badminton	1	118	8	6.8
Bowling	5	30643	2237	7.2
Bicycle	1	2685	12	0.5
Cageball	1	2685	150	5.6
Diamond Ball	1	7492	904	12.1
Freethrow	2	6750	553	8.1
Handball	14	40536	1458	3.5
Hare & Hound	1	3885	250	6.4
Hiking	1	118	11	9.3
Horseshoes	12	41606	2830	6.7
Indoor Baseball	2	1463	316	21.5
Mass Track	1	2685	480	17.9
Playground Ball	5	18865	4622	24.4
Pushball	1	1922	149	7.8
Relay	1	2685	939	34.9
Squash	1	7492	15	0.2
Speedball	3	14058	2478	17.6
Volley Ball	7	26011	1875	7.2

SUMMARY

Including duplicates	33	82570	69466	84.1
Exclusive of duplicates	6	21426	13593	63.4
Including duplicates	67	129558	29692	22.9
Exclusive of duplicates	13	34029	6024	17.7
Including duplicates	37	85895	54175	63.1
Exclusive of duplicates	14	38212	19241	50.4

VI

THE POPULARITY OR UTILITY OF THE BRANCHES OF ATHLETICS

TABLE J

*Total Participation as Indicating Relative Popularity or Utility of the
Branches of College Athletics*

Sports arranged on the basis of number of participants engaged*	Number of participants	Sports arranged on the basis of percentage of participants engaged to registration†	Per cent
1. Basketball (1)	13200	1. Basketball (1)	20.9
2. Baseball (4)	10215	2. Football (4)	12.4
3. Tennis (3)	6147	3. Tennis (3)	10.3
4. Football (2)	4319	4. Baseball (2)	10.1
5. Swimming (6)	3597	5. Rowing (10)	10.0
6. Boxing & Wrestling (9)	3290	6. Swimming (5)	8.4
7. Cross-Country (8)	2615	7. Lacrosse (15)	7.5
8. Golf (13)	1287	8. Cross-Country (7)	7.1
9. Track & Field (10)	574	9. Boxing & Wrestling (6)	6.7
10. Rowing (5)	550	10. Track & Field (9)	5.5
11. Soccer (12)	371	11. Rifle or Pistol (14)	5.1
12. Fencing (16)	336	12. Soccer (11)	4.0
13. Gymnasium (14)	308	13. Golf (8)	3.4
14. Rifle or Pistol (11)	295	14. Gymnasium (13)	2.1
15. Lacrosse (7)	112	15. Water Basketball (16)	2.0
16. Water Basketball (15)	55	16. Fencing (12)	1.1

TABLE K

*Participation as Indicating Relative Popularity or Utility of the Branches
of Intercollegiate Athletics*

Sports arranged on the basis of number of participants engaged*	Number of participants	Sports arranged on the basis of percentage of participants engaged to registration†	Per cent
1. Football (1)	7286	1. Football (1)	5.6
2. Track & Field (2)	5455	2. Track & Field (2)	4.9
3. Baseball (5)	3283	3. Lacrosse (13)	4.1
4. Basketball (7)	2892	4. Rowing (10)	3.5
5. Boxing & Wrestling (9)	1631	5. Baseball (3)	3.4
6. Swimming (10)	1331	6. Soccer (11)	2.9
7. Tennis (14)	1285	7. Basketball (4)	2.5
8. Cross-Country (12)	1160	8. Hockey (12)	2.2
9. Golf (13)	640	9. Boxing & Wrestling (5)	1.9
10. Rowing (4)	614	10. Swimming (6)	1.7
11. Soccer (6)	556	11. Polo (17)	1.5
12. Hockey (8)	432	12. Cross-Country (9)	1.4
13. Lacrosse (3)	402	13. Golf (9)	1.3
14. Gymnasium (18)	207	14. Tennis (7)	1.2
15. Fencing (17)	184	15. Rifle or Pistol (16)	1.2
16. Rifle or Pistol (15)	164	16. Water Basketball (18)	0.87
17. Polo (11)	68	17. Fencing (15)	0.7
18. Water Basketball (16)	25	18. Gymnasium (14)	0.5

* Figures in parentheses indicate relative position on percentage basis.
† Figures in parentheses indicate relative position on basis of numbers engaged.

TABLE L

Participation as Indicating Relative Popularity or Utility of the Branches of Intramural Athletics

Sports arranged on the basis of number of participants engaged*	Number of participants	Sports arranged on the basis of percentage of participants engaged to registration †	Per cent
1. Baseball (7)	6782	1. Relay (18)	34.9
2. Basketball (10)	6315	2. Playground Ball (4)	24.4
3. Track & Field (9)	5222	3. Indoor Baseball (29)	21.5
4. Playground Ball (2)	4622	4. Mass Track (25)	17.9
5. Tennis (17)	4375	5. Speedball (9)	17.6
6. Swimming (13)	3659	6. Diamond Ball (19)	12.1
7. Horseshoes (19)	2830	7. Baseball (1)	10.0
8. Football (11)	2822	8. Hiking (36)	9.3
9. Speedball (5)	2478	9. Track & Field (3)	8.9
10. Cross-Country (22)	2450	10. Basketball (2)	8.5
11. Bowling (16)	2237	11. Football (8)	8.5
12. Volley Ball (15)	1875	12. Freethrow (23)	8.1
13. Soccer (25)	1622	13. Swimming (6)	7.9
14. Golf (32)	1553	14. Pushball (32)	7.8
15. Boxing (31)	1527	15. Volley Ball (12)	7.2
16. Handball (30)	1458	16. Bowling (11)	7.2
17. Wrestling (33)	1104	17. Tennis (5)	7.0
18. Relay (1)	939	18. Badminton (37)	6.8
19. Diamond Ball (6)	904	19. Horseshoes (7)	6.7
20. Lacrosse (24)	772	20. Hare & Hound (30)	6.4
21. Gymnasium (27)	676	21. Rowing (26)	6.1
22. Hockey (26)	673	22. Cross-Country (10)	5.8
23. Freethrow (12)	553	23. Cageball (31)	5.6
24. Polo (29)	539	24. Lacrosse (20)	4.4
25. Mass Track (4)	480	25. Soccer (13)	4.2
26. Rowing (21)	469	26. Hockey (22)	3.9
27. Rifle or Pistol (28)	463	27. Gymnasium (21)	3.9
28. Fencing (34)	389	28. Rifle or Pistol (27)	3.8
29. Indoor Baseball (3)	316	29. Polo (24)	3.5
30. Hare & Hound (20)	250	30. Handball (16)	3.5
31. Cageball (23)	150	31. Boxing (15)	3.3
32. Pushball (14)	149	32. Golf (14)	3.1
33. Water Basketball (35)	32	33. Wrestling (17)	2.9
34. Squash (37)	15	34. Fencing (28)	1.2
35. Bicycle (36)	12	35. Water Basketball (33)	1.1
36. Hiking (8)	11	36. Bicycle (35)	0.5
37. Badminton (18)	8	37. Squash (34)	0.2

* Figures in parentheses indicate relative position on percentage basis.
† Figures in parentheses indicate relative position on basis of numbers engaged.

INDEX

INDEX